MW00510238

Achieving Economic Growth and Welfare Through Green Consumerism

Punitha Sinnappan
Sunway Business School, Sunway University, Malaysia

A volume in the Advances in
Marketing, Customer Relationship
Management, and E-Services
(AMCRMES) Book Series

Titles in this Series

For a list of additional titles in this series, please visit:
http://www.igi-global.com/book-series/advances-marketing-customer-relationship-management/37150

Handbook of Research on Achieving Sustainable Development Goals With Sustainable Marketing
Iza Gigauri (St. Andrew the First-Called Georgian University, Georgia) Maria Palazzo (Universitas Mercatorum, Italy) and Maria Antonella Ferri (Universitas Mercatorum, Italy)
Business Science Reference • copyright 2023 • 455pp • H/C (ISBN: 9781668486818) • US $305.00 (our price)

Global Developments in Nation Branding and Promotion Theoretical and Practical Approaches
Andreas Masouras (Neapolis University, Cyprus) Sofia Daskou (Neapolis University, Cyprus) Victoria Pistikou (Democritus University of Thrace, Greece) Dimitrios Dimitriou (Democritus University of Thrace, Greece) and Tim Friesner (University of Winchester, UK)
Information Science Reference • copyright 2023 • 320pp • H/C (ISBN: 9781668459027) • US $240.00 (our price)

Origin and Branding in International Market Entry Processes
Carlos Francisco e Silva (Universidade Europeia, Portugal)
Business Science Reference • copyright 2023 • 320pp • H/C (ISBN: 9781668466131) • US $250.00 (our price)

Global Applications of the Internet of Things in Digital Marketing
Arshi Naim (King Kalid University, Saudi Arabia) and V. Ajantha Devi (AP3 Solutions, India)
Business Science Reference • copyright 2023 • 410pp • H/C (ISBN: 9781668481660) • US $250.00 (our price)

Applications of Neuromarketing in the Metaverse
Monika Gupta (Chitkara Business School, Chitkara University, India) Kumar Shalender (Chitkara University, India) Babita Singla (Chitkara Business School, Chitkara University, India) and Nripendra Singh (PennWest University, Clarion, USA)
Business Science Reference • copyright 2023 • 338pp • H/C (ISBN: 9781668481509) • US $255.00 (our price)

701 East Chocolate Avenue, Hershey, PA 17033, USA
Tel: 717-533-8845 x100 • Fax: 717-533-8661
E-Mail: cust@igi-global.com • www.igi-global.com

Table of Contents

Detailed Table of Contents

Chapter 1

Nandana Ranjith, CHRIST University (Deemed), India
D. Preethi, CHRIST University (Deemed), India
Krishna Prasath S., CHRIST University (Deemed), India

Green marketing research is becoming more and more well-liked in academia and business. Both companies and customers today recognize the value of eco-friendly products due to increased awareness of how companies respond to various factors contributing to environmental degradation. One should understand the meaning, opportunities, and threats associated with green marketing to harness the benefits of green marketing. This book chapter aims to explore various aspects of green marketing, including its evolution throughout the years, opportunities, threats, the future of green marketing, etc. To sum up, this chapter aims to gain an in-depth understanding of green marketing and how companies could use it to their advantage. Successful implementation will be possible only if associated threats are carefully analyzed and understood. Therefore, a part of this chapter will be dedicated to understanding the threats associated with green marketing strategies.

Chapter 2

Mehvish Riyaz, Islamic University of Science and Technology, India
Anisa Jan, Islamic University of Science and Technology, India

The chapter presents an overview of environmentally responsible consumer behavior by focusing on its core aspects, such as its evolution, significance, influencing factors, and consequences of practicing the behavior on businesses, individuals, and the environment. Second, the chapter explores the numerous theories utilized by scholars to explain and predict this behavior. In addition, the chapter also attempts to establish a connection between the concept of environmentally responsible consumption behavior and the pursuit of environmental sustainability, which is crucial in today's world, and emphasizes how engaging in this behavior can contribute to the achievement of the United Nations sustainable development goal 12.

Chapter 3

Pınar Yürük-Kayapınar, Trakya University, Turkey
Burcu Ören Özer, Trakya University, Turkey

The aim of this chapter is to engage with the concepts of green consumer and green consumerism and to perform a bibliometric analysis of the related publications. To this end, the studies are examined in WoS and Scopus between 1965 and 2023, using the keywords "green consumer" and "green consumerism." The study imposed certain constraints, resulting in the acquisition of a total of 7238 articles derived from 1728 sources. For this analysis, the Bibliometrix R Package Program was applied. An initial phase of the study was to conduct a descriptive analysis to provide an overview of the data. The subsequent phase involved examining several elements: the number of publications and citations by year; the most published journals on these subjects and their H-index values; the number of publications and H-index values of the authors; productivity of countries; most frequently used words; and collaboration networks of words, countries, and authors. Additionally, a factor analysis was carried out within the scope of the study to facilitate the observation of cluster formations.

Chapter 4

Shafiu Ibrahim Abdullahi, Bayero University, Kano, Nigeria
Kamal Kabiru Shehu, Federal University, Kashere, Nigeria
Mohammed B. Adamu, Adamawa State Polytechnic, Yola, Nigeria
Husayn Mahmud Muhammad, Federal College of Education, Yola,
*   Nigeria*

The main purpose of the chapter is to find out the effects of renewable energy on economic growth and household consumption in Nigeria. Renewable energy supply and environmentally sustainable consumption are key ingredients in achieving sustainable economic growth and development all over the world. The chapter aims at highlighting the positive contributions of green energy to sustainable consumption and economic growth. The main methods of analysis for the study are Granger causality tests, VAR impulse response function, and Variance decomposition. The findings show strong links between renewable electricity supply, economic growth, and household consumption in Nigeria. This was expected a priori, as overwhelming empirical and theoretical literature has attested to the effects of renewable electricity on economic growth of other nations around the world.

Chapter 5
    Sejana Jose V, CHRIST University (Deemed), India
    H. Sandhya, CHRIST University (Deemed), India
    Bindi Varghese, CHRIST University (Deemed), India

Emerging technological advancements and sustainability concerns have initiated the integration of smart technologies into the transportation infrastructure at major cities and tourist hubs. The rising environmental concerns have called for a shift in focus from conventional methods to innovative green transport initiatives being formulated by DMOs and destination planners. The use of data analytics and artificial intelligence in transportation has been proven to be a reasonable method for sustainable transportation. This study focuses on assessing the value propositions of smart transportation systems in enriching the tourist experience by providing convenient travel solutions. The chapter focuses on understanding the value proposition of smart transport designs at destinations and the long-term prospects of installing such sustainable infrastructure at major tourist hubs. The study also aims to evaluate the tourist experience in using smart transportation services and the potential benefits and challenges involved in the practical implementation of such systems.

Chapter 6
    Ahmet Bilgehan Kandemir, Gazi University, Turkey
    Başak Gök, Gazi University, Turkey
    Hadi Gökçen, Gazi University, Turkey

The increase in the human population in the world, the rapid rate of digitization, the support of more services using digital technology during this transformation, and the increase in the number of users lead to the emergence of large volumes of data and information. In the global context, it is one of the most important problems of today to produce sustainable solutions together with the effective and efficient use of all kinds of resources. Regarding their energy usage and effects on the ICT carbon footprint, data centers are regarded as sustainable goods and services. In this study, within the framework of sustainability, data centers were discussed, and basic concepts, global standards, world examples, and suggestions to make data centers more efficient were shared.

Expansion of the tourism sector can lead to environmental deterioration. In response, initiatives for sustainable tourism have emerged, followed by certification schemes to promote sustainable consumption, and align consumer preferences and behavior. However, many destinations struggle to satisfy these standards, particularly in smaller developing countries. This chapter aims to analyze the possibility of certification for a spa destination in Serbia, an emerging economy in South-East Europe, using it as a case study to understand the certification process and draw a conclusion about the capacity of small destinations to meet requirements. The research is focused on green destination standard as the most notable validation of the GSTC criterion in the case of Sokobanja Spa. Although the destination in the case study could not receive certification, the results and examples of successful destinations in the region indicate that certification is achievable with the systematic effort of the destination's management and national-level support, particularly in the infrastructure segment.

Body and beauty care are considered essential in everyday life of a young adult. This has attracted the attention of the cosmetic industry to respond with products that serve these varying interests. Not only are the youth interested in using cosmetic products, but they also consider the greenness of the cosmetic products. This has forced the corporate world to churn out products that are considered safe for the environment and also engage in practices that are considered green. Drawing on the theory of planned behavior, the chapter assesses how students' exposure to green marketing practices influences their purchase of cosmetic products over time. The chapter uses eco-label, eco-brand, and environmental advertising as predictors of students' purchasing behaviour of cosmetic products. Further, PLS-SEM is used to examine the effect of green marketing tools on students' purchasing decisions. The study's findings suggest that eco-label and environmental advertising influence the purchase of cosmetic products. Implications of the findings are discussed.

In modern societies, the need for a high degree of mobility in transportation systems
is increasingly evident. Consequently, the establishment of a sustainable transport
system that aligns with social needs, economic growth, and environmental concerns
becomes paramount. This chapter aims to shed light on the role of transport in
sustainable development and the challenges associated with achieving sustainable
mobility. A thorough analysis of the primary factors contributing to the growing
demand for mobility is provided. Additionally, the chapter examines the key decision-
makers involved in shaping transportation systems, with a particular focus on the
pivotal role of intelligent transportation systems. These systems are considered a vital
component in addressing road congestion and enhancing overall traffic performance,
such as reducing congestion and noise levels while promoting sustainable mobility.

Green economy and its relevant concepts have gained popularity during the last
decade to promote and support equitable and sustainable development. Developing
countries have deliberately undertaken initiatives that float responsible development,
valuing the magnanimity and foresight of these principles despite their barriers to the
progress of a developing nation. The repeating idea of placing a tax on the production,
use, and emission of carbon by industry has been recognized and implemented by
governments worldwide. The principle addressed in this chapter advocates for the
implementation of carbon tax measures in a selective and authoritative manner, which
historically led to non-conformity, restlessness, and inefficiency. The objective of
this article is to utilize Petri Nets to legalize the behavior of a multi-level marketing
system to assure an effective carbon tax hierarchy to promote a green economy, to
optimize it, and to model it.

Preface

Environmental challenges have far-reaching social, economic, and ecological implications. Climate change, for instance, poses risks to food security, water availability, and public health. Biodiversity loss threatens ecosystem stability and resilience. Pollution in various forms negatively impacts air and water quality, affecting human health and ecosystems. A shift towards more sustainable practices is desirable and essential for the long-term well-being of our planet and future generations. Green consumerism has emerged as a response to these challenges, driven by a desire to minimize environmental impact and promote a more sustainable future.

Green consumerism, also known as sustainable or conscious consumption, refers to purchasing decisions that prioritize environmental sustainability and ethical considerations. It is a proactive approach that recognizes the power of consumers to influence market dynamics and drive positive change. By prioritizing sustainable and environmentally friendly products and services, green consumerism can drive economic growth while enhancing the welfare of individuals and communities.

The economic growth is stimulated by creating new market opportunities and innovations. As consumers increasingly demand sustainable products and services, businesses are incentivized to invest in research and development, improve their sustainability practices, integrate eco-friendly manufacturing processes and adopt eco-friendly technologies (i.e., renewable energy solutions, efficient waste management systems and energy-efficient technologies). This innovation leads to the emergence of green industries and the creation of new jobs, which in turn, fosters economic growth.

Moreover, green consumerism often involves opting for healthier or more ethically produced products. For example, choosing organic food, non-toxic materials, eco-friendly personal care products, or sustainably sourced clothing not only reduces exposure to harmful chemicals but also promotes healthier lifestyles. These choices can improve physical health, quality of life, ethical satisfaction, and a greater sense of connectedness to the environment. Engaging in sustainable practices also fosters community and social cohesion through collective actions, such as participating in community recycling programs, supporting local farmers' markets, or advocating for environmental policies. These shared endeavors can strengthen social bonds, promote collaboration, and enhance the community's welfare.

It should be emphasized that green consumerism is a collective effort that necessitates the participation and collaboration of all parties involved. It is not solely the responsibility of individuals or consumers, but also requires the engagement of businesses, governments, and non-governmental organizations. Consumers play a crucial role by making conscious and sustainable choices in their purchasing decisions, creating demand for greener alternatives and sending a powerful message to businesses. In turn, companies can drive change by embracing sustainable practices, implementing eco-friendly policies, and offering a more comprehensive range of sustainable options. Governments contribute by creating an enabling environment through policies, regulations, incentives, and investments in sustainable infrastructure. Additionally, organizations and non-governmental entities are vital in raising awareness, advocating for sustainability, and fostering collaboration among businesses, governments and consumers. Through this shared commitment and action, we can achieve lasting positive impacts on both the economy and the well-being of people.

A holistic approach to green consumerism becomes indispensable for a future green world. It means considering sustainability and making conscious choices across all areas of our lives, not just focusing on one aspect in isolation. A truly sustainable and environmentally conscious society requires us to examine and address the environmental impact of our choices in energy, transportation, food, fashion, housing, finance, education, tourism and more. By embracing green consumerism holistically, we can create a synergy of sustainable practices across various sectors, leading to a more interconnected and harmonious relationship with the environment. This holistic approach ensures that our efforts towards a green world are comprehensive, impactful and address the sustainability challenges we face thoroughly.

A Description of the Target Audience

While this book may comprise a limited number of chapters, it serves as a valuable starting point for a wide range of readers seeking to delve into green consumerism. Incorporating the latest empirical and analytical research offers much information for academics, interdisciplinary researchers, policymakers, professionals, and practitioners alike. This insightful resource provides knowledge and practical applications that will empower readers to enhance their understanding of green consumerism and initiate meaningful actions towards achieving economic growth and welfare through sustainable consumption.

Organization of the Book

The book is organized into ten chapters, each offering unique insights into different aspects of green consumerism. Here is a brief introduction to each chapter.

Chapter 1 provides an in-depth exploration of green marketing, focusing on its evolution, opportunities, and threats. Businesses can leverage its benefits by gaining a deeper understanding of green marketing. The chapter also emphasizes the importance of carefully analyzing and understanding the potential threats to green marketing strategies for successful implementation.

Chapter 2 focuses on environmentally responsible consumption behavior. It provides a comprehensive overview of this behavior, discussing its evolution, significance, and the factors influencing it. The chapter also explores the consequences of environmentally responsible consumption behavior on businesses, individuals, and the environment. The connection between this behavior, the pursuit of environmental sustainability, and its contribution to the United Nations Sustainable Development Goal 12 are emphasized.

Chapter 3 presents a bibliometric analysis of research trends in green consumerism. Examining studies published between 1965 and 2023 provides insights into the number of publications and citations over the years, the most published journals and authors, the productivity of countries, and the collaboration networks in this field. The analysis aims to identify the key trends and contributions in green consumerism research.

Chapter 4 examines the application of green consumerism in the energy sector, specifically in Nigeria. It analyzes the impact of adopting renewable energy sources on economic growth and household consumption using methods such as Granger causality tests and VAR impulse response functions. The chapter highlights the potential benefits of transitioning to renewable energy, including reduced reliance on fossil fuels and job creation. It also discusses policy frameworks and government initiatives necessary to support renewable energy adoption.

Chapter 5 focuses on sustainable transportation systems. It explores the integration of emerging technologies, such as Artificial Intelligence and Data Analytics, into transportation infrastructure to enhance the efficiency and sustainability of travel. The chapter emphasizes the value propositions of smart transportation systems in improving the tourist experience and providing convenient travel solutions. It also discusses the long-term prospects and challenges of implementing sustainable transportation infrastructure at significant tourist hubs. By examining the intersection of technology, sustainability and tourism, this chapter sheds light on the potential of smart green transportation to contribute to a more sustainable future.

Chapter 6 delves into the significance of data centers in promoting sustainability and green computing practices. It highlights the challenges posed by the increasing volumes of data generated worldwide and the need for effective resource utilization. The chapter explores the concept of sustainability in data centers and shares global standards, examples, and recommendations to enhance their efficiency. It provides valuable insights for optimizing data centers and promoting a greener approach to data management and computing.

In the tourism domain, chapter 7 examines the feasibility of implementing green tourism practices in small emerging economies in Europe. Using a case study of a spa destination in Serbia, it analyzes the potential for meeting certification standards and promoting sustainable tourism. The chapter explores the challenges faced by smaller destinations in aligning with sustainable tourism standards and discusses the role of destination management and national-level support in achieving certification.

Chapter 8 explores the impact of green marketing tools on consumer purchasing behavior in the cosmetic industry. It examines the influence of eco-label, eco-brand, and environmental advertising on students' purchasing decisions, in reference to the Theory of Planned Behavior. Through Partial Least Squares Structural Equation Modeling (PLS-SEM), the chapter reveals the significant role of eco-label and environmental advertising in shaping consumer choices. The findings contribute to a better understanding of how green marketing strategies drive sustainable consumption in the cosmetic industry.

Chapter 9 delves into the challenges of road traffic congestion and proposes innovative measures to achieve a sustainable transportation system. It emphasizes the critical role of transport in sustainable development and highlights the growing demand for mobility. The chapter examines vital decision-makers in shaping transportation systems, focusing on intelligent transportation systems. These systems are identified as instrumental in addressing road congestion, reducing noise levels, and promoting sustainable mobility. By exploring the role of intelligent transportation systems, the chapter aims to enhance overall traffic performance and contribute to a more sustainable and efficient transportation infrastructure.

Chapter 10 focuses on the implementation of carbon tax measures, emphasizing the need for a selective and authoritative approach to ensure effectiveness. By introducing Petri Nets, the chapter aims to provide a framework for modeling and optimizing a multi-level marketing system that supports a green economy and facilitates the effective implementation of carbon tax policies.

Punitha Sinnappan
Sunway University, Malaysia

Chapter 1
Green Marketing:
Exploring Concepts, Strategies, and Future Trends

Nandana Ranjith
CHRIST University (Deemed), India

D. Preethi
CHRIST University (Deemed), India

Krishna Prasath S.
CHRIST University (Deemed), India

ABSTRACT

Green marketing research is becoming more and more well-liked in academia and business. Both companies and customers today recognize the value of eco-friendly products due to increased awareness of how companies respond to various factors contributing to environmental degradation. One should understand the meaning, opportunities, and threats associated with green marketing to harness the benefits of green marketing. This book chapter aims to explore various aspects of green marketing, including its evolution throughout the years, opportunities, threats, the future of green marketing, etc. To sum up, this chapter aims to gain an in-depth understanding of green marketing and how companies could use it to their advantage. Successful implementation will be possible only if associated threats are carefully analyzed and understood. Therefore, a part of this chapter will be dedicated to understanding the threats associated with green marketing strategies.

DOI: 10.4018/978-1-6684-8140-0.ch001

INTRODUCTION

Marketing is how a company promotes purchasing or selling a product or service. Contrary to popular belief, marketing is more than just selling and promoting. It also addresses managerial and social issues related to producing value for a product or service (Kotler & Armstrong, 2023). Marketing is essential for every organization because it raises consumer awareness of the firm's products or services, engages them, and assists the customers in making purchase decisions (Emeritus, 2022). Marketing is critical to every profit-seeking organization since it serves as a channel between customers and other stakeholders. In this age of information influx, it has become difficult for organizations to attract the attention of the mass. Marketers are forced to develop new and innovative methods to connect with their audience making it a hectic job. Marketers are trying to relate to their ultimate consumers and attract new ones. They are often chasing the new trends in the market to seem more relatable and be accepted by the mass. Sustainability and environmental consciousness are some terms that we come across on a daily basis. Due to a greater understanding of how firms react to numerous elements causing environmental degradation, both businesses and customers today recognize the value of eco-friendly products. Research on green marketing is gaining popularity in both academia and business.

Moreover, the impact of industrialization on the environment and other man-made environmental catastrophes have made people view businesses as a threat to the environment. Organizations are motivated to produce ecological products as a result of environmental damage. Increased consumption and a favorable attitude towards environmentally friendly items promote the growth of green products and marketing (Vilkaite-Vaitone & Skackauskiene, 2019). As consumers' awareness of environmental issues grew, businesses started to capitalize on people's interests.

Aim and Purpose of the Chapter

In the current generation of information influx, it has become challenging for companies to grasp customers' attention to their products or services. Considering the hype for environmental consciousness, green marketing could be used as an effective tool to reach the audience.

To get the maximum benefit from green marketing, it is essential to know what green marketing is, assess the evolution of green marketing since the early 1960s and provide a criticism of both theories and practices to understand how the marketing discipline may still progress toward improved sustainability.

Finally, this chapter aims to identify current trends in green marketing in the contemporary marketing world.

An in-depth understanding of the concept of green marketing would enable easy identification of opportunities and threats associated with green marketing, which in turn helps marketers adopt green marketing strategies successfully.

This chapter could provide ample information about green marketing to researchers and students for a better understanding of concepts relating to green marketing.

To sum up, the chapter's main objective is to provide readers with a thorough grasp of green marketing and its advantages for businesses. Examining the possible hazards connected with green marketing is essential before exploring the benefits it offers altogether. Organizations may work to get the best outcomes in their attempts at green marketing by carefully analyzing and managing these risks. By doing a thorough literature study on the topic and providing actual instances of businesses that have successfully utilized green marketing methods, this chapter strives to improve our understanding of green marketing. The ultimate goal is to compile all facts and insights available to help different organizational stakeholders better understand the concept and make appropriate decisions.

As discussed in this chapter, these fundamental aspects of green marketing will enable stakeholders, especially decision-makers, to fully understand various aspects of green marketing and may effectively use such tactics. Moreover, this chapter will provide useful information for researchers carrying out or planning to conduct studies in related areas.

Methodology

The primary objective of this chapter is to gain a comprehensive understanding of green marketing, including the advantages it brings to an organization. In discussing the opportunities presented by green marketing, it is essential to examine the potential risks involved thoroughly. Without carefully analyzing and mitigating these risks, achieving optimal results from green marketing cannot be assured. Thus, through this chapter, the concept of green marketing, its emergence, and its associated threats are explained. Through this chapter, the readers will get an in-depth understanding of the phenomenon of green marketing through an extensive literature review on the topic. The chapter also put forward real-life examples of companies that use green marketing to give readers a better understanding of the topic. Thus, the primary objective of the chapter is to collect all the available information to understand better the concept that, in turn, would help various stakeholders of an organization to understand the concept and make decisions accordingly.

There are various methods of conducting research viz review, experimental, observational, survey, and case study, few to name. Since the nature of this book chapter is to understand the given concept in depth, the review method has been adopted. The review method seeks to provide a complete and critical analysis of the pertinent literature and research. It requires meticulously locating, evaluating, and synthesizing the findings of critical studies in order to address research issues or advance understanding of a particular subject (Baumeister & Leary, 1997). To sum up, the primary goal of review research is to synthesize and compile the available information on a particular subject. Its primary goals are to give an in-depth summary, fill in any gaps in the literature, and make wise suggestions for ongoing and future projects. This aligns perfectly with the objective of this chapter.

A narrative review is employed to be more specific with the methodology. A systematic review has been considered for the chapter, but considering the flexibility that comes with opting narrative review, the goal is to provide a broad overview of a topic or field rather than conducting an exhaustive and systematic search of the literature. Moreover, systematic reviews demand a lot of time and effort due to the laborious nature of their tasks, which include thorough literature searches, quality evaluation, data extraction, and maybe meta-analysis. A narrative review becomes a more practical choice when there are time and budget limitations. A narrative review can nevertheless provide insightful analysis and effectively advance our understanding of a subject despite variations in technique.

What is Green Marketing?

Let us first examine some definitions of green marketing to get insights into the concept.

According to Henion and Kinnear (1976), ecological marketing (also known as green marketing) "is concerned with all marketing activities:(1) that served to help environmental problems, and (2) that may serve to provide a remedy for environmental problems".

Pride and Ferrell (1993) defined green marketing as "an organization's effort of designing, promoting, pricing and distributing products that will not harm the environment".

Polonsky (1994) defined green marketing as a phenomenon "consisting of all activities designed to generate and facilitate any exchanges intended to satisfy human needs, such that the satisfaction of these needs and wants occurs, with minimal detrimental impact on the natural environment".

Tiwari et al. (2011) defined green marketing as a "holistic marketing concept wherein the production, marketing consumption and disposal of products and services happen in a manner that is less detrimental to the environment with growing awareness about the implications of global warming, non-biodegradable solid waste, harmful impact of pollutants, etc.".

According to Groening et al. (2018), "Green marketing involves marketing (e.g., price and promotion) combined with the goal of reducing environmental impact, although not necessarily with the goal of reducing consumption, rather to persuade the consumer to purchase green products and services."

A wide range of collective actions are referred to as green marketing, including changes to packaging, advertising, the manufacturing process, and the products themselves (Polonsky, 1994); this is clear from the definitions that have been examined earlier. From the definitions, it is also clear that, unlike traditional marketing techniques, green marketing involves not only merely marketing the products, it expects the firm to make the product itself or the process more environmentally friendly.

An article by Vaibhav et al. (2015) tries to understand and resolve challenges faced by green marketers by assimilating green marketing and the 4 Ps of the marketing mix.

Four P's of Green Marketing

Green Products: Those products whose environmental and social performance, in manufacturing, usage, and disposal, is noticeably better and getting better when compared to traditional or comparable products available in the market (Peattie, 1995). According to Vaibhav et al. (2015), green products should incorporate a better design, eco-friendly technology, and packing while not compromising on quality, usefulness, and value.

Green Pricing: Green products are generally costlier (D'Souza et al., 2006). This could be because of considerable investments in research and development of such products. Like most other types of innovative activity, green product creation is fraught with risk and uncertainty (Chen, 2001). A premium price is usually charged for the additional benefits offered. Consider sustainable clothing, they are generally on the pricey side (de Brito et al., 2008), and it is a niche market (Niinimäki, 2010); many people do not understand the amount of money they save up in the long run if they switch to sustainable clothing. Similar is the case with energy-efficient equipment. People see the price tag and immediately reject it but may not consider potential cost benefits in the long run. People choose choices that require a smaller initial financial outlay, not recognizing that another option is less expensive in the long term while also being better for the environment (Gleim et al., 2013). It is stated that buyers are not interested in paying more for a "green" product, so marketers must emphasize the pricing policy (Ottman, 1998). This is why marketing is essential, and marketing campaigns should highlight the benefits of green products and be able to justify the reasons for a premium price.

Green Place: Place in the marketing mix is that element that ensures that the product is supplied and is accessible to the customers at the right time (Mahmoud, 2018). It involves the process of delivering things from the manufacturer to the consumer. In order for green businesses to successfully establish themselves and achieve competitive pricing, companies need to ensure that their distributors prioritize environmental concerns and implement a green distribution strategy (Mahmoud, 2018). The green place is nothing but using green distribution channels to reach consumers. Green distribution includes efforts to reduce the environmental effect of moving goods and services from supplier to customer and vice versa (Håkansson & Waluszewski, 2005; Taş & Akcan, 2022). Firms could achieve a green distribution channel by evaluating their existing supply chain and bringing in necessary changes.

Green Promotion: Using environmentally friendly marketing techniques to publicize a company's goods or services is referred to as green promotion (Kalama, 2007). Firms could highlight their eco-friendly features more in promotional activities. An excellent example of green promotion could be Patagonia's campaign in 2011. The campaign was featured in New York Times, with a picture of Patagonia jacket telling readers not to buy the jacket. The advertisement briefed the reasons why they are asking the readers not to the jacket. The advertisement also briefed why they should not buy the jacket and showed the reader that producing one such jacket causes a trail of environmental damages. The advertisement included a list of things that will result, or the purchase of the jacket will constitute. They advertised that with one purchase made, 20 pounds of carbon dioxide were released, which is 24 times the weight of the jacket, the 36 gallons of water needed to make the jacket (enough to meet the daily needs of 45 people), and the volume of garbage generated (two-thirds of its weight in waste) (Kenji, 2020). The main motive here was to encourage people to reuse their jackets or buy second-hand rather than buy a new one. Switching to digital marketing methods instead of print promotions could reduce the use of paper in the organization, a green practice that could bring down the cost of production.

The four Ps of green marketing are integral to the process, and each element should be carefully examined.

Traditional Marketing Versus Green Marketing

Marketing is an essential aspect of any business as it helps to promote and sell products or services to consumers. However, as the world becomes more environmentally conscious, businesses are starting to adopt a new approach to marketing known as green marketing. Green marketing focuses on promoting products and services that are environmentally friendly and sustainable (Dangelico & Vocalelli, 2017), while traditional marketing focuses on promoting products and services without considering the environment. Promoting and selling goods and services to customers is the primary goal of conventional marketing (Kotler et al., 2015). Print commercials, television advertising, radio advertising, and billboards are examples of traditional marketing techniques. Conventional marketing aims to influence as many people as possible to buy a specific good or service. Traditional marketing does not emphasize environmentally friendly methods or contemplate how a product or service will affect the environment.

Traditional marketing strategies include print advertisements, television commercials, radio ads, and billboards. These strategies focus on reaching as many people as possible and persuading them to purchase a particular product or service (Abebe et al., 2018). Traditional marketing does not take into consideration the impact that the product or service has on the environment, and it does not focus on sustainable practices.

Green marketing strategies focus on promoting environment-friendly and sustainable products and services. These strategies include eco-friendly packaging, renewable energy, and sustainable materials. Green marketing emphasizes the importance of sustainability and encourages businesses to adopt environmentally friendly practices. Green marketing also uses social media platforms and online advertising to reach environmentally-conscious consumers who want to make sustainable choices (Ginsberg & Bloom, 2004).

The success of conventional marketing tactics relies on the intended audience and the advertised product or service. While it can effectively appeal to a wide range of consumers and convince them to buy a particular product or service, conventional marketing is inadequate in promoting eco-friendly and sustainable products and services. It fails to understand the significance of sustainability and does not motivate businesses to adopt eco-friendly practices (Piercy, 1998).

On the other hand, green marketing is useful in reaching out to environmentally aware consumers who prioritize sustainable choices. It prioritizes sustainability and encourages businesses to incorporate eco-friendly practices. Furthermore, green marketing effectively promotes eco-friendly and sustainable products and services. Consumers prioritizing environmental sustainability are more inclined to purchase such products and services.

History

With the end of World War II, environmental concerns began to receive more attention in the US, where green marketing first became well-known. After the Second World War, several environmental problems in the 1960s and 1970s, including the Santa Barbara Oil Spill of 1969, sparked discussions about environmental preservation in the US.

The news of ozone depletion at the tail end of the 1970s significantly increased people's sensitivity to environmental problems. This increased concern for the environment sparked many socio-political responses, including the creation of the Clean Air Act in 1963 and the Endangered Species Act in 1973, among others.

Green marketing has come about as a result of businesses being compelled to operate more responsibly due to the public's increased awareness of environmental concerns (Trandafilovic et al., 2017).

There have been numerous early adopters of environment friendly marketing techniques, making it difficult to pinpoint which firm tried it first. Nevertheless, Patagonia is widely considered to be one of the pioneers in Green Marketing. Yvon Chouinard started Patagonia by producing mountain climbing gear. A climbing gear called piton made the majority of Patagonia's sales in the early 1970s. A piton is a spike made of hammered metal inserted into a rock's cracks. The climbing rope is then attached to a carabiner, which is in turn attached to the piton. All of this equipment is required to ensure climbers' safety when ascending. As soon Chouinard realized his pitons were damaging the rocks, he started reducing the production of these pitons. This was one of Patagonia's first steps to conserve the environment. Soon they came up with an alternative for pitons and introduced it to the customers through a 14-page essay in their catalog. The essay briefed about how this newly formed alternative for pitons where more environment friendly, laying the groundwork for future environmental essays in Patagonia collections. Patagonia is today known for its environment-friendly initiatives.

Ecover is another excellent example of companies trying to be more environmentally conscious in the 1970s. Ecover is a company that produces eco-friendly cleaning products. Ecover had its humble beginnings in the late 1970s when a group of Belgian scientists came together to create phosphate-free cleaning solutions to decrease the harm cleaning supplies do to the environment. Green marketing was not practiced as it is today in the 1970s. To be more correct, various organizations have become more conscious of the environment in response to rising environmental concerns.

The 1980s was the time when firms started taking Green marketing more seriously. The 1980s witnessed a lot of environmental catastrophes, like the Exxon Valdez oil spill in 1989, Chornobyl in 1986, the Bhopal disaster in 1984, and the ozone hole in Antarctica that was discovered in 1985. As a result of the media's coverage of these and other disasters, public concern for the environment grew, making the topic popular (Peattie, 2001). Several firms and organizations began to employ green marketing methods in order to target clients who were growing more environmentally conscious. In the 1980s, several companies started integrating environmental statements and themes into their advertising and marketing materials as part of the green marketing movement. The Body Shop, a British cosmetics company that opened its doors in 1976, pioneered in the environmentally conscious and ethical beauty segment. In the 1980s, The Body Shop began advertising its products as eco-friendly, and the company's founder, Anita Roddick, became a proponent of eco-friendly business practices. While McDonald's is not commonly associated with environmental activism, the fast-food corporation publicized its environmental efforts in the 1980s.

McDonald's issued its first environmental report in 1989, detailing the company's efforts to reduce pollution and preserve resources.

During the 1990s, consumers' awareness of environmental issues and green marketing grew. During this time, many businesses started making even more efforts to promote their green credentials through marketing and advertising and increased their environmental efforts. In 1992, Nike launched its Reuse-A-Shoe initiative, which gathered and repurposed used sports shoes into new products. Additionally, the firm began involving reused materials in its shoeboxes and made environmentally friendly bundling materials. In 1997, Toyota introduced the Prius, the first mass-produced hybrid vehicle in history. The company made a big deal of the environmental benefits of the car, like lower emissions and better fuel economy, through marketing campaigns. The Body Shop's Community Trade initiative, which sourced goods from fair trade vendors, was launched in the 1990s to further its commitment to environmental sustainability. In addition, the business began actively promoting and advertising its eco-friendly products and developed its first eco-friendly packaging.

Green marketing grew more popular in the 1990s, and many firms began to make significant efforts to improve their environmental policies and publicize and sell them. However, the major problem in this era was the allegations of greenwashing. Greenwashing is the practice of presenting misleading or inflated environmental claims regarding goods or services in an effort to win over environmentally conscientious. In response to rising environmental consciousness, businesses started incorporating rhetorical fallacies about their eco-friendly practices into their advertising and marketing efforts in the 1980s, which is when greenwashing first became a problem. Customers are now skeptical about genuine claims made by companies as a part of their green marketing efforts.

The 2000s saw a rise in green marketing and eco-friendly products, but it was also a time when many companies engaged in greenwashing. Greenwashing refers to making false or exaggerated environmental claims to appeal to environmentally-conscious consumers without making significant changes to their production or business practices. Green marketing became increasingly popular in the 2000s as consumers and businesses become more aware of environmental issues and the need for sustainable practices. Many businesses started incorporating green marketing into their branding and advertising strategies in the 2000s. This included emphasizing the use of recycled or sustainable materials in their goods, minimizing their carbon footprint, and showcasing their ecologically responsible production practices. In the early 2000s, BP started a rebranding campaign with a new logo that featured a green and yellow sunflower. In addition, the company began to promote its environmental initiatives and investments in renewable energy sources like wind and solar power. However, BP was later criticized for its poor safety record and its contribution to climate change through the production of fossil fuels. BP spent significantly more money on activities that extract oil than it did on renewable energy. BP only invested $45 million in the solar energy company Solarex in 1999, compared to the $26.5 billion it spent to acquire ARCO to diversify its oil drilling operations (Landman, 2010). In 2008, McDonald's debuted several eateries advertised as using sustainable resources and green energy. However, detractors cited the eateries' continued reliance on unsustainable practices, such as providing food in single-use containers. In 2009, ExxonMobil introduced a brand of gasoline that it promoted as being ecologically benign and lowering pollution. Critics countered that the fuel did little to lower pollution and was hardly distinguishable from regular gasoline. Overall, the rise of green marketing in the 2000s reflected a growing awareness of environmental issues among consumers and businesses and a desire to promote more sustainable practices and products. Nevertheless, greenwashing has become a common practice ever since more and more companies have started adopting green marketing. Various well-known companies have been alleged to be greenwashing, which is a significant threat to green marketing.

Opportunities

We often read about the consequences that human beings and other living beings face as a result of climate change, global warming, rising sea levels, melting glaciers, etc. As a result, people are becoming more aware of the importance of protecting the environment in which they live. People want to ensure that future generations inherit a clean planet. Numerous studies conducted by environmentalists indicate that people are changing their behavior to be more environmentally friendly because they are concerned about the environment (Mishra & Sharma, 2010).

Some of the opportunities of green marketing are listed down:

1.   Attract environmentally conscious consumers

Environmental concerns are becoming more and more prevalent around the world (Chang, 2011). Moreover, various reports claim that customers are becoming more environmentally conscious day by day. According to surveys conducted in the United States and Europe in the 2000s, environmental awareness has increased (Eurobarometer, 2008; Saad, 2007). According to Eurobarometer (2008), over ninety-five percent of European respondents agree that environmental protection is essential. Eighty percent of people believe it impacts their quality of life and that they should contribute to its protection. According to a news report by Gallup in 2007, concern for the environment among US citizens has increased. This trend of increasing awareness and sentiments towards environmental issues continues to grow. In the wake of the pandemic, individuals are more dedicated to addressing environmental concerns and modifying their own behavior to improve sustainability, according to a new BCG survey of more than 3,000 people across eight countries (Kachaner et al., 2020).

As people are becoming more conscious about the environment, there is an opportunity for companies to capitalize on such emotions.

Companies may cultivate strong customer relationships through green marketing by showcasing their dedication to environmental sustainability. Companies can boost brand recognition by demonstrating to their customers that they are taking steps to minimize their environmental effects. When the brands that consumers favor work to safeguard the environment, they are pleased and proud of them (Tanwari, 2020). Moreover, currently, available works of literature indicate that brand performance is influenced by ethical business behavior (Sharma & Sharma, 2014).

According to Mainieri et al. (1997), improper labeling and poor marketing may often be reasons why pro-environment consumerism trailed behind their ideals. This shows the importance of green marketing for green products and services. Green marketers must properly communicate their green features, whether associated with the product, price, promotion, or place. Considering this increase in demand for green alternatives, not many companies have fully utilized green marketing to their advantage.

2.   Differentiate from competitors

Competitive advantage is the capacity to operate at a greater level than rivals in the same market or industry with better and more efficient utilization of resources (Porter, 1998). The distribution system, intellectual property, cost structure, branding, product quality, customer service, and cost structure are just a few factors that contribute to competitive advantages (Twin, 2022). In an era of stiff competition, companies are looking for ways to set them apart from their competitors. Green marketing could be one way of differentiating the brand or company from its competitors.

Seventh Generation, an American company that sells household cleaning products, has set a unique place in the market through its green product attributes. In addition to using biodegradable, plant-based phosphate- and chlorine-free ingredients in its products, the company uses recycled and post-consumer materials in its packaging. Similarly, Patagonia has many competitors, Canada Goose, and Columbia Sportswear, to name a few popular ones. However, in its market, Patagonia created an image that set them apart from its competitors via green marketing.

3.   Creates a good image

Green marketing initiatives will improve the company's brand image and ultimately influence consumer purchasing decisions (Nguyen & Nguyen, 2018). Many businesses strive to establish a good brand reputation because it offers a variety of advantages, such as the ability to withstand aggressive marketing tactics from rival businesses, increased support and cooperation from intermediaries, and possibilities for brand expansion (Delgado-Ballester & Munuera-Alemán, 2005).

4.   Reduce the cost of production:

Green Marketing focuses on creating and promoting goods considered safe for the ecosystem and aimed at reducing adverse environmental impacts. Unlike traditional marketing, green marketing aims to satisfy the customers' needs while minimizing the ecological impact (Sinnappan & Rasdi, 2013). According to American Marketing Association, green marketing "refers to the development and promotion of products that are presumed to be environmentally safe (i.e., designed to minimize negative effects on the physical environment or to improve its quality)." To sum up, green marketing does not imply merely selling a product. It encompasses a wide range of activities, including modifications to packaging, promotions, and manufacturing processes, as well as product modifications (Polonsky, 1994). This requires the firm to include more greener approach in its production process. Green marketing reduces the cost of production; for example, if the firm uses simplified packaging, costs are reduced while harmful waste like emissions and toxic byproducts are eliminated with simplified and sustainable packaging. This results in lower fees and penalties for safe disposal and containment. By using chemicals that are not harmful, green manufacturing also saves water and reduces waste disposal. Recycling water also reduces the need for freshwater, which can be used for cleaning and irrigation, among other things. Solar panels and lighting that uses less energy are also effective ways to save money and money spent on energy (NJMEP, 2016).

Apart from the opportunities mentioned, there are a few others like a chance to connect more closely with stakeholders and customers. Businesses that can demonstrate their commitment to sustainability and social responsibility gain the trust and appreciation of stakeholders and customers. Customer loyalty, effective word-of-mouth advertising, and brand reputation may all improve as a result. The price of sustainable goods and services is another problem. Although people are eager to pay more for eco-friendly items, not everyone can. As a result, businesses must figure out how to lower the cost of sustainable goods and services while increasing their availability to a wider variety of customers.

Last but not least, there are a number of green marketing prospects. One of the most significant opportunities is the possibility of expanding markets for sustainable products and services. As consumers become more aware of their choices' effects on society and the environment, they are more likely to look for new products and services that meet their needs and values.

Threats

One of the major threats associated with using green marketing strategies is the confusion between green marketing and greenwashing. It is important to remember that no campaign will be effective if the company does not practice the idea being promoted. In plain English, this is acting on your promises or walking the talk. This is a section where a company's credibility is evaluated (de Bakker, 2009).

The failure to translate words into actions is one of the critical faults that has caused green marketing tactics to backfire in the past.

1.   Greenwashing

Green marketing refers to the promotion of items that are thought to be ecologically safe. While greenwashing refers to deceiving customers about a company's environmental policies or false marketing claims made about the advantages of a product or service to the environment (Tinne, 2013). Businesses have used green marketing techniques to convey their environmental initiatives in order to increase their competitive edge and lure environmentally conscientious customers (Szabo & Webster, 2020). With the increase in demand for green products, more companies have started emphasizing the sustainability of their operations and products in order to capitalize on these expanding green markets (Delmas & Burbano, 2011). Often the claims made by organizations appear to be false or misleading. According to the study by Szabo and Webster (2020), customers' perceptions of a company's products might be harmed by perceived greenwashing.

The main issue with greenwashing is that consumers become confused about products that are actually green. Because of this, genuine attempts made by companies are often confused with being greenwashing; hence, the firm cannot derive the full benefits of green marketing (Furlow, 2010).

2.   Green marketing myopia

"Green marketing must satisfy two objectives: improved environmental quality and customer satisfaction. Misjudging either or overemphasizing the former at the expense of the latter can be termed green marketing myopia" (Ottman et al., 2006). A situation wherein an undertaking tries to fulfill its environmental goals while neglecting to fulfill its obligations to the customers, creating an imbalance between the company's marketing goals (Hernández-Zelaya et al., 2021).

In 2008, Frito Lay came up with biodegradable packaging for the SunChips product line. The company claimed that the bag is made up of decomposable natural fibers. Soon after the release, the company received much backlash online for the noisy corn-based packaging. As mentioned before, green marketing has two objectives: that the brand's environmental features deliver obvious advantages to customers and that the cost of the green attribute to consumers does not outweigh the product's benefits (Ottman et al., 2006). In this example, customers did not place a high value on compostability, while many found the noisy packing extremely unpleasant (Ottman & Eisen, 2010).

3.   Products become expensive.

Goods may become more expensive if we try to go green. Green or environmentally safe products are an integral part of green marketing strategies. The expense of producing green products is generally higher than the cost of producing conventional products (Li & Cai, 2009). Utilizing cutting-edge technology to prevent contamination and purchasing ecologically friendly materials through legitimate sources require substantial monetary investments. They are making the cost of green marketing higher than that of traditional marketing. Developing green goods in itself is expensive as massive amounts are to be spent on research and development (Keegan & Green, 2000). Because of this, some businesses continue to pursue a wait-and-see strategy rather than making a firm commitment to the creation of green products (Roome, 1992). A company which is aiming to harness the benefits of green marketing should be involved in the creation and promotion of goods that are environmentally friendly or be ready to bring in necessary changes to its products and processes to reduce its negative impacts on the environment.

4.   Socio-Economic Factors

The pandemic of coronavirus disease 2019 (COVID-19) and its repercussions on an individual's life have changed consumer behavior. A movement from conventional to green purchasing has been seen in the context of buying and consumption (Sajid et al., 2022). A series of consumer surveys conducted by Deloitte in the UK from 2020-2022 give insights about how consumers' attitudes and behavior have changed over the years. They first conducted the survey before the worst of the COVID-19 pandemic and the second one again in March 2021. The results showed that consumers adopted more sustainable lifestyles during the pandemic, like shopping more locally and spending only on necessities. The same survey carried out in 2021 and 2022 suggests that this was due more to the impact of COVID-19 rather than a conscious choice to adopt a more sustainable lifestyle.

According to the survey in 2022, consumers are finding it hard to save money and are in a quest to find ways to save money, such as by adopting a more sustainable lifestyle and selecting more durable goods that can be reused or repaired simply. This is because they have fewer options and opportunities as a result of the impact of inflation and supply chain disruptions. 2022 added to the problems of economic uncertainty (Deloitte, 2023). Two main groups of factors are causing the present wave of global inflation. On the supply side, the COVID-19 pandemic's effects on the world's circumstances are causing prices of goods like food and gasoline to rise (CNBCTV18, 2021).

Green Marketing in the 21st Century

Green marketing, also called eco-marketing or sustainable marketing, is the practice of promoting products or services with environmentally friendly characteristics. Green marketing aims to heighten consumer awareness about sustainable practices and encourage them to make environmentally responsible choices. Over the past few decades, green marketing has grown in popularity as people have become more concerned about the impact of human activities on the environment.

In the early 2000s, green marketing was still a novel concept. Although a few companies have been promoting eco-friendly products and services, most companies have not yet embraced the idea of sustainability. Nevertheless, this began to change as more consumers demanded eco-friendly products and services.

One of the major driving forces behind the growth of green marketing in the 2000s was the mounting awareness of climate change. People began to realize that their daily actions significantly impacted the environment, and they recognized the need to take measures to reduce their carbon footprint. As a result, they started to seek out eco-friendly products and services. Many companies perceived this as an opportunity to differentiate themselves from their competitors by highlighting their eco-friendly credentials. They began to use green marketing as a means of appealing to consumers who were concerned about the environment. This led to an expansion in the availability of eco-friendly products and services, such as organic food and hybrid cars. However, not all companies were genuine in their efforts to promote sustainability. Some companies engaged in "greenwashing," which involved making false or misleading claims about the environmental benefits of their products or services. This practice was problematic for both consumers and legitimate green businesses, as it made it challenging for consumers to distinguish which companies were truly committed to sustainability. Various organizations, such as the Federal Trade Commission (FTC), implemented guidelines for green marketing claims to address this issue. These guidelines mandate that companies provide clear and truthful information about the environmental benefits of their products or services.

They also prohibited companies from making vague or unverifiable claims about their eco-friendliness.

Another challenge for green marketing in the 2000s was the cost of eco-friendly products and services. Although many consumers were willing to pay a premium for sustainable products, there was a limit to how much they were willing to spend. Consumers would often choose a less expensive, non-eco-friendly alternative if a product or service cost were too high; this made it difficult for businesses to price their eco-friendly products and services competitively. To overcome this challenge, some businesses focused on making their eco-friendly products and services more affordable. They searched for ways to reduce their costs, such as by utilizing recycled materials or optimizing their production processes. This helped to make eco-friendly products and services more accessible to a wider range of consumers.

Green marketing was crucial in raising consumer awareness about sustainability and encouraging businesses to adopt more eco-friendly practices in the 2000s. While there were obstacles to overcome, such as greenwashing and pricing, the trend towards sustainability continued to gain momentum. Nowadays, green marketing has become more prevalent and accepted, and consumers have more choices than ever before when it comes to eco-friendly products and services.

While in the 20th century, consumers were often a victim of greenwashing practices, in the 21st century, people and the media have become quick to point out the claims that seem unrealistic and hold them accountable for false claims made in the name of green marketing.

Future of Green Marketing

The growing demand for environmentally friendly goods and services is one of the most critical trends in green marketing. Due to the increasing number of green customers worldwide, marketers have struggled to comprehend consumers' purchasing intentions for green products (D'Souza et al., 2006). Our literature review suggests that more people are becoming aware of environmental issues and ready to contribute to positive change. It turns out that people are ready to shell out more money for goods and services that are ecologically beneficial. Future predictions say that this tendency will continue as consumers grow more conscious of their decisions' effects on society and the environment. Long-term success is likely for businesses that can provide sustainable goods and services that satisfy customer demands.

In green marketing, openness and cooperation are increasingly becoming more crucial. Cooperation among private sector, nonprofit, and governmental groups may aid in promoting sustainability and developing a more sustainable economy. Moreover, more governments are pushing businesses to go green or at least adopt some green practices. Consumers and stakeholders are more inclined to trust businesses that are open and honest about their sustainability strategies and results. In order to protect consumers from greenwashing, the need for robust verification and certification systems to validate green claims has become the priority of governments.

CONCLUSION AND RECOMMENDATION FOR FUTURE RESEARCH

The practice of marketing goods or services that are ecologically benign, morally responsible, and fiscally viable is known as green marketing or sustainable marketing. Through the review of the literature, it was found that people's sentiments toward environmental concerns are increasing. Business organizations are liable as each individual in protecting the environment, but are they eco-conscious? At present, not to the extent they have to be. Moreover, several business organizations have been held liable for various environmental damages that have been caused. These allegations have built a negative image of big corporations in people's minds. Green marketing could help organizations regain some of their lost glory. Unlike traditional marketing, green marketing focuses on growing green consciousness.

This chapter has discussed some of the significant opportunities available if the company goes green. Green marketing does not, however, come without challenges. One of the biggest challenges is the lack of international standardization for what defines sustainable or ecologically friendly products and services. This has led to a lot of misinformation and "greenwashing," in which companies claim how much more ecologically responsible they are than they actually are.

To sum up, green marketing gives firms a bunch of opportunities. Ultimately it is in the hands of the firm how well they utilize the opportunities available to them.

The chapter only discusses various fundamental aspects of green marketing and associated terminologies, but by examining relevant literature and analyzing available statistical data, it can be concluded that the general public is becoming more environment-conscious. However, a lot of literature argues that these environment-conscious attitudes do not necessarily turn into eco-friendly purchase decisions. A detailed qualitative study could be conducted to understand the deviations in the attitude and behavior of consumers.

REFERENCES

Abebe, R., Adamic, L., & Kleinberg, J. (2018). Mitigating Overexposure in Viral Marketing. *Proceedings of the AAAI Conference on Artificial Intelligence*, *32*(1). doi:10.1609/aaai.v32i1.11282

Baumeister, R. F., & Leary, M. R. (1997). Writing Narrative Literature Reviews. *Review of General Psychology*, *1*(3), 311–320. doi:10.1037/1089-2680.1.3.311

Chang, C. (2011). Feeling ambivalent about going green: Implications for green advertising processing. *Journal of Advertising*, *40*(4), 19–31. doi:10.2753/JOA0091-3367400402

Chen, C. (2001). Design for the Environment: A Quality-Based Model for Green Product Development. *Management Science*, *47*(2), 250–263. doi:10.1287/mnsc.47.2.250.9841

CNBCTV18. (2021). Explained: Why inflation rates are increasing across the globe. *CNBCTV18*. https://www.cnbctv18.com/economy/explained-why-inflation-rat es-are-increasing-across-the-globe-11565352.htm

D'Souza, C., Taghian, M., Lamb, P., & Peretiatkos, R. (2006). Green products and corporate strategy: An empirical investigation. *Society and Business Review*, *1*(2), 144–157. doi:10.1108/17465680610669825

Dangelico, R. M., & Vocalelli, D. (2017). "Green Marketing": An analysis of definitions, strategy steps, and tools through a systematic review of the literature. *Journal of Cleaner Production*, *165*, 1263–1279. doi:10.1016/j.jclepro.2017.07.184

de Bakker, F. G. A. (2009). Book Review: Jennifer Howard-Grenville. Corporate culture and environmental practice: Making change at a high-technology manufacturer. Cheltenham, UK: Edward Elgar, 2007. *Organization & Environment*, *22*(2), 257–260. doi:10.1177/1086026609338170

de Brito, M. P., Carbone, V., & Blanquart, C. M. (2008). Towards a sustainable fashion retail supply chain in Europe: Organisation and performance. *International Journal of Production Economics*, *114*(2), 534–553. doi:10.1016/j.ijpe.2007.06.012

Delgado-Ballester, E., & Munuera-Alemán, J. L. (2005). Does brand trust matter to brand equity? *Journal of Product and Brand Management*, *14*(3), 187–196. doi:10.1108/10610420510601058

Delmas, M. A., & Burbano, V. C. (2011). The drivers of greenwashing. *California Management Review*, *54*(1), 64–87. doi:10.1525/cmr.2011.54.1.64

Deloitte. (2023). *How consumers are embracing sustainability*. Deloitte. https://www2.deloitte.com/uk/en/pages/consumer-business/articles/sustainable-consumer.html

Emeritus. (2022). *What is the Importance of Marketing for Businesses? Discover the Undiscovered*. Emeritus. https://emeritus.org/blog/what-is-the-importance-of-marketing-for-business/

Eurobarometer. (2008). *Attitudes of Europeans towards the Environment*. European Union. https://europa.eu/eurobarometer/surveys/detail/673

Furlow, N. E. (2010). Greenwashing in the new millennium. *The Journal of Applied Business and Economics*, *10*(6), 22–25.

Ginsberg, J. M., & Bloom, P. N. (2004). Choosing the right green marketing strategy. *MIT Sloan Management Review*, *46*(1), 79–84.

Gleim, M. R., Smith, J. S., Andrews, D., & Cronin, J. J. Jr. (2013). Against the Green: A Multi-method Examination of the Barriers to Green Consumption. *Journal of Retailing*, *89*(1), 44–61. doi:10.1016/j.jretai.2012.10.001

Groening, C., Sarkis, J., & Zhu, Q. (2018). Green marketing consumer-level theory review: A compendium of applied theories and further research directions. *Journal of Cleaner Production*, *172*, 1848–1866. doi:10.1016/j.jclepro.2017.12.002

Håkansson, H., & Waluszewski, A. (2005). Developing a new understanding of markets: Reinterpreting the 4Ps. *Journal of Business and Industrial Marketing*, *20*(3), 110–117. doi:10.1108/08858620510592722

Henion, K. E., & Kinnear, T. C. (1976). *A guide to ecological marketing. Ecological Marketing*. American Marketing Association.

Hernández-Zelaya, S. L., Reyes-Reina, F., & Rodríguez Benito, M. E. (2021). Evolution and Future of the Marketing and Sustainability Linkage: Towards a Civil Marketing Approach. In Financial Management and Risk Analysis Strategies for Business Sustainability (pp. 105-123). IGI Global.

Kachaner, N., Nielsen, J., Portafaix, A., & Rodzko, F. (2020). *The Pandemic Is Heightening Environmental Awareness*. Boston Consulting Group.

Kalama, E. (2007). *Green marketing practices by Kenya petroleum refineries: A study of the perception of the management of oil marketing companies in Kenya* [Doctoral dissertation, University of NAIROBI].

Keegan, W. J., & Green, M. S. (2000). *Global marketing* (2nd ed.). Prentice-Hall.

Kenji. (2020). "Don't Buy This Jacket" — Patagonia's Daring Campaign. *Medium*. https://bettermarketing.pub/dont-buy-this-jacket-patagonia-s-daring-campaign-2b37e145046b

Kotler, P., & Armstrong, G. (2023). Principles of Marketing. Pearson College Div.

Kotler, P., Burton, S., Brown, L., & Armstrong, G. (2015). *Marketing*. Pearson Higher Education AU.

Landman, A. (2010, May 3). *BP's "Beyond Petroleum" Campaign Losing its Sheen*. Prwatch.

Li, H., & Cai, W. (2009). Green marketing and sustainable development of garment industry-A game between cost and profit. *International Journal of Biometrics*, *3*, 81.

Mahmoud, T. O. (2018). Impact of green marketing mix on purchase intention. *International Journal of Advanced and Applied Sciences*, *5*(2), 127–135. doi:10.21833/ijaas.2018.02.020

Mainieri, T., Barnett, E. G., Valdero, T. R., Unipan, J. B., & Oskamp, S. (1997). Green Buying: The Influence of Environmental Concern on Consumer Behavior. *The Journal of Social Psychology*, *137*(2), 189–204. doi:10.1080/00224549709595430

Mishra, P., & Sharma, P. (2010). Green marketing in India: Emerging opportunities and challenges. *Journal of Engineering. Science and Management Education*, *3*, 9–14.

Nguyen, N. H., & Nguyen, D. N. (2018). Impacts of green marketing on the green brand image and equity in banking sector. *WSEAS Transactions on Business and Economics*, *15*, 452–460.

Niinimäki, K. (2010). Eco-clothing, consumer identity and ideology. *Sustainable Development (Bradford)*, *18*(3), 150–162. doi:10.1002d.455

NJMEP. (2016). *How Green Manufacturing & Sustainability Reduces Costs & Improves Efficiencies*. NJMEP. https://www.njmep.org/blog/how-green-manufacturing-sustainability-reduces-costs-improves-efficiencies/

Ottman, J. (1998). *Green Marketing: Opportunity for Innovation* (2nd ed.). NTC/ Contemporary Publishing Company.

Ottman, J., & Eisen, M. (2010). *Green Marketing Myopia and the SunChips Snacklash*. Green Marketing. http://www.greenmarketing.com/site/green-marketing-myopia-and-the-sunchips-snacklash/

Ottman, J. A., Stafford, E. R., & Hartman, C. L. (2006). Avoiding Green Marketing Myopia: Ways to Improve Consumer Appeal for Environmentally Preferable Products. *Environment*, *48*(5), 22–36. doi:10.3200/ENVT.48.5.22-36

Peattie, K. (1995). *Environmental Marketing Management*. Pitman.

Peattie, K. (2001). Towards sustainability: The third age of green marketing. *The Marketing Review*, *2*(2), 129–146. doi:10.1362/1469347012569869

Piercy, N. F. (1998). Marketing implementation: The implications of marketing paradigm weakness for the strategy execution process. *Journal of the Academy of Marketing Science*, *26*(3), 222–236. doi:10.1177/0092070398263004

Polonsky, M. J. (1994). An introduction to green marketing. *Electronic Green Journal*, *1*(2). Advance online publication. doi:10.5070/G31210177

Porter, M. E. (1998). *The competitive advantage: Creating and sustaining superior performance*. Free Press. doi:10.1007/978-1-349-14865-3

Pride, W. M., & Ferrell, O. C. (1993). *Marketing* (8th ed.). Houghton Mifflin.

Roome, N. (1992). Developing environmental management strategies. *Business Strategy and the Environment*, *1*(1), 11–24. doi:10.1002/bse.3280010104

Saad, L. (2007, March 26). *Environmental concern holds firm during past year*. Gallup News Service. https://news.gallup.com/poll/26971/environmental-concern-holds-firm-during-past-year.aspx

Sajid, K. S., Hussain, S., Hussain, R. I., & Mustafa, B. (2022). The Effect of Fear of COVID-19 on Green Purchase Behavior in Pakistan: A Multi-Group Analysis Between Infected and Non-infected. *Frontiers in Psychology*, *13*, 826870. doi:10.3389/fpsyg.2022.826870 PMID:35422735

Sharma, N. K., & Sharma, B. (2014). Ethical marketing as a tool for developing customer relations: An empirical analysis. *International Journal on Customer Relations*, *2*(2), 26.

Sinnappan, P., & Rasdi, R. M. (2013). Corporate social responsibility: Adoption of green marketing by hotel industry. *Asian Social Science*, *9*(17), 79. doi:10.5539/ass.v9n17p79

Szabo, S., & Webster, J. (2020). Perceived greenwashing: The effects of green marketing on environmental and product perceptions. *Journal of Business Ethics*, *171*(4), 719–739. doi:10.100710551-020-04461-0

Tanwari, A. (2020). A study on assessing the relationship between green marketing and brand loyalty in manufacturing sector of Greece: A moderating role of green supply chain practices. *Journal of Business Management and Accounting*, *4*(1), 44–55.

Taş, M. A., & Akcan, S. (2022). *Investigation of green criteria with clustering analysis in green supplier selection* (pp. 207–228). IGI Global. doi:10.4018/978-1-7998-8900-7.ch012

Tinne, W. S. (2013). Green Washing: An Alarming Issue. *ASA University Review*, *7*(1), 81–88.

Tiwari, S., Tripathi, D. M., Srivastava, U., & Yadav, P. K. (2011). Green marketing-emerging dimensions. *Journal of Business Excellence*, *2*(1), 18–23.

Trandafilovic, I., Conic, V., & Blagojevic, A. (2017). Impact of demographic factors on environmentally conscious purchase behavior. *Ekonomika Poljoprivrede*, *64*(4), 1365–1377. doi:10.5937/ekoPolj1704365T

Twin, A. (2022). *Competitive Advantage Definition with Types and Examples*. Investopedia. https://www.investopedia.com/terms/c/competitive_advantage.asp

Vaibhav, R., Bhalerao, V., & Deshmukh, A. (2015). Green marketing: Greening the 4 Ps of marketing. *International Journal of Knowledge and Research in Management and E-Commerce*, *5*, 5–8.

Vilkaite-Vaitone, N., & Skackauskiene, I. (2019). Green marketing orientation: Evolution, conceptualization and potential benefits. *Open Economics*, *2*(1), 53–62. doi:10.1515/openec-2019-0006

Chapter 2
An Overview of Environmentally–Responsible Consumption Behavior:
Evolution, Significance, Antecedents, and Consequences.

Mehvish Riyaz
iD https://orcid.org/0000-0001-9625-2867
Islamic University of Science and Technology, India

Anisa Jan
iD https://orcid.org/0000-0002-1792-2410
Islamic University of Science and Technology, India

ABSTRACT

The chapter presents an overview of environmentally responsible consumer behavior by focusing on its core aspects, such as its evolution, significance, influencing factors, and consequences of practicing the behavior on businesses, individuals, and the environment. Second, the chapter explores the numerous theories utilized by scholars to explain and predict this behavior. In addition, the chapter also attempts to establish a connection between the concept of environmentally responsible consumption behavior and the pursuit of environmental sustainability, which is crucial in today's world, and emphasizes how engaging in this behavior can contribute to the achievement of the United Nations sustainable development goal 12.

DOI: 10.4018/978-1-6684-8140-0.ch002

INTRODUCTION

We are living in an era of globalization that is characterized by a rapid increase in the consumption of goods and services. It is pertinent to mention that the majority of environmental issues are caused by excessive and irresponsible consumption habits of people. Many nations throughout the world are coming to the realization of the seriousness of the issue, and as a result, they have begun taking steps to mitigate the negative effects that their economic activities have on the surrounding environment. This recognition and concern for the environment and humanity have led to the emergence of a concept known as "sustainable development." For both national and international policies on environmental conservation and sustainable development, altering the consumption patterns of people has been a key goal. In the past few decades, there has been a gradual development in consumers' interest in ecological issues affecting their consumption choices. Nowadays consumers have started recognizing the positive and negative influences of their purchase decisions on the environment. It is presumed that sustainable consumption habits of people can eradicate or at the very least minimize environmental issues caused by humans. Consumers have started to evaluate their purchases for environmental responsibility by choosing products with a higher number of environmental benefits and boycotting products that are harmful to the environment. The shift from a conventional consumption pattern toward a more sustainable and responsible consumption pattern delivers them the twin benefit of better healthcare as well as the chance to contribute to environmental sustainability. Promoting the idea of responsible consumerism to further promote sustainable models of production has become a top priority for international policymakers. It is very important for researchers and practitioners in the field to emphasize how important it is to consume in a responsible manner and to try to make responsible consumption behavior stronger over time by investigating and strengthening the drivers of the behavior.

EVOLUTION

The idea of environmentally conscious consumption behavior first emerged in the year 1973, when Fisk (1973) used the term "responsible consumption" and referred to it as an attempt towards "rational and efficient use of resources concerning the global human population." In early works Webster (1975) and Kilbourne & Beckmann (1998) also emphasized researching environmentally conscious consumers. Mayer (1976) first differentiated between environmentally responsible and socially responsible consumption. Roberts (1995) was the first to distinguish between social and environmental issues and suggested a two-dimensional scale (social and environmental) for measuring conscious consumer behavior. Environmentally responsible consumption behavior has evolved over time, and most of the published research studies have examined the interactions between various precursors and environmentally friendly consumer behavior. De Young (1985) studied the behavior of consumers concerning recycling, reusing, and saving materials while examining the driving forces behind conservation actions in the US.

Balderjahn (1988) investigated the behaviors of consumers in Germany with respect to home insulation, energy curtailment, ecologically responsible buying, environmental concern, and ecologically responsible use of cars while analyzing the role of environmental attitudes and personality traits in forecasting environmentally friendly consumption behaviors. Roberts & Bacon (1997) in the US investigated the connection between environmental concern and environmentally conscious consumer behavior while studying the use of reusable products, buying environmentally safe products, reducing energy, and conserving fuel when driving a car. Kaiser & Wilson (2004) in Switzerland studied behaviors relating to energy conservation (for example, using energy-efficient products), mobility and transportation (for example, carpooling), waste avoidance (for example, using reusable shopping bags), recycling (for example, paper), and socially motivated conservation (for example, enrolling in environmental organizations). Francois-Lecompte & Roberts (2006) tried to measure responsible consumption behavior in France while studying behaviors having positive impacts on the environment like avoiding the purchase of harmful product offerings, lowering and restricting one's consumption habits, etc.

Barr (2007) performed a study in the UK in which he investigated how environmental values, situational traits, and psychological elements influence the forecast of waste management behavior. Ballantine & Creery (2010) investigated the disposal practices of willing simplifiers while studying preference for commodities that are socially responsible, ecologically friendly, and of high quality among consumers in the US and also studied behaviors like borrowing or hiring items; purchasing second-hand or used items; cultivating one's food; and fixing goods instead of discarding them. Khare (2014) investigated the impact of consumer susceptibility to interpersonal influence and demographics on environmentally responsible consumption behavior in India while studying the behaviors like utilizing recyclable materials, conserving energy, and cutting down on energy usage. In the year 2015, Khare (2015) examined the impact of past environmental attitudes, social and personal environmental norms, social influence, and green self-identity on Indian consumers' green consumption behavior while studying the behaviors like recycling and reusing product packaging. Biswas & Roy (2015) investigated the impact of consumption values on sustainable consumption behavior among Indian consumers while examining the behaviors like buying eco-friendly products, recycling, and buying products with minimalistic packing.

Sudbury-Riley & Kohlbacher (2016) performed a cross-cultural study in UK, Germany, Hungary, and Japan in their attempt to measure ethically minded consumer behavior while studying various environmentally responsible consumption behaviors such as using products that can be recycled and boycotting products that are harmful to the environment. Sharma & Jha (2017) identified a group of value dimensions that motivate consumers in India to behave in an environmentally friendly manner, Getting rid of things that can still be used by donating, selling, or swapping them instead of just sitting them around unused. Further, researchers tried to highlight the impact of several other factors on behaviour in the form of mediators and moderators. Besides this researchers like Ivanova et al. (2019) tried to monitor the impact of multigroup moderators like age, gender, income, generation, etc in order to generate new findings and future implications. Researchers are trying to further explore the various dimensions of the behavior and unfold the knowledge gaps which still need to be addressed.

ENVIRONMENTALLY RESPONSIBLE CONSUMPTION BEHAVIOR

Environmentally Responsible Consumption Behavior encompasses a wide variety of actions taken by consumers before, during, and after the purchase, use, and disposal of consumer goods. Researchers have from time to time given several definitions for environmentally responsible consumption behavior. But among these researchers, Gupta & Agrawal (2018) after performing a thorough review of the literature have highlighted the nine core Environmentally responsible consumption behaviors that contribute to a reduction in the detrimental effect that one's day-to-day consumption has on the surrounding environment which include:

1. Making purchases of things that are less harmful to the environment such as products that are regional, energy-saving, or recyclable.
2. Buying products that have ecologically friendly packaging such as products that have minimal or no packaging at all.
3. Acquiring items after doing an in-depth analysis of one's own needs and requirements.
4. Indulging in methods of consumption that include multiple people, such as pooling, leasing, lending, and sharing.
5. Consciously consuming things such as need-based and zero-waste consumption,
6. Handling products with care such as looking after one's assets, most of which are durables, and using them in a way that extends their lifespan.
7. Repair and reuse items rather than carelessly throwing them away.

8. Getting rid of things that can still be used by donating, selling, or swapping them instead of just sitting them around unused.
9. Waste sorting which includes the safe management of toxic and hazardous waste, recycling, and other procedures.

While indulging in ecologically responsible consumption behavior buyers consider the effects that purchasing a product will have on the surrounding environment. To gain an understanding of environmentally responsible consumption behaviors, it is necessary to investigate all of the behaviors that consumers engage in intending to mitigate the adverse impact that consumption has on the environment. Taking clues from these nine behaviors we can conclude that environmentally responsible consumption behavior is a multi-dimensional construct which can be practiced at three different phases of consuming a product which include:

Acquisition phase: This phase will include a consumer's environmentally conscious behavior with respect to product acquisition. At this point, a customer can make intelligent use of his or her purchasing power by purchasing goods from businesses that offer environmentally responsible goods and avoid purchasing goods from businesses that sell environmentally irresponsible goods. Hence, at this stage, a consumer directly or indirectly with help of their purchasing power promotes fair and responsible products by increasing public pressure on firms to accept a greater share of responsibility for the effects of their actions on society and the environment.

Usage phase: At this point, the customer is aware that they are consuming a product and is doing so while keeping in mind the effects that the product will have on the environment. Because the vast majority of products are already hazardous to the environment at this point in the consumption process, this stage is extremely significant when it comes to the protection of the environment.

Disposal phase: Responsible actions at the disposal stage of the consumption process include recycling, reusing, and disposing of the products responsibly. This stage is one of the toughest stages to handle since most countries are still lacking the proper channels to dispose of the various types of waste generated after the product's life span gets over. For example, the wastes generated from electronic products are a huge concern for many countries like the US, China, India, etc since they are the source of toxic substances such as lead, cadmium, mercury, chromium, and polybrominated biphenyls.

THEORETICAL MODELS FOR ENVIRONMENTALLY RESPOSIBLE CONSUMPTION BEHAVIOR INVESTIGATION

The predominant theoretical frameworks for investigating environmentally responsible consumption behavior in contexts such as sustainable packaging, food selection behavior, recycling behavior, eco-tourism, and organic food purchasing, etc are as follows:

Theory of Reasoned Action

Fishbein and Ajzen (1975) developed TRA to explain the motives behind customer behavior. The model was initially established with the goal of forecasting people's intentions to take reasoned action in everyday life situations, such as the use of birth control pills. TRA is useful in explaining mental and cognitive processes that help us understand how consumers make decisions in different situations. This theory says that a consumer's intention to buy sustainable goods shows how inclined or wanting they are to purchase environmentally friendly goods or use eco-friendly choices or alternatives. But TRA only talks about voluntary control and doesn't talk about who owns the necessary facilities and resources to perform a behavior. For examples, some people may have a favorable opinion of environmentally friendly items, but they might not be capable of purchasing them owing to financial constraints or a lack of product accessibility. In order to increase the scope of TRA, a perceived behavioral control component was added to TPB, which increases the framework's ability to predict behavioral intentions.

Theory of Planned Behavior

According to the TPB, the likelihood of one engaging in the action that is sought increases proportionately with the level of purpose that is directed toward that conduct (Ajzen, 1991). Individuals' behavioural intentions are formed by taking into consideration three dimensions, including attitude toward a behavior, subjective norms, and perceived behavioural control. The theory of planned behavior (TPB) also considers behavioural intentions to be a central construct. An individual's positive or negative evaluation of the results of a particular activity might be used to infer the nature of their attitudes toward a particular behavior. Subjective norms are the social expectations that are placed on an individual to participate in a particular activity, and perceived behavior control is an individual's personal view of how simple or difficult it is to carry out a particular action. In addition, the TPB can be utilized to analyze any behaviors that call for the utilization of planning. The TPB is a well-defined framework that may be widely applied to research sustainable human behaviors through several concerns, including cutting carbon emissions, cooling behavior, renewable power investment, entrepreneurial behavior, and sustainable behavior. The majority of studies have used TPB to study green purchase behaviors.

Value Orientation Theory

The value orientation model is one of the first attempts to create a cross-cultural philosophy of values (Kluckhohn & Strodtbeck, 1961). According to environmental psychologists, people's values and attitudes toward their surroundings are among the most important determinants of their actions. Concerns about sustainable consumption patterns are also intrinsically tied to human values. The choices that customers make are in turn determined by a varied range of value orientations, which may include social and environmental considerations. Value has therefore been identified as one of the most essential guides of evaluated attitudinal measures in environmentally friendly behavior by a large number of behavioral research investigations on environmentalism.

Norm Activation Theory

The purpose of this theory is to investigate how feelings of future achievement and shame motivate people to take environmentally responsible actions (Schwartz, 1977). According to this theory, the first step toward norm activation is for an individual to become conscious of the potential adverse effects of their actions and to accept personal responsibility for their failure to act in an environmentally responsible manner. Prior research that combined the NAM with the TPB discovered that intentions serve as a mediator between personal norms and behavior. When considered as a whole, the results indicate that an integrated NAM–TPB model is the one that can best describe environmentally responsible behavior.

Diffusion of Innovations Theory

The theory of the diffusion of innovations is a concept that outlines how new technology as well as other developments move throughout civilizations, from the initiation to the mass acceptance of these innovations. Creating profitable unique ideas is what innovation is all about. The theory of diffusion of innovation has been used on multiple occasions to investigate customers' intentions and levels of willingness to try new environmentally friendly product categories of the intended audience, such as organic foods. This theory can be further used to study people's willingness concerning new product innovation adoption in pro-environmental product categories.

Table 1. Research articles incorporating the above-mentioned theoretical models:

Theory of reasoned action	TRA is successful in highlighting psychological and cognitive neural mechanisms in order to understand how customers make decisions in specific contexts. Subjective norms along with the attitude of a consumer plays an important role in determining behavioural intentions with respect to Eco-friendly buying.	(Kotchen & Reiling, 2000; Masrom, 2007)
Theory of planned behavior	Attitudes, perceived behavioural control, and subjective norms can all be used to predict environmentally friendly buying behaviour. TPB has been used extensively in the context of obtaining and consuming organic food, organic apparels, organic milk, organic vegetables, etc. Due to its broad interpretation and ability to frequently adjust to the different settings in which studies are conducted, the TPB is applicable in many academic fields.	(Aschemann-Witzel & Zielke, 2017; Carfora et al., 2019; Dorce et al., 2021; Echegaray & Hansstein, 2017; Hosta & Zabkar, 2021a; Khare, 2015b; Stall-Meadows & Davey, 2013)
Value orientation theory	Many behavioral scientists consider values that can be measured as the primary benchmark for envisioned attitude changes towards environmentally responsible consumption behaviour. Results have shown that the level of a positive environmental attitude increased with the increasing level of value orientation, further increasing environmentally conscious behavioural intentions	(Buerke et al., 2017; Kautish & Sharma, 2019)
Norm activation theory	The framework claims that personal norms are influenced by two elements: the knowledge that engaging in a given action (or not engaging) has specific repercussions and the sense of accountability for engaging in that behavior. The majority of the studies using this paradigm to study green behaviors have been conducted in developed countries.	(Corraliza & Berenguer, 2000; Duong et al., 2022; Follows & Jobber, 2000)
Diffusion of innovations theory	Researchers have employed diffusion of innovation theory to investigate the intentions of consumers and their readiness to try products that are environmentally friendly such as organic foods across various population segments and discovered that customers sense of innovativeness may impact consumer intention to purchase eco-friendly products. But the theory has not been widely tested in different cross-cultural settings.	(Dilotsotlhe, 2021; Zhen & Mansori, 2012)

SIGNIFICANCE OF ENVIRONMENTALLY RESPONSIBLE CONSUMPTION BEHAVIOR

In addition to humans, millions of creatures and plants call Earth home. Not only is the world around us our home, but it also contains everything that ensures our continued existence. Life is only conceivable due to the availability of both waters at the surface and air at higher altitudes. As the only habitable planet in the solar system, we should respect every form of the ecosystem and defend our planet from harmful actions. It is essential to our survival in many ways, including the provision of the food and water we consume, the air we breathe, the shelter we have, and many other things. When we do more to protect the natural world around us, our homes will be cleaner and more pleasant to live in. If, in contrast, we choose to ignore the environment and engage in activities that are harmful to it, then we are increasing the challenges we face in gaining access to clean necessities such as food, water, and shelter. It is essential to be aware that there is nowhere else for any of us to flee towards, even though most of us can often view this as unimportant. If we do something to ruin what we've got here, we will be expected to deal with the repercussions of our doings and instead, if we take care of the surrounding environment, then the natural world will likewise look after us in exchange.

A responsible approach to consumption is extremely valuable since it enables us to safeguard the environment in a variety of different ways, including the following:

Protection Against the Degradation of Natural Resources

The depletion of the earth's natural resources is one of the most pressing issues that the world must deal with in the present day. Whenever a resource is utilized at a rate that is greater than the rate at which it can regenerate itself, the resource is said to be depleted. The beginning can be traced back to the dawn of the industrial revolution. Our society has progressed culturally, and our civilization has developed a great deal of technology that does make our lives simpler; consequently, the amount of raw resources we require for industrial as well as household consumption has skyrocketed. The issue is that we are consuming far too much with little to no consideration. Our world is just not capable of satisfying the ever-increasing requirements we place upon it. If we do not exercise caution in the management of the utilization of natural resources by humans, we will observe a depletion of these resources. Natural resources that require a greater amount of time to regenerate are at a greater risk of experiencing irreversible exhaustion. The habit of responsible individual consumption on the part of people can bring about a shift on a larger scale. If people will begin to consume responsibly by carefully evaluating and monitoring the, need they have for these natural resources it can certainly save the resources from getting depleted. Promoting environmentally responsible consumption behavior can be very significant to protect our natural resources.

Protection Against the Global Warming

Human actions, especially fossil fuel burning, increase heat-trapping greenhouse gas levels in Earth's atmosphere. The phenomenon referred to as global warming takes place as a result of the accumulation of carbon dioxide (CO_2) and other harmful emissions in the air, where they then absorb sunlight and other forms of solar radiation. In a normal situation, this radiation would be ejected into space; however, because of the presence of these impurities, which can remain in the atmosphere for years or even decades, the heat is trapped and the temperature of the planet continues to rise. These heat-trapping pollutants are collectively referred to as greenhouse gas emissions; more particularly, carbon dioxide, methane, nitrous oxide, water vapor, and chlorofluorocarbons. The effect that these gases have is also referred to as the greenhouse effect. Overexposure to acid rain or CO2 will have an adverse effect on marine life, which will eventually have an adverse effect on the entire ecosystem. Once more, the growing demand from customers is the driving force behind industries' excessive consumption of fossil fuels in order to meet production needs leading to greenhouse gas emissions. People will be less likely to engage in wasteful and excessive spending patterns if responsible models of consumption are encouraged, which will have the effect of lowering demand for goods to some extent. As a result, it has the potential to significantly cut the emission of greenhouse gases by companies of this type.

Promoting Fair and Responsible Models of Production

Consumption and production are inextricably linked to one another. Whatever is made, is made for consumption, whether that consumption is direct or indirect. Both of them represent different aspects of the same coin. When consumers demand products that have a low impact on the environment and only spend their money on things that help the planet remain habitable, it will immediately put pressure on corporations to shift their production methods to be more righteous and accountable for the harm they create. Because the client is considered to be the most important aspect of a business, every aspect of a company's operations is tailored to meet the demands and expectations of the customer.

Conserving Biodiversity

The term "biodiversity conservation" refers to the process of safeguarding, enhancing, and managing the world's various forms of life to ensure long-term advantages for both current and future generations. The loss of habitat, carbon emissions, overuse of resources, the introduction of exotic species, and global warming are the five primary factors that threaten biodiversity. The other dangers are the direct results of the rise in the human population and the consumption of resources. Biodiversity is the cornerstone that supports the functioning of ecosystems and the flourishing of humanity. If there wasn't enough variety of plants and animals in an environment, we wouldn't have nearly the number of organisms including ourselves that we do today. The conversion of forest land to agricultural and urban land, as well as the production of pollutants that degrade habitats and damage species, are two ways in which population expansion and greater resource usage threaten biodiversity.

The state of the environment is deteriorating, which means that the possibility of living organisms on earth surviving is getting worse. Thus, promoting responsible models of consumption, in this case, is also very important because it will have a direct impact on biodiversity conservation. Consuming a lesser number of socially and environmentally irresponsible products can be very helpful to protect the flora and fauna of this planet.

Promoting Sustainable Development

Sustainable practices aim to save Planet, limit climate change, and advance societal progress without jeopardizing the viability of existing life forms or leaving no one behind. The idea behind this is to ensure that our current requirements are met without risking those of future generations. One of the key principles of sustainable development is limiting human impact on the environment. The notion of Sustainable development is encompassed by environmentally responsible consumption behavior, where a person assesses his consumption based on sustainability and only consumes goods that do not harm or impede the development of future generations. Therefore, this behavior holds a futuristic approach when it comes to consuming different products.

Proper Waste Handling

Both production and consumption of goods result in a significant amount of garbage. Therefore, waste management is an important part of the work being done in the area of environmentally responsible consumption behavior. A large amount of waste is generated on daily basis from both organized as well as unorganized sectors. This waste needs to be disposed of through the proper channels. The behaviors which are included in the post-usage phases include recycling, donating, selling, etc.

SUSTAINABLE DEVELOPMENT GOAL 12 AND ERCB

The Brundtland Report, which was initially released in 1987, is credited with being the source of the contemporary notion of sustainability. The Brundtland Report, also known as Our Common Future, was the initial report of its kind to be released by the United Nations. It was the first document of its kind to notify of the negative environmental impact of economic developments and globalization. Additionally, it was the initial report of its kind to aim to offer solutions that addressed issues that emerged as a result of industrialization and population expansion. Years later, in 2010, the Millennium Development Goals (MDGs) were adopted during the same-named United Nations Summit. The objectives provided a blueprint for reducing poverty and hunger as well as enhancing health, education, living circumstances, environmental sustainability, and gender equality. Targets that the Member States agreed to attempt to attain until 2015. In September 2015, 193 nations convened at the United Nations to approve and pledge to a long-term, all-encompassing strategy to address the world's largest challenges to worldwide sustainable development. The outcome was the Sustainable Development Goals, a list of seventeen objectives to build a more equitable and sustainable future for everybody by 2030.

Among these 17 sustainable development goals, the 12th goal stands for responsible consumption and production. The key to responsible consumption and production is finding ways to get more done with fewer resources. In addition to this, it is about uncoupling growth in the economy from the deterioration of the environment, improving the effectiveness with which resources are used, and promoting green lifestyles. Both sustainable production and consumption have the potential to make significant contributions to the fight against poverty as well as the shift toward environmentally friendly economies. Unsustainable consumption and production have presently increased greenhouse gas emissions, air pollution, and agricultural productivity, which threatens livelihoods and social cohesion, and water scarcity. The shift toward sustainable and responsible production and consumption of goods and services is essential if we are to lessen our detrimental effects on the climate and the environment, as well as on the health of individuals and populations.

Environmentally responsible consumption behavior if truly promoted can create an ease for the policymakers to attain the targets of sustainable goal number 12. Encouraging the adoption of responsible individual consumer behavior can bring about change in overall consumption patterns throughout the globe. On the other side identifying the potential drivers and inhibitors of the behavior can be of tremendous importance in attaining SDG-12, since, the behavior is also aligned with the notion of sustainability and it can reveal the various psychological barriers that can come in the way of sustainable and responsible consumption. Also, consumption and the production of material commodities are closely intertwined; in fact, one cannot exist independently of the other. When people start consuming goods which are eco-friendly in nature and abstain from buying goods that are harmful for the environment, production patterns will automatically shift from unsustainable to sustainable ones.

Companies Embracing Sustainable Development Goals Globally

1. **Refurbed (Vienna, Austria)**: Refurbed serves as a digital marketplace for repaired goods. In comparison to their fresh, bought at the store equivalents, it offers refurbished mobile devices, laptops, and tablets that are up to 40%

less expensive and 100% safer for the environment. Refurbished renewal is a 40-step procedure that gives things a brand-new appearance and functionality.

2. **Phenix (Paris, France):** The company offers an online and mobile-based marketplace for reselling, recycling, and exchanging things from various industries. Consumers can purchase customised baskets of items that remain unsold (fruits and veggies, bread and pastries, etc.) from such businesses at cheaper rates via the Phenix App. By giving things a second life, Phenix hopes to minimise wastage and promote the shift to an economy based on circularity.

3. **The Littery (Riga, Latvia):** The Littery has developed lottery rewards that uses artificial intelligence to encourage consumers to organise and dispose of the trash they produce. The preliminary results suggest that 100% of the trash goes into the trash bins, accurately sorted where needed.

4. **Vinted (Vilnius, Lithuania):** Vinted is a Lithuanian internet store where users may purchase, sell, and trade items mostly apparel and accessories new or used. The organization's objective is to make second-hand products preferred option globally. Second-hand clothing has a significantly good social and environmental effect. It saves a lot of resources, water, and energy while lowering the release of greenhouse gases.

5. **Land Life Company (Amsterdam, Netherlands):** The Land Life Company is a technology-driven reforestation firm which grows trees in large quantities. It provides businesses and organisations with a safe and open method of addressing climate change and offsetting greenhouse gas emissions by the rehabilitation of the natural world. Initiatives of Land Life Company are strengthening natural environment, reviving significant ecological systems, and benefiting communities nearby on both the economic and social scales.

6. **Planetiers (Lisbon, Portugal):** A variety of ecologically friendly goods can be purchased on Planetiers. The enterprise additionally organises conferences and recruits' executives, academics, entrepreneurs, and financiers to serve as representatives. The 17 SDGs are adhered to in all of Planetiers' operations.

7. **Biopipe (Zürich, Switzerland):** Without producing sludge, the Biopipe system, a revolutionary biological sewage treatment technology, changes water into a state suited for agriculture. The Biopipe system offers the following significant advantages: Zero Sludge, No Odour, No Noise, No Chemicals, and Low Energy Consumption.

8. **SOMA (Belgrade, Serbia):** The company aims at creating innovative ideas, techniques, and biological substances with the goal of enhancing the concept of circular economy, facilitating sustainable industry, and minimizing pollution. Using fungi-based technological advances, SOMA develops recyclable substitutes to plastic. The company's primary goal is to introduce ecological, ethical and sustainable practices to the biotech sector.

India has also made significant progress in the recent year with its initiatives for sustainability. SDGs are already being used as a guideline by the Indian government in developing various national level schemes such as Zero Defect Zero Effect Scheme, Smart Cities, Swachh Bharat Abhiyan (Clean India Mission), Waste Management Rules, Star Labelling Programme, Perform Achieve and Trade (PAT) Scheme, and others in order to attain the sustainable India. Many companies in India are now actively support environmental protection by building ecologically sound brands and producing products that are environmentally friendly. HDFC was among the highest scorers owing to its ecologically conscious financing policies, encouragement of green housing, and the participation of staff into environmental programme. With Wipro's corporate office in Pune being the most sustainable organisational structure within its sector in all of India, it has also contributed to the development of technology that assists with waste prevention and energy conservation. Apart from such organisations IndusInd Bank is one of the initial financial institutions in India that discouraged the use of paper for ATM counterfoils and to promote the use of electronic communications, which has contributed significantly to the decrease of deforestation. Mahindra also received recognition for its data-driven approach to environmentalism and for efficiently using commercial skills to benefit communities. Other companies in India evaluated according to criteria such as resource effectiveness, philanthropic endeavour, financial leadership, well-being of staff members, ethical income include Godrej Consumer Products, Marico, Piramal Enterprises, Hindustan Lever, HCL Technologies, Godrej Industries, Tata Chemicals, Tata Power, Infosys, Tata Motors, ICICI Bank, Gail India, Cipla, Ultratech Cement, Eicher Motors and Aditya Birla Fashion Retail.

ANTECEDENTS OF ENVIRONMENTALLY RESPONSIBLE PURCHASE INTENTION

It is a commonly held belief that the intention of consumers to buy ethical products will lead to their actual purchase behavior. As a result, the process of intentional creation is an essential component in the decisions that pertain to moral pursuits Throughout the course of research on environmentally responsible consumption behavior, many frameworks have been offered to elucidate its antecedents. The majority of work has been done by several researchers in the field to explore various antecedents that affect the behavior positively or negatively. Some of the major antecedents which have been repeatedly tested by the researchers in different scenarios under different frameworks are as:

Attitude

Attitude toward the behavior is defined as the "degree to which a person has a favorable or unfavorable evaluation of the behavior in question" (Ajzen, 1991). It is generally accepted that attitudes are one of the most important factors in accurately predicting pro-environmental behaviors. Consumers who have a favorable attitude toward sustainable products as a result of their beliefs and evaluations are more likely to buy such products because of the belief that it is better for them and the environment. Although there has been a rise in both the public's interest and favorable consumers' attitudes toward the subject of sustainability, in reality, customers' behavioral intentions do not coincide with their actual behaviors. This phenomenon is referred to as the intention-behavior gap, and it is something that is still not explored fully in the literature. Numerous research have supported the idea that attitudes towards the environment in general have a significant positive impact on Environmentally responsible consumption behavior (Dorce et al., 2021; Taufique & Islam, 2020; Vu et al., 2021).

Subjective Norm

Subjective norms were characterized as consumers' perceptions of specific conduct that are heavily influenced by the opinions of others such as family, colleagues, spouses, and educators (Ajzen, 1991). Subjective norm is another key predictor of customers' intentions to make environmentally responsible purchases. This shows that employing "opinion leaders" like celebrity endorsers to encourage intentions in purchasing sustainable and responsible products could effectively translate these choices into a social norm. As a result, here the individual makes an effort to absorb the standards and values that are held by his significant group. There have been multiple investigations on the relationship between subjective norms and the intention to purchase Eco-friendly goods (Hsu et al., 2017; Kumar et al., 2021; Sheoran & Kumar, 2022).

Perceived Behavioural Control

It relates to a person's perceived competence and self-efficacy to carry out a specific behavior (Ajzen, 1991). The feeling that one has control over their behavior has a favorable impact on their desire, which in turn has a significant impact on the activity one intends to engage in. It is believed to be one of the main components that contribute to an increase in an individual's level of want because an individual's level of desire may become more intense when there are adequate possibilities for that individual to engage in a certain action. Researchers in the field of sustainable consumption make extensive use of this antecedent. An abundance of studies has associated the use of environmentally friendly goods with perceived controlled behaviour (Bhutto et al., 2019; Hosta & Zabkar, 2021b; Khare, 2015b).

Media Exposure

Businesses typically disseminate information about their sustainability efforts through a variety of media, ranging from traditional communication channels (such as television broadcasts, newspapers, radio, and so on) to new media (such as organizational social media, websites, and so on). In a variety of settings, such as communication on health and sustainability, it has been discovered that people's exposure to and attention to messages sent by the media increases their level of knowledge, influences the audiences' intentions, and encourages them to engage in the following behaviors. The exposure of younger generations to the media is a crucial component of the strategy for fostering environmentally responsible behavior (Ivanova et al., 2019; Lee & Cho, 2020; Soomro et al., 2020; Yang & Zhang, 2021).

Perceived Value

The perceived value of anything is determined by the amount of perceived quality that is sacrificed in exchange for that something. When people believe that they are getting more value for their money than they are giving up, this is viewed as favorable. A considerable connection has been found by researchers between the value that is perceived and the ambition to behave more sustainably. As a result, low perceived value may cause consumers to change their minds about making a purchase. In light of the recent growth in concern for the environment, perceived value is an essential component of green purchase intention. Thus, the perceived benefit of being environmentally friendly plays a more significant part in the modern environmental age. Many studies have revealed that perceived value had an impact on an individual's environmental responsibility (Agrawal & Gupta, 2018; Chiu et al., 2014; Lin & Chen, 2022; Yadav & Pathak, 2017)

Environmental Concerns

Environmental concern refers to the degree to which buyers are aware of problems that are associated with the ecosystem and demonstrate a desire or propensity to contribute to finding solutions to such problems. The level of environmental consciousness exhibited by a consumer as well as their acceptance of environmentally friendly things influence the motivations and intentions a consumer has to purchase sustainable products. One of the earliest ideas to be integrated into studies on the environment was the concept of environmental concern, which was meant to characterize actions that were responsible for the environment. Behavior that is motivated by concern for the environment often has an emotional component (strong feelings of anger, disappointment).Many studies have identified that consumer's Environmental concern and acceptance of environmentally friendly products may impact their reasons for buying products that are environmentally friendly (Duong et al., 2022; Durmaz & Akdoğan, 2023; Tandon et al., 2020).

Green Self-Identity

Green self-identity is crucial to differentiate one's identity from others who do not value the environment as well as adhering to the values and practices of the group of individuals to which a person wants or believes he belongs, such as those who care about environmental issues. Within the realm of environmental or "green" issues, there is a widespread opinion that self-identity takes the shape and label of green self-identity due to its rising relevance and specificity. Recently, the concept of green self-identity has been promoted as a stronger antecedent of purchase intention for sustainable products and, more generally, as a driver of ecologically friendly actions (Carfora et al., 2019; Khare & Pandey, 2017; Neves & Oliveira, 2021)

Ethical Ideologies

The ethical ideology of customers is another aspect that impacts the consumers' decision to buy ecologically responsible items and can be considered a significant influencer in this area. The antecedent in question has not been the subject of extensive inquiry. It calls for additional research and investigation (Hosta & Zabkar, 2021b; Pekerti & Arli, 2017).

   In addition to the antecedents that have already been explained, several additional important antecedents have been used by various researchers. These antecedents include personal norms, willingness to pay, availability of environmentally responsible products, availability of knowledge, and so on.

CONSEQUENCES OF BEHAVING RESPONSIBLY DURING THE CONSUMPTION PROCESS

1. **With respect to people**: The protection of the natural world ought to be a moral obligation for humans. Humans are accountable for environmental protection. Protecting the environment would be a way for them to satisfy their compulsions. There are two different ways to be motivated to consume in a

sustainable way. First, it's based on what each person wants and needs. Second, it's based on "moral and personal beliefs" or hopes for "social harmony and sustainability." In addition to fulfilling, one's commitments to one's moral code, the behavior in question can have positive effects on people in several different ways. Importantly, a person should consume responsibly because the unsustainable consumption habits of people lead to environmental destruction the destruction of the environment is harmful because it endangers the long-term health of all living things, including humans, animals, and plants. The primary objective of environmental protection is to ensure that both current and future generations will be able to continue living in a healthy environment. The following things could be regarded as the consequences of performing the behavior:

1. Contributes to a healthier lifestyle.
2. Protection against depletion of resources.
3. Better quality of air and water.
4. Protection against the destruction of forests.
5. Protection against climatic changes etc.

2. **With respect to businesses**: The vast majority of customers are becoming increasingly conscious, on daily basis, of the impact that their purchases have on the environment, which is causing businesses to be held more and more accountable for their unsustainable manufacturing processes. Businesses are gradually beginning to feel the effects of environmentally conscious consumer behavior on a population-wide scale. But it may also have a positive impact on businesses, since it may make it easier for them to adapt to the preferences of customers who want sustainable products while also enabling them to take advantage of a variety of tax breaks and other financial incentives offered by the government. It may also entice lenders or investors who are committed to environmental or ethical concerns and when purchasing energy-saving equipment, businesses may be eligible for financial assistance and loan programs.

3. **With respect to the environment:** By engaging in the behavior many harmful activities which deteriorate the quality of the environment can be minimized such as carbon emissions can be reduced by switching to sources of renewable energy or investing in products that have a lower impact on the environment. Additionally, we can have the ability to preserve natural resources by selecting goods and services that make use of recycled materials or trash as raw materials or resources. When people use products that are better for the environment, they are helping to protect and preserve the natural resources that the universe provides, such as metals, forests, and even water. Therefore, each person who engages in the behavior contributes to the protection and maintenance of these natural resources. If a greater number of people utilized products that were

better for the environment, it would be to the benefit of all of the inhabitants on the planet as well as nature itself.

METHODOLOGY

The systematic review of literature method was used for the chapter, that entails finding, collecting, and analysing the relevant literature. A systematic evaluation of articles from published research on environmentally responsible consumption behavior was done. To confirm that the review of literature omits unimportant investigations, we examined all the extracted research articles. These articles were then carefully scrutinised for their relevance, which resulted in the removal of several research articles and the final inclusion of 40 research articles for the purpose of review. This chapter primarily examines the attitude-behavior irregularities with an emphasis on understanding the psychological, social, and cultural elements that influence consumers' intentions to buy environmentally friendly products. According to our review of the literature, there are a number of studies on consumers' environmentally conscious purchase behaviours in both developed as well as developing nations.

MANAGERIAL IMPLICATIONS

Based on the review, this study provides several managerial implications. To begin, businesses and policymakers must seize every chance to explain the advantages of making environmentally responsible choices in order to improve consumer health and encourage sustainability. Businesses and policymakers may try to raise consumers' perceptions of their capacity to buy sustainable products. For the purpose of doing so, companies should bring ecologically responsible products to customers' homes, and governmental organisations would possibly promote the growth of regional sustainable marketplaces making such products freely available. For the purpose of influencing the behaviour of young and adult population, who have a relatively emotional approach towards ecological issues, marketers should put greater effort into reaching audiences through social as well as traditional media sources. Additionally, businesses ought to explicitly state information about the product, such as the proven material distinctions between non-green commodities and green commodities with the goal to convince buyers to accept higher prices for a particular product. Also, publicly verifiable industry standards and certification processes must be created. Therefore, businesses and organisations will be obligated to establish relationships based on trustworthiness, giving the environmentally sensitive entrepreneurs the opportunity to develop an appealing green brand for the consumers.

FUTURE RESEARCH DIRECTIONS

The concept of environmentally responsible consumption behaviour being multidimensional in nature, researchers may have possibly ignored some potentially important characteristics that should be researched further. In India, there is a lack of understanding of the aspects impacting customers' green purchasing behaviour, and eco-consciousness. Future studies may consider mediators and/or moderators in relation to ecologically friendly consumption behaviour in order to improve the proposed conceptual model's ability to predict consumer purchasing behaviour. Future research should also incorporate characteristics such as price of environmentally friendly products, their quality requirements, and social concerns to provide additional insight into customers' green buying behaviour. The impact of consumer-related factors, such as standard of living, lifestyle, eating habits, and health concerns, have additionally not been taken into account on a larger sample. Also, instead of predicting future behaviour on the basis of attitudes as done in previous studies, future studies should focus on finding and understanding the purchase situations where attitudes fail to translate into actual buying behaviour. To have a better understanding of why purchasing intentions sometimes do not translate into actual decisions, the important social and psychological elements should be examined through a longitudinal approach.

CONCLUSION

The continuation of life on Earth is contingent upon the existence of favorable environmental conditions. There are obvious indications that it is deteriorating at an increasing rate. The biophysical environment is deteriorating in an irreversible manner as a direct result of excessive consumption, rising rates of population, and the accelerating pace of technological advancement. Because of humans and their irresponsible behavior toward the environment in a variety of countries, a significant portion of the Earth's natural resources is now in a precarious state in the present scenario. In addition, pollution is growing at an alarming rate each year, which results in the harming of natural surroundings. Because of this, it is therefore imperative that efforts be taken to safeguard the environment. The current environmental catastrophe calls for the most dramatic shift in consumer behavior in contemporary history Sustainability through consumption is also a significant marketing challenge. Consumer behavior researchers are still trying to figure out what motivates customers to behave in an environmentally responsible manner and purchase ethical items, and it's a matter of speculation. In practice, consumers' evaluations and judgments regarding possible socially and environmentally responsible purchases are not always ideal, optimal, or linear; rather, they are frequently dynamic and fluctuate from day to day and depending on the context in which they are made. Therefore, having an understanding of this behavior is extremely important because it may one day change the whole process of consumption and production making them fully sustainable. Additionally, this behavior needs to be further investigated in light of all of the possible constructs that might affect it in order to understand all the potential psychological drivers and inhibitors of this behavior.

REFERENCES

Agrawal, R., & Gupta, S. (2018). Consuming Responsibly: Exploring Environmentally Responsible Consumption Behaviors. *Journal of Global Marketing, 31*(4), 231–245. doi:10.1080/08911762.2017.1415402

Ajzen, I. (1991). The theory of planned behavior. *Organizational Behavior and Human Decision Processes, 50*(2), 179–211. doi:10.1016/0749-5978(91)90020-T

Aschemann-Witzel, J., & Zielke, S. (2017). Can't Buy Me Green? A Review of Consumer Perceptions of and Behavior Toward the Price of Organic Food. *The Journal of Consumer Affairs, 51*(1), 211–251. doi:10.1111/joca.12092

Balderjahn, I. (1988). Personality variables and environmental attitudes as predictors of ecologically responsible consumption patterns. *Journal of Business Research, 17*(1), 51–56. doi:10.1016/0148-2963(88)90022-7

Ballantine, P. W., & Creery, S. (2010). The consumption and disposition behaviour of voluntary simplifiers. *Journal of Consumer Behaviour, 9*(1), 45–56. doi:10.1002/cb.302

Barr, S. (2007). Factors influencing environmental attitudes and behaviors: A U.K. case study of household waste management. In Environment and Behavior, 39(4). doi:10.1177/0013916505283421

Bhutto, M. Y., Zeng, F., Soomro, Y. A., & Khan, M. A. (2019). Young chinese consumer decision making in buying green products: An application of theory of planned behavior with gender and price transparency. *Pakistan Journal of Commerce and Social Science, 13*(3), 599–619.

Biswas, A., & Roy, M. (2015). Green products: An exploratory study on the consumer behaviour in emerging economies of the East. *Journal of Cleaner Production, 87*(1), 463–468. doi:10.1016/j.jclepro.2014.09.075

Buerke, A., Straatmann, T., Lin-Hi, N., & Müller, K. (2017). Consumer awareness and sustainability-focused value orientation as motivating factors of responsible consumer behavior. *Review of Managerial Science*, *11*(4), 959–991. doi:10.100711846-016-0211-2

Carfora, V., Cavallo, C., Caso, D., Del Giudice, T., De Devitiis, B., Viscecchia, R., Nardone, G., & Cicia, G. (2019). Explaining consumer purchase behavior for organic milk: Including trust and green self-identity within the theory of planned behavior. *Food Quality and Preference*, *76*(March), 1–9. doi:10.1016/j.foodqual.2019.03.006

Chiu, Y. T. H., Lee, W.-I., & Chen, T.-H. (2014). Environmentally responsible behavior in ecotourism: Antecedents and implications. *Tourism Management*, *40*, 321–329. doi:10.1016/j.tourman.2013.06.013

Corraliza, J. A., & Berenguer, J. (2000). Environmental values, beliefs, and actions: A situational approach. *Environment and Behavior*, *32*(6), 832–848. doi:10.1177/00139160021972829

De Young, R. (1985). *Encouraging environmentally appropriate behavior: The role of intrinsic motivation.*

Dilotsotlhe, N. (2021). Factors influencing the green purchase behaviour of millennials: An emerging country perspective. *Cogent Business and Management*, *8*(1), 1908745. doi:10.1080/23311975.2021.1908745

Dorce, L. C., da Silva, M. C., Mauad, J. R. C., de Faria Domingues, C. H., & Borges, J. A. R. (2021). Extending the theory of planned behavior to understand consumer purchase behavior for organic vegetables in Brazil: The role of perceived health benefits, perceived sustainability benefits and perceived price. *Food Quality and Preference, 91*. doi:10.1016/j.foodqual.2021.104191

Duong, C. D., Doan, X. H., Vu, D. M., Ha, N. T., & Van Dam, K. (2022). The Role of Perceived Environmental Responsibility and Environmental Concern on Shaping Green Purchase Intention. *Vision (Basel)*, 1–15. doi:10.1177/09722629221092117

Durmaz, Y., & Akdoğan, L. (2023). The effect of environmental responsibility on green the effect of environmental responsibility on green consumption intention: The moderator role of price sensitivity and the mediator role of environmental concern. A case study in Turkey. *Environment, Development and Sustainability*, *0123456789*. Advance online publication. doi:10.100710668-023-03083-6

Echegaray, F., & Hansstein, F. V. (2017). Assessing the intention-behavior gap in electronic waste recycling: The case of Brazil. *Journal of Cleaner Production*, *142*, 180–190. doi:10.1016/j.jclepro.2016.05.064

Fishbein, M., Ajzen, I., & Belief, A. (1975). *Intention and Behavior: An introduction to theory and research.* Addison-Wesley.

Fisk, G. (1973). Criteria for a Theory of Responsible Consumption. *Journal of Marketing, 37*(2), 24–31. doi:10.1177/002224297303700206

Follows, S. B., & Jobber, D. (2000). Environmentally responsible purchase behaviour: A test of a consumer model. *European Journal of Marketing, 34*(5/6), 723–746. doi:10.1108/03090560010322009

Francois-Lecompte, A., & Roberts, J. A. (2006). Developing a measure of socially responsible consumption in France. *Marketing Management Journal, 16*(2).

Gupta, S., & Agrawal, R. (2018). Environmentally responsible consumption: Construct definition, scale development, and validation. *Corporate Social Responsibility and Environmental Management, 25*(4), 523–536. doi:10.1002/csr.1476

Hosta, M., & Zabkar, V. (2021a). Antecedents of Environmentally and Socially Responsible Sustainable Consumer Behavior. *Journal of Business Ethics, 171*(2), 273–293. doi:10.100710551-019-04416-0

Hosta, M., & Zabkar, V. (2021b). Antecedents of Environmentally and Socially Responsible Sustainable Consumer Behavior. *Journal of Business Ethics, 171*(2), 273–293. doi:10.100710551-019-04416-0

Hsu, C. L., Chang, C. Y., & Yansritakul, C. (2017). Exploring purchase intention of green skincare products using the theory of planned behavior: Testing the moderating effects of country of origin and price sensitivity. *Journal of Retailing and Consumer Services, 34*, 145–152. doi:10.1016/j.jretconser.2016.10.006

Ivanova, O., Flores-Zamora, J., Khelladi, I., & Ivanaj, S. (2019). The generational cohort effect in the context of responsible consumption. *Management Decision, 57*(5), 1162–1183. doi:10.1108/MD-12-2016-0915

Kaiser, F. G., & Wilson, M. (2004). Goal-directed conservation behavior: The specific composition of a general performance. *Personality and Individual Differences, 36*(7), 1531–1544. doi:10.1016/j.paid.2003.06.003

Kautish, P., & Sharma, R. (2019). Value orientation, green attitude and green behavioral intentions: An empirical investigation among young consumers. *Young Consumers, 20*(4), 338–358. doi:10.1108/YC-11-2018-0881

Khare, A. (2014). Consumers' susceptibility to interpersonal influence as a determining factor of ecologically conscious behaviour. *Marketing Intelligence & Planning, 32*(1), 2–20. doi:10.1108/MIP-04-2013-0062

Khare, A. (2015). Antecedents to green buying behaviour: A study on consumers in an emerging economy. *Marketing Intelligence & Planning, 33*(3), 309–329. doi:10.1108/MIP-05-2014-0083

Khare, A., & Pandey, S. (2017). Role of green self-identity and peer influence in fostering trust towards organic food retailers. *International Journal of Retail & Distribution Management, 45*(9), 969–990. doi:10.1108/IJRDM-07-2016-0109

Kilbourne, W. E., & Beckmann, S. C. (1998). Review and critical assessment of research on marketing and the environment. *Journal of Marketing Management, 14*(6), 513–532. doi:10.1362/026725798784867716

Kluckhohn, F. R., & Strodtbeck, F. L. (1961). *Variations in value orientations.* Grand Valley State University.

Kotchen, M. J., & Reiling, S. D. (2000). Environmental attitudes, motivations, and contingent valuation of nonuse values: A case study involving endangered species. *Ecological Economics, 32*(1), 93–107. doi:10.1016/S0921-8009(99)00069-5

Kumar, A., Prakash, G., & Kumar, G. (2021). Does environmentally responsible purchase intention matter for consumers? A predictive sustainable model developed through an empirical study. *Journal of Retailing and Consumer Services, 58*, 102270. doi:10.1016/j.jretconser.2020.102270

Lee, J., & Cho, M. (2020). The Effects of Consumers' Media Exposure, Attention, and Credibility on Pro-environmental Behaviors. *Journal of Promotion Management, 26*(3), 434–455. doi:10.1080/10496491.2019.1699629

Lin, P. H., & Chen, W. H. (2022). Factors That Influence Consumers' Sustainable Apparel Purchase Intention: The Moderating Effect of Generational Cohorts. *Sustainability (Basel), 14*(14), 8950. doi:10.3390u14148950

Mayer, R. N. (1976). The socially conscious consumer—Another look at the data. *The Journal of Consumer Research, 3*(2), 113–115. doi:10.1086/208659

Neves, J., & Oliveira, T. (2021). Understanding energy-efficient heating appliance behavior change: The moderating impact of the green self-identity. *Energy, 225*, 120169. doi:10.1016/j.energy.2021.120169

Pekerti, A. A., & Arli, D. (2017). Do Cultural and Generational Cohorts Matter to Ideologies and Consumer Ethics? A Comparative Study of Australians, Indonesians, and Indonesian Migrants in Australia. *Journal of Business Ethics, 143*(2), 387–404. doi:10.100710551-015-2777-z

Roberts, J. A. (1995). Profiling Levels of Socially Responsible Consumer Behavior: A Cluster Analytic Approach and Its Implications for Marketing. *Journal of Marketing Theory and Practice*, *3*(4), 97–117. doi:10.1080/10696679.1995.11501709

Roberts, J. A., & Bacon, D. R. (1997). Exploring the Subtle Relationships between Environmental Concern and Ecologically Conscious Consumer Behavior. *Journal of Business Research*, *40*(1), 79–89. doi:10.1016/S0148-2963(96)00280-9

Schwartz, S. H. (1977). In L. Berkowitz (Ed.), *Normative Influences on Altruism*, pp. 221–279. Academic Press.

Sharma, R., & Jha, M. (2017). Values influencing sustainable consumption behaviour: Exploring the contextual relationship. *Journal of Business Research*, *76*, 77–88. . doi:10.1016/j.jbusres.2017.03.010

Sheoran, M., & Kumar, D. (2022). Conceptualisation of sustainable consumer behaviour: Converging the theory of planned behaviour and consumption cycle. *Qualitative Research in Organizations and Management*, *17*(1), 103–135. doi:10.1108/QROM-05-2020-1940

Soomro, R. B., Mirani, I. A., Sajid Ali, M., & Marvi, S. (2020). Exploring the green purchasing behavior of young generation in Pakistan: Opportunities for green entrepreneurship. *Asia Pacific Journal of Innovation and Entrepreneurship*, *14*(3), 289–302. doi:10.1108/APJIE-12-2019-0093

Stall-Meadows, C., & Davey, A. (2013). Green marketing of apparel: Consumers' price sensitivity to environmental marketing claims. *Journal of Global Fashion Marketing*, *4*(1), 33–43. doi:10.1080/20932685.2012.753293

Sudbury-Riley, L., & Kohlbacher, F. (2016). Ethically minded consumer behavior: Scale review, development, and validation. *Journal of Business Research*, *69*(8), 2697–2710. doi:10.1016/j.jbusres.2015.11.005

Tandon, A., Dhir, A., Kaur, P., Kushwah, S., & Salo, J. (2020). Why do people buy organic food? The moderating role of environmental concerns and trust. *Journal of Retailing and Consumer Services, 57,* 102247. doi:10.1016/j.jretconser.2020.102247

Taufique, K. M. R., & Islam, S. (2020). Green marketing in emerging Asia: Antecedents of green consumer behavior among younger millennials. *Journal of Asia Business Studies*, *15*(4), 541–558. doi:10.1108/JABS-03-2020-0094

Vu, D. M., Ha, N. T., Ngo, T. V. N., Pham, H. T., & Duong, C. D. (2021). Environmental corporate social responsibility initiatives and green purchase intention: An application of the extended theory of planned behavior. *Social Responsibility Journal*. doi:10.1108/SRJ-06-2021-0220

Webster, F. E. Jr. (1975). Determining the Characteristics of the Socially Conscious Consumer. *The Journal of Consumer Research, 2*(3), 188. doi:10.1086/208631

Yadav, R., & Pathak, G. S. (2017). Determinants of Consumers' Green Purchase Behavior in a Developing Nation: Applying and Extending the Theory of Planned Behavior. *Ecological Economics, 134,* 114–122. doi:10.1016/j.ecolecon.2016.12.019

Yang, X., & Zhang, L. (2021). Understanding residents' green purchasing behavior from a perspective of the ecological personality traits: The moderating role of gender. *The Social Science Journal, 00*(00), 1–18. doi:10.1080/03623319.2020.1850121

Zhen, J. S. S., & Mansori, S. (2012). Young female motivations for purchase of organic food in Malaysia. *International Journal of Contemporary Business Studies, 3*(5), 61–72.

Chapter 3
Analyzing Research Trends in Green Consumerism:
A Bibliometric Study Using RStudio

Pınar Yürük-Kayapınar
iD https://orcid.org/0000-0002-7460-6465
Trakya University, Turkey

Burcu Ören Özer
Trakya University, Turkey

ABSTRACT

The aim of this chapter is to engage with the concepts of green consumer and green consumerism and to perform a bibliometric analysis of the related publications. To this end, the studies are examined in WoS and Scopus between 1965 and 2023, using the keywords "green consumer" and "green consumerism." The study imposed certain constraints, resulting in the acquisition of a total of 7238 articles derived from 1728 sources. For this analysis, the Bibliometrix R Package Program was applied. An initial phase of the study was to conduct a descriptive analysis to provide an overview of the data. The subsequent phase involved examining several elements: the number of publications and citations by year; the most published journals on these subjects and their H-index values; the number of publications and H-index values of the authors; productivity of countries; most frequently used words; and collaboration networks of words, countries, and authors. Additionally, a factor analysis was carried out within the scope of the study to facilitate the observation of cluster formations.

DOI: 10.4018/978-1-6684-8140-0.ch003

INTRODUCTION

The world has come to a consensus on the need for a sustainable, ecological, and green environment, as the consequences of damage to the natural order are felt increasingly with each passing day. All segments of society—particularly nations, statesmen, businesses, and consumers—are making a concerted effort to address these challenges. Environmental problems, ecological imbalances, non-recyclable waste, ozone layer depletion, reduction of natural resources, toxic emissions, and global warming pose a threat to our present and future. Thus, the journey towards sustainability should be pursued urgently, and green consciousness should be instilled in every segment of society. This constitutes a social duty incumbent upon us for the betterment of society. Businesses have responded by adopting a green marketing approach, a strategy that has significantly reshaped the behavior of both enterprises and consumers.

In implementing green marketing strategies, businesses have begun to produce goods and services that either prevent or minimize environmental pollution, while simultaneously catering optimally to consumer demands and needs. In response, consumers have gravitated back towards green practices, showing a preference for eco-friendly businesses, and demonstrating increased awareness about this issue. Unfortunately, not all consumers are equally cognizant of the importance of sustainability. A significant portion of society still fails to comprehend the importance of the 'green' concept, is unable to distinguish between green and non-green products and remains unaware of businesses' green initiatives. Conversely, some consumers, despite their awareness, continue to choose non-green options. As a result, businesses have started to emphasize green initiatives more prominently in their promotional activities, underscoring the concepts of green products, green consumers, and green consumption. This trend is reflected in industries across the board, as seen in automobile advertisements featuring electric cars, banks refusing loans to environmentally harmful businesses, and home appliance advertisements promoting the use of recyclable materials.

In light of the prevailing belief that the planet is on the brink of environmental catastrophes due to climate change, the European Union seeks to catalyze a sustainable green transition. In response to the threats posed by global warming, climate change, and air pollution, the European Commission has proposed the "European Green Deal," demonstrating its leadership in this critical area. The European Green Deal strives for a fair and competitive transition to zero greenhouse gas emissions by 2050 for the countries and citizens of the European Union (European Commission, 2021).

The Green Deal action plan seeks to increase resource efficiency, restore biodiversity, and reduce pollution by transitioning to a clean, circular economy. This plan encompasses various policy areas, including clean energy, sustainable industry (i.e., sustainable, environmentally friendly production cycles), green construction and renovation, sustainable food systems (from farm to fork), pollution elimination, sustainable mobility (more sustainable means of transportation), and biodiversity (measures to protect fragile ecosystems) (Akilli Hayat 2030 Blog, 2022).

The policy areas in question aim to achieve zero carbon emissions, decarbonize the energy sector, invest in environmentally friendly technologies, stimulate innovation in production, and terminate dependency on resource extraction. In reaching these objectives, the plan ensures that no region or community is left behind, signifying an inclusive enhancement in quality of life. The realization of these goals necessitates the participation of all sectors and stakeholders.

Recognizing the global significance of the green movement, this chapter, inclusive of a literature review and bibliometric analysis, is designed specifically to delve into the concepts of the green consumer and green consumerism. This chapter is designed s as follows: Initially, it explores the green marketing process and the role of green consumers within it, as well as the concept of green consumerism. The behaviors of green consumers, who demonstrate environmental consciousness and friendliness, are described, and their characteristics and market segments are identified. The green marketing strategies of businesses are examined in relation to these consumer segments and characteristics. Thereafter, a bibliometric analysis of publications in the Web of Science and Scopus concerning the concepts of green consumer and green consumerism is conducted. By entering the keywords 'green consumer' and 'green consumerism,' a total of 1,728 sources were identified between 1965 and 2023, resulting in a total of 7,238 publications. These publications are subsequently subjected to a bibliometric analysis—comprising performance analysis (publication-related metrics, citation-related metrics, citation, and publication), scientific mapping (citation analysis, co-citation analysis, bibliographic coupling, co-word analysis, co-authorship analysis), and network analyses (network metrics, clustering, and visualization)-and interpreted.

BACKGROUND

Green Consumerism and Green Consumer Behavior

Green marketing, which aspires to fulfill consumer demands and needs without harming the environment or with minimal damage, encompasses all environmental and eco-friendly marketing activities. The development of green marketing is delineated in three stages. The first is ecological marketing, which emerged between 1960 and 1980, with the goal of reducing dependence on harmful products. The second is environmental marketing, which between 1981 and 2000 aimed to lessen environmental damage. Lastly, from 2001 onwards, sustainable marketing has aimed to offset production and consumption costs to establish a sustainable economic order. This period is considered the green marketing era. The question of how environmental concerns would impact consumer behavior arose during the second stage, i.e., environmental marketing. The outcome of these investigations led to the emergence of a new consumer concept, the 'Green Consumer' (Peattie, 2001). This concept has remained at the heart of green marketing practices to the present day. With the advent of the green consumer concept, considerations related to green consumption, green consumerism, and green product purchase decisions started to gain prominence. The underlying sentiment propelling these concepts is the notion of accountability toward the ecosystem. Consequently, green consumption is a sophisticated form of consumption, wherein consumers incorporate environmental and ethical concerns into their consumption behavior, driven by a sense of ecosystem accountability. This form of consumption pertains to energy saving, recycling, usage of energy-efficient devices, and proper waste disposal. The greening of a product encompasses activities related to its design, raw material selection, production, storage, transportation, usage, and recycling. Typically, green consumers are cognizant of most of these processes. This is because environmentally aware consumers recognize the negative effects and additional costs on the environment, from a product's development, production, distribution, consumption, to disposal, and aim to minimize them (Omar et al., 2015). There are five types of behaviors exhibited by consumers with this inclination (Hofmeister-Toth et al., 2011):

- Reducing consumption of conventional products,
- Adjusting demand – purchasing environmentally friendly products instead of traditional ones,
- Consuming environmentally friendly products,
- Participating in recycling and waste collection,
- Engaging in environmental complaints or protests.

Environmentally conscious and eco-friendly green consumers avoid purchasing the following types of products (Peattie, 2001):

- Products that endanger the health of consumers or others,
- Products that cause significant environmental damage during production, use, or disposal,
- Products that consume disproportionately large amounts of resources,
- Products that have excessive packaging, unnecessary waste due to excess features, or an extremely short lifespan,
- Products that use materials from endangered species or environments,

- Products that involve cruelty to animals,
- Products that negatively impact other countries

Given these behaviors, green consumers refrain from purchasing products that they perceive as posing health risks, causing environmental harm during production, use, or disposal, consuming excessive energy, featuring excessive packaging, and containing ingredients from threatened habitats or species (Akehurst et al., 2012).

To ascertain whether a product possesses these characteristics, green consumers require information at every stage, from the product's production to its delivery and even post-sale services. Terms such as environmental awareness, being green, eco-conscious, environmentally friendly, and pro-environment have come into existence as a result of these behaviors.

Green Consumer Characteristics and Segments

In the nascent stages of green marketing, environmental awareness and adopting green practices were confined to specific segments of society. However, over time, environmental concerns ceased to be the prerogative of a singular group. Factors such as rising education levels, heightened awareness, more research on consumer purchases, changes in socio-economic spheres, and increases in welfare levels are among the pivotal reasons for this shift. Consequently, consumers began to express increasing concern for the environment, and these concerns directly impacted their behaviors. Businesses, in turn, swiftly adapted their practices to cater to these evolving behaviors.

Each green consumer displays different motivations towards the product content when purchasing green products. This makes it challenging for marketers and manufacturers to design and position green products in the market (Peattie & Charter, 2002). Therefore, it's essential to analyze the diverse preferences, needs, motivations, and especially the characteristic features of green consumers and their market segments. As a result of this analysis, green consumers can answer the questions of *"what they think, what they feel, what they do and how they behave"*.

Being a green consumer is closely tied to the pro-environmental culture of consumers (Akhtar et al., 2021). Therefore, the social and cultural characteristics of consumers influence their green status and degree. Demographics, economic status, and education levels are other attributes that affect green behavior. For instance, in a study examining green behaviors across generations, it was found that consumers belonging to Generation X exhibited more green behavior than those in Generations Y and Z (Yürük-Kayapınar et al., 2019). Hence, businesses need to be cognizant of these behavioral changes in consumers when formulating and implementing their green marketing Studies examining the green status and levels of consumers have looked at different segments of green consumers in the market. While these segments generally signify the same concept, they are named differently in different studies:

- Activists, Realists, Complacent, Alienated (Rex & Baumann, 2007);
- The Uncommitted, The Green Activists, The Undefined (Paço, 2009)
- Green, Ambiguous, Un-Devoted, Explorers (Awad, 2011).

Though green consumers are segmented differently in various studies, the most widely accepted and utilized market segmentation of green consumers consists of five categories (Ginsberg & Bloom, 2004; Rex & Baumann, 2007):

- *True Blue Greens:* This segment embodies strong environmental values. They are interested in continually improving their green behavior. If a business is not environmentally friendly, they will not purchase its products, and they are more likely to avoid such businesses. They are major green purchasers and recyclers. They are also referred to as 'Faithful Greens'.
- *Greenback Greens:* Politically, they are not active environmental consumers and do not spend much time being green. However, they still tend to buy more green products than the average consumer. They do not make a change in their lifestyle. They are also known as 'Fake Greens'.
- *Sprouts:* This segment is environmentally friendly in theory, but not in practice. If buying green means spending more, they may refrain from purchasing the green product. They occasionally buy a green product but can also revert to non-green habits. They can act both ways. If provided with a suitable environment, they may be persuaded to buy green. They are also known as 'Those Improving'.
- *Grousers:* They lack a high degree of education in environmental awareness, and they resist change. They believe that green products are expensive compared to others and that these products do not perform well. They argue that environmental issues are someone else's problem. They are also known as 'Complainants'.
- *Basic Browns:* Their environmental concerns are fleeting. They quickly forget and show indifference towards environmental and social problems. They are also known as 'Those Not Caring'.

There are consumers who behave differently according to these segments and exhibit different levels of green behavior. However, as the social, cultural, demographic, and psychological characteristics of green consumers vary, there are distinctive differences within each segment. These differences significantly impact their behavior. Thus, these characteristics of green consumers need to be scrutinized for businesses to execute their green strategies more effectively. Cultural factors wield the most significant influence on a consumer's decision-making process, as culture is inseparable from the individual. Social acceptance and reference groups are other critical factors. Moreover, demographic characteristics exert considerable influence as they determine consumption types. Psychological factors shape individual behavior, particularly when environmental sensitivity is involved, the significance of this factor escalates. The individual amasses a wealth of information throughout life, learning what to consume and how. Therefore, all the characteristics of an individual play a significant role in shaping consumer behavior, serving as a decision mechanism for the type of consumer they will become. When operators and marketers aim to identify green consumers, they should first consider the decision-making criteria in their segmentation and targeting strategies. The characteristics of green consumers have been studied in different research based on varying attributes (Awad, 2011; Chanpaneri & Jog, 2020; Finisterra do Paço et al., 2009; Finisterra do Paço & Raposo, 2008; Oliveira & Sousa, 2019; Omar et al., 2015; Samarasinghe, 2012). Therefore, in this study, all research examining these characteristics was considered and discussed as follows:

- *Socio-Demographic Characteristics:* Age, Gender, Marital Status, Household, Religion, Subculture, Education, Job, Income, Social Class
- *Psychographic Characteristics:* Lifestyle, Personality, Motivation, Values, Environmental concern, altruism.
- *Behavioral Characteristics:* Knowledge, Attitude, Product Usage, Brand Loyalty, Purchase Behavior, Benefits.
- *Environmental Characteristics*: Concern, Ecological Consciousness, Subjective Norms, Environmentally Friendly Behavior, Willingness to Pay, Recycling, Scepticism towards Environmental Claims, Information Search.

Having examined all market segments of green consumers and the distinctive characteristics within each segment, the question remains: how should businesses determine and implement a strategy? To answer this, businesses need to ask themselves two crucial questions: First, how important is the green consumer segment to the business, and will the business suffer financially if consumers perceive the business as not being sufficiently green? Secondly, to what extent can the brand or business differentiate itself in green strategy and outcompete rivals in this arena? The answers to these questions will aid businesses in determining the degree to which 'green' should be emphasized in their marketing strategies. The following strategies can guide businesses on how they can answer these questions (Ginsberg & Bloom, 2004):

Lean Green: These businesses strive to be responsible corporate entities but do not particularly endeavor to promote and market their green initiatives. They engage in environmentally responsible activities not for the sake of being green, but to reduce costs. They do not perceive significant gains from green market segments and fear not differentiating themselves from competitors, which dissuades them from promoting their green activities.

Defensive Green: They perceive green marketing as a precautionary measure, accept green segments as profitable, and aim to bolster the brand image with green strategies. Their environmental sensitivities are sincere, but their efforts to publicize them are sporadic. They lack the ability to differentiate from their competitors in green. They partake in or sponsor small-scale eco-friendly events.

Shaded Green: These businesses make long-term investments in green strategies. They view green as a significant opportunity to create a competitive advantage and can differentiate from their competitors with green strategies. They primarily emphasize and promote consumer benefits, with environmental benefits being promoted as a secondary factor.

Extreme Green: Green strategies are central to these businesses. They serve niche markets and deliver products to consumers through private channels. Environmental awareness is integrated into all activities of these businesses and has been the main driving force since the inception of the business.

The state of the consumer determines which of the above green strategies businesses will opt for. Today's consumers, especially the greenest among them, exhibit high environmental sensitivity. They expect businesses to promptly respond to this high sensitivity with green marketing strategies. At the same time, they demand instant access to products with desired features. Consequently, the consumer focuses on both production and consumption simultaneously. Thus, it can be asserted that green consumers direct marketing activities in their respective businesses. Pleasing this conscious consumer depends on the business's position in green marketing.

Given that all product production involves some degree of waste production and energy consumption, any business can implement green innovations and marketing. However, in practice, different companies employ green marketing based on their evaluations of its financial and non-financial value; some even incorporate green initiatives as a key component of their strategic plan. The following are examples of environmentally friendly marketing:

- *Ben and Jerry's* was among the first businesses to weave environmental values into their organizational purpose. They support the use of organic products and conduct business sustainably. With the aid of environmentally friendly products and packaging that is easily recyclable or biodegradable, its parent company,
- Unilever, which manages more than 400 brands, has cut its greenhouse gas emissions in half over the past 15 years (Dillon, 2021).

- **Starbucks** has long incentivized environmentally friendly coffee growing practices by offering farmers increased payments for adopting such practices. Through its 'Shared Planet Programme', it promotes sustainability practices among customers, employees, and business owners. Starbucks uses single-use cups, avoids plastic, and employs eco-friendly packaging materials as part of its efforts to reduce waste in its packaging and products (Davey, 2022).
- **İkea,** a globally renowned company known for its emphasis on sustainable sourcing and renewable energy, has developed a strategy named "People and Planet Positive" that promotes green living, renewable energy, and environmental restoration. The objective of this green marketing initiative is to mitigate the negative effects of the company's operations on the local ecosystem (Rock Content, 2021; Weisman, 2023).
- **Johnson and Johnson,** the second-largest commercial consumer of clean energy in the USA, has consistently reduced production pollution over the past 20 years. In January 2011, it initiated the development of a plan to become the most environmentally conscious corporation. Johnson & Johnson offers bandages and other products for babies and children. It is also highly regarded for the micro-environmental practices it has instituted, which include training employees in the workplace on how to integrate environmental principles into their work (Weisman, 2023).
- **Timberland,** assigns an ecological impact score to each pair of shoes it sells. Moreover, it restructured its store designs to use 30% less energy. Timberland, one of the world's most recognized clothing companies, employs environmental narratives to promote its products. To devise and execute a green marketing strategy, the company is broadening its partnerships and experimenting with new technologies. The company aims to use only organic and renewable materials, and soon, all its products will comply with environmental standards, known as TEPS (Staff, 2022).

METHODOLOGY

Aim, Method of the Research, and Sampling

The aim of this research is to describe the literature on the concepts of green consumer and green consumerism, which is one of the main focal points of green marketing, which is an important approach in the field of marketing. It is aimed to discover the structure and trends of publications in this field. The analysis results will provide important information into new research areas and future studies will be guiding.

In the research, publications on the concepts of green consumer and green consumerism in Web of Science and Scopus databases between 1965 and 2023 were examined and analyzed. First, the keywords that would best explain the subject and scope of the research "green consumer" and "green consumerism" were identified. Then the data were preprocessed, and the constraints were applied.

1.   The first constraint is the selection of platforms to search for keywords. Two basic platforms were chosen, namely Web of Science (WoS) and Scopus, which scan SSCI, SCI, ESCI, Scopus and ISI databases. Keywords were entered separately on these platforms and the total number of articles on this subject was examined. A total of Green Consumerism: 401, Green Consumer: 17123, Green Consumerism or Green Consumer: 17287, and Green Consumerism and Green Consumer: 237 articles were found in WoS. In Scopus, Green consumerism: 444, Green Consumer: 13991, Green Consumerism or Green Consumer: 14181 articles were found.

2.   As the second constraint, the type of documents was determined as article, review article and early access. Thus, by eliminating other document types, a total of 14503 documents were found in WoS, including Article: 13402, Review Article: 1101 and Early Access: 404. In Scopus, a total of 10660 documents, including Article: 9798 and Review: 862, were accessed.

3.   The third constraint is the selection of domain categories of documents. Social science fields were selected. A total of 4212 from the categories of Business, Management, Economics, Hospitality Leisure Sport Tourism, Social Science Interdisciplinary, Family Studies, Social Issues, Cultural Studies, Psychology Social, Public Administration, Behavioral Science, Business Finance, Psychology, Operational Research in WoS; In Scopus, a total of 4814 documents were accessed from the fields of Business, Management and Accounting, Social Sciences, Economics, Econometrics and Finance, Psychology.

4.   Another constraint is the selection of the date range. According to the analysis of studies on green consumers and green consumerism, the first study was carried out in 1965. Since there is not a very long history related to these two issues, no date limitation was made, and the analysis was carried out with the documents from the first published date to the present (1965-2023).

When all the above constraints were applied, a total of 7238 articles were reached from the WoS and Scopus databases. These data were loaded into Bibliometrix R Package Program, duplicates in both WoS and Scopus were identified, and data were edited. Duplicate entries of the publications were deleted and a total of 7238 publications were analyzed.

Bibliometrics refers to a set of statistical and mathematical techniques used to quantify and evaluate the volume and quality of books, papers, and other publications (Durieux & Gevenois, 2010). Bibliometric research provides quantitative analysis of the creation, consumption, and use of data collected from library collections and services, such as WoS, generating information and communication activities as well as scientific documentation. Therefore, the aim of bibliometric studies is to augment our understanding of the scientific research process (Osareh, 1996). This type of analysis provides information about the theoretical scope of the research subject, the intellectual framework, and the development of specific research areas (Zupic & Čater, 2015). Bibliometric analysis is categorized into two divisions: performance analysis and science mapping. Science mapping focuses on the relationships between research components, whereas performance analysis predominantly considers the accomplishments of research components (Donthu et al., 2021).

The bibliometric method carrying out these analyses is performed with a range of software including VOSviewer, R package program, Gephi, Leximancer, and others (Donthu et al., 2021). This study employed the R package program, as Bibliometrix, a unique bibliometric tool developed in R, performs statistical calculations according to a logical workflow and can generate graphs. R is an extensible, object-oriented, and functional programming language, making it easy to automate analyses and create new functionalities. This open software offers flexibility, quick upgrades, and integration with other statistical R packages, making it particularly useful in a continually evolving scientific discipline such as bibliometrics. It encompasses all the basic bibliometric analysis methods, but is particularly useful for science mapping (Seyhan & Özzeybek Taş, 2021).

Findings

A total of 7238 articles from 1728 sources, published between 1965 and 2023, were identified. When is examined, it is seen that the annual growth rate of 7238 studies obtained from a total of 1728 sources is 8.68%, the average age of the documents is 7.07, and the average citation per document is 32.14. The total reference number of all the studies obtained is 340491. The keywords plus derived by WoS and Scopus are 10563, and the author's keywords are 14947, according to the analysis of the content of the documents. 7238 publications were written by a total of 13345 authors, and a total of 1251 of these publications were written by a single author. The number of co-authors per document is 2.84, and the rate of international co-authorships is 9.008%.

The bibliometric analysis results of these obtained data are explained with the following figures, tables, and comments. Within the scope of the bibliometric analysis, productivity analysis, citation analysis, co-citation analysis, bibliographic

Table 1. Main information about data

Keyword Selection	Green Consumer Green Consumerism Green Consumerism or Green Consumer		
Data Preprocessing (Restrictions)	Platform		Web of Science (WoS) Scopus
	Date range		1965-2023
	Document Type		Article, Review Article, Early Access
	Categories	WoS	Business, Management, Economics, Hospitality Leisure Sport Tourism, Social Science Interdiciplinary, Family Studies, Social Issues, Cultural Studies, Psychology Social, Public Administration, Behavioral Science, Business Finance, Psychology, Operational Research
		Scopus	Business, Management and Accounting, Social Sciences, Economics, Econometrics and Finance Psychology
Total Numbers of	Sources		1728
	Documents		7238
	Annual Growth Rate %		8.68
	Document Average Age		7.07
	Average Citations Per Doc		32.14
	References		340491
Document Contents	Keywords Plus (Id)		10563
	Author's Keywords (De)		14947
Authors	Authors		13345
	Authors Of Single-Authored Docs		1043
Authors Collaboration	Single-Authored Docs		1251
	Co-Authors Per Doc		2.84
	International Co-Authorships %		9.008
Analysis	Performance Analysis		Publication-related metrics, Citation-related metrics, Citation and publication related metrics
	Scientific Mapping		Citation analysis, Co-citation analysis, Bibliographic coupling, Co-word analysis, Co-authorship analysis
	Network Analysis		Network metrics, clustering and visualization

coupling, co-word analysis, co-authorship analysis, Network metrics, clustering and visualization analyses of the studies published on green consumer and green consumerism were conducted. The most cited studies and authors, the countries, and journals with the most publications, the most used concepts with these concepts,

Figure 1. Distribution of articles by year and number of citations

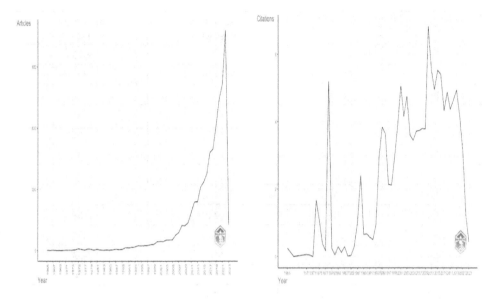

the collaborations of authors and countries with each other, maps created with the keywords on green consumer and green consumerism of the obtained studies were tested.

Figure 1 shows the total number of publications on green consumer and green consumerism and their annual change between 1965 and 2023. In addition, the annual citation numbers per year are discussed.

When the articles in the WoS and Scopus databases on green consumer and green consumerism were examined, it was determined that the first article was published in 1965. While only one article was published in 1965 and the following years, 14 articles were published in 1990, and an increase in the number of articles published each year began to be observed. Although there are ups and downs after 1990, there is generally an increase in the number of articles every year. But the real leap was in the late 1990s and early 2000s. After this date, it has continued to increase rapidly. The most important data is observed in 2022. In 2022, the total number of articles on these subjects increased to 1079, and although it was in the first months of 2023, 125 articles were published. It is thought that this data will exceed the score of 2022 by the end of 2023.

Considering the average citation rates per article for each article in Table 2, it is seen that the highest average in the last 20 years was in 2003 with 99.71 citations. When the average citation rates are examined on a yearly basis, it is revealed that it was made in 2010 with 6.83 in the last 20 years, although the highest citation is from 2003. Contrary to the continuous increase in the number of publications

Table 2. Number of documents and average citations by article and year

Year	Articles	MeanTCper Article	MeanTCper Year
2003	51	99.71	4.75
2004	51	71.96	3.6
2005	52	65.52	3.45
2006	75	66.93	3.72
2007	87	63.61	3.74
2008	122	60.84	3.8
2009	121	56.73	3.78
2010	136	95.65	6.83
2011	187	72.03	5.54
2012	237	59.54	4.96
2013	238	60.85	5.53
2014	311	54.01	5.4
2015	336	38.93	4.33
2016	376	39.02	4.88
2017	480	30.6	4.37
2018	497	27.9	4.65
2019	612	24,69	4.94
2020	743	16.69	4.17
2021	816	9.24	3.08
2022	1079	2.43	1.22
2023	125	0.43	0.43

published every year, there is a continuous increase and decrease in the number of annual citations.

One of the most important factors that make the subject attract more academic attention is the sources in which the article is published. Especially the first 20 journals and the impact values of these journals are of great importance. In figure 2 below, H index values are given to show the effect size of the journals.

Looking into the publications where papers on green consumers and green consumerism were published found that the "Sustainability" journal had the highest number of articles published (429) for the articles considered in this research. This is followed by the "Journal of Cleaner Production" (325), "Energy Policy" (141) and "Business Strategy and The Environment" (122), respectively. Although the most published journal is Sustainability, it is seen to be in the 6th place in the H index

Figure 2. The most published journals and H index values

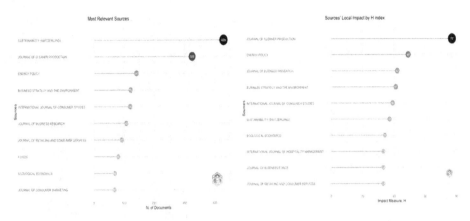

ranking. Journal of Cleaner Production is in the 1st place with an H index value of 77. The h index value of 77 means that 77 articles on this subject have at least 77 or more citations. It is followed by Energy Policy journal with an H index value of 49, Journal of Business Research with an H index value of 42, and Business Strategy and The Environment with an H index value of 41.

In Figure 3 below, the productivity of the authors related to green consumer and green consumerism is discussed. The authors who published the most on these topics, how many publications they made and the authors with the highest H index value were examined.

As seen in Figure 3, the author who published the most on these subjects was Wang Y. with a total of 50 publications. However, it is in the 2nd place in the H index value ranking. This author is followed by Wang L. with 42 publications, Na N. with 41 publications, and Wang J. with 39 publications. According to the H index values, Han H., who is in the 8th place with 32 publications, has the highest value in this regard with the 24 H index value. Wang Y. with 21H index, Kim Y. with 20 H index value, Chen Y. with 17 H index value, and Green P. and Wang J. with 16 H index values make up the top 6.

In Figure 4, the countries that publish the most on green consumer and green consumerism and how many publications they make are seen. The productivity levels of the countries were examined.

When the number of publications of the countries is investigated, it is seen that the country with the highest number of publications is USA (2803). China (1464), UK (795), India (755) and Australia (441) are next, respectively, making up the top five broadcasting countries. Turkey, on the other hand, is in the 19th place with 131 publications. The most cited countries, on the other hand, constitute the top 5,

Figure 3. Authors' production over time

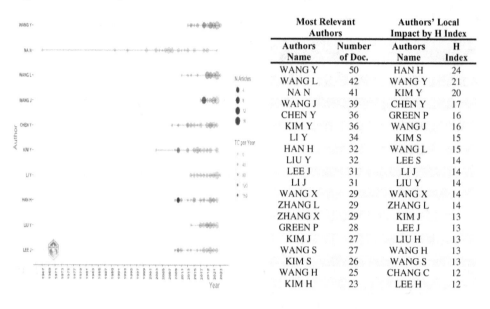

Most Relevant Authors		Authors' Local Impact by H Index	
Authors Name	Number of Doc.	Authors Name	H Index
WANG Y	50	HAN H	24
WANG L	42	WANG Y	21
NA N	41	KIM Y	20
WANG J	39	CHEN Y	17
CHEN Y	36	GREEN P	16
KIM Y	36	WANG J	16
LI Y	34	KIM S	15
HAN H	32	WANG L	15
LIU Y	32	LEE S	14
LEE J	31	LI J	14
LI J	31	LIU Y	14
WANG X	29	WANG X	14
ZHANG L	29	ZHANG L	14
ZHANG X	29	KIM J	13
GREEN P	28	LEE J	13
KIM J	27	LIU H	13
WANG S	27	WANG H	13
KIM S	26	WANG S	13
WANG H	25	CHANG C	12
KIM H	23	LEE H	12

Figure 4. Country scientific production

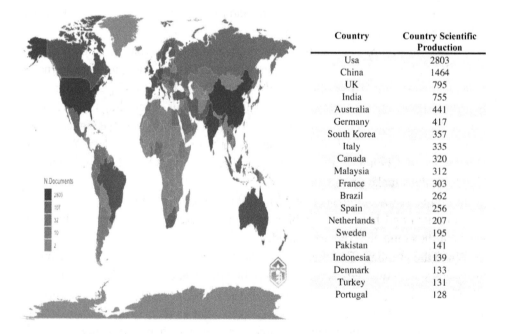

Country	Country Scientific Production
Usa	2803
China	1464
UK	795
India	755
Australia	441
Germany	417
South Korea	357
Italy	335
Canada	320
Malaysia	312
France	303
Brazil	262
Spain	256
Netherlands	207
Sweden	195
Pakistan	141
Indonesia	139
Denmark	133
Turkey	131
Portugal	128

Figure 5. Most relevant words

respectively, USA (56138), China (23866), UK (19361), Canada (9410) and India (9292). In the citation ranking, Turkey ranks 27th with 1164 citations.

The most frequently used words in publications on green consumer and green consumerism between 1965 and 2023 are analyzed in Figure 5. Analysis results are shown as Word Cloud (left) and Tree Map (right).

Figure 5 contains the first 50 most used words. When the most used words are examined, it is seen that the most used word in all publications is "Green" (723). Immediately after, the word "Sustainability" was used 446 times, "Sustainable Development" was used 412 times, and "Consumption Behavior" was used 411 times. The word "China" is also among the most used words. In the ranking of countries, China was identified as the second country with the most publications on this subject. Among these 50 words, the least repeated word is "Choice" (100).

In Figure 6, trending topics are given according to the keywords of the authors. In this figure, the size and color of the circles indicate how often the term is used, and the length of the lines indicates how long the term has been studied.

According to the keywords used by the author, "Covid-19" and "PLS-SEM" seem to be trending topics in recent years. "Green attitude, green trust, electric vehicles, and social media" seem to be other important trend topics used together with research topics. According to the keywords used by the authors, it is seen that the most used keyword is "sustainability" (650). After this word, it has been determined that there are "green marketing" (473), "green products" (208), "sustainable consumption" (205), and "consumer behavior" (184). The frequency of the words "Covid-19, PLS-SEM", which are trend topics in recent years, has been observed as 44 and 20, respectively. Again, 'electric vehicles' was used as a keyword 48 times and social media was used as a keyword 42 times.

Figure 6. Trend topics based on keywords

Terms	Freq.
covid-19	44
pls-sem	20
green attitude	20
green trust	57
electric vehicles	48
purchase intention	170
theory of planned behavior	114
social media	42
green consumption	150
green products	208
sustainable consumption	205
consumer behavior	184
sustainability	650
corporate social responsibility	142
green	103
green marketing	473
sustainable development	152
green consumer	66
marketing	95
consumption	94

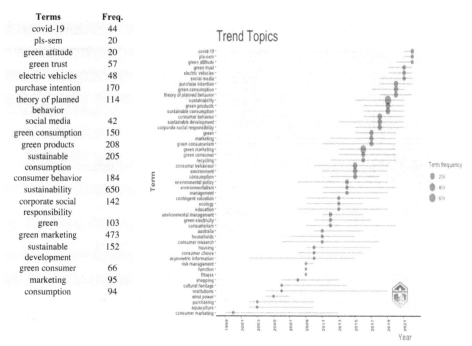

In Figure 7, the collaboration network of keywords (left), countries (right) and authors are given. Each color in these networks forms a different cluster. It is explained that the words, countries, and authors in the same color and in the same cluster are in collaboration with each other. For example, the upper left figure showing the collaboration of the keywords shows that the green-colored words are mostly used with each other, that is, there is a collaboration between them. Likewise, words in clusters of different colors collaborate with each other to a lesser extent.

When the upper left figure showing the collaboration of the keywords in Figure 5 is examined, it is seen that the words "sustainability", "green marketing", "green consumer", "green consumerism", "marketing", "environmental", "consumer behavior", "corporate social responsibility", "innovation" in the same color is most in collaboration with each other and they form a separate cluster.

Similarly, when the collaboration of the countries in the upper right corner is investigated, it has been determined that the countries in orange color "USA", "China", "Turkey", "Korea", "Russia", "Malaysia", "Hungary", "Japan" are in collaboration with each other the most and they form a separate cluster. When the author collaboration at the bottom is investigated, it is observed that Han H., Lee J., Kim Y., and Lee M. in green are in collaboration with each other.

Figure 7. Collaboration network of keywords, countries, and authors

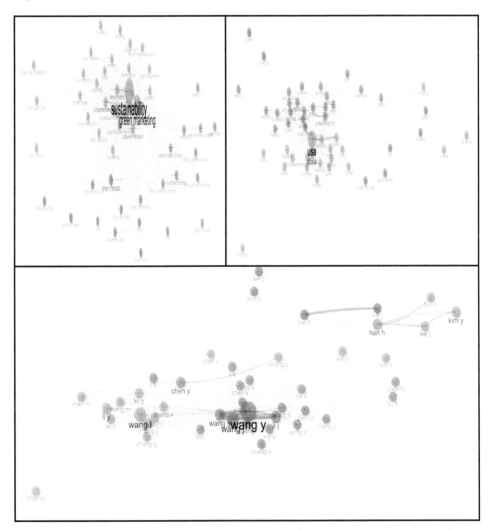

Figure 8 shows the conceptual structure map showing the density of the frequently used words using two different colors and two different clusters.

Upon conducting a factor analysis on the titles of studies pertaining to the concepts of green consumer and green consumerism, it becomes evident that they are categorized into two distinct groups denoted as "blue" and "red." When the blue color cluster is considered, it has been determined that the words "sustainable", "green", "consumption", "consumer", "marketing" and "environmental" are related and connected to each other. When the cluster in red color is examined, it is seen that the words "recycling", "attitude", "theory of planned behavior", "green purchase

Figure 8. Conceptual structure map

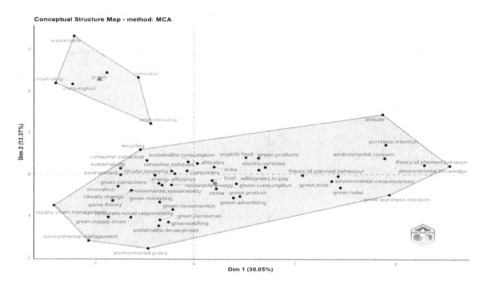

intention" "sustainable consumption", "trust", "electric vehicles", "climate change" are related and connected to each other.

FUTURE RESEARCH DIRECTIONS

This study includes a general theoretical framework on green consumer and green consumerism, as well as a bibliometric analysis of these concepts. The green consumer segments and characteristics included in the study will make it easier for practitioners and marketers who apply green marketing strategies and define themselves as green to recognize their consumers. Thus, businesses will be able to clarify which strategies they will attach more importance to, which issues they should focus more on, and at which green strategy stage they can define themselves. However, the literature review in this study was handled in general. For this reason, future studies detailing this issue may help businesses to put their green marketing strategies on a more solid basis.

In addition, a bibliometric analysis of green consumer and green consumerism was made in this study. Data were obtained from Web of Science and Scopus. Data drawn from different databases or adding a different database such as Google Scholar may lead to different results. Another constraint occurred in the selection of the research area/category. By choosing different categories, the concept of green consumer and green consumerism can be analyzed based on different disciplines in future studies. Bibliometrix R Package program was used. Using a different programming package such as VOSviewer will enable different visualization of the results obtained and additionally different analysis.

This study guides researchers, marketers and businesses that do or do not implement a green marketing strategy and contributes to the literature. It is hoped that this study will be a source for future studies in addition to previous studies. It is thought that the findings obtained because of the study will contribute to future research.

CONCLUSION

The shifting world order facilitates expedited efforts each day toward a sustainable, ecological, and greener environment. In anticipation of this green world order, the European Union has devised the "European Green Deal" action plan. As part of this, nations, businesses, practitioners, and consumers are all urged to fulfill their respective responsibilities. While executing this plan, the quality of life for each community is set to improve.

Environmental issues pose a significant threat to the current and future existence of all life forms on Earth. Consequently, consumers, businesses, and nations are gradually adopting green practices and promoting environmental awareness. The rise in environmental consciousness among consumers is shaping them into green consumers, while enterprises are growing closer to green marketing each day. In this evolving world order, the concepts of green consumers, green businesses, and green consumption are gaining prominence.

This study, focusing on green consumers and green consumerism, employs a bibliometric analysis. Publications on these concepts in the "Web of Science and Scopus" databases between 1965 and 2023 were examined and analyzed. After applying constraints on document types, categories, and date range, a total of 7,238 articles were obtained from 1,728 sources. The total number of references is 340,491, and the total number of authors is 13,345.

While only one article was published in 1965 and the years that followed, 14 articles were published in 1990. The significant surge occurred in the late 1990s and early 2000s. The most substantial data was observed in 2022. In that year, the total number of articles on these subjects increased to 1,079, and although only in the early months of 2023, 125 articles have been published. When examining the average citation rates on an annual basis, the highest citation was from 2003, though the last 20 years' peak was in 2010 with a rate of 6.83. While the number of publications has typically increased, it is observed that there are fluctuations and variations in the number of citations. The concepts of adopting green practices, green thinking, and green consumption contribute to the establishment of a new world order. The

European Union's "The European Green Deal" project, in particular, invites all nations to go green. This call is also mirrored in the increase in the number of publications.

When examining the sources in which these articles were published, it was revealed that the most articles were published in "Sustainability" with 429 articles. Although "Sustainability" is the most published journal, it ranks sixth in the H index ranking. "Journal of Cleaner Production" occupies the first place with an H-index value of 77. The sources in which the studies are published indicate the academic strength of the publications, and their H-indexes support this. "Sustainability" can be regarded as the strongest journal in this field.

In another analysis, the productivity of the authors was examined. The author who published the most on these subjects was "Wang Y" with a total of 50 publications. However, it ranks second in the H-index value ranking. According to the H-index values, "Han H," who is in the eighth place with 32 publications, has the highest value in this regard with an H-index value of 24. Knowledge of the most prominent authors and their H-indexes provides essential information for researchers seeking future collaborations or support.

The number of publications by country was also examined. The country with the highest number of publications is the USA, with 2,803 publications. The most cited countries constitute the top five, respectively: the USA (56,138), China (23,866), UK (19,361), Canada (9,410), and India (9,292). When examining the most frequently used words, it is seen that the word "Green" was used most often in all publications (723 times), closely followed by the word "Sustainability," which was used 446 times. According to the keywords used by the authors, "Covid-19" and "PLS-SEM" appear to be trending topics in recent years. The frequency of author keywords in the studies reflects the most studied variables, the direction of the subject, and opportunities for future studies. It is expected that the concept of green consumerism has focused on the words "Covid-19" and "PLS-SEM," especially in recent years. The Covid-19 pandemic has affected the entire world and changed consumer behavior. PLS-SEM is the most widely used quantitative method in recent years.

The collaboration of keywords was examined. The words "sustainability," "green marketing," "green consumer," "green consumerism," "marketing," "environmental," "consumer behavior," "corporate social responsibility," and "innovation" appear most frequently in the same cluster and they form a separate cluster. Similarly, when the collaboration of the countries was investigated, it was found that the countries colored in orange—USA, China, Türkiye, Korea, Russia, Malaysia, Hungary, Japan—are most frequently in collaboration with each other and form a distinct cluster. The relationship between keywords in studies provides valuable insights to enrich future research and facilitates literature review.

Finally, a factor analysis was performed. Two clusters emerged from the factor analysis. The first cluster links the words "sustainable," "green," "consumption," "consumer," "marketing," and "environmental." The second cluster connects the words "recycling," "attitude," "theory of planned behavior," "green purchase intention," "sustainable consumption," "trust," "electric vehicles," and "climate change."

Based on the results above, there is an important area of investigation, especially in the field of social sciences, with the increase in publications in recent years. The most cited studies appear in significant journals. These concepts contribute to the formation of a new world order. Thus, each study on this subject will be beneficial. There are variations in consumers' green behavior between countries and within regions of the same country. Understanding the sources of motivation that cause these differences will yield significant findings for the literature. It will also provide guidance for businesses conducting or planning to conduct international marketing activities.

This study has offered a comprehensive understanding of bibliometric variables related to green consumers and green consumerism. It provides a timely and useful examination of the current status and scientific progress of green consumerism, a new concept that has been the subject of increased study in recent years. Additionally, the study highlights unexplored issues that could be further researched by scholars and addressed from the policy-making and management perspectives of businesses. This study has revealed which issues the studies on green consumerism have focused more on and which issues previous studies have paid less attention to.

This study has identified areas that research has not addressed, thus illuminating gaps for future studies. According to the study's results, business managers can adopt green marketing strategies, and researchers can determine which topics they should explore. It is anticipated that future studies will focus more on this concept. This analysis provides vital information for researchers and will guide and enlighten new studies that will contribute to the development of the concept. Researchers can also benefit from this analysis and the integration of multidisciplinary fields in their future studies.

REFERENCES

Akehurst, G., Afonso, C., & Martins Gonçalves, H. (2012). Re-examining green purchase behaviour and the green consumer profile: New evidences. *Management Decision, 50*(5), 972–988. doi:10.1108/00251741211227726

Akhtar, R., Sultana, S., Masud, M. M., Jafrin, N., & Al-Mamun, A. (2021). Consumers' environmental ethics, willingness, and green consumerism between lower and higher income groups. *Resources, Conservation and Recycling, 168*, 105274. doi:10.1016/j.resconrec.2020.105274

Akilli Hayat 2030 Blog. (2022, March 25). *Yeşil mutabakat nedir?* Zorlu. https://www.zorlu.com.tr/akillihayat2030/yazilar/yesil-mutabakat-nedir

Awad, T. (2011). Environmental segmentation alternatives: Buyers' profiles and implications. *Journal of Islamic Marketing, 2*(1), 55–73. doi:10.1108/17590831111115240

Chanpaneri, A., & Jog, D. (2020). The role of consumer typology on the consumers' green involvement and its effect on green purchase behaviour. *4th International Marketing Conference Marketing Technology and Society.* Indian Institute of Management Kozhikode.

Davey, L. (2022). *15 Green marketing examples to inspire you in 2022.* GIVZ. https://www.givz.com/blog/green-marketing-examples

Dillon, V. (2021). Ben and Jerry: Founders striving towards sustainability. *The Momentum.* https://www.themomentum.com/articles/ben-and-jerry-founders-striving-towards-sustainability

Donthu, N., Kumar, S., Mukherjee, D., Pandey, N., & Lim, W. M. (2021). How to conduct a bibliometric analysis: An overview and guidelines. *Journal of Business Research, 133,* 285–296. doi:10.1016/j.jbusres.2021.04.070

Durieux, V., & Gevenois, P. A. (2010). Bibliometric indicators: Quality measurements of scientific publication. *Radiology, 255*(2), 342–351. doi:10.1148/radiol.09090626 PMID:20413749

European Commission. (2021, July 14). *A European Green Deal.* European Commission. https://commission.europa.eu/strategy-and-policy/priorities-2019-2024/european-green-deal_en

Finisterra do Paço, A. M., Barata Raposo, M. L., & Filho, W. L. (2009). Identifying the green consumer: A segmentation study. *Journal of Targeting. Measurement and Analysis for Marketing, 17*(1), 17–25. doi:10.1057/jt.2008.28

Finisterra do Paço, A. M., & Raposo, M. L. B. (2008). Determining the characteristics to profile the "green" consumer: An exploratory approach. *International Review on Public and Nonprofit Marketing, 5*(2), 129–140. doi:10.100712208-008-0010-9

Ghvanidze, S., Velikova, N., Dodd, T. H., & Oldewage-Theron, W. (2016). Consumers' environmental and ethical consciousness and the use of the related food products information: The role of perceived consumer effectiveness. *Appetite, 107,* 311–322. doi:10.1016/j.appet.2016.08.097 PMID:27554182

Ginsberg, J. M., & Bloom, P. N. (2004). Choosing the right green marketing strategy. *MIT Sloan Management Review*, *46*(1), 79–84.

Hofmeister-Toth, G., Kasza-Kelemen, K., & Piskti, M. (2011). The shades of green living in Hungary. *International Journal of Management Cases*, *13*(2), 5–14. doi:10.5848/APBJ.2011.00027

Kumar, P., & Ghodeswar, B. (2015). Factors affecting consumers' green product purchase decisions. *Marketing Intelligence & Planning*, *33*(3), 330–347. doi:10.1108/MIP-03-2014-0068

Oliveira, C., & Sousa, B. (2019). Green consumer behavior and its implications on brand marketing strategy. In V. Naidoo & R. Verma (Eds.), *Green marketing as a positive driver toward business sustainability* (pp. 69–95). IGI Global. doi:10.4018/978-1-5225-9558-8.ch004

Omar, N., Osman, L., Alam, S. S., & Othman, A. (2015). Ecological conscious behaviour in Malaysia: The case of environmental friendly products. *Malaysian Journal of Consumer and Family Economics*, *18*, 17–34.

Osareh, F. (1996). Bibliometrics, citation analysis and co-citation analysis: A review of literature I. *Libri*, *46*(3), 149–158. doi:10.1515/libr.1996.46.3.149

Paço, A. (2009). Adam werbach, strategy for sustainability. A business manifesto. *International Review on Public and Nonprofit Marketing*, *6*(2), 187–188. doi:10.100712208-009-0039-4

Peattie, K. (2001). Towards sustainability: The third age of green marketing. *The Marketing Review*, *2*(2), 129–146. doi:10.1362/1469347012569869

Peattie, K., & Charter, M. (2002). Green marketing. In M. Baker (Ed.), *The marketing book* (5th ed.). Routledge.

Rex, E., & Baumann, H. (2007). Beyond ecolabels: What green marketing can learn from conventional marketing. *Journal of Cleaner Production*, *15*(6), 567–576. doi:10.1016/j.jclepro.2006.05.013

Rock Content. (2021, August 21). *What is green marketing? 5 examples to inspire your business*. Rock Content. https://rockcontent.com/blog/green-marketing-examples/

Samarasinghe, R. (2012). A green segmentation: Identifying the green consumer demographic profiles in Sri Lanka. *Int. J. Mark. Technol.*, *2*(4), 318–331.

Seyhan, F., & Özzeybek Taş, M. (2021). Sağlık turizmi konusunda yapılan çalışmaların "R tabanlı" bibliyometrix analizi. *Social Sciences Studies Journal, 7*(81), 1569–1586. doi:10.26449ssj.3117

Staff, W. B. E. (2022, October 25). Green marketing. *Website Builder Expert.* https://www.websitebuilderexpert.com/grow-online/green-marke ting-examples/

Weisman, J. (2023, January 12). 9 green marketing examples to ınspire you. *Content Writers.* https://contentwriters.com/blog/brands-doing-green-marketing-right/

Yürük-Kayapınar, P., Kayapınar, Ö., & Ergan, S. (2019). Tüketicilerin yeşil ürün satın alma davranışlarının kuşaklar bakımından incelenmesi. *OPUS Uluslararası Toplum Araştırmaları Dergisi, 11*(18), 2055–2070. doi:10.26466/opus.565155

Zupic, I., & Čater, T. (2015). Bibliometric methods in management and organization. *Organizational Research Methods, 18*(3), 429–472. doi:10.1177/1094428114562629

ADDITIONAL READING

Dangelico, R. M., Nonino, F., & Pompei, A. (2021). Which are the determinants of green purchase behaviour? A study of Italian consumers. *Business Strategy and the Environment, 30*(5), 2600–2620. doi:10.1002/bse.2766

Dhir, A., Sadiq, M., Talwar, S., Sakashita, M., & Kaur, P. (2021). Why do retail consumers buy green apparel? A knowledge-attitude-behaviour-context perspective. *Journal of Retailing and Consumer Services, 59*, 102398. doi:10.1016/j. jretconser.2020.102398

Kumar, G. A. (2021). Framing a model for green buying behavior of Indian consumers: From the lenses of the theory of planned behavior. *Journal of Cleaner Production, 295*, 126487. doi:10.1016/j.jclepro.2021.126487

Machová, R., Ambrus, R., Zsigmond, T., & Bakó, F. (2022). The impact of green marketing on consumer behavior in the market of palm oil products. *Sustainability (Basel), 14*(3), 1364. doi:10.3390u14031364

Munerah, S., Koay, K. Y., & Thambiah, S. (2021). Factors influencing non-green consumers' purchase intention: A partial least squares structural equation modelling (PLS-SEM) approach. *Journal of Cleaner Production, 280*, 124192. doi:10.1016/j. jclepro.2020.124192

Niedermeier, A., Emberger-Klein, A., & Menrad, K. (2021). Which factors distinguish the different consumer segments of green fast-moving consumer goods in Germany? *Business Strategy and the Environment, 30*(4), 1823–1838. doi:10.1002/bse.2718

Nittala, R., & Moturu, V. R. (2023). Role of pro-environmental post-purchase behaviour in green consumer behaviour. *Vilakshan-XIMB Journal of Management, 20*(1), 82–97. doi:10.1108/XJM-03-2021-0074

Taufique, K. M. R. (2022). Integrating environmental values and emotion in green marketing communications inducing sustainable consumer behaviour. *Journal of Marketing Communications, 28*(3), 272–290. doi:10.1080/13527266.2020.1866645

Testa, F., Pretner, G., Iovino, R., Bianchi, G., Tessitore, S., & Iraldo, F. (2021). Drivers to green consumption: A systematic review. *Environment, Development and Sustainability, 23*(4), 4826–4880. doi:10.100710668-020-00844-5

KEY TERMS AND DEFINITION

Bibliometric Analysis: It is a quantitative data compilation method that makes use of secondary data that numerically analyzes the books, articles and other publications produced by individuals or institutions in a certain area, in a certain period and in a certain region, and the relations between these publications.

Conscious Consumer: It is referred as a responsible, sensitive consumer who researches before purchasing a product, thinks about the economy and limited resources by not buying more than they need, and calculates not only the purchasing stage but all the steps after the purchase.

Environmental Friendly Product: It can be defined as ecological and environmentally friendly products that take their raw materials from nature, do not contain chemicals that harm nature and living things, and whose waste does not harm nature.

Green Consumer: It refers to individuals or organizations that do not buy or do not want to buy the products of enterprises that endanger the health of living things and negatively affect the environment, are environmentally conscious, examine all stages from the production of the product to after use, and make efforts to make the environment more livable with these decisions.

Green Consumerism: It indicates to a consumption style that aims to sensitively approach the relationship of the goods or services offered for consumption with nature, in which the criteria for the efficient use of recyclable environmental resources, produced by consumers, are observed.

Green Marketing: With the awareness of social responsibility, it is the creation of marketing activities covering the processes from the production of environmentally friendly products to the after-use of the products without harming the environment and the living things in the environment or with minimal damage to satisfy the needs of the society and consumers and to achieve the goals of the enterprise.

Network Analysis: Network metrics is the bibliometric analysis phase, which includes clustering and visualization analysis, and is used to enrich the evaluation of bibliometric analysis.

Performance Analysis: It is the bibliometric analysis stage that shows the evaluation of the research and publications of individuals and institutions, and performs publication-related metrics, citation-related metrics, citation, and publication analyzes.

Scientific Mapping: It is a bibliometric analysis stage that examines the relationships between research components, reveals interactions and structural connections, and includes citation analysis, co-citation analysis, bibliographic coupling, co-word analysis, and co-authorship analysis.

Chapter 4

An Analysis of Relationships Between Renewable Electricity, Household Consumption, and Economic Growth in Nigeria

Shafiu Ibrahim Abdullahi
Bayero University, Kano, Nigeria

Kamal Kabiru Shehu
Federal University, Kashere, Nigeria

Mohammed B. Adamu
Adamawa State Polytechnic, Yola, Nigeria

Husayn Mahmud Muhammad
Federal College of Education, Yola, Nigeria

ABSTRACT

The main purpose of the chapter is to find out the effects of renewable energy on economic growth and household consumption in Nigeria. Renewable energy supply and environmentally sustainable consumption are key ingredients in achieving sustainable economic growth and development all over the world. The chapter aims at highlighting the positive contributions of green energy to sustainable consumption and economic growth. The main methods of analysis for the study are Granger causality tests, VAR impulse response function, and Variance decomposition. The findings show strong links between renewable electricity supply, economic growth, and household consumption in Nigeria. This was expected a priori, as overwhelming empirical and theoretical literature has attested to the effects of renewable electricity on economic growth of other nations around the world.

DOI: 10.4018/978-1-6684-8140-0.ch004

INTRODUCTION

According to Andrews and Friis (n.d.), 'widespread use of fossil fuels, rapid deforestation, and activities related to the production of goods and services are causing exponential increases in greenhouse gas emissions that are changing the earth's climate'. Production of electricity that is used in houses and industries has been important source of environmental deterioration and climate change. This, therefore, called for searching for environmentally sustainable sources of electricity production. Modern consumption and economic growth cannot be possible without electricity; it has been argued that it is the current mad rush for unsustainable consumption and economic growth that landed the world in the present climate crisis. It is also the same thing that causes the unreasonable thirst for environmentally harmful electricity supply by nations around the world by all means possible. Sustainable consumption involves ensuring reasonable use of resources without unnecessarily damaging the environment. According to Karuppannan and Sivam (2009) and Yigitcanlar et al. (2015), environmentally conscious consumers prefer places where there are less environmental damages than where environment is not given any consideration. Consumers now a day patronize environmentally friendly goods, especially with labels that indicate they are carbon free (Feucht & Zander, 2017).

Consumers are now eager to adopt green living than before. The concept of ethical consumption has become widespread and has gotten wider applications in different fields. Ethical consumption also includes changing individual behavior to avoid consumption habit that result in damage been caused to the environment. Example, include turning electricity appliances off when not in use or patronizing environmentally friendly sources of energy such as solar, wind and hydroelectric dams. According to Andrews and Friis (n.d.), there are three widely recognized dimensions of sustainable development; they are materials and energy use, land use, and human development. Coal has been recognized as an important source of greenhouse effect that affect the environment, hence the widespread movement away from coal as major source of electricity to renewable sources of energy. Nigeria is not left behind in this transition toward renewable energy. Though the global climate conference COP 27 that held in Egypt pointed out the constraints facing developing countries such as Nigeria and the need for developed countries to pay poor countries through climate financing, Nigeria generates large amount of its electricity through hydroelectric dams located around the country.

Around the world, the role of energy in economic development of nations has remained a hot topic at the centre of public discussions. The Russia-Ukraine war has further shed light on the strategic role of energy in global economics, politics and diplomacy. Europeans countries that depend on Russian energy were left scrambling to find alternative sources of energy or else their economies suffer severe consequence, not least was the slowdown in economic growth and looming recession. Among the various sources of energy, the role of electricity in the growth of modern economies cannot be overemphasized. Its role as complement to other factors of production is legendary. One of the major problems faced by developing countries, Nigeria inclusive, is shortage of electricity. This has a direct negative effect on economic growth and development. There is huge gap between electricity demand and supply in Nigeria (Abdullahi, 2018). But, this is despite the abundant resources that Nigeria is endowed with, but Nigeria has failed to harness these resources to provide the needed electricity for economic development. The power sector problem in Nigeria has affected the generation, transmission and distribution of power. But, only about 25% of generated electricity in Nigeria is delivered to consumers; the remaining 75% is lost during generation, transmission, and distribution process (World Energy Council, 2019). The failure of successive governments to provide adequate electricity supply has been described as the main obstacle to Nigerian industrialization. Because of the seriousness of the problem of electricity supply in Nigeria many households provide their own electricity through using generators or micro solar panels; this has been described as sometime dangerous and efficient alternatives to the main power grid. Households in Nigeria depend very much on electricity as source of energy for the running of their houses.

Nigeria's population is ravaged by poverty which has contributed to the lower standard of living enjoyed by the larger population. There exists a nexus between poverty and energy; the poor are theorized to use low efficient and environmentally damaging sources of energy. Poor nations are also the most ravaged by problem of poor energy supply. The role of consumption in the general welfare of households cannot be overemphasized; in fact, it is the most important barometer in measuring standard of living around the world. The role of electricity in household consumption and from there on general welfare has been overlooked by successive studies. The list of developmental challenges facing Nigeria cannot be complete without the mentioning of power problems. It is accepted that power supply shall be in line with demand for power in order for meaningful economic development to be achieved. Data has shown that countries with high use of electricity are in most cases the countries that are most industrialized and developed. But studies such as that of Ozturk (2010) show that there is a negative relationship between grow of a given economy and energy consumption. This, therefore, call for reduction in energy consumption through the use of innovative technologies. Despite, it owns poor electricity supply, Nigeria exports electricity to the neighboring Niger and Benin republics. How Nigeria manages to do that has been a mystery to many observers of the power supply-demand equilibrium in Nigeria.

Unlike previous studies that focused on relationship between combinations of different types of energies productions and economic growth, this study focus is on renewable electricity production, household consumption and economic growth. The main purpose of the chapter is to find out the effects of renewable energy on economic growth and household consumption in Nigeria. Renewable energy supply and environmentally sustainable consumption are key ingredients in achieving sustainable economic growth and development all over the world. The chapter serves four main purposes: one, measure the effects of renewable electricity supply on economic growth and household consumption; two, find the direction of causality between the variables in the respective models used for the study; three, measure how volatility in renewable electricity supply affect both economic growth and household consumption; fourth, measure how shock to the independent variable (renewable electricity supply) affect the dependent variables (economic growth and household consumption). Overall, the chapter aims at highlighting the positive contributions of green energy to sustainable consumption and economic growth. The main methods of analysis for the study are Granger causality tests, VAR impulse response function and Variance decomposition. It is hypothesized that positive shock from renewable electricity supply is economic growth and household consumption enhancing. Generally, electricity supply is a sensitive variable; it is far more sensitive to shocks than economic growth or household consumption. The chapter is subdivided into introduction, literature review, theoretical framework, data and methodology, results and discussions, implications and conclusion and recommendations.

Literature Review

Energy is a crucial factor in the rapid industrialization we are witnessing today in the modern world; and of course, energy is a citadel without which other economic sectors would have collapsed. A successful functioning of an economy majorly relies on how well other sectors relate directly or indirectly with the energy sector. The nexus between Electricity Supply and Economic Growth have been fairly analyzed and are there in the literature. The reviewed literature in this work is divided into two main compartments: those studies that were conducted on Nigeria and those that were conducted elsewhere around the world on other countries. The range of the literatures is wide in term of timeframe, econometric methodology and variables involves.

Studies From Around the World

Khobai (2018) conducted an empirical study using quarterly time series data spanning first quarter of 1997 to fourth quarter of 2012 in order to examine the causal relationship between renewable electricity and economic growth in South Africa. The study used economic growth as endogenous variable and renewable electric power, employment, capital formation, carbon dioxide emission as exogenous variables. To detect the direction of causation and evaluate its magnitude, Vector Error Correction Model was employed for the purpose of analyzing the data. The result of the analysis shows that there is one-way causation from renewable electricity to economic growth. It confirms the significance of renewable electric power in socio-economic development of South Africa. The result of a research conducted by Fazal et al. (2020), on the impact of the renewable-energy consumption on the economic development of Thailand, for the period 1990 to 2018, confirmed a significant impact of the renewable energy consumption on economic development of Thailand. The paper made use of Autoregressive and Distributed Lag Model for analysis. The result also revealed a uni-directional relationship between renewable energy and economic growth established using Granger Causality Approach.

Another research work by Azam et al. (2020) is related to the study of the nature and magnitude of causation between Gross Domestic Product and electricity supply in Pakistan, covering the timeframe 1990 to 2015. GDP as usual is the dependent variable while electricity supply is the independent variable, alongside other macroeconomic indicators (such Gross Capital Formation, Export and Investment, that were made the controlled variables). All the study variables were found to be in first order I (1) in the two-unit root tests conducted: Augmented Dickey Fuller and Philip Peron tests. The paper made use of Johansen Co-integration and Granger causality tests to measure both the long run and short run relationship and causation between the dependent and independent variables. The result of the analysis revealed that both the dependent (GDP) and independent variable (Electricity Supply) are co-integrated. Though the variables put together display long-term connectivity, but causality was absent from Gross Domestic Product to export and from export to investment. Conclusively, Gross Domestic Product causes electricity consumption in the long run based on the work, but economic growth progresses irrespective of electricity supply. Increase in electricity demand has usually resulted from higher economic growth, noted the findings of the work. Another empirical investigation by Stungwa et al. (2022) in South Africa, using annual time series data covering 1971 to 2014, study the impact of electricity supply on economic growth. The short run result of the analysis revealed that the relationship between the variables is positive and statistically significant. While in the long run, relationship was negative and insignificant. Mabugu et al. (2022) employed Autoregressive Distributed Lag model to investigate the possible effects of disequilibrium in the demand and supply of electricity in South Africa on economic growth in the period 1985 to 2019. The result of the analysis shows that there is possible expansion in economic growth in the long run, when the disequilibrium is in favour of the supply side of the electric supply and demand relationship. Hence, the paper advises the authorities concern to consolidate their strategy on how to boost the production and efficient supply of electricity in order to boost economic growth.

Studies Covering Nigeria

Umeji et al. (2023) conducted an empirical analysis that covered 1990 to 2020 to study the impact of renewable energy consumption on the Nigeria's economic growth. In order to examine the nature of the relationship between the dependent variable (economic growth) and independent variable (renewable energy consumption), they made use of Toda-Yamamoto Augmented Granger Causality Test, and Autoregressive Distributed Lag Model (ARDL) Bound Testing Approach to oversee the impact of renewable energy consumption on Nigeria's economic growth. The result of the study discovered a bi-directional relationship between the renewable energy consumption and economic growth in Nigeria. The result also shows a significant positive impact of the renewable energy consumption on the economic growth in Nigeria. Using Non-Linear Autoregressive Distributed Lag Model, Somoye et al. (2022) conducted a research that covered 1990Q1 - 2019Q4 to investigate the impact of renewable energy consumption on Nigeria's economic growth. From the result, a cointegration among variables was discovered and confirmed. Unlike many existing literatures, the result of this research further revealed that, economic growth in Nigeria decreases due to a positive shock of renewable energy consumption, but, in the long run, the economic growth of Nigeria increases, due to the negative shock of renewable energy consumption.

Mukhtar et al. (2020) have examined the effects of energy consumption, interest rate and import on household consumption in Nigeria. They used data for the period ranging from 1985 to 2018. The result shows that interest rate and energy consumption affect household consumption, while import is not statistically significant. The negative and statistically significant relationship between interest rate and household consumption means that monetary authorities can boost household consumption by lowering the interest rate. The positive and statistically significant relationship between energy consumption and household consumption means that high household consumption will lead to high energy consumption. Nnaji et al. (2013) investigated the causal relationship among electricity supply, fossil fuel consumption, CO_2 emissions and economic growth in Nigeria for the period 1971-2009; the Granger causality results indicate that electricity supply has not impacted significantly on economic growth. Chitedze et al. (2021) examined the level at which electricity consumption (EC) contributed to real sector performance in Nigeria. They used time series data, covering the period between 1981 and 2015. The findings show that EC displays a little and insignificant impact on manufacturing, as well as agriculture and service outputs. The empirical result from causality test suggests bidirectional causality between EC and manufacturing sector. Nathaniel and Bekun (2020) explored the link between electricity consumption, urbanization and economic growth in Nigeria using data from 1971-2014. The results have affirmed cointegrating relationship; it shows that electricity consumption increases economic growth, while the impact of urbanization appears to inhibit growth. Ogundipe et al. (2016) examined relationship between electricity consumption and economic development for the period 1970-2013. The study found long-run cointegration with electricity consumption inversely related to economic development. The study also found evidence of unidirectional causal relationship running from economic development to electricity consumption.

Ekeocha et al. (2020) re-evaluated the relationship between energy consumption and economic growth in Nigeria over the period between 1999Q1 to 2016Q4. The results show that the role of energy consumption as a driver of economic growth is negligible. Granger causality tests revealed a unidirectional causality running from energy consumption to economic growth. Oyaromade et al. (2014) investigated the relationship between total energy consumption and economic growth in Nigeria. The study found no clear relationship between energy consumption and economic growth. Ali et al. (2020) examined electricity consumption and economic growth nexus in a trivariate framework by incorporating urbanization, using annual frequency data from 1971-2014. Results confirmed that electricity consumption drives economic growth. A unidirectional causality from urbanization to electricity consumption and economic growth was found. Iyke (2014) examined dynamic causal linkages between electricity consumption and economic growth in Nigeria for the period 1971-2012. The results show causal flow from electricity consumption to economic growth.

Okoye et al. (2021) analyzed energy consumption and economic growth nexus in Nigeria using data of between 1981 and 2017. The results show that energy consumption significantly determined growth of economic activities. Onakoya et al. (2013) evaluated nexus between energy consumption and economic growth in Nigeria for the period of 1975 to 2010. The result shows that in the long run, energy consumption moved with economic growth except for coal. The results also revealed that petroleum, electricity and total energy consumption have positive relationship with economic growth. Ogbonna et al. (2016) examined the impact of power generation on economic growth in Nigeria during the period 1980 - 2015. The study found no causality between power generation and economic growth in Nigeria.

An Autoregressive Distributed Lag Model, Co-integration and Granger Causality tests were employed by Abur (2022) to determine correlation between economic growth and electricity supply in Nigeria within the time frame of 1986 to 2019. At the end, a long run relationship was observed between electricity supply and economic growth in Nigeria. The result of the co-integration analysis posited a two-way causation between the variables under study. Thus, the paper suggested a consolidated effort towards improvement of the electricity supply by the relevant policy makers for the growth of Nigerian Economy. Onayemi et al. (2020) employed Autoregressive Distributed Lag Model and time series data of 1986 to 2017, in order to empirically study the inter-relationship that explained how steady electrification directed and encouraged the inflows of Foreign Direct Investment (FDI) with impacts on the Economic Growth of Nigeria. The study used Gross Domestic Product as endogenous variable and foreign direct investment, labor force, Gross Fixed Capital Formation and Electric Power Supply were the exogenous variables in the model. From the results of the analysis, it is noticeable that all the explanatory variables are statistically significant. Meanwhile according to the study, the impact of foreign direct investment on economic growth was significant in the long run, with addition of almost 27% above the 3% short run impact of foreign direct investment on economic growth in Nigeria. The result further revealed that there is propensity for economic growth to go up by 6% at every 1% increment in electricity supply; this imperatively shall give direction to policy makers in making sure that power sector is up to standard in order to efficiently produce steady electricity supply in Nigeria.

Ugbaka et al. (2019) investigated whether there could be positive and significant effects on economic growth of Nigeria from existing supply of electricity and more investment in the sector by policy makers and private investors within sampled period of 1980 to 2017 using Wald Test and ARDL Model. The result of the analysis disclosed that there is a positive and significant impact from the studied external variable to Nigerian economic growth in the short and long. The study further recommended that government initiate policies that would move the power sector forward so as to expedite sound economic growth and development of Nigeria. In a different study, an Autoregressive Distributed Lag (ARDL) Bound testing approach was employed by Yakubu et al. (2015) to investigate the relationship between output of manufacturing sector and electricity supply in Nigeria for the period spanning 1971 to 2010. The result of the research indicated that the dependency of manufacturing output on electricity supply is significant and positive in the long run. The significance of electricity supply on output of the manufacturing sector in Nigeria for the period of the analysis was found to be important; manufacturing sector output increased by 2.175% from a 1% Electricity Supply increment in the long-term. Apinran et al. (2022) in a study that covered from year 1981 to 2019, taking capital, carbon emissions and labor force into account, employed ARDL model to empirically examine the impact of supply and consumption of electricity on Nigerian economic growth. The results of the analysis showed positive effects of labor force, capital and electricity consumption on Nigerian economic growth. But the effect of carbon emission on economic growth was found to be negative. The paper suggested serious commitment by government in maintenance of the power sector, so as to have a stable electricity supply which would help to accelerate economic growth.

To check the causal relationship between electric power consumption and economic growth in Nigeria, a multivariate empirical analysis was carried out by Akomolafe et al. (2014). The empirical work checked whether there is a negative, neutral or positive effect of electricity consumption on economic growth in Nigeria from 1990 to 2011. It employed ADF and PP tests for stationarity tests. Vector Error Correction, Johansen Co-integration tests and Granger causality test were also used to analyze the relationship between the variables. The result of the study, however, confirmed long run positive relationship between real GDP and electricity consumption within the study's time frame. Adedokun (2015) employed Wald test, Granger Causality test and Vector Error Correction model to empirically analyze how efficient and smooth could trajectory of economic growth in Nigeria be when electricity consumption is considered as an independent variable and economic growth as dependent variable. The result of the Granger causality test shows that either of the two variables has power of causation and prediction on the other; only that causation is stronger from electricity consumption to economic growth.

Theoretical Framework

In developing countries, poverty has led people into putting too much pressure on the environment. But meeting the demands of modern economies, which mainly centered on all kinds of consumptions while maintaining environmental balance, is a herculean task. According to World Commission on Environment and Development (1987), sustainability refers to 'meeting the needs of the present generation without compromising the needs of future generations'. To Pearce and Warford (1993), development is sustainable 'if and only if the stock of overall capital assets remains constant or rises over time'. The exclusion of the environment from GNP calculations is blamed for the absence of environmental considerations from development economics (Todaro and Smith, 2003). To account for environment in calculating national income, Pearce and Warford (1993) proposed that capital assets shall include not only manufacturing capital but human capital and environmental capital such as forest, soil quality and clean water. According to this, sustainable national income or sustainable net national product (NNP) is the amount that can be consumed without diminishing the capital stock.

$$NNP = GNP - DM - DN \tag{1}$$

Where, D_m = depreciation in manufactured capital assets, D_n = depreciation in environmental capital. A more complex but better measure is:

$$NNP = GNP - DM - DN - R - A \tag{2}$$

Where, R = expenditure required to restore environmental capital, A = expenditure required to avert destruction of environmental capital.

The main theoretical models use for this work revolve round general production function and its extensions such as in Solow (1956), Romer (1982 & 1986) and Barro (1996) models. Consumption model explains how households conduct their consumption activities and how electricity use comes into the equation. In traditional consumption models, household source of income money include income receive from labor and returns from investments made (Abdullahi & Shuaibu, 2022); in return households pay taxes to the government and decide how much of the remaining money to save and consume. Household consumption according to Tobit and Golub (1998) is:

$$\max E \left\{ \sum_{t=0}^{T} U\left(C_t, t\right) \right\} \tag{3}$$

Where U = Utility, C = Consumption, t = time and household seek to maximize expected utility over time between t=0 and t=T, subject to the requirement that consumption is given by income minus saving. Some of the most well-known theories of consumption include Keynes absolute income hypothesis where income is theorized to be the main determinant of consumption. Friedman's permanent income hypothesis, on the other hand, theorizes that consumption is a function of both current and expected income. While Modigliani's Lifecycle hypothesis shows that households stabilize consumption overtime as they relate consumption to expected lifetime income. Keynes (1936) absolute income hypothesis is of the form:

$$C = \mathbb{C} + cY, \mathbb{C} > 0, 0 < c < 1 \tag{4}$$

Where C - consumption, Y - disposable income, $\mathbb{C}$ - constant or autonomous consumption, c - MPC

But, there is no way one would talk about electricity supply without talking of its environmental impacts. This is one of the three most important components of this chapter, the others being consumption and economic growth. Because of this the chapter looks at the existing theories that explain energy-environment relationship. According to Dasgupta and Maler (1991), development economics has failed to recognize renewable environmental resources in a way they deserve. Dasgupta and Maler (1991) put an economy production function taking into consideration the use of renewable resources as:

$$dk/dt = F(K,L) - C - Q - R \tag{5}$$

Where, K – Capital goods, L – Labor efforts, C – Resource consumption, Q – Spending on environmentally friendly technology, R – Rate of production that counters the damages to the environment. In traditional economic analysis, there are many models that try to explain economic growth. The much popular Solow growth model is of the form:

$$Y=f(K,L,T) \tag{6}$$

Where Y – output, K – capital stock, L- labor and T- technology But, the more empirically inclined Cobb-Douglas production function is:

$$F(K,L) = AK^{\alpha} L^{1-\alpha} \tag{7}$$

Where, K – Capital, L – Labor, A – Variable representing the state of technology, α – Parameter determining capital share of total output. Stern (1993, 1997, 2000, 2004) has put forward a model that linked energy usage to economic growth. He revisited the neoclassical theories of growth to examine the factors that could reduce or strengthen linkage between energy use and economic growth over time.

Data and Methodology

Data

Data for the study was sourced from The World Bank, Central Bank of Nigeria (CBN) and National Bureau of Statistics (NBS) for the period 1989 to 2019. The variables whose data was used for the study include renewable electricity supply, household consumption, economic growth, physical capital, credit available to the private sector (as proxy for entrepreneurial investment), income, interest rate and Dependency ratio. The variable credit to the private sector has dual functions, it acts as proxy for entrepreneurship level and it also acts as source of capital money needed for economic growth and development. For example, Shuaibu et al. (2021) found that saving which serves as primary source of credit for the private sector served as an important source of economic growth in Nigeria.

Models

Model 1
Model 1 is energy-growth model that tests the effects of energy especially electricity on economic growth in Nigeria. The dependent variable is economic growth

with physical capital, labor force, credit available to the private sector (as proxy for entrepreneurial investment) and electricity supply as independent variables.

$$G = \partial_0 + \partial_1 P + \partial_2 L + \partial_3 C + \partial_4 E + \varepsilon \qquad (8)$$

Where, G – economic growth, P – physical capital, L – labor force, C – credit to private sector, E – electricity supply, ε – error term

Model 2

Model 2 is consumption-energy model that measures effects of electricity supply on household consumption. Here the dependent variable is household consumption while income, interest rate, dependency ratio and electricity supply are the independent variables.

$$H = \theta_0 + \theta_1 I + \theta_2 R + \theta_3 D + \theta_4 E + \epsilon \qquad (9)$$

Where, H – household consumption, I – income, R – interest rate, D – dependency ratio, E – electricity supply, ϵ - error term

Methodology

The paper uses Granger causality to measure the direction of causality between variables, VAR impulse response function and Variance decomposition to measure effects of shocks in the independent variables on the dependent variable. Unit root tests were conducted to find out whether the series are stationary or not.

Granger Causality

Granger causality is a statistical concept that is used for and based on prediction. Its mathematical formulation is based on linear regression modeling of stochastic processes (Granger, 1969). Granger causality was developed in the 1960s and has seen various applications in economics. As an econometric model it is used to verify the usefulness of one variable to forecast another.

VAR Impulse Response Function

VAR model provides a channel by which the data, rather than the econometrician, determine the dynamic structure of the model. Hence, after VAR estimation impulse response function and variance decomposition provide an opportunity to characterize the dynamic structure of the model. The impulse response function traces the response of the endogenous variable to a shock in that variable and in every other endogenous variable (Pindyck & Rubinfeld, 1998).

Results and Analysis

Summary Statistics

Granger Causality Results

The results of the causality tests show that there is one-way causality from electricity supply to economic growth and electricity supply to household consumption, see table 1 and 2.

VAR Impulse Response Function and Variance Decomposition Results

The results of the impulse response function show that one standard deviation shock to electricity (in model 1) led to a much higher increase in electricity than in economic growth, see figure 1. In the case of the household consumption model (model 2), the change in electricity as a result of one standard deviation shock to electricity is much higher than in the case of economic growth model (model 1). It also shows that the effect on consumption (model 2) as a result of shock to electricity is lower than the respective effect on economic growth in model 1, see figure 2. In the case of the model 1, in the subsequent periods, electricity falls and economic growth rises and as time goes by they all approach zero. In the same subsequent period in the case of model 2, electricity falls while consumption mostly remains constant; but as time moves they all approach zero. The results of variance decomposition for period one show that when there is a shock to electricity, 2.7% of the change is attributable to economic growth while 97.3% is attributed to change in electricity itself, see table 4. This is the forecasted change in electricity supply in the case of model 1 attributed to each of electricity and economic growth. For model 2, the result of the variance decomposition for period one shows that about 1% of forecasted change in supply of electricity in Nigeria is attributed to consumption, while 99% is

Table 1. Summary statistics

	Electr.	GDP	H. Cons.	Physicalcap	Income	Credit	Interest	Labour	Dependency
Mean	21.92000	2.23E+11	1.51E+11	4.61E+10	2.23E+11	9.941290	12.11607	45878947	88.36548
Median	21.11000	1.36E+11	8.11E+10	3.55E+10	1.36E+11	8.460000	10.82000	45940926	87.88000
Maximum	36.51000	5.68E+11	4.15E+11	1.21E+11	5.68E+11	19.63000	23.99000	62151626	92.33000
Minimum	12.81000	4.95E+10	1.68E+10	1.88E+10	4.95E+10	4.960000	4.704871	31787602	86.62000
Std. Dev.	7.147105	1.79E+11	1.38E+11	2.53E+10	1.79E+11	3.641084	5.231871	9277286.	1.647173
Skewness	0.440746	0.486329	0.590058	0.889471	0.486329	0.933335	0.822377	0.008890	1.079416
Kurtosis	1.851621	1.655339	1.784005	3.394179	1.655339	3.511839	2.821002	1.751954	3.141756
Jarque-Bera	2.707081	3.557477	3.708788	4.288345	3.557477	4.839141	3.535622	2.012332	6.045837
Probability	0.258324	0.168851	0.156548	0.117165	0.168851	0.088960	0.170706	0.365618	0.048659
Sum	679.5200	6.90E+12	4.67E+12	1.43E+12	6.90E+12	308.1800	375.5981	1.42E+09	2739.330
Sum Sq. Dev.	1532.433	9.62E+23	5.70E+23	1.92E+22	9.62E+23	397.7247	821.1743	2.58E+15	81.39537
Observations	31	31	31	31	31	31	31	31	31

Source: Authors' Analysis Using Eview

attributed to electricity itself, see table 5. It is noticeable that when the two models are compared the influence of economic growth on forecasted change in electricity supply is higher than that of consumption. In the subsequent periods, it can be seen that the respective influence of electricity in the two models reduces while that of both economic growth and consumption increase relatively as time goes by.

Table 2. Causality results for model one

Lags: 2			
Null Hypothesis:	**Obs**	**F-Statistic**	**Prob.**
PHYSICALCAP does not Granger Cause GDP	29	0.16666	0.8475
GDP does not Granger Cause PHYSICALCAP		0.57049	0.5727
LABOUR does not Granger Cause GDP	29	11.8266	0.0003
GDP does not Granger Cause LABOUR		0.29623	0.7463
CREDIT does not Granger Cause GDP	29	1.46598	0.2508
GDP does not Granger Cause CREDIT		6.99814	0.0040
ELECTRICITY does not Granger Cause GDP	29	1.46806	0.2503
GDP does not Granger Cause ELECTRICITY		3.50323	0.0462

Source: Authors' Analysis using Eview

Table 3. Causality results for model two

Lags: 2			
Null Hypothesis:	**Obs**	**F-Statistic**	**Prob.**
INCOME does not Granger Cause CONSUMPTION	29	7.09425	0.0038
CONSUMPTION does not Granger Cause INCOME		0.61897	0.5469
INTEREST does not Granger Cause CONSUMPTION	29	0.67817	0.5170
CONSUMPTION does not Granger Cause INTEREST		0.35986	0.7015
DEPENDENCY does not Granger Cause CONSUMPTION	29	2.29435	0.1225
CONSUMPTION does not Granger Cause DEPENDENCY		0.53091	0.5948
ELECTRICITY does not Granger Cause CONSUMPTION	29	0.90103	0.4195
CONSUMPTION does not Granger Cause ELECTRICITY		3.42514	0.0491

Source: Authors' Analysis using Eview

Implications

There are a number of implications that arise from the conduct of this study. First of all it testifies to the important of renewable electricity on economic growth and household consumption in Nigeria. With the links between electricity in one hand and economic growth and household consumption on the other, the urgency of increasing electricity supply in order to boost economic growth and household consumption become more imperative. Previous studies such as that of Mukhtar et al. (2020) have also found strong link between energy supply and household consumption, only that this study has focus on renewable electricity supply instead of the whole of energy

Figure 1. Impulse response function for economic growth-electricity supply
Source: authors' analysis using Eview

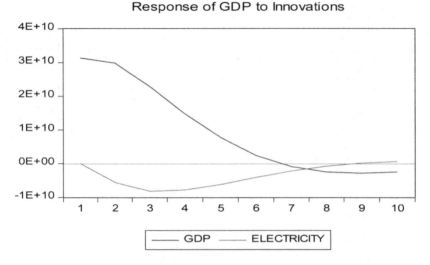

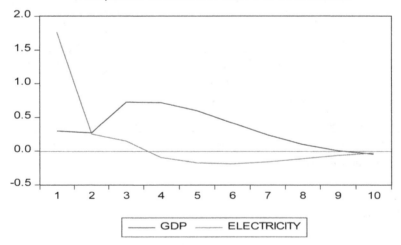

sources aggregated together. Theoretical and empirical literature has also testified to the strong link between economic growth and household consumption. To the extent that anything that increase anyone of the two increase the other. Hence by this, increase in electricity serves the two main goals of increasing economic growth and household consumption. The study finding that volatilities from electricity supply

Figure 2. Impulse response function for household consumption-electricity supply
Source: Authors' Analysis using Eview

Response to Cholesky One S.D. (d.f. adjusted) Innovations

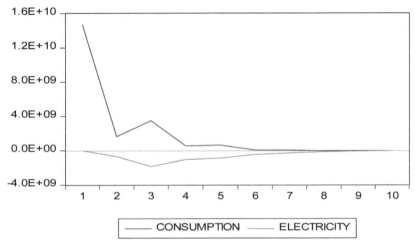

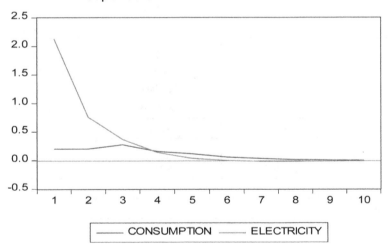

to economic growth and household consumption further strengthen the enduring links between electricity supply and the two main variables. Hence, positive shock from electricity supply is economic growth and household consumption enhancing. Electricity supply is a sensitive variable as this study has shown; it is far more sensitive to shocks within the model than either of economic growth or household

Table 4. Variance decomposition analysis for economic growth-electricity supply

Variance Decomposition of GDP:			
Period	S.E.	GDP	ELECTRICITY
1	3.14E+10	100.0000	0.000000
2	4.36E+10	98.36126	1.638744
3	5.00E+10	96.07084	3.929157
4	5.27E+10	94.26610	5.733902
5	5.36E+10	93.13905	6.860954
6	5.38E+10	92.61696	7.383038
7	5.39E+10	92.46642	7.533578
8	5.39E+10	92.46430	7.535699
9	5.40E+10	92.48449	7.515514
10	5.41E+10	92.48866	7.511343
Variance Decomposition of ELECTRICITY:			
Period	S.E.	GDP	ELECTRICITY
1	1.789367	2.745292	97.25471
2	1.826850	4.793732	95.20627
3	1.971836	17.72632	82.27368
4	2.101004	27.32110	72.67890
5	2.191811	32.58400	67.41600
6	2.238853	34.67045	65.32955
7	2.257126	35.22390	64.77610
8	2.262060	35.25581	64.74419
9	2.263041	35.22549	64.77451
10	2.263717	35.24792	64.75208
Cholesky Ordering: GDP ELECTRICITY			

Source: Authors' Analysis using Eview

consumption. The electricity supply industry in Nigeria is more responsive to changes in economic growth than changes in household consumption.

Table 5. Variance decomposition analysis for household consumption-economic growth

Variance Decomposition of CONSUMPTION:			
Period	**S.E.**	**CONSUMPTION**	**ELECTRICITY**
1	1.47E+10	100.0000	0.000000
2	1.48E+10	99.78267	0.217326
3	1.54E+10	98.33901	1.660987
4	1.54E+10	97.89024	2.109756
5	1.54E+10	97.58210	2.417896
6	1.54E+10	97.49443	2.505567
7	1.54E+10	97.46084	2.539163
8	1.55E+10	97.45300	2.547001
9	1.55E+10	97.45097	2.549033
10	1.55E+10	97.45064	2.549361
Variance Decomposition of ELECTRICITY:			
Period	**S.E.**	**CONSUMPTION**	**ELECTRICITY**
1	2.142986	0.905657	99.09434
2	2.283339	1.597644	98.40236
3	2.329467	2.945159	97.05484
4	2.339342	3.385167	96.61483
5	2.342591	3.627529	96.37247
6	2.343414	3.695218	96.30478
7	2.343728	3.717960	96.28204
8	2.343825	3.722922	96.27708
9	2.343860	3.724015	96.27598
10	2.343871	3.724152	96.27585
Cholesky Ordering: CONSUMPTION ELECTRICITY			

Source: Authors' Analysis using Eview

CONCLUSION AND RECOMMENDATION

Government after government have shown a nonchalant attitude towards ending the problem of electricity supply, instead focusing resources on short term goals. But providing a stable power supply to a nation of over 200 million is certainly a long term goal that cannot be achieved when view as short term goal. This study has shown that to boost economic growth and household consumption, Nigerian government needs to repair the damage done to the electricity sector. With far less than 10,000 megawatts been produced currently, government most start massive investment in the sector if rapid economic growth and development is to be guaranteed. The privatization of the Nigerian power sector in the last one decade has not achieved the desire result of boosting the amount of electric power supply in the country. The private sector investors have refused to make the huge investment require to move the sector forward, instead they manage with short term borrowings from commercial banks in order to fill short term deficit in their daily operations funds. Thus, Nigerian government most either invest it own funds in the sector or invite new investors to partner with the existing investors in order to achieve desire results. Countries in Africa, that are less materially endowed, have far better electric power supply than Nigeria; this tells you that something is bad somewhere else in how Nigerian authority manage the power sector. During the last two decades, billions of dollars was reported to have been stolen in relation to the power sector revitalization. Considering the importance of consumption in determining human welfare, any factor that will help boost consumption shall not be taken for granted by any government that is serious about the welfare of its people. The same thing applies to any variable that boost economic growth. Renewable sources of energy are very important in achieving these goals.

This chapter used Granger causality test, VAR impulse response and variance decomposition to measure causality, shock and volatility in renewable electricity supply in Nigeria with reference to economic growth and household consumption. At the end its findings show strong links between renewable electricity supply, economic growth and household consumption in Nigeria. This was expected a priori, as overwhelming empirical and theoretical literature have attested to the effects of renewable electricity on economic growth of other nations around the world. As Nigeria moves toward high and sustainable economic growth in the 21st century, there is no alternative to rapid and sustain investment in the power sector. Power sector shall be a catalyst for economic growth and development not otherwise. Other factors that together with efficient power supply help economic growth such as physical capital provision, educated pool of manpower and availability of credit shall also be given priority, if Nigeria is to achieve it macroeconomic targets. Likewise, factors that boost household consumption such as increase money available to household through fighting of poverty and entrenching entrepreneurship, provision of affordable consumption loan and reduction in inequality. Nigeria cannot afford the continuous nationwide blackout of recent years, if indeed it is serious about economic growth and the need to free it citizens from the clutch of poverty and wastefulness.

REFERENCES

AbdullahiS. I. (2018). Nigerian economy: Business, governance and investment in period of crisis. *Social Science Research Network*. https://ssrn.com/abstract=3310120

Abdullahi, S. I., & Shuaibu, M. (2022). Can Stock Market Capitalization and Financial Development Predict Household Consumption in Nigeria? *CBN Bullion*, *46*(2), 39–48.

Abur, C. C., Angahar, J. S., & Terande, T. J. (2022). Electricity Generation and Economic Growth in Nigeria: Is There Any Link? *Asian Journal of Current Research*, *7*(1), 1–7. doi:10.56557/ajocr/2022/v7i17560

Adedokun, A. (2015). Can Electricity Consumption be Useful in Predicting Nigerian Economic Growth? Evidence From Error Correction Model. *OPEC Energy Review*, *39*(2), 125–140. doi:10.1111/opec.12042

Akomolafe, K. J., & Danladi, J. D. (2014). Electricity Consumption and Economic Growth in Nigeria: A Multivariate Investigation. *International Journal of Economics Financial Management*, *3*(1), 143–159.

Ali, H. S., Nathaniel, S. P., Uzuner, G., Bekun, F. V., & Sarkodie, S. A. (2020). Trivariate modelling of the nexus between electricity consumption, urbanization and economic growth in Nigeria: Fresh insights from Maki Cointegration and causality tests. *Heliyon*, *6*(2), e03400. doi:10.1016/j.heliyon.2020.e03400 PMID:32123762

Andrews, C. J., & Friis, R. H. (n.d.). Green Living: Reducing the Individual's Carbon Footprint. In. (Eds.), The Praeger Handbook of Environmental Health (pp. 455-475).

Apinran, M. O., Usman, N., Akadiri, S. S., & Onuzo, C. T. (2022). The Role of Electricity Consumption, Capital, Labor Force, Carbon Emissions on Economic Growth: Implication for Environmental Sustainability Targets in Nigeria. *Environmental Science and Pollution Research International*, *29*(11), 15955–15965. doi:10.100711356-021-16584-6 PMID:34636018

Azam, A., Rafiq, M., Shafique, M., Ateeq, M., & Yuan, J. (2020). Causality Relationship Between Electricity Supply and Economic Growth: Evidence From Pakistan. *Energies, 13,* 837. doi: 13040837. doi:10.3390/en

Barro, R. J. (1996). *Determinants of economic growth: A cross-country empirical study*. National Bureau of Economic Research.

Chitedze, I., Nwedeh, C. C., Adeola, A., & Abonyi, D. C. (2021). An econometric analysis of electricity consumption and real sector performance in Nigeria. *International Journal of Energy Sector Management, 15*(4), 855–873. doi:10.1108/IJESM-04-2020-0003

Dasgupta, P., & Maler, K. (1991). *The environment and emerging development issues.* The World Bank.

Ekeocha, P. C., Penzin, D. J., & Ogbuabor, J. E. (2020). Energy Consumption and Economic Growth in Nigeria: A Test of Alternative Specifications. *International Journal of Energy Economics and Policy, 10*(3), 369–379. doi:10.32479/ijeep.8902

Fazal, S., Gillani, S., Amjad, M., & Haider, Z. (2020). Impact of the Renewable-Energy Consumption on Thailand's Economic Development: Evidence from Cointegration Test. *Pakistan Journal of Humanities and Social Sciences*, 857-67. https://doi.org/. doi:1052131/pjhss.2020.0802.0103

Feucht, Y., & Zander, K. (2017). Consumers' attitudes on carbon footprint labelling: Results of the SUSDIET project. *Thünen Working Paper, No. 78, Johann Heinrich von Thünen-Institut, Braunschweig.* DNB. doi:10.3220/WP1507534833000

Granger, C. W. J. (1969). Investigating causal relations by econometric models and cross-spectral methods. *Econometrica, 37*(3), 424–438. doi:10.2307/1912791

Iyke, B. N. (2014). *Electricity consumption and economic growth in Nigeria: A revisit of the energy-growth debate.* MPRA Paper No. 70001. https://mpra.ub.unimuenchen.de/70001/

Karuppannan, S., & Sivam, A. (2009). *Sustainable development and housing affordability, institute of sustainable systems and technologies.* University of South Australia. https://tasa.org.au/wp-content/uploads/2008/12/Sivam-Alpana_-Karuppannan-Sadasivam.pdf

Keynes, J. M. (1936). *The General Theory of Employment, Interest and Money.* Macmillan.

Khobai, H. (2018). *The Causal Linkages Between Renewable Electricity Generation and Economic Growth in South Africa.* MPRA Paper No. 86485, UTC.

Mabugu, M., & Inglesi-Lotz, R. (2022). *Energy Sources. Part B, Economics, Planning, and Policy,* 1–18.

Mukhtar, S., Abdullahi, S. I., & Murtala, I. (2020). Do Energy Consumption, Interest Rate and Import affect Household Consumption in Nigeria: What did the Empirical Evidence says? *Lapai Journal of Economics, 4*(2), 98–106.

Nathaniel, S. P., & Bekun, F. V. (2020). *Electricity consumption, urbanization and economic growth in Nigeria: New insights from combined cointegration amidst structural breaks.* AGDI Working Paper, No. WP/20/013, African Governance and Development Institute (AGDI), Yaoundé.

Nnaji, Chukwu, & Moses. (2013). Electricity Supply, Fossil fuel Consumption, Co2 Emissions and Economic Growth: Implications and Policy Options for Sustainable Development in Nigeria. *International Journal of Energy Economics and Policy*, *3*(3), 262–271.

Ogbonna, O. S., Idenyi, O. S., & Nick, A. (2016). Power Generation Capacity and Economic Growth in Nigeria: A Causality Approach. *European Journal of Business and Management*, *8*(32), 74–90.

Ogundipe, A. A., Akinyemi, O., & Ogundipe, O. M. (2016). Electricity Consumption and Economic Development in Nigeria. *International Journal of Energy Economics and Policy*, *6*(1), 134–143.

Okoye, L. U., Omankhanlen, A. E., Okoh, J. I., Adeleye, N. B., Ezeji, F. N., Ezu, G. K., & Ehikioya, B. I. (2021). Analyzing the Energy Consumption and Economic Growth Nexus in Nigeria. *International Journal of Energy Economics and Policy*, *11*(1), 378–387. doi:10.32479/ijeep.10768

Onakoya, A. B., Onakoya, A. O., Salami, O. A., & Odedairo, B. O. (2013). Energy consumption and Nigerian economic growth: An empirical analysis. *European Scientific Journal*, *9*(4), 25–40.

Onayemi, S. O., Olomola, P. A., Alege, P. O., & Onayemi, O. O. (2020). Foreign Direct Investment, Electricity Power Supply and Economic Growth in Nigeria. *International Journal of Energy Economics and Policy*, *10*(5), 243–247. doi:10.32479/ijeep.7774

Oyaromade, R., Mathew, A., & Abalaba, B. P. (2014). Energy Consumption and Economic Growth in Nigeria: A Causality Analysis. *International Journal of Sustainable Energy and Environmental Research*, *3*(1), 53–61.

Ozturk, I. (2010). Literature survey on energy–growth nexus. *Energy Policy*, *38*(1), 340–349. doi:10.1016/j.enpol.2009.09.024

Pearce, D. W., & Warford, J. J. (1993). *World without end: Economics, environment and sustainable development – A summary.* World Bank.

Pindyck, R. S., & Rubinfeld, D. L. (1998). *Econometric models and economic forecasts.* McGraw.

Romer, P. M. (1982). The Origins of endogenous growth. *The Journal of Economic Perspectives, 8*(1), 3–22. doi:10.1257/jep.8.1.3

Romer, P. M. (1986). Increasing returns and long run growth. *Journal of Political Economy, 94*(5), 1002–1038. doi:10.1086/261420

Shuaibu, M., Yusufu, M., Abdullahi, S. I., Shehu, K. K., & Adamu, M. B. (2021). What explains economic growth in Nigeria in the last three decades?—A dynamic modelling approach. *East African Scholars Multidiscip Bull, 4*, 75–84.

Solow, R. M. (1956). A Contribution to the Theory of Economic Growth. *The Quarterly Journal of Economics, 70*(1), 65–94. doi:10.2307/1884513

Somoye, O. A., Ozdeser, H., & Seraj, M. (2022). The Impact of Renewable Energy Consumption on Economic Growth in Nigeria: Fresh Evidence from a Non-linear ARDL Approach. *Environmental Science and Pollution Research International, 29*(41), 62611–62625. doi:10.100711356-022-20110-7 PMID:35404038

Stern, D. (2000). A multivariate cointegration analysis of the role of energy in the US economy. *Energy Economics, 22*(2), 267–283. doi:10.1016/S0140-9883(99)00028-6

Stern, D. I. (1993). Energy and economic growth in the USA: A multivariate approach. *Energy Economics, 15*(2), 137–150. doi:10.1016/0140-9883(93)90033-N

Stern, D. I. (1997). Limits to substitution and irreversibility in production and consumption: A neoclassical interpretation of ecological economics. *Ecological Economics, 21*(3), 197–215. doi:10.1016/S0921-8009(96)00103-6

Stern, D. I. (2004). Factors affecting linkage Between energy and growth. Encyclopedia of Energy, 2.

Stungwa, S., Hlongwane, N. W., & Daw, O. D. (2022). Consumption and Supply of Electricity on Economic Growth in South Africa: An Econometric Approach. *International Journal of Energy Economics and Policy, 12*(1), 266–274. doi:10.32479/ijeep.12542

Tobin, J., & Golub, S. S. (1998). *Money credit and capital*. McGraw-Hill international.

Todaro, M. P., & Smith, S. C. (2003). *Economic development*. Pearson Education.

Ugbaka, M. A., Awujola, A., & Isa, G. H. (2019). Electricity Supply and Economic Growth in Nigeria: A Bound Testing and Co-integration Approach. *Lapai Journal Economics; 3*(2).

Umeji, G., Agu, A. O., Eleanya, E. E., Chinedum, E. M., Nwabugwu, O. O., & Obumnene, M. T. (2023). Renewable Energy Consumption and Economic Growth in Nigeria. *African Journal of Social Science and Humanities Research.*, 6(1), 34–48. doi:10.52589/AJSSHR-BNHM472F

World Commission on Environment and Development. (1987). Our common future. Oxford University Press.

World Energy Council. (2019). *WEC Trilemma: Country Profile*. World Energy Council.

Yakubu, Y., Manu, S. B., & Bala, U. (2015). Electricity Supply and Manufacturing Output in Nigeria: Autoregressive Distributed Lag (ARDL) Bound Testing Approach. *Journal of Economics and Sustainable Development*, 6(17).

Chapter 5
Artificial Intelligence Towards Smart Green Transportation:
A Path Towards Sustainability

Sejana Jose V.
CHRIST University (Deemed), India

H. Sandhya
CHRIST University (Deemed), India

Bindi Varghese
CHRIST University (Deemed), India

ABSTRACT

Emerging technological advancements and sustainability concerns have initiated the integration of smart technologies into the transportation infrastructure at major cities and tourist hubs. The rising environmental concerns have called for a shift in focus from conventional methods to innovative green transport initiatives being formulated by DMOs and destination planners. The use of data analytics and artificial intelligence in transportation has been proven to be a reasonable method for sustainable transportation. This study focuses on assessing the value propositions of smart transportation systems in enriching the tourist experience by providing convenient travel solutions. The chapter focuses on understanding the value proposition of smart transport designs at destinations and the long-term prospects of installing such sustainable infrastructure at major tourist hubs. The study also aims to evaluate the tourist experience in using smart transportation services and the potential benefits and challenges involved in the practical implementation of such systems.

DOI: 10.4018/978-1-6684-8140-0.ch005

INTRODUCTION TO SUSTAINABILITY

The concept of sustainability gained more emphasis through the development of the world commission on Environment and Development in 1987. The report popularly known as the Brundtland Report highlighted the environmental issues globally as the cause of poverty in many underdeveloped nations. In the 1960s, the concept of sustainability started gaining more importance. The reason for this is a high increase in population, overutilization of resources, and an increase in pollution (Shiva, 1992). The core theme of sustainability is to develop a plan which allows humans to utilize natural resources by safeguarding them for future generations (World Commission on Environment and Development, 1987). It is also explained as the process of distributing social and economic wealth keeping the environment in mind (Lumley & Armstrong, 2004). The sustainable plan is evolved based on the evaluation of the present and future conditions and repercussions of human activities on the generations (Vogt & Weber, 2019). In the mid-eighteenth century and at the beginning of the nineteenth century, conservation, equality, and social and environmental justice gained prominence. Many concerns were raised and the experts realized the importance of integration in the policies for local, state, and national development (Lumley & Armstrong, 2004). The United Nations also addressed the environmental concerns in the conference conducted in Stockholm. And also, some of the general principles were initiated to overcome the environmental problems due to unsustainable development. During that phase, sustainable development gained more focus and started considering the transportation sector (Barbosa et al., 2014). Sustainable development is mainly about inculcating eco-friendly practices in every stage of the product life cycle.

Sustainability focuses mainly on three factors. They are economic, social, and environmental. Various research studies have interpreted these factors differently. Some of the studies have discussed these three factors as the pillars of sustainability. Whereas, other researchers have interpreted social, environmental, and economic as intersecting points and as a coextensive approach (Purvis et al., 2018). The organization has a major role in the sustainable development domain to maintain consistency between environmental, economic, and social factors (Swarbrooke, 1999). Environmental sustainability mainly focuses on the balance between ecology and biology. It also emphasizes the protection of flora and fauna and creates environmental behavior. Similarly, social sustainability works on the improvisation of human life. Here, it focuses on gender equality, fair distribution of basic human needs between generations, cultural enhancement, and community development. On the other hand, economic sustainability strives to generate income by offering products and services which are eco-friendly. The economic dimension boosts the economy of the country without surpassing the environmental and cultural activities (Herremans & Reid, 2002).

According to recent studies, it is claimed that the transport industry is one of the major air pollutants. It has significantly contributed to carbon emissions due to the non-renewable energy usage in transport. This has led to serious issues in damaging the global system. Many prominent authors have recommended incorporating sustainability and green mode of transport to overcome the issues caused due to conventional transportation systems (Larina et al., 2021). The transportation industry is rigorously working on the transformation of the entire system into a more eco-friendly manner. However, studies have highlighted that most developing countries are still following unsustainable modes of transportation.

Objectives of the Study

Transportation enabled tourists to access different destinations around the globe. Assimilating the green concept with intrinsic artificial intelligence embedded in the vehicles will address the current issues faced due to the unsustainable model of the transportation system. Green transportation mainly aims to address the future of social, environmental, and economic factors. In many countries, Hop-on and hop-off buses are mostly preferred by tourists during their movement in tourist destinations. Electrifying the bus with the infusion of intelligence will enhance the tourist experience and will bring equilibrium among society, the economy, and the environment.

Significance of the Study

Intelligent transportation system are gaining prime focus in smart cities as it enhances productivity and efficiency in the transportation sector. It is also proven that artificial intelligence application in the transportation sector leads to sustainability. This chapter focuses on the integration of intelligence application tools in tourist electric hop-on and hop-off buses in smart cities. The chapter also discusses the different aspects of the intelligence applications such as e-ticketing services, QR codes to avail the destination information with pictorial representations, geographical location details, GPS tracker, and passenger feedback and passenger concern facilities within the electric hop-on and hop-off buses. This chapter proposes a globally accepted transportation model for sustainable and smart cities. Thus this chapter is an indicator of a sustainable and friendly intelligent electric hop-on hop-off for the tourists in the destination.

LITERATURE REVIEW

Modern Approaches to Sustainability

The modern world has realized the significance of functioning nature friendly. Every industry has infused sustainability into its operations. The transportation industry is one of the major sectors contributing to the excess emission of carbon and causing air pollution. They are rigorously striving to attain sustainability in their operations. Technology plays an eminent role in modern transportation systems to attain sustainability goals (Bamwesigye & Hlavackova, 2019). The major factors considered to attain sustainability in transportation systems are sustainable education, technology, green transportation, hub and spoke systems in road transport, green construction for urban mobility, renewable energy usage, and accommodating population growth (Sodiq et al., 2019). On the other hand, Banwesigye and Hlavackova (2019), stated that sustainable transportation should cover the main three core themes, they are (I) safe and reconcilable (II) sustainable transportation should be affordable and also have multiple options for travelers to choose from and, (III) it should be eco-friendly in terms of greenhouse gas emission-free. It is also observed that most of the developing countries are including sustainability in national-level policies and also encouraging public-private partnerships to promote sustainable development (Law et al., 2017; Kantawateera et al., 2014).

As one of the sustainability initiatives, slow travel is becoming a trend among tourists. Tourists prefer slow travel as it gives way to them to explore and meet people from different cultures (Lin, 2018). Greening is also a new approach that has been implemented in the transportation sector. The green concept addresses the negative impact on the environment. It aims to reduce GHG emissions and increase efficiency and reliability in the transportation sector (Law et al., 2017). Technology is one of the main indicators of the green concept in the transportation sector. Though technology is superseding human resource power, it is proven that it gains sustainable development goals. In the modern era, building smart cities have become a trend and most of the prominent cities are converting their conventional cities to smart. One of the main criteria for a smart city is implementing green transportation and green infrastructure. For every destination to be enabled with sustainable practices, community acceptance, and support are vital. It is empirical that some Western cities have smart communities that easily adapt and take part in sustainable and green practices (Ramírez-Moreno et al., 2021).

Practices Followed by Developed Countries

Developed countries are the ones who follow more advanced sustainable practices than developing countries. Developed countries are well-equipped and flexible in terms of infrastructure, advanced technologies, and communities that easily engage in sustainable practices when compared to developing countries. In the UK, there is an initiative called the national network cycle to meet sustainable development goals. The National Network Cycle (NNC) is a scheme that was initiated in the year 2000 to enhance the green transportation system in the country. They have developed cycle lanes in a wider network that connects to all the major centers of the cities. NNC was also implemented to enhance the tourist experience in tourist destinations. It was an effective initiative to attain sustainable principles in the transportation sector (Lumsdon, 2000). In addition, autonomous vehicles are also being integrated into the cities of the UK as one of the initiatives to increase social, economic, and environmental welfare (Lim & Taeihagh, 2018). Similarly, as a green initiative and to enhance mobility services, Lisbon has equipped with the software named Maas (Mobility as a Service) to enable travelers to use multiple modes of transportation in a single application. Mobility as a service initiative has enhanced transportation services and also has resulted in less harming the environment. The app features the booking of shared cars, taxis, ferries, e-bikes, trams, buses, and trains and e-parking facilities in and around Lisbon (Cruz & Sarmento, 2020). Countries named Dubai, Canada, Australia, and Russia have enabled artificial intelligence in their mobility services. The introduction of autonomous vehicles has also led to a drastic transition in the transportation sector. Most of the developed countries have converted their conventional cities into smart cities by enabling technology in their mobility services. For example, Dubai has initiated an autonomous transportation strategy by aiming to meet sustainable goals. On the other hand, Canada integrated sustainable last-mile delivery in the smart city of Toronto (Golubchikov & Thornbush, 2020).

Transit-oriented development is also given a large weightage in Western countries. Cervero and Sullivan (2011) proposed that the implementation of transit-oriented developments in Sweden, Germany, and Australia have resulted in a positive impact on the environment and reduced carbon emission. To promote green transportation the cities in Sweden have trams in the heart of the cities and companies are offering car-sharing services. They are also limited with car parking spaces and the parking space for the cars is charged which led to the discouragement of car ownership. Similarly, Kogarah Town Square in Australia and Freiberg in Germany have well-developed transit infrastructure and pedestrian and bike lanes which have made the communities shift to public vehicles.

Green Initiatives

The term green initiatives are conceptualized as the amalgamation of green or eco-friendly practices aiming in achieving environmental sustainability (Centobelli et al., 2019). Green initiatives are considered to be one of the major factors to achieve environmental sustainability. Due to the repercussions faced by the entire ecosystem, it has become very crucial to all industries (Hamid et al., 2020), especially the transportation industry. Since the transport industry is considered to be one of the major polluters it has become crucial to transform the conventional system into green and sustainable (Bamwesigye & Hlavackova,, 2019). The influencing factors to implement green initiatives are high demand from travelers who are environment conscious, competitors who follow green practices, support from the government, and also to contribute environmental protection (Evangelista, 2014). Due to the high accessibility and reach about the significance of environmental conservation, the approach is more inclined toward eco-friendly and green behavior. The emerging green practices in transportation services are low environmental impact vehicles. Low-impact or green transport vehicles are electric vehicles, walking, bicycles, carpooling, biofuel cell vehicles, solar vehicles, hybrid vehicles, and autonomous vehicles (Li, 2016). Other green practices in the transportation sector are green infrastructure, reuse and recycling of production cycles, mobility at the services, electronic ticketing system, pedestrian system, green code of behavior in destinations, and green administration.

The New York Department of Transportation has initiated Green leadership in transportation environmental sustainability (GreenLITES) to enhance the bottom line of sustainability (Eisenman, 2012). It is a transportation metric program that was initiated to measure sustainability. The GreenLITES mainly aims to conduct a continuous assessment of sustainability to offer the best green initiatives in the transportation sector for the state. GreenLITES programs have different levels of certification programs which are awarded based on the scorecard. The certification level starts from GreenLITES certification to GreenLITES evergreen certification. In addition, Muench et al. (2010) have also discussed the significance of the National Environmental Policy Act and it is being accessed through the INVEST tool. INVEST tool is a metric that is exclusively used to measure road transportation highways. The INVEST tool is implemented to transform and design the road highways to be sustainable.

In the logistics sector, the main factors for initiating green initiatives are environmental policies, competency framework on the environment, and strong communication (Seroka-Stolka, 2016). Environmental policy can be shown as the organizational commitment to attaining sustainable culture. The other variables namely competency framework and strong communication are mostly linked to managerial behavior to incline green initiatives among the personnel in the organization. Developing knowledge and skills on the sustainable factors and communicating the significance to the participants will bring environmental behavior. It also results in taking responsibility for initiating and following green initiatives.

Sustainable Development Goals and Plans

United Nations General Assembly in the year 2015, developed sustainable development goals to address global environmental, social, and economic issues. It is the compilation of seventeen integrated global plans designed to achieve by 2030. The main motto in developing sustainable development goals is to achieve well-being and peace for both the planet and human beings in the present and the future (Nundy et al., 2021; Ho & Goethals, 2019). These seventeen SDGs address the impact of biodiversity, climate change, economic growth, and sustainable utilization of resources (Bakker et al., 2017). Since the transportation sector is considered to be one of the major resources that act as a bridge in the movement of people in the tourism industry (Pande, 2022). A sustainable mode of transport is possible by introducing green transportation. This green transportation contributes to 17 sustainable development Goals. No poverty is the first SDG. Green transportation supports ending poverty in all its possible ways by providing employability. The next SDG is zero hunger and it promotes sustainable agriculture. Green transportation can support sustainability in agriculture through the introduction of a rural transport system. Green and sustainable transportation also helps to achieve the goal of good health and well-being for all ages as it uses eco-friendly practices (Gudmundsson & Regmi, 2017). Improved environmental condition is attained by educating the tourism stakeholders about the benefits of green transportation and its positive impact on the environment. The ease of handling green transportation provides employability to all ages and gender and leads to gender equality. The green transportation system attempts to create a positive impact on the environment. It preserves good water and sanitation by reducing toxic emissions. As green transportation attempts to render sustainable and modern energy, it is considered the most reliable source of transportation. The utilization of green transportation systems paves the way for a regenerative and sustainable economy, employment, industrialization, and infrastructure. It is attained in its best way because the green transportation system reduces carbon emissions and increases green practices.

Green transportation can be an ideal medium to reduce inequality among countries as it uses similar technology with reasonable manufacturing costs. The movement of resources is majorly done through the transportation system. The involvement of green transportation in this movement leads to green and sustainable smart cities. It also enables sustainable production and consumption as it inculcates eco-friendly principles (Brussel et al., 2019). Green Transportation also supports the marine, sea, and terrestrial ecosystems by generating productive impacts. The implementation of green transportation in any destination involves all tourism stakeholders. In a nutshell, the utilization of green transport makes a destination peaceful, generates quality revenue, and makes the environment friendly to all living organisms.

INTRODUCTION TO ARTIFICIAL INTELLIGENCE

The majority of definitions of artificial intelligence center on how robots can replicate human intelligence or how it is a branch of computer science. John McCarthy initially used the phrase "artificial intelligence" in the 1950s, defining it as "the science and engineering of constructing intelligent machines, especially intelligent computer programs" (McCarthy, 2007, n.p.). In the Encyclopaedia Britannica, Artificial intelligence is described as "the ability of a digital computer or computer-controlled robot to accomplish tasks generally associated with intelligent beings''. Marinchak et al. (2018) have advised that mechanical, analytical, intuitive, and emotional intelligence are the four skills used in service-related employment. Service automation can take the place of human labor since AI systems are capable of performing activities requiring these talents better than people, from mechanical to emotional duties.

Pervasive robotics are the type of robots that are present everywhere (in surroundings with connected smart things), and it is a combination of artificial intelligence, robots, and the Internet of Things. These robots are equipped to carry out multiple tasks without human assistance. The best example to relate is the collaborative robot (cobot)-a run automated supermarket that operates without human supervision. These are essential components of intelligent robotization in tourism, where devices and services are developed and implemented in invasive environments both before and after tourists arrive at their destinations (Özdemir & Hekim, 2018).

Role of AI in the Tourism Industry

Most of the industries are transforming themselves into automated and tourism is one among them. The travel and tourism industry vendors have incorporated intelligent machines into their business operation. Similar to the manner in which KLM Royal Dutch Airlines launched Care-E to help passengers carry their bags to the gate in 2018, Amsterdam Airport Schiphol deployed Spencer, an android robot, in 2015 to help travelers. Care-E is a smart self-driving trolley (Marvin et al. 2018). The first fully automated hotel is the Henna Hotel established in the year 2015 at Japan's Huis Ten Bosch amusement park. Since then, it has spread its operations to numerous other destinations. In addition to the automated room services, the hotels have also equipped with dinosaur receptionists, robot cloakroom attendants, and robot porters (Feng et al., 2018). Intelligent advancements in travel and tourism have paved the way for increased comfort, cost savings, and convenience however, it also worries about how technology may affect the community and the society as a whole (Gurkaynak et al., 2016). The (possible) loss of human interaction throughout the travel experience is a significant realization brought on by the automation of tourist services (Danilina & Slepnev, 2018). The tourism experience is mapped based on the specific apps that are programmed to offer services and assistance throughout the trip journey, and these applications include benefits as well as hazards for tourists (consumers) and tourism destinations (authorities and service providers). Intelligent automation can be utilized to attract tourists even during the pre-trip stage and that helps them to avail relevant information search, and in reservations that paves on pre-arrival experience procedures. The deployment of artificial intelligence is fundamental for service providers and harness Omni channel marketing automation to scale up marketing materials globally, offer clients targeted offers, foster leads, and simpler route to purchase (Tussyadiah, 2020).

Artificial Intelligence is one of the emerging trends and will be the future of all human operations. Technology imitates the functioning of the human intellect (Yigitcanlar & Cugurullo, 2020). AI applications can be used as a mechanism to overcome some of the challenges of environmental degradation, safety concerns, and carbon emission, and increase the travel demand for passenger and cargo services (Dubey & Gunasekaran, 2015). The foundation for the development of smart cities is artificial intelligence applications. The prospect of any smart city is through the AI application to expand the infrastructural facilities, engage the people, reduce pollution, develop green concepts, improvising the efficiency of the urban area and commercial activities (Yigitcanlar et al., 2020).

The prime focus of the nations is to convert the cities into smart cities inculcating sustainability in their planning and development. The infusion of sustainable concepts in smart city development is essential as it contains the core activities of the society and the economy. The conveyance system is one of the main components of any development of the smart city. And it provides a pathway to revolutionize, transform, and prosper the outlook of the city. The development of any smart city may not be complete without foreseeing the future of the transportation system (Nikitas et al., 2020). To achieve the vision of the city, the transportation sector and the related sector needs to be involved in the planning and development stage of the smart city (Dubey & Gunasekaran, 2015).

Nikitas et al. (2020) have discussed the various fields of AI in the transport sector. Some of the AI methods adopted in the transportation sector are artificial neural networks, artificial immune systems, ant colony optimizers, bee colony optimization, simulated annealing, genetic algorithms, automated vehicle location, and fuzzy logic model. AI application in the transport sector is especially seen in the shared mobility concept which has benefited in many aspects. AI applications in shared mobility had addressed fraudulent driver services, provided personalized passenger services, and also led to enhancing reliability and efficiency in the transport sector (Abduljabbar et al., 2019). On the other hand, public buses play an important role in the transportation sector. The studies have identified that some of the AI methods, namely hybrid colony algorithms and automated vehicle location, have been adopted in the buses. The artificial neural network is considered to be the core function of transportation infrastructure systems and it is used in problem-solving and the maintenance process of the system (Gharehbaghi, 2016). These applications are used to schedule the bus, improve the vehicle's operational efficiency, and reduce the waiting period of the passengers by enabling them to predict the bus arrivals' timings. Intelligent transportation systems include autonomous vehicle systems, transportation networking, automated vehicle detection, foreseeing traffic congestion, AI traffic control system, and driver behavior detection applications (Joseph et al., 2020). AI applications are also used in automated buses. Unlike conventional vehicles, autonomous vehicles can pick up and drop off passengers almost anywhere in a city. Instead of looking for a free parking spot, the autonomous vehicle parks itself in a remote area on the outskirts of the city where cheap land is more easily accessible. As a result, there won't be a need for huge parking lots near airports as there is now (Wiseman, 2022). Application-based automated buses are being implemented in major countries and the application is capable of detecting the fastest route and also picking up from the location of the passenger based on the request made (Abduljabbar et al., 2019).

The transportation industry will notably shift as a result of autonomous vehicles. Autonomous vehicles will increase road safety and our quality of life. There will be a sharp decline in road accidents. Additionally, autonomous vehicles can solve parking problems by enabling distant parking on the rural outskirts of cities. These cars will use less gasoline and have less expensive insurance. Additionally, this technology can be very helpful to people with disabilities, and military autonomous vehicles can reduce the number of combat-related injuries and fatalities (Wiseman, 2022).

Regarding the effective management of space available for parking in cities and transportation hubs, there is no need for a vast parking lot because parking for autonomous vehicles is not expected to be close to where a passenger has to arrive. Additionally, because vehicles will be parked exactly in the proper position with nearly no unused space, parking lots will be built more densely. Furthermore, the parking spaces will be designated based on the type of car, therefore they won't be as large as possible to accommodate the largest vehicle (Wiseman, 2017).

Artificial Intelligence, Smart city, and sustainable transportation can be aligned together. Artificial Intelligence will help to overcome the challenges faced by the urban and transportation sector. Whereas, Smart cities are considered to be the representation of potential smart cities. On the other hand, the transportation system is one of the core for any urban area, inculcating robotic applications in the development of transportation systems and smart cities will improvise the productivity of the entire urban area, it also leads to sustainability, and effective planning, wellbeing and sound governance in the city.

PROSPECTS OF ARTIFICIAL INTELLIGENCE-ENABLED TRANSPORTATION

By integrating technological applications like Artificial Intelligence, Machine Learning, and Robotics, cities globally are in the transformation process of becoming 'Smart Cities' (Ramdoss et al., 2018). The application of AI enables spatial navigation and through interactive automated systems uses data processing technology to reveal the dynamics of the grid in modern cities (Marvin et al. 2018). The main artificial intelligence (AI) strategies used in a smart transport design include automation of services through big data and machine learning, smart decision-making through e-governance, smart education through robotics and one-stop-shop solutions, smart infrastructure through sensors and remote monitoring and tracking systems, smart education through robotics, and smart mobility through smart traffic management and smart parking facilities (Feng et al., 2018; Ramdoss et al., 2018; Boenig-Liptzin, 2017).

The prospective uses of robotic automation systems (RAS) in security, the military, transportation, healthcare, education, construction, sustainability, energy management, etc. have been widely publicized through research. According to Golubchikov and Thornbush (2020), self-driving automobiles, autonomous vehicles, and hyperloop technologies are being adopted in the transportation industry and are part of a transport revolution (Rehena & Janssen, 2019). Automatic autonomous vehicles (AVs) make it possible to use transportation infrastructure more effectively. They also significantly reduce the need for parking in urban areas, ensuring that there is always room available for housing and recreational activities (Girardi & Temporelli, 2017). The main advantages of automated vehicles are the advancement of social and economic sustainability. AVs can uplift fuel efficiency directly upsetting economic efficiency by lowering congestion, expanding the overall capacity of the road, and enhancing the traffic flow (Mora & Bolici, 2016). The automated vehicles can link to the external communication network, which allows them to control and allocate data while they are in motion (Bakıcı et al., 2013). Improvisation of traffic congestion, spatial efficiency, and road competence is possible through vehicular platooning. Vehicular platooning is the practice of driving a group of vehicles together (Esposito et al., 2021). Given the enormous costs of congestion, which total more than $120 billion and £30 billion annually in the US and the UK, respectively, the economic benefits are significant (Ng et al., 2022). AI-enabled Automated Traffic Control Systems that use real-time sensor data and unmanned aerial vehicles (UAV) also make it possible to use uncharted airspace efficiently (Danilina & Slepnev, 2018).

Applications for smart mobility are competent in gathering a variety of data types. This calls for the availability of monetary resources for developing and incorporating smart-mobility automation, as well as data, a partnership between the public and private sectors, ICT professionals, and citizen participation (Wu, 2020). The practical performance of the smart city concept poses a variety of challenges. For a smart city, the most important aspect is the availability of data and the free flow of information throughout the various sectors and sub-sectors of the economy. The openness of data and the over usage of information can result in a variety of barriers which are institutional, communicational, statutory, and technological (Yigitcanlar et al., 2021). Many IoT applications still struggle with data privacy, which makes it difficult to involve citizens more effectively while safeguarding user data. Although the concept of "smart cities" seems highly promising and upbeat from a positive perspective, there are a lot of obstacles to overcome when putting it into action (Ng & Kim, 2021).

Urban mobility must take sustainability into account by enhancing the state of the environment, social cohesion, and economic competitiveness (Noh et al., 2020). Therefore, research has identified several methods like co-modality between public and private transportation (Andersen & Skrede, 2017); transportation optimization (Alizadeh, 2015), and the creation and execution of sustainable mobility plans (Gaffney & Robertson, 2018); which could help achieve these sustainability objectives.

METHODOLOGY

The study is purely conceptual and based on careful analysis of the literature based on Green Transportation, Sustainability, Artificial Intelligence, and the influence of smart technologies on developing sustainable transport at destinations. This study's methodology involves a thorough analysis of the state of the literature, research, innovations, developments, trends, and applications in the fields of intelligent and sustainable transportation, as well as AI. The current study contributes to ongoing scholarly conversations regarding AI and smart, green sustainable vehicles. The study's conclusions are intended to help urban policymakers, planners, and other stakeholders in establishing a smart, green transport system in their decisions about the sustainable deployment of AI.

RESULTS AND DISCUSSIONS

Green mobility could undergo many revolutions thanks to artificial intelligence (AI). The following are a few conceptual ramifications of AI in green transportation. Using real-time data to optimize traffic lights and redirect vehicles in real-time to prevent congestion and cut emissions, artificial intelligence (AI) can assist in the supervision of traffic flow (Centobelli et al., 2019). By analyzing data from the battery, motor, and other systems to maximize energy efficiency and increase the vehicle's range, AI can help electric vehicles perform at their best (Abduljabbar et al., 2019). AI can be used to manage and monitor sustainable transportation infrastructure, such as electric vehicle charging stations, to make sure they are being utilized properly and efficiently. AI can optimize routes, cut down on idle, and reduce energy usage in cars by analyzing data from sensors, traffic patterns, and other factors (Golubchikov & Thornbush, 2020). AI can facilitate the creation of autonomous vehicles, which have the potential to reduce emissions by doing away with the need for human drivers who might stop or accelerate too abruptly or fail to adhere to fuel-efficient driving techniques (Bamwesigye & Hlavackova, 2019).

Outcome and Implications

The chapter focuses on offering a sustainable and environment-friendly Intelligent Transportation system for destinations by integrating Artificial Intelligence and smart technology applications.

The outcome of the chapter is to provide clarity on the concept of AI-enabled transportation systems and the effective implementation of such systems in tourist transportation. The implications of developing such sophisticated systems are the digital transformation of cities and the development of a much more sophisticated and globally accepted model for managing urban transportation systems.

Cities are already implementing several smart mobility solutions, which may influence the modal split and behavior of residents. These solutions include an e-parking system, in-car navigation services, e-ticketing, e-pass, info-mobility signage, autonomous vehicles, demand-responsive transportation, vehicle pooling, services live tracking, biometric scanning, and dynamic queue management (Rehena & Janssen, 2019; Bwalya, 2019; Girardi & Temporelli, 2017; Ma & Lam, 2019). Numerous urban disciplines, including business, data analytics, health, education, energy, environmental monitoring, land use, transport, governance, and security, are being employed rapidly to increase efficiency. This directly affects the planning, development, and management of modern cities. But because heterogeneous AIs target heterogeneous problems and objectives without adopting a comprehensive strategy, the various applications of AI commonly occur to be fragmented (Mohammed et al., 2014).

Artificial intelligence in green-mode vehicles will create value propositions for the entire transport industry. Implementation of artificial intelligence will enhance the tourist experience and will help them to have hassle-free travel. The integration of computer applications in vehicles will ease many tedious procedures and can have increased efficiency in sector operations. AI also solves problems such as construction for facilitating parking and congestion in urban cities. The introduction of autonomous vehicles can solve the parking issue in the town as the vehicle can drive itself to the nearest rural place. The movement of autonomous vehicles for parking from the city to the nearest rural place will prevent the construction of under-passage and over-bridge parking spaces. It also enables physically able passengers to move around without any dependency.

Given that sustainability is about understanding and responding in terms of the whole rather than isolated components, coordination of the numerous AIs present in the cities is required for developing a sustainable ecosystem (Danilina & Slepne, 2018). AI has the potential to transform cities and communities for the better and advance multiple SDGs. Despite these promising developments, we still need to exercise caution when choosing the appropriate AI technology for a given situation, as well as when verifying its cost and compliance with sustainability guidelines and taking into account challenges related to community acceptance (Robert et al., 2017). Instead of imposing AI on society and cities, local community discussions about AI should be held while taking into account regional, cultural, demographic, and economic diversity (Prasad et al., 2021). The pressing need to advance not only technologically but also socially and politically stems from the fact that sustainability can only be realized through a balanced combination of technology, community, and policy drivers (Hämäläinen, 2020).

CONCLUSION

Human safety and certainty is the prime consideration in any innovation. Though the cities are transformed into smart cities, it is very important to ensure the security of the society and community through digitization and inter-institutional cooperation (Girardi & Temporelli, 2017). To design and develop safe and ethical behavior, it is imperative to generate and foster a culture of safety in a modern digital world (Danilina & Slapen, 2018). Finally, it is also essential to collaborate with government entities for executing the recommended smart city solutions (Robert et al., 2017). To bring clarity over the implementation and key relationship between sectors (such as transport-energy, energy-water-food, resource efficiency, and recovery, etc.) enhancement and a deep understanding of financial sustainability, political viability, equity, and transparency are required. These strategic movement results to hold community engagement, robust planning, and utilization of technologies in the urban infrastructure (Golubchikov & Thornbush, 2020). The shift from tedious manual operations to automation has enhanced the tourist experience. Some of the automated initiatives are e-ticketing which avoids carrying liquid money, a GPS tracker inbuilt into the vehicle, parking congestion issues, and also supports physically abled tourists who can rely on an autonomous vehicle for their movement in the cities. The future of smart cities can be made more sustainable, inclusive, and livable through smarter communities and it will be highly appreciated by the world how technological advancement can improve the quality of society, environment, and economy. Emerging technological advancements and sustainability concerns have initiated the integration of smart technologies into the transportation infrastructure at major cities and tourist hubs. The rising environmental concerns have called for a shift in focus from conventional methods to innovative green transport initiatives being formulated by DMOs and destination planners. The use of Tourist Data Analytics and Artificial Intelligence in transportation has been proven to be a reasonable method for sustainable transportation. Developed nations like Australia, Finland, Singapore, and China have already initiated the integration process much earlier and have been successful in creating a pollution-free and eco-friendly alternative to transportation. This study focuses on assessing the value propositions of smart transportation systems in enriching the tourist experience by providing convenient and hassle-free travel solutions. Smart Transportation infrastructure includes the installation of free wifi in tourist buses, GPS-enabled tracking systems, multilingual audio guides, automated ticket counters, and QR code scanners. The ease and convenience of usage, real-time information dissemination, and safety and reliability of the system create value for tourists. The paper focuses on understanding the value proposition of smart transport designs at destinations and the long-term prospects of installing such sustainable infrastructure at major tourist hubs. The study also aims to evaluate the tourist experience in using smart transportation services and the potential benefits and challenges involved in the practical implementation of such systems. The outcome of the chapter is to provide clarity on the concept of AI-enabled transportation systems and the effective implementation of such systems in tourist transportation. The implications of developing such sophisticated systems are the digital transformation of cities and the development of a much more sophisticated and globally accepted model for managing urban transportation systems. AI has the potential to transform cities and communities for the better and advance multiple SDGs. The implementation of artificial intelligence enhances the tourist experience as it avoids the tedious procedure of manual transport operations, e-ticketing facility which avoids carrying liquid money, a GPS tracker inbuilt into the vehicle, parking congestion issues, and also supports physically abled tourists who can rely on an autonomous vehicle for their movement in the cities. AI also solves problems such as construction for facilitating parking and congestion in urban cities. The introduction of autonomous vehicles can solve the parking issue in the town as the vehicle can drive itself to the nearest rural place. Smarter communities will be driving the future of cities towards a more liveable, inclusive, zero carbon and sustainable future as societies throughout the world start to appreciate better how technological progress can improve quality of life and support clean economic development. The study also emphasizes the importance of working in partnership with government entities is essential to execute the suggested smart city solutions Smarter communities will be driving the future of cities towards a more liveable, inclusive, zero carbon and sustainable future as societies throughout the world start to appreciate better how technological progress can improve quality of life and support clean economic development.

Scope for Future Research

The present study revolves around the prospects of Artificial intelligence in promoting sustainable transportation with specific reference to the tourism industry. Further, the study can be broadened to include the implementation of AI-enabled transportation in multiple sectors in urban cities. The technical implications and challenges while developing such a system can be further investigated. The prospects of Artificial intelligence have been discussed in detail in the present study, however, the negative social impacts of technological applications replacing human resources can be researched in depth.

REFERENCES

Abd Hamid, M., & Mohd Isa, S. (2020). Exploring the sustainable tourism practices among tour operators in Malaysia. *Journal of Sustainability Science and Management*, *15*, 68–80.

Abdel Wahed Ahmed, M. M., & Abd El Monem, N. (2020). Sustainable and green transportation for better quality of life case study greater Cairo–Egypt. *HBRC Journal*, *16*(1), 17–37. doi:10.1080/16874048.2020.1719340

Abduljabbar, R., Dia, H., Liyanage, S., & Bagloee, S. A. (2019). Applications of artificial intelligence in transport: An overview. *Sustainability (Basel)*, *11*(1), 189. doi:10.3390u11010189

Alizadeh, T. (2015). A policy analysis of digital strategies: Brisbane vs. Vancouver. *International Journal of Knowledge-Based Development*, *6*(2), 85–103. doi:10.1504/IJKBD.2015.071469

Andersen, B., & Skrede, J. (2017). Planning for a sustainable Oslo: The challenge of turning urban theory into practice. *Local Environment*, *22*(5), 581–594. doi:10.1080/13549839.2016.1236783

Bakıcı, T., Almirall, E., & Wareham, J. (2013). A smart city initiative: The case of Barcelona. *Journal of the Knowledge Economy*, *4*(2), 135–148. doi:10.100713132-012-0084-9

Bakker, S., Major, M., Mejia, A., & Banomyong, R. (2017). ASEAN cooperation on sustainable transport: Progress and options. *Transport and Communications Bulletin for Asia and the Pacific*, *87*, 1–16.

Bamwesigye, D., & Hlavackova, P. (2019). Analysis of sustainable transport for smart cities. *Sustainability (Basel)*, *11*(7), 2140. doi:10.3390u11072140

Barbosa, G. S., Drach, P. R., & Corbella, O. D. (2014). A conceptual review of the terms sustainable development and sustainability. *Journal of Social Sciences*, *3*(2), 1.

Boenig-Liptsin, M. (2017). AI and robotics for the city: Imagining and transforming social infrastructure in San Francisco, Yokohama, and Lviv. *Field Actions Science Reports. The journal of field actions*, (17), 16-21.

Bwalya, K. J. (2019). The smart city of Johannesburg, South Africa. In *Smart city emergence* (pp. 407–419). Elsevier. doi:10.1016/B978-0-12-816169-2.00020-1

Centobelli, P., Cerchione, R., Esposito, E., & Shashi. (2020). Evaluating environmental sustainability strategies in freight transport and logistics industry. *Business Strategy and the Environment*, *29*(3), 1563–1574. doi:10.1002/bse.2453

Cervero, R., & Sullivan, C. (2011). Green TODs: Marrying transit-oriented development and green urbanism. *International Journal of Sustainable Development and World Ecology*, *18*(3), 210–218. doi:10.1080/13504509.2011.570801

Cruz, C. O., & Sarmento, J. M. (2020). "Mobility as a service" platforms: A critical path towards increasing the sustainability of transportation systems. *Sustainability (Basel)*, *12*(16), 6368. doi:10.3390u12166368

Danilina, N., & Slepnev, M. (2018, June). Managing smart-city transportation planning of "Park-and-ride" system: Case of Moscow metropolitan. *IOP Conference Series. Materials Science and Engineering*, *365*(2), 022002. doi:10.1088/1757-899X/365/2/022002

Dubey, R., & Gunasekaran, A. (2015). The role of truck driver on sustainable transportation and logistics. *Industrial and Commercial Training*, *47*(3), 127–134. doi:10.1108/ICT-08-2014-0053

Eisenman, A. (2012). *Sustainable streets and highways: an analysis of green roads rating systems*. Bureau of Transportation Statistics.

Esposito, G., Clement, J., Mora, L., & Crutzen, N. (2021). One size does not fit all: Framing smart city policy narratives within regional socio-economic contexts in Brussels and Wallonia. *Cities (London, England)*, *118*, 103329. doi:10.1016/j.cities.2021.103329

Feng, L., Liu, F., & Shi, Y. (2018, May). City brain, a new architecture of smart city based on the Internet brain. In *2018 IEEE 22nd International Conference on Computer Supported Cooperative Work in Design ((CSCWD))* (pp. 624-629). IEEE. 10.1109/CSCWD.2018.8465164

Gaffney, C., & Robertson, C. (2018). Smarter than smart: Rio de Janeiro's flawed emergence as a smart city. *Journal of Urban Technology*, *25*(3), 47–64. doi:10.1080/10630732.2015.1102423

Girardi, P., & Temporelli, A. (2017). Smartainability: A methodology for assessing the sustainability of the smart city. *Energy Procedia*, *111*, 810–816. doi:10.1016/j.egypro.2017.03.243

Golubchikov, O., & Thornbush, M. (2020). Artificial intelligence and robotics in smart city strategies and planned smart development. *Smart Cities, 3*(4).

Gudmundsson, H., & Regmi, M. B. (2017). Developing the sustainable urban transport index. *Transport and sustainable development goals*, 35.

Gurkaynak, G., Yilmaz, I., & Haksever, G. (2016). Stifling artificial intelligence: Human perils. *Computer Law & Security Report*, *32*(5), 749–758. doi:10.1016/j.clsr.2016.05.003

Hämäläinen, M. (2020). A framework for a smart city design: Digital transformation in the Helsinki smart city. *Entrepreneurship and the community: a multidisciplinary perspective on creativity, social challenges, and business*, 63-86.

Herremans, I. M., & Reid, R. E. (2002). Developing awareness of the sustainability concept. *The Journal of Environmental Education, 34*(1), 16–20. doi:10.1080/00958960209603477

Ho, L. T., & Goethals, P. L. (2019). Opportunities and challenges for the sustainability of lakes and reservoirs in relation to the Sustainable Development Goals (SDGs). *Water (Basel), 11*(07), 1462. doi:10.3390/w11071462

Holdgate, M. W. (1987). Our Common Future: The Report of the World Commission on Environment and Development. Oxford University Press, Oxford & New York: xv+ 347+ 35 pp., 20.25× 13.25× 1.75 cm, Oxford Paperback,£ 5.95 net in UK, 1987. *Environmental Conservation, 14*(3), 282–282. doi:10.1017/S0376892900016702

Joseph, S. I. T., Velliangiri, S., & Chandra, C. S. (2020). Investigation of deep learning methodologies in intelligent green transportation system. *Journal of Green Engineering, 10*, 931–950.

Kantawateera, K., Naipinit, A., Sakolnakorn, T. P. N., & Kroeksakul, P. (2015). Tourist transportation problems and guidelines for developing the tourism industry in Khon Kaen, Thailand. *Asian Social Science, 11*(2), 89.

Larina, I. V., Larin, A. N., Kiriliuk, O., & Ingaldi, M. (2021). Green logistics-modern transportation process technology. *Production Engineering Archives, 27*(3), 184–190. doi:10.30657/pea.2021.27.24

Law, A., DeLacy, T., & McGrath, G. M. (2017). A green economy indicator framework for tourism destinations. *Journal of Sustainable Tourism, 25*(10), 1434–1455. doi: 10.1080/09669582.2017.1284857

Li, H. R. (2016). Study on green transportation system of international metropolises. *Procedia Engineering, 137*, 762–771. doi:10.1016/j.proeng.2016.01.314

Lim, H. S. M., & Taeihagh, A. (2018). Autonomous vehicles for smart and sustainable cities: An in-depth exploration of privacy and cybersecurity implications. *Energies, 11*(5), 1062. doi:10.3390/en11051062

Lin, L. P. (2018). How would the contextual features of a destination function together with individual factors to enhance tourists' intention toward ST in Taiwan? *Journal of Sustainable Tourism, 26*(9), 1625–1646. doi:10.1080/09669582.2018.1491586

Lumley, S., & Armstrong, P. (2004). Some of the nineteenth century origins of the sustainability concept. *Environment, Development and Sustainability, 6*(3), 367–378. doi:10.1023/B:ENVI.0000029901.02470.a7

Lumsdon, L. (2000). Transport and tourism: Cycle tourism–a model for sustainable development? *Journal of Sustainable Tourism, 8*(5), 361–377. doi:10.1080/09669580008667373

Ma, R., & Lam, P. T. (2019). Investigating the barriers faced by stakeholders in open data development: A study on Hong Kong as a "smart city". *Cities (London, England), 92*, 36–46. doi:10.1016/j.cities.2019.03.009

Macrorie, R., Marvin, S., & While, A. (2021). Robotics and automation in the city: A research agenda. *Urban Geography, 42*(2), 197–217. doi:10.1080/02723638.20 19.1698868

Marinchak, C. M., Forrest, E., & Hoanca, B. (2018). Artificial intelligence: Redefining marketing management and the customer experience. [IJEEI]. *International Journal of E-Entrepreneurship and Innovation, 8*(2), 14–24. doi:10.4018/IJEEI.2018070102

McCarthy, J. (2007). From here to human-level AI. *Artificial Intelligence, 171*(18), 1174–1182. doi:10.1016/j.artint.2007.10.009

Mohammed, F., Idries, A., Mohamed, N., Al-Jaroodi, J., & Jawhar, I. (2014, March). Opportunities and challenges of using UAVs for dubai smart city. In *2014 6th international conference on new technologies, mobility and security (NTMS)* (pp. 1-4). IEEE. 10.1109/NTMS.2014.6814041

Mora, L., & Bolici, R. (2015). How to become a smart city: Learning from Amsterdam. Bisello A., Vettorato D., Stephens R., Elisei P.(eds) Smart and sustainable planning for cities and regions. Edinburgh University.

Muench, S. T., Anderson, J. L., & Söderlund, M. (2010). Greenroads: A sustainability performance metric for roadways. *Journal of Green Building, 5*(2), 114–128. doi:10.3992/jgb.5.2.114

Ng, M. K., Koksal, C., Wong, C., & Tang, Y. (2022). Smart and sustainable development from a Spatial planning perspective: The case of Shenzhen and Greater Manchester. *Sustainability (Basel), 14*(6), 3509. doi:10.3390u14063509

Ng, M. K., Koksal, C., Wong, C., & Tang, Y. (2022). Smart and sustainable development from a Spatial planning perspective: The case of Shenzhen and Greater Manchester. *Sustainability (Basel), 14*(6), 3509. doi:10.3390u14063509

Nikitas, A., Michalakopoulou, K., Njoya, E. T., & Karampatzakis, D. (2020). Artificial intelligence, transport and the smart city: Definitions and dimensions of a new mobility era. *Sustainability (Basel), 12*(7), 2789. doi:10.3390u12072789

Noh, S. M., Kang, H. S., & Jang, S. Y. (2020). The Effects of Smart Tolling for the Improvement of Traffic Flow on the Seoul Tollgate with ARENA. *Journal of Advanced Simulation in Science and Engineering*, *7*(2), 279–290. doi:10.15748/jasse.7.279

Nundy, S., Ghosh, A., Mesloub, A., Albaqawy, G. A., & Alnaim, M. M. (2021). Impact of COVID-19 pandemic on socio-economic, energy-environment and transport sector globally and sustainable development goal (SDG). *Journal of Cleaner Production*, *312*, 127705. doi:10.1016/j.jclepro.2021.127705 PMID:36471816

Özdemir, V., & Hekim, N. (2018). Birth of industry 5.0: Making sense of big data with artificial intelligence, "the internet of things" and next-generation technology policy. *OMICS: A Journal of Integrative Biology*, *22*(1), 65–76. doi:10.1089/omi.2017.0194 PMID:29293405

Pande, K (2017). Mainstreaming sdgs in national policies: the case of transport sector in nepal. *Transport and Sustainable Development Goals*, *16*.

Pfeffer, K. P., Zuidgeest, M. Z., van Maarseveen Maarseveen, M., & Brussel, M. B. (2019). Access or Accessibility? A Critique of the Urban Transport SDG Indicator.

Prasad, D., Alizadeh, T., & Dowling, R. (2021). Multiscalar smart city governance in India. *Geoforum*, *121*, 173–180. doi:10.1016/j.geoforum.2021.03.001

Purvis, B., Mao, Y., & Robinson, D. (2019). Three pillars of sustainability: In search of conceptual origins. *Sustainability Science*, *14*(3), 681–695. doi:10.100711625-018-0627-5

Ramadoss, T. S., Alam, H., & Seeram, R. (2018). Artificial intelligence and Internet of Things enabled circular economy. *The International Journal of Engineering and Science*, *7*(9), 55–63.

Ramírez-Moreno, M. A., Keshtkar, S., Padilla-Reyes, D. A., Ramos-López, E., García-Martínez, M., Hernández-Luna, M. C., Mogro, A. E., Mahlknecht, J., Huertas, J. I., Peimbert-García, R. E., Ramírez-Mendoza, R. A., Mangini, A. M., Roccotelli, M., Pérez-Henríquez, B. L., Mukhopadhyay, S. C., & Lozoya-Santos, J. D. J. (2021). Sensors for sustainable smart cities: A review. *Applied Sciences (Basel, Switzerland)*, *11*(17), 8198. doi:10.3390/app11178198

Rehena, Z., & Janssen, M. (2019). The smart city of Pune. In *Smart City Emergence* (pp. 261–282). Elsevier. doi:10.1016/B978-0-12-816169-2.00012-2

Robert, J., Kubler, S., Kolbe, N., Cerioni, A., Gastaud, E., & Främling, K. (2017). Open IoT ecosystem for enhanced interoperability in smart cities—Example of Métropole De Lyon. *Sensors (Basel)*, *17*(12), 2849. doi:10.339017122849 PMID:29292719

Salomonson, N., & Fellesson, M. (2014). Tricks and tactics used against troublesome travelers—Frontline staff's experiences from Swedish buses and trains. *Research in Transportation Business & Management*, *10*, 53–59. doi:10.1016/j.rtbm.2014.04.002

Seroka-Stolka, O. (2016). Green initiatives in environmental management of logistics companies. *Transportation Research Procedia*, *16*, 483–489. doi:10.1016/j.trpro.2016.11.045

Shiva, V. (1992). Recovering the real meaning of sustainability. D. Cooper and J. Palmer (eds.), The environment question: Ethics and global issues. Taylor and Francis.

Swarbrooke, J. (1999). *Sustainable tourism management*. Cabi. doi:10.1079/9780851993140.0000

Tussyadiah, I. (2020). A review of research into automation in tourism: Launching the Annals of Tourism Research Curated Collection on Artificial Intelligence and Robotics in Tourism. *Annals of Tourism Research*, *81*, 102883. doi:10.1016/j.annals.2020.102883

Vogt, M., & Weber, C. (2019). Current challenges to the concept of sustainability. *Global Sustainability*, *2*, e4. doi:10.1017us.2019.1

Wiseman, Y. (2017). Remote parking for autonomous vehicles. *International Journal of Hybrid Information Technology*, *10*(1), 313–324. doi:10.14257/ijhit.2017.10.1.27

Wiseman, Y. (2022). Autonomous vehicles. In *Research Anthology on Cross-Disciplinary Designs and Applications of Automation* (pp. 878–889). IGI Global. doi:10.4018/978-1-6684-3694-3.ch043

Wu, W. N. (2020). Features of smart city services in the local government context: a case study of San Francisco 311 system. In *HCI in Business, Government and Organizations: 7th International Conference, HCIBGO 2020, 22*, (pp. 216–227). ACM.

Yigitcanlar, T., & Cugurullo, F. (2020). The sustainability of artificial intelligence: An urbanistic viewpoint from the lens of smart and sustainable cities. *Sustainability (Basel)*, *12*(20), 8548. doi:10.3390u12208548

Yigitcanlar, T., Desouza, K. C., Butler, L., & Roozkhosh, F. (2020). Contributions and risks of artificial intelligence (AI) in building smarter cities: Insights from a systematic review of the literature. *Energies*, *13*(6), 1473. doi:10.3390/en13061473

Yigitcanlar, T., Kankanamge, N., & Vella, K. (2021). How are smart city concepts and technologies perceived and utilized? A systematic geo-Twitter analysis of smart cities in Australia. *Journal of Urban Technology*, *28*(1-2), 135–154. doi:10.1080/10630732.2020.1753483

Yusof, N. A., Abidin, N. Z., Zailani, S. H. M., Govindan, K., & Iranmanesh, M. (2016). Linking the environmental practice of construction firms and the environmental behaviour of practitioners in construction projects. *Journal of Cleaner Production*, *121*, 64–71. doi:10.1016/j.jclepro.2016.01.090

Chapter 6

Data Centers in Sustainability and Green Computing

Ahmet Bilgehan Kandemir
iD https://orcid.org/0000-0002-0009-9384
Gazi University, Turkey

Başak Gök
iD https://orcid.org/0000-0002-8687-5961
Gazi University, Turkey

Hadi Gökçen
Gazi University, Turkey

ABSTRACT

The increase in the human population in the world, the rapid rate of digitization, the support of more services using digital technology during this transformation, and the increase in the number of users lead to the emergence of large volumes of data and information. In the global context, it is one of the most important problems of today to produce sustainable solutions together with the effective and efficient use of all kinds of resources. Regarding their energy usage and effects on the ICT carbon footprint, data centers are regarded as sustainable goods and services. In this study, within the framework of sustainability, data centers were discussed, and basic concepts, global standards, world examples, and suggestions to make data centers more efficient were shared.

DOI: 10.4018/978-1-6684-8140-0.ch006

INTRODUCTION

Today, the methods of obtaining, using and sharing information are changing rapidly. In the knowledge economy, it is inevitable to evaluate the production, storage and correct management of knowledge, which can be positioned as both capital and product, within the scope of sustainability. Realizing that the information economy will provide a competitive advantage both for today and for the future, governments, institutions and companies attach importance to the sustainability of the products and services they have developed in the matter of data and information management.

While the world's digital transformation continues at an extraordinary pace, the rise of the human population, the support of more services with digital technology and the increase in the use of digital services by users cause the emergence of large volumes of data and information. With the effect of globalization, the need and desire of human beings to access information anytime, anywhere has caused institutions to adopt cloud computing as an architecture. Cloud computing can be defined as a pool of shared resources that provides software and hardware services from a basic source, usually over a network such as the internet. The fact that cloud computing can meet today's computing needs, is less costly than traditional infrastructures, and reduces energy consumption, electronic waste and carbon footprint thanks to its advantages such as increase in the demand for cloud computing thanks to virtualization.

Green Computing is a technology awareness that aims at minimizing environmental damage to resources, equipment, design, and operations used by information technologies, computer and technology by-products. The concept of Green Computing originated in the United States in the early 1990s. It is based on the Environmental Protection Agency's "Energy Star" program. In general, information technology means the production and use of products and services without harm to the environment, and is environmentally sustainable (Pal, 2018). Green computing, green IT, or ICT sustainability is defined at Wikipedia, and is the study and practice of environmentally sustainable computing or IT (Wikipedia, 2022). The cloud covers the deployment of IT services such as server, storage, databases, network, while the green aims to make the most effective use of all resources in running computing operations. While operational processes are the main purpose of cloud computing, such as energy consumption, energy waste, reduction of carbon footprint additionally green IT includes sustainable processes such as reducing harmful waste, increasing the use of effective energy. Data centers are a service that includes information economically access, storage and services under cloud computing, providing a competitive advantage within green computing with sustainability.

Data centers serve as facilities where a massive amount of information is collected, stored and/or presented to customers. Data centers are one of the most compute-intensive and power consuming facilities. According to the National Energy

Agency's 2022 report, the number of Internet users has increased and data center workloads have changed. In 2015, the number of Internet users was 3 Billion and increased to 4.9 Billion in 2021 (International Energy Agency, 2022). Regardless of the speed of Internet users increasing, users of Internet are generating and consuming more data every day. Internet traffic was reported as 0.6 ZB in 2015 and 3.4 ZB in 2021, up 40% (International Energy Agency, 2022). The number of data centers is expected to increase even further, especially due to the rapid increase in demand for data-intensive services, such as video services, interest in IoT devices, cloud games, and augmented virtual reality applications. Therefore the increase in data centers could create major problems for the infrastructure of cities' power grids in some areas. Thus, global efforts to reduce the impact from IT production and use have become much more important.

It is inevitable that the problems of access to food and water, rapid consumption of natural resources, climate change, global warming, loss of biodiversity, waste and pollution, which concern the whole world, will threaten human life in the future as well as today. This situation has led to an increase in efforts to produce sustainable solutions with the effective and efficient use of all kinds of resources in the global context. Following the findings published by the Intergovernmental Panel on Climate Change in 2022, the increase in human-induced global warming has increased and it has been stated that it causes significant climate changes (IPCC Climate Change 2022, pages 59-62). According to the report, it is stated that with the measures that can be taken, a strong and continuous reduction in carbon dioxide (CO_2) and other greenhouse gas emissions can rapidly improve air quality and lower global temperatures (IPCC Climate Change 2021, pages 64-71). Effective use of world energy resources in line with climate change and global warming has become the focus of both environmentalists and governments, institutions and businesses.

Data centers, where electricity consumption is intense, strive to provide more efficient service in order to both provide nature-friendly services and gain competitive advantage by reaching low costs. In this context, the concept of data center efficiency has arisen. Data centers have set some standards by producing various methods to increase efficiency and productivity. Today, governments, institutions and organizations are doing a lot of work on energy consumption, environmental problems and sustainability that will shape our future and reviewing their ways of doing business processes.

Green Information Systems focuses on the design and implementation of information technologies that contribute to sustainable business processes, whereas Green Information Technologies generally focus on the cost savings and energy efficiency of deploying IT resources. Green Information Systems and Green Information Technologies are two key elements of environmental sustainability the first is information technology as a solution, the second is information technology as a problem. Subjects such as carbon footprints and electronic waste play a crucial role in the development of green computing. The carbon footprint can be described as a measure of the amount of greenhouse gasses produced by activities undertaken by individuals, institutions, or countries, and the amount of damage inflicted on the environment, in terms of carbon dioxide. According to the World Health Organization (WHO), "the carbon footprint is a measure of the impact of your activities on the amount of carbon dioxide (CO_2) produced by burning fossil fuels, and is represented as a weight in tons of CO_2 emissions produced" (YouMatter, 2020). The term "e-waste" is generally used for consumer and commercial electronic equipment that is near or near the end of its life (California Government, 2022). Electronic waste is also a danger to human health (World Health Organization, 2021). Reducing the carbon footprint and electronic waste that arise with the increasing use of technology, producing environmentally friendly and sustainable solutions that consume less energy are within the scope of green computing studies.

For sustainability, efficiency of services and products and effective energy use are important. Energy efficiency can be expressed as a way to manage and tame energy consumption growth. If something can provide fewer energy inputs or more services with the same energy input, this is called energy efficient (International Energy Agency, 2016). For sustainability, the preference for energy-efficient products is unavoidable. According to the GeSI Smart 2020 report, the entire ICT sector in the world produces 2% of the world's global greenhouse gasses, and the part of data centers is 15% in all ICT. In other words, 0.3% of global greenhouse gasses in the world come from data centers. The global greenhouse gas rate generated by data centers in the same report was 0.1% in 2008 (GeSI, 2008), and has increased considerably today. For this reason, data centers tend to reduce energy consumption and carbon footprint, increase energy efficiency, move towards environmentally friendly sustainable structures, and set standards recently.

In this study, which was organized in a conceptual analysis model as a methodology, researches on the efficiency of data centers were examined by scanning method; definitions, standards, solutions are presented in detail. This conceptual review includes the basic and technical concepts of data centers, which have an important place in information management, green computing and its future, special data center projects, and discussions and evaluations for increasing data center efficiency.

BASIC CONCEPTS

What is a Data Center?

A data center is a physical facility consisting of networked computers, servers, storage systems, and computing infrastructure that organizations use to data-merge, process, store, and publish large amounts of data. Data centers have their roots in the gigantic computer rooms of the 1940s, symbolized by one of the earliest examples, ENIAC (Bartels, 2011). With the development of technology and the rapid rise of the microcomputer industry, IT operations began to grow in complexity and companies needed to control their IT resources. As a solution to this problem, companies have created server rooms in order to control and manage all IT resources in a hierarchical structure thanks to network configurations and cabling, by placing the servers in a specific room in their campus. This process, which started with server rooms, has developed and has created data centers today. The rapid development of the internet infrastructure in the world has led to the desire of companies to use the internet more to gain competitive advantage, the globalization of data centers and the increase in their numbers. Data centers are structured as facilities with redundant connections, security infrastructures and cooling systems. Data centers, which can serve multiple businesses at the same time, can be used by both large and small-sized businesses. For reasons such as internet access and secure use, and the difficulty of managing data and IT equipment, large and small-sized businesses prefer to run their business processes by getting service from data centers instead of providing services with their own servers.

Data centers bring the critical IT infrastructure required to deliver resources and services to business employees, partners and clients around the globe. Because these critical IT operations are crucial to business continuity, they often include infrastructure that include uninterruptible power supply, data communication links, peripheral controls (air conditioning, firefighting infrastructures, etc.) and redundant or redundant components for various security devices. For many businesses, a data center facility can represent the largest and most expensive asset the business can have, both in terms of capital investment and recurring operating expenses.

Data Center Types

There are a huge amount of data center types and service models available across the globe. Their classification depends on whether they belong to single or multiple organizations, how they meet the standards of the topology of other data centers (if they do), what technologies they use for computing and storage, and even their energy efficiency. There are six main data center types:

Enterprise Data Centers

They are facilities established and operated by companies themselves that are optimized only for those company users and their stakeholders. Such data centers are best suited for companies with unique network requirements or doing enough to benefit economies of scale. They are often found inside the company.

Data Centers Managed Services

These data centers are managed by a third party (or a managed service provider) on behalf of a company. The company that wishes to obtain service will rent the equipment and infrastructure instead of buying them. The technical responsibility of the equipment provided belongs to the data center.

Common Layout (Multi-Tenant) Data Centers

Common location data centers, also defined as "co-location" in the industry, offer data center space to businesses looking to host compute equipment and servers off-site. Companies without space for their own enterprise data centers or an IT team to manage them often choose a public location data center. While the data center firm undertakes building, cooling, bandwidth, network redundancy, security, the customer company provides and manages server components (sometimes included network components).

Hyperscale Data Centers

Hyperscale data centers are designed to support a very large-scale IT infrastructure. These facilities were born to meet the growing demand for cloud computing. Data and applications are available from most of the world on the cloud services provider's servers with high redundancy infrastructure. Serving these types of data centers, the company can focus on its business without having to undertake the responsibilities and costs of managing a data center. According to the Synergy Research Group, "there are only 700 hyperscale data centers, but that number has increased twice as much as five years ago" (SRG, 2021).

Despite the fact that this represents a relatively small portion of the world's data centers—there are reportedly more than 7 million of them—hyperscale data centers are on the rise. Hyperscale data centers are owned and run by the organization they serve, much like enterprise data centers are. They only function on a much greater scale for huge data storage and cloud computing platforms. Examples include

Amazon Web Services (AWS), Google Cloud, Microsoft (Azure), and IBM Cloud, some of the most popular options worldwide.

A typical hyperscale data center has at least 5000 servers, 500 cabins, 40 MW capacity, and 10,000 square feet of floor space. Because design is defined by the need for fast activation, everything from servers, storage, rack enclosures, power and cooling systems is often standardized to make deployment easier, increase efficiency, and reduce costs.

Micro/Edge Data Centers

The instant high demand for connectivity, the need for analytics and automation by expanding the IoT, revealed the need for extreme solutions to make computing closer to the actual data.

Such data centers are small and real-time data processing, analysis, and facilities that aim to be near the people they serve to perform the action, thereby enabling low-latency communication with smart devices. By positioning and processing data services as close to end users as possible, edge data centers enable businesses to lower communication latency and enhance customer experience.

As we continue to transform the way we live and work innovating technologies, from robots, telehealth and 5G, to autonomous vehicles, wearable technologies and smart power grids, we may continue to see the dissemination of such data centers.

Container/Modular Data Centers

Container data center is usually made up of a module or shipping containers packaged with ready, plug and play data center components. "The concept of container / modular data center was first introduced about 15 years ago and is now used in temporary and permanent deployments" (Sechrist, 2022). Modular data centers and temporary operations often occur at construction sites or in disaster zones. An example of these is supporting alternative care facilities during the pandemic. For persistent operations, they can be set up to allow rapid scalability of an organization to accommodate new technology, such as opening space inside a building or adding IT infrastructure to an educational institution to support digital classes.

The management, monitoring and maintenance of physical hardware and software in a data center facility requires good planning. This planning must include uninterrupted power supplies (UPS), power supply subsystems, cooling infrastructure, ventilation systems, fire suppression systems, redundant power generators and redundant links to external networks. Energy consumption and cost of all these systems are expected to be low, productivity, efficiency and sustainability. In this context, the concepts of PUE, WUE, CUE have been developed to measure and compare the efficiency, carbon footprint, and water use of data centers.

TECHNICAL CONCEPTS

Power Usage Effectiveness (PUE)

PUE (Power Usage Effectiveness) is a metric that originated in 2006 to measure the effectiveness of data centers (Malone & Belady, 2006) and is now becoming a standard in the industry. PUE can be calculated for both the entire datacenter and the components (cooling, security...) separately (Avelar, Azevedo, & French, 2012). The PUE calculation method is as follows.

PUE= (Total Facility Energy)/(IT Equipment Energy)

Total power consumed at the facility is composed of energy consumed by IT equipment such as UPS, batteries, rack cabinets, power cords, lighting equipment, air conditioners, pumps, fans, and products for air conditioning, servers, databases. The PUE value can range from 1 to infinite, and the approximation of value to 1 indicates increased activity (Avelar, Azevedo, & French, 2012). The ideal PUE value is 1. Data centers are working to bring the PUE value closer to 1.

The Uptime Institute researches and annually publishes data from data centers from 2007 to the present. The report also includes the PUE trend, where the global PUE average for 2022 is 1.55 on average and is generally on a downward trend, as shown in Figure 1.

Global companies regularly share PUE values and PUE objectives in a clear and transparent manner. As a measure of energy-efficient use, PUE provides businesses a competitive advantage. In addition, effective use of energy from limited world resources is important for sustainability. Some global companies and PUE values that offer PUE values for open access are included in Figure 2.

With enterprise and hyperscale data centers that reduce PUE value to highly effective levels and serve only their products, companies like Facebook (Meta), Google, and Amazon have seen considerable success in productivity across the globe. Equinix, one of the largest data center operators in the world, unlike other hyperscale data centers listed above Equinix serves a wide range of customers from outside and has different types of facilities in different continents, has shown that it can handle a very significant productivity burden on its global average.

Figure 1. Average global PUE values
(Davis, Bizo, Lawrence, Rogers, & Smolaks, 2022)

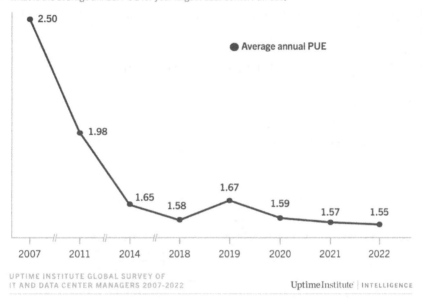

Figure 2. Average annual PUE values for some global companies
Sources: (Google, 2023) (Walsh, 2022) (NREL, 2023) (Lefdal Mine Datacenter, 2022) (Equinix, 2021)
(Amazon, 2020) (DigitalRealty, 2023) (Microsoft, 2022)

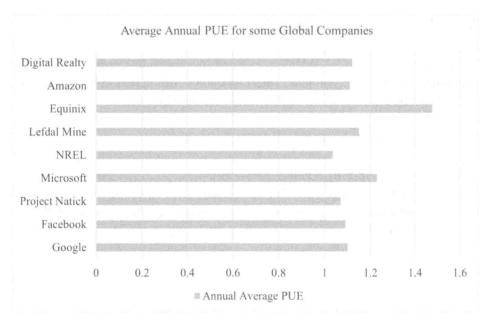

Data Center Infrastructure Efficiency (DCIE)

DCIE (data center infrastructure efficiency) is derived from the total facility energy ratio of IT equipment energy used. This metric takes a value between 0 and 100, and it is preferable to approach 100. The following formulas are used to obtain the DCIE value.

DCIE = IT Equipment Power/Total Facility Power x 100%

or DCIE = 1/PUE.

Pue and DCIE defined their level in Yüzgeç & Günel articles as in *Table 1*.;

Table 1. PUE and DCIE levels

PUE	DCIE	Level
3.0	33%	Quite Inefficient
2.5	40%	Inefficient
2.0	50%	Average
1.5	67%	Efficient
1.2	83%	Very Efficient

(Yüzgeç & Günel, 2015)

Water Usage Effectiveness (WUE)

Water Usage Effectiveness (WUE) is a variant introduced by Green Grid in 2011 to measure the efficiency of data centers in water consumption. It measures how much water the facility uses for cooling and other building needs.

WUE= (Annual Water Usage)/(IT Equipment Energy)

It is a value obtained by dividing the water consumption of the facility in liters by the electricity consumption of the IT equipment. The water consumption here is the value used for cooling, humidity regulation and on-site electricity metering (Watkins, 2013).

Carbon Usage Effectiveness (CUE)

Carbon-handling activity (CUE) is a measuring tool used to measure carbon gas emissions that a data center emit daily. The units used by the CUE metric are carbon dioxide (kgCO2-eq) per kilogram per hour (kWh).

CUE= (Total CO2 emissions caused by the Total Data Center Energy)/(IT Equipment Energy)

Ideally, measures such as PUE, WUE, CUE and processes associated with them will help organizations determine whether an existing data center can be optimized before a new data center is needed. The Green Grid therefore recommends using CUE, a new measure for addressing carbon emissions associated with data centers. The impact of operational carbon consumption is revealed as crucial to the design, location and operation of existing and future data centers. When used in conjunction with the PUE metric, data center operators can quickly assess the sustainability of data centers, compare results, and determine whether any energy efficiency and/or sustainability improvements are required.

Both PUE and CUE simply cover their operations inside the data center. They do not cover the entire environmental impact of the lifecycle of the data center and IT equipment. It does not involve other measurement, calculation or metrics, such as identifying the carbon produced in the manufacture of IT equipment and then sending it to the data center, and it is difficult to determine the consumptions in these processes (Belady, 2010).

Like the PUE, the CUE uses the total known IT energy value in the calculation. Once specified for PUE, the same value should be used as a denominator in CUE. Unlike PUE, CUE has dimensions, and PUE is non-unit; their value is energy divided by energy. Another major difference is the value range. The ideal value of PUE is 1.0, which means that all the energy used in the field goes to IT equipment, and there is no theoretical upper limit for PUE. CUE ideal value is 0.0, indicating that there is no carbon footprint associated with the operations of the data center. Like PUE, CUE has no theoretical upper limit.

An alternative approach to calculating CUE is to multiply the carbon emission factor (CEF) by the annual PUE of the data center: $CUE = CEF \times PUE$

PUE is the annual PUE for the data center, and CEF is the plant's carbon emission factor (kgCO2eq/kWh) based on government data for the region of operation for that year. For such regional information, there are numerous resources, including reports from the primary public service provider/suppliers, and various government-based and NGO-based reports.

We need more sustainable development because energy use, carbon emissions, and data center power footprint are influencing businesses' growth, building locations, and outsourcing tactics. With more environmentally friendly data centers, IT firms may better manage expanding computing, networking, and storage demands, lower total cost of ownership (TCO), stay competitive, and satisfy upcoming business objectives (Belady, 2010).

Data Center Design and Infrastructure Standards

It is important where you keep your data, so it is important to know the differences between the sites that hold your information. During the development and proliferation of Data Centers, a number of standards, including the design of the facility, infrastructure requirements, and sustainability requirements, have emerged. Some of these are:

ANSI/TIA 942-B

This standard includes many variables, such as the planning, design of a data center facility, fire protection, IT equipment placement, network design, cabling, and cable labeling standard that determine the minimum requirements for most data centers.

The TIA-942 specification refers to specific and public data center requirements for applications and procedures such as network architecture, electrical design, file storage, backup and archiving, system redundancy, network access control and security, database management, web hosting, content deployment, environmental control, physical hazards protection (fire, flooding, storm) and power management, and application hosting (ANSI, 2022).

ASHRAE

The American Association of Heating, Cooling and Air Conditioning Engineers (ASHRAE) instructions are not exclusive to IT or data centers only; they relate to the design and implementation of heating, ventilation, air conditioning, cooling and related areas.

The interior has 87 active standards and guideline project committees addressing areas such as air quality, thermal comfort, energy saving in buildings, reducing cooling emissions, and security classification. This association regularly shares working temperatures for IT equipment best suited to the entire industry (ASHRAE, 2021).

LEED Certificate

LEED is short for Leadership in Energy and Environmental Design. It is an eco-friendly building certification system which means energy use and leadership in environmental building design. In the LEED certification introduced from 1998 and developed by the American Council of Green Buildings (USGBC), structures score on measures such as energy efficiency, resource use, carbon emissions. This certification is also applicable for data center facilities (U.S. Green Building Council, 2022).

The level of certification based on the total of the points received is as follows:

Certified (Standard) : 40-49 points range
Silver Level : 50-59 points range
Gold Level : 60-79 points range
Platinum Level : 80-110 points range

Uptime Institute Tier Standards

The Uptime Institute is an organization focused on improving performance, efficiency and reliability of critical business infrastructure through innovation, collaboration, and independent certifications, regardless of technology and vendor. Although headquartered in New York City, it has offices and employees in many countries, and is an industry-leading benchmark for data center performance, durability, sustainability and efficiency (Internet time). It evaluates data centers objectively with certifications that set standards for data centers at 4 levels. These levels are as follows.

Tier One (Basic Capacity)

This tier represents an entry level with data center standards and features non-redundant capacity components and a single non-redundant deployment path to service a critical IT infrastructure. 12-hour fuel storage available for on-site power generation (generator) or additional power requirements. A facility at this level is vulnerable to critical IT infrastructure service interruption for both planned and unplanned maintenance work or downtime. Disruption of the facility infrastructure will be required to ensure the necessary preventive annual maintenance recovery. Failure to provide these maintenance will result in unplanned failures and the resulting losses will increase in severity. Operating time is set to 99.671%. The annual downtime period for a site at this level is set to a maximum of 28.8 hours.

Tier Two (Redundant Capacity Components)

Facilities at this level include, in addition to those at layer 1, partially redundant critical capacity components for power and cooling that provide security against interruptions. A single and non-redundant distribution path is available. On this site, the deployment path must be enabled to serve critical IT infrastructure while the components are off-line. His power supplies can withstand 24-hour power cuts. A facility at this level is vulnerable to critical IT infrastructure service interruption for both planned and unplanned maintenance work or downtime. Twelve hours of fuel storage available at the facility for 'N' capacity. Operating time is 99.749%. The maximum number of hours is 22.7 per year in a facility at this level.

Tier Three (Concurrently Maintainable)

With a Tier 3 site infrastructure, simultaneous maintenance, this means that each capacity or distribution component can be removed on a schedule to support IT resources without affecting IT resources. While the electric power backbone and mechanical deployment path require only one deployment path at any time to service critical environments, the Tier 3 facility has multiple distribution paths. All IT equipment is packed with dual power sources and is set up correctly to comply with the topology of the plant architecture. His power supply can withstand up to 72 hours of power failure. Each capacity component and element in the deployment path can be removed from service on a planned basis without any impact to the critical environment.

There is sufficient permanent installed capacity to meet the needs of the facility should backup components and distribution paths be removed from service for any reason. The facility is subject to disruption due to unplanned activities. Business (human) failures on site infrastructure components can cause compute interruption. Unplanned deactivation or failure of any capacity component or distribution item may affect the critical environment.

Level 3 data centers are the industry standard that provides customers with high-quality space, power and cooling, providing sufficient redundancy and flexibility to support a customer's mission-critical computing and storage needs. Operating time is set at 99.982%. A maximum time of year's downtime is set at this level of facility.

Tier Four (Fault Tolerant)

Also known as Fault-Tolerant Facility Infrastructure, this facility infrastructure includes multiple, independent, physically isolated systems that deliver redundant capacity components, as well as active deployment paths that simultaneously serve critical environments at a Tier 3 level. Distribution lines that feed the entire Data Center (piping for cooling, energy, and cabling for IT) should be redundant. Both of the lines will be active (50% and 50%), and in the event of any failure, a solid line will automatically take over the failed line's task. A single failure of any capacity system, capacity component, or deployment item will not affect the critical environment. The infrastructure control system responds to an autonomous failure while maintaining a critical environment. With critical capacity components and distribution paths divided into segments, each capacity component and element can be disposed of on a planned basis without any impact to the critical environment.

The facility is not susceptible to disruption due to any planned infrastructure maintenance or unplanned activity. His power supply can withstand power cuts up to 96 hours. This power must not depend on any external source. Operating time is set at 99.95%. The annual downtime of a site at this level is set to a maximum of 26 minutes.

Table 2. Uptime institute level comparison (tier standard topology, Uptime Institute)

Criterion	Tier 1	Tier 2	Tier 3	Tier 4
Working Time Warranty	99.61%	99.741	99.982	99.95%
Annual Outage	<28.8 hours	<22.7 hours	<1.6 hours	<26 minutes
Minimum Capacity Components to Support IT Load	N	Partial N+1	Full N+1	2N or 2N+1 Error Tolerant
Deployment Roads-Electric Power Backbone	1	1	1 Active and 1 Alternative	2 Concurrent Active
Critical Power Distribution	1	1	2 Concurrent Active	2 Concurrent Active
Synchronous Maintenance	No	No	Yes	Yes
Fault-Tolerant	No	No	No	Yes
Partitioning	No	No	No	Yes
Continuous Cooling	No	No	No	Yes
Customer Type	Small companies with simple requirements	SMBs	Growing and Large Business	Government Institutions, Large Business
Level Preference Main Reason	Best value data center	A good balance of price/performance	High performance and affordability	Continuously high traffic and data processing, fault-tolerant facility

In Table 2, the tier comparison is shown in detail. Uptime Institute's Data Center Tier certification does not require the use of specific technologies or design options.

Companies are allowed to select from a variety of options, giving them flexibility in achieving certification objectives. This enables each data center to decide how to best meet requirements and receive the desired rating. It is not always a good idea to choose tier 3 or 4 when offering a more reliable service. The tier of data center that best suits a decision maker's demands should be selected.

Cost and uptime are often the 2 primary factors to be taken into account when choosing a level. When a less expensive facility can handle your business, paying for a tier 3 data center can be a waste of money. Additionally, deploying on a tier 2 site when you require improved uptime might have an adverse effect on your earnings, productivity, customer satisfaction, and brand reputation due to potential interruption.

GREEN COMPUTING AND THE FUTURE OF IT

Today, organizations are doing a lot of work to determine the future of energy consumption, environmental issues, and sustainability, and are looking at the way business is done. In information technology, the work done within the framework of this goal is called green computing. "Green information technologies, or in other words, may be derived from the early 1990s, when the United States Environmental Protection Agency launched its energy star program, issued a directive on the European Union's energy label, and worldwide activity like this emerged" (Jouma & Kadry, 2012).

With IT being used in every aspect of our lives, the concept of green computing has become even more important. Many definitions of this concept have been made to date. Some of these definitions include: "Green computing, also called green technology, is an effective and efficient use of resources such as monitors, printers, storage tools and networking and communications systems associated with computers and computers in the name of environmental sustainability" (Shinde, Nalawade, & Nalawade, 2013).

Goksen, Damar, and Dogan, (2016) described green computing as "extending from the production of information technology products to the transformation of it without harming nature at the end of its life" (Yılmaz, Damar, & Doğan, 2016).

In the development of green computing, topics such as carbon footprint, electronic waste, energy efficiency, and so on have become important. Carbon footprints can be described as a measure of the amount of greenhouse gasses produced by individuals, institutions, or countries' activities, and the amount of damage done to the environment, in terms of carbon dioxide. According to the WHO, "the carbon footprint is a measure of the impact of your activities on the amount of carbon dioxide (CO2) produced by burning fossil fuels, and is expressed as the weight of CO2 emissions produced in tons" (YouMatter, 2020). It is called electronic waste or e-waste, and it is called electronic products that have reached the end of useful life. It is widely seen as a major issue throughout the world, whether out-of-use, out-of-date PCs and electrical electronics are eliminated regardless of how any equipment is disposed of without damaging nature (Hepkul & Polatoğlu, 2013). Energy efficiency can be expressed as a way to manage and rein in energy consumption growth. Energy-efficient products are called energy-efficient products. If something can serve more with less energy input, or with the same energy input, that thing is called energy efficient (International Energy Agency, 2016).

According to IPCC statistics, the greenhouse gas that most causes climate change in the world is carbon dioxide emitted by the use of fossil fuels in the energy sector" (IPCC, 2022). Electricity, heat generation, industry and transport are the most common components for carbon dioxide emissions. The amount of greenhouse gas emissions from the IT sector worldwide is published in the GeSI Smart 2020 report. According to this report, the entire ICT sector produces 2% of the world's global greenhouse gasses, the most greenhouse-generated IT technologies are telecoms infrastructure and devices, PC's, peripherals and printers, and the share of the data center is 15%. 0.3% of global greenhouse gasses in the world come from servers, while large internet data centers produce 0.1% of global greenhouse gasses (GeSI, 2008).

Future of Workload in Internet Traffic and Data Centers

The increasing use of the internet in every aspect of both work and private life affects the use of data centers. It is common for researchers to expect that the strong increase in demand for data network services will continue, especially due to data-intensive activities like video services, interest in IoT devices, cloud gaming, and augmented virtual reality applications.

According to a 2022 report from the International Energy Agency, internet user, internet traffic, data center workload, data center energy use and transfer have been increasing worldwide. The fact that the growth in energy consumption is less given the components' growth rates in this report indicates that the steps are taken in terms of sustainability.

According to the International Energy Agency's 2022 report, an increase in the number of Internet users and the change in data center workloads were shown in Table *3*. While internet usage increased by 60% from 2015 to 2021, this increase was determined as 40% for internet traffic and 260% for data center workload. Data center energy usage is expected to increase between 10% and 60%, and data transfer energy usage is expected to be between 20% and 60%.

Table 3. Interchange of use for internet and data centers (IEA 2022)

Features	2015	2021	Change
Internet Users	3 Billion	4.9 Billion	+ 60%
Internet Traffic	0.6 ZB	3.4 ZB	+ 40%
Data Center Workload	180 Million	650 Million	+ 260%
Data Center Energy Usage	200 TWh	220-360 TWh	+ 10-60%
Data Transfer Energy Usage	220 TWh	260-340 TWh	+ 20-60%

Given the prediction that demand for IT products and services is likely to increase rapidly in all areas, AKCP's 2022 energy projections are that data centers will be much more available, as seen in *Figure 3* (AKCP, 2022).

Figure 3. AKCP energy forecast
(AKCP, 2022)

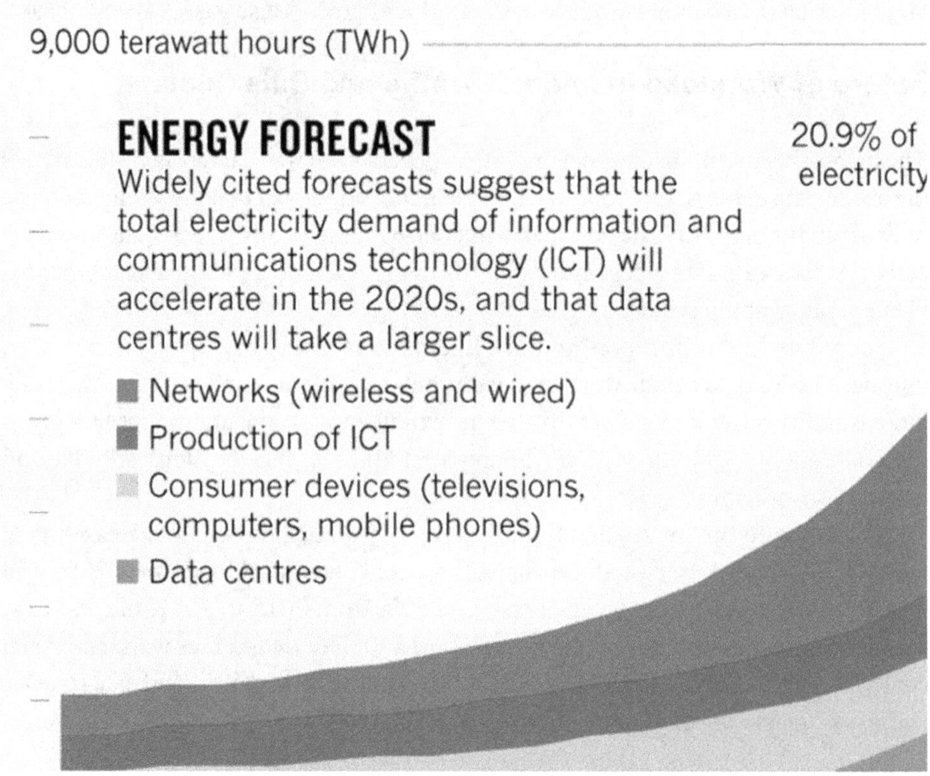

9,000 terawatt hours (TWh)

ENERGY FORECAST
Widely cited forecasts suggest that the total electricity demand of information and communications technology (ICT) will accelerate in the 2020s, and that data centres will take a larger slice.

20.9% of electricity

■ Networks (wireless and wired)
■ Production of ICT
▨ Consumer devices (televisions, computers, mobile phones)
■ Data centres

Climate Neutral Data Center Agreement

In January 2021, European data center operators and industry associations launched the "Climate Harmless Data Centers" Agreement, which has a commitment to make data centers climate neutral by 2030, and is an intermediate (2025) target for power use effectiveness and zero carbon production. Under this agreement, new data centers established by 1 January 2025 are projected to have an annual PUE of 1.3. For existing data centers, this target is expected to be achieved on January 1, 2030 (Climate Neutral Data Center Pact, 2022). Data Centers will acquire clean energy to supply electricity. Data center electricity demand is projected to reach 75% renewable energy or carbon-free energy by December 31, 2025 and 100% by December 31, 2030.

Server and Equipment Refresh Frequency

The Uptime Institute survey answers the question, "How often does your organization refresh its servers?" Shown that in *Figure 4*, refresh times have increased with each passing year. "Several factors can be found, such as a continuing semiconductor shortage that began in 2020 and caused both high prices and longer delivery times for some IT equipment" (Davis, Bizo, Lawrence, Rogers, & Smolaks, 2022).

Figure 4. Server refresh frequency decrease
(Uptime Institute, 2022)

Server refresh cycles are slowing down

How often does your organization typically refresh its servers?

The upward trend here may also reflect a slowdown in server power efficiency gains. Especially innovation with Intel-powered servers making up most of the market means underperforming performance and energy improvements, so organizations may be worried about refresh costs.

Electronic Waste Policy

Electronic waste policy covers industrial processes such as the ability to re-evaluate electronics after they have expired, supplying new products to their production. Data Centers have developed an electronic waste policy. Electronic waste policy covers industrial processes such as re-evaluating electronics after the expiration date, supplying new products to their production.

Efficiency and Special Projects in Global Data Centers

It is aimed to develop more effective and sustainable data center designs by sharing information in data center processes. In addition, special projects have been developed to increase the efficiency of data centers, taking advantage of geographical advantages such as underwater and mining. Some studies in this context are as follows.

Open Computing Project (Open Compute Project): Facebook (Meta)

Facebook (Meta) is one of the largest global businesses of the world. The company, which wants to turn the difficulties of managing the world's largest social media company and thus a huge IT load into an opportunity, has opened all the processes of its new data center, which it calls the Open Compute Project (OCP), to everyone. OCP includes all studies and research on data center design, IT equipment design and data center efficiency. The aim of the project is to enable the data and IT center industries to be more efficient and effective beyond their current boundaries and to help meet industry-wide standards.

In the OCP, organizations, industries, open source utilization enables simple access to data center designs, hardware schematics, software codes, and all sorts of important documents. It also paves the way for a whole new philosophy, cutting off the logic of classical markets that "what I've discovered is my company's private knowledge".

Today, stakeholders in the OCP have become a project and a platform for the industry's biggest players such as AMD, Intel, ARM, Microsoft, Nvidia, Siemens, IBM, DELL and HP, and other companies developing hardware and software. Drawing on the expertise of the OCP community, it produces projects that provide

Figure 5. Microsoft Project Natick, Scott Eklund - Jonathan Banks

OCP members and the data center industry (vendors, suppliers and end users) with an open framework and resources to enable industry best practices that promote reusability and sustainability (OpenCompute, 2023).

Microsoft Natick Project (Underwater Data Center)

The Microsoft Natick Project is a project where Microsoft explores the viability of the idea of setting up an underwater data center. Phase 1 tests and trials were carried out in the project in 2013 and 2015. Phase 2 studies, which started in 2015 and are still ongoing, investigate whether the concept is practical in terms of logistics, environment and economy. A 40 inch container is designed to adapt to submarine conditions and make the most of space (See *Figure 5*). In the project that is still a concept: "In the matter of cooling IT resources, significant amount of efficiency achieved and 1,07 PUE value measured" (Microsoft, 2022). Besides the advancement of the facility, to provide power underwater, projects that will transform tides into electric energy are being researched.

Lefdal Mine Project

Known as one of the most energy efficient data centers in the world, the Lefdal Mine (*Figure 6*) is located in the Sogn og Fjordane region on the west coast of Norway.

The facility, which used to serve as a mine and was later converted, consists of six levels divided into 75 rooms with 120,000 square meters of potential white space, and is located next to a deep, cold fjord with a stable and abundant source of CO_2 neutral energy (hydroelectric). Located just below sea level, the facility has year-round access to unlimited 8°C seawater, and they aimed to cool IT resources by using natural resources by transforming cold water into cold air with their seawater and freshwater conversion circuits, heat exchangers.

Figure 6. Lefdal mine data center

The design and documentation of the security-minded facility's infrastructure installations is highly confidential and is not shared publicly. The facility serves as a sub mountain facility and has natural protection for attack types such as EMP (Electro Magnetic Pulse).

Its emphasis on sustainability and renewable energy is "PUE value is 1.15, WUE and CO_2 emissions are 0, while carbon footprint is limited by the footprint it occupies" (Lefdal Mine Datacenter, 2022).

HOW TO IMPROVE DATA CENTER EFFICIENCY

Measures that can be taken to increase the efficiency of data centers are discussed in this section. In this context, it is expected to contribute to decision makers in the planning, management and evaluation of data centers.

Cold-Hot Corridor Creation, Parsing, and Preventing Leaks

Temperature-intensive points in the facility must be detected using thermal cameras and heat monitoring systems. In order to make the most efficient use of the cold air produced by the on-site cooling technology, IT equipment needs to be disconnected from the hot air it produces. Along with this decomposition, unused cabins, gaps and leaks between equipment for reasons such as defects or displacement should be covered by the appropriate products, preventing the passage of temperature between the two corridors. This will enable servers running at an ideal temperature range to consume more efficient power, which can result in lower PUE.

Cabling Standard and Sustainability

Wiring in the data center is a process that needs to be evaluated and planned in the design phase. Proper cabling and planning for air ducts with the right equipment will affect cooling performance. This will reflect positively on the PUE. It is important to maintain the same standard, not only during initial setup, but also in scenarios such as future capacity building, site relocation, and data center technical staff being rigorous about cabling.

Energy Consumption Monitoring and Optimization Outside IT Equipment

It is important to detect the presence of electrical consumption except products used by IT equipment in order to reduce PUE. For example, if older generation equipment is used for lighting, refreshing them can be done only at the time of need, making them sensor-proof. Consumption outside the white space will be monitored and will reduce overall facility consumption if savings can be made. This could help bring down the PUE.

Using Data Center Management Tools

Regularly monitoring data centers and measuring efficiency requires top management commitment. "Although a simple Excel spreadsheet can help in this regard, you can perform regular audits with environmental monitoring systems or more advanced DCIM (Data Center Infrastructure Management) systems, and compare your productivity figures by making continuous improvements" (Doğuş Pazarlama, 2022). Measuring more real time will make a big difference for PUE.

Free Cooling

Free cooling are industrial solutions that enable the facility to use less energy by utilizing natural climate and zone benefits, making air and liquid cooling systems more efficient. Examples such as Facebook (Meta), with hyperscale data centers serving global scale, prefer regions where it can use free cooling in data center location selection and can reduce PUE data.

Renewable Energy Use in Data Centers

IT companies invest significant sums in renewable energy projects to protect themselves from fluctuations in electricity prices, reduce environmental impact and

Figure 7. Top five enterprise buyers of shape renewable energy purchase agreements

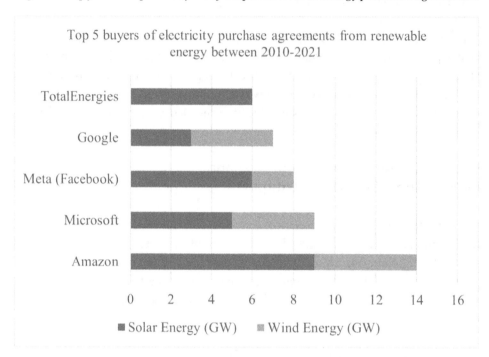

improve brand reputations. With the price of renewable energy sources having the advantages of long-term budgeting and cost-cutting, it may make sense for companies to purchase energy sources in that direction, given that there are far fewer variables than the energy that comes from mines such as coal. The use of renewable energy in data centers is a method that can directly increase plant efficiency.

In particular, hyperscale data center operators lead the way in the supply of enterprise renewable energy through energy purchase agreements (ESA). As seen in *Figure 7*, "Amazon, Microsoft, Meta and Google are the four largest recipients of corporate renewable energy ESAs, with contracts totaling over 38 GW to date" (International Energy Agency, 2022).

It is no coincidence that Facebook, Amazon, Google, Microsoft, and others are investing in energy, especially in data centers where PUE data points out.

Ingrid Burrington wrote in a magazine, "The decision to use renewable energy in data centers is as commercial a calculation as a public connection is, especially in America, where big companies like Facebook and Google can put pressure on energy companies and decision makers, but only on such scale can be done by companies" (Burrington, 2015).

With this in mind, it is possible for energy companies to feel more strongly about building renewable energy infrastructure and concluding deals that can be expected to cover operational costs.

Equipment that has finished its lifecycle, broken down or unused in data centers should be included in the recycling process by making the right agreements so that it can be used by the industry. The policy of updating internal equipment and extending its life cycle if required during their lifetime can also provide an enhancement to produce less waste and reduce costs.

Given this transformation policy, a facility that reduces carbon emissions to the environment can show how seriously a data center takes the concept of efficiency and green computing.

Considering the increasing energy prices recently, it may be necessary for the relevant institutions and organizations to support data center operators with certain tax reductions and incentives by establishing the right policies in order to continue the sustainability of the industry.

Factors such as the environmental climatic conditions of the location of the data center, the design of the facility, the reduction of cooling costs by using natural resources and free cooling of the IT equipment within the data center can reduce the PUE figure to be obtained. It would be beneficial to measure the PUE figure frequently and periodically with accurately placed devices.

In today's technology and information age, data centers have an important place in the management of information. Developing more efficient and nature-friendly data centers within the scope of sustainability and green computing is among the working issues of both today and the future. This study, which presents concepts, standards, current examples and suggestions about data centers, is expected to contribute to decision makers in data center design and planning.

REFERENCES

AKCP. (2022, February). *The Amount of Datacenter Energy Use.* AKCP Monitoring. https://www.akcp.com/blog/the-real-amount-of-energy-a-data-center-use/

Amazon. (2020, June 17). Four trends driving global utility digitization. *Amazon AWS Blog.* Amazon. https://aws.amazon.com/tr/blogs/industries/four-trends-driving-global-utility-digitization/

ANSI. (2022). *ANSI/TIA-942 Standard.* TIA Online. https://tiaonline.org/products-and-services/tia942certification/ansi-tia-942-standard/

ASHRAE. (2021). *2021 Thermal Guidelines for Air Cooling.* Kasım. https://www. ashrae.org/file%20library/technical%20resources/bookstore/supplemental%20files/ referencecard_2021thermalguidelines.pdf

Avelar, V., Azevedo, D., & French, A. (2012, October 02). *White Paper#49 - PUE: A Comprehensive Examination of the Metric.* The Green Grid. https://www. thegreengrid.org/en/resources/library-and-tools/237-PUE%3A-A-Comprehensive-Examination-of-the-Metric

Bartels, A. (2011, August 31). *[INFOGRAPHIC] Data Center Evolution: 1960 to 2000.* Rackspace Blog. https://web.archive.org/web/20181024232055/https://blog. rackspace.com/datacenter-evolution-1960-to-2000

Belady, C. (2010, December 02). *Carbon Usage Effectiveness (CUE): A Green Grid Data Center Sustainability Metric.* [White paper 32]. The Green Grid. https://www. thegreengrid.org/en/resources/library-and-tools/241-Carbon-Usage-Effectiveness-%28CUE%29%3A-A-Green-Grid-Data-Center-Sustainability-Metric

Burrington, I. (2015, December 16). *The Enviromental Impact of Data-Center Industry.* The Atlantic. https://www.theatlantic.com/technology/archive/2015/12/ there-are-no-clean-clouds/420744/

California Goverment. (2022). *What Is E-Waste?* CalRecycle. https://calrecycle. ca.gov/electronics/whatisewaste/

Climate Neutral Data Center Pact. (2022). *Self-Regulatory Initative.* Aralık. https:// www.climateneutraldatacentre.net/wp-content/uploads/2022/07/20220725__Self-Regulatory-Initiative.pdf

Davis, J., Bizo, D., Lawrence, A., Rogers, O., & Smolaks, M. (2022). *Global Data Center Survey 2022.* Uptime Institute.

DigitalRealty. (2023). *Driving Efficiency in Design and Performance through Sustainability.* Digital Realty - Green Datacenters. https://www.digitalrealty.com/ data-center-solutions/green-data-centers

Doğuş Marketing. (2022). *PUE Değeri Nedir, Ne İşe Yarar?* Doğuş Marketing. https://dogus.com.tr/pue-degeri-nedir-nasil-dusurulur/

Equinix. (2021). *2021 Sustainability Report.* Kapost. https://cloud.kapostcontent. net/pub/fae282ef-8d29-4266-96cd-b1bc91164299/sustainability-report-fy2021?ku i=nKl648GVlEjEXFAjNIzzuw

GeSI. (2008, June). *Smart 2020: Enabling the low carbon economy in the information age*. GeSI. https://gesi.org/research/smart-2020-enabling-the-low-carbon-economy-in-the-information-age

Google. (2023). *Google*. Efficiency Datacenters. https://www.google.com/about/datacenters/efficiency/

Hepkul, A., & Polatoğlu, V. (2013). Türkiye'de Kurumsal Sosyal Sorumluluk Olarak E-Atıkların Bertarafı. *Social Business@Anadolu*, 169-170.

International Energy Agency. (2016, November). *Energy, Climate Change and Environment 2016 Insights*. International Energy Agency. https://www.iea.org/reports/energy-climate-change-and-environment-2016-insights

International Energy Agency. (2022, September). *Data Centres and Data Transmission Networks*. International Energy Agency. https://www.iea.org/reports/data-centres-and-data-transmission-networks

IPCC. (2021). *Climate Change 2021 The Physical Science Basis*. IPCC. https://report.ipcc.ch/ar6/wg1/IPCC_AR6_WGI_FullReport.pdf

IPCC. (2022). *Climate Change 2022: Mitigation of Climate Change (The Working Group III Report)*. IPCC. https://www.ipcc.ch/report/ar6/wg3/downloads/report/IPCC_AR6_WGIII_FullReport.pdf

Jouma, C., & Kadry, S. (2012). Green IT: Case Studies. *2012 International Conference on Future Energy, Environment and Materials, (vol.* 16, pp. 1052-1058). Energy Procedia.

Lefdal Mine Datacenter. (2022, December 1). *Cooling*. Lefdal Mine Datacenter. https://www.lefdalmine.com/facility-2/cooling/

Malone, C., & Belady, C. L. (2006). *Metrics to Characterize Data Center & IT Equipment Energy Use*. Digital Power Forum, Richardson, TX.

Microsoft. (2022, December 14). *Project Natick Phase 2*. Project Natick Research. https://natick.research.microsoft.com/

NREL. (2023). *National Renewable Energy Laboratory*. High-Performance Computing Data Center. https://www.nrel.gov/computational-science/hpc-data-center.html

OpenCompute. (2023). *Sustainability*. Open Compute Project. https://www.opencompute.org/projects/sustainability

Pal, K. (2018, May 3). *How Green Computing Can Improve Energy Efficiency in IT*. Technopedia. https://www.techopedia.com/how-green-computing-can-improve-energy-efficiency-in-it/2/32212

Sechrist, S. (2022, May 18). *Understanding the Differences Between 5 Common Types of Data Centers*. Datacenter Frontier. https://www.datacenterfrontier.com/voices-of-the-industry/article/11427373/understanding-the-differences-between-5-common-types-of-data-centers

Shinde, S., Nalawade, S., & Nalawade, A. (2013). Ekim). Green Computing: Go Green and Save Energy. *International Journal of Advanced Research in Computer Science and Software Engineering*, *3*(7), 1033–1037.

SRG. (2021, September 13). *Hyperscale Data Center Count Grows to 659 – ByteDance Joins the Leading Group*. Synergy Research Group. https://www.srgresearch.com/articles/hyperscale-data-center-count-grows-to-659-bytedance-joins-the-leading-group

Uptime Entitüsü. (2022). *Uptime Institute Issued Awards*. Uptime Institute. https://uptimeinstitute.com/uptime-institute-awards/achievements

U.S. Green Building Council. (2022). *U.S. Green Building Council*. LEED Project Profiles. https://www.usgbc.org/projects/?Country=%5B%22Turkey%22%5D

Walsh, N. (2022, 4 22). *How Microsoft measures datacenter water and energy use to improve Azure Cloud sustainability*. Microsoft Azure. https://azure.microsoft.com/en-us/blog/how-microsoft-measures-datacenter-water-and-energy-use-to-improve-azure-cloud-sustainability/

Watkins, E. (2013, July). What is WUE (water usage effectiveness)? . *TechTarget*. https://www.techtarget.com/searchdatacenter/definition/WUE-water-usage-effectiveness

Wikipedia. (2022). *Green Computing*. Retrieved December 2022, from Wikipedia: https://en.wikipedia.org/wiki/Green_computing

World Health Organization. (2021, June 15). *Soaring e-waste affects the health of millions of children, WHO warns*. World Health Organization. https://www.who.int/news/item/15-06-2021-soaring-e-waste-affects-the-health-of-millions-of-children-who-warns

Yılmaz, G., Damar, M., & Doğan, O. (2016, October). *Yeşil Bilişim: Bir Kamu Kurumu Örneği ve Politika Önerileri*. 673-686. Ege Akademik Bakış.

YouMatter. (2020). *What Is A Carbon Footprint? A Carbon Footprint Definition.* Retrieved Aralık 2022, from YouMatter. https://youmatter.world/en/definition/definitions-carbon-footprint/

Yüzgeç, U., & Günel, A. (2015). Üniversitelere Yönelik Bir Veri Merkezinin Enerji Planlaması. *Bilecik Şeyh Edebali Üniversitesi Fen Bilimleri Dergisi, 2*(2), 18–19.

ABBREVIATIONS

ASHRAE American Association of Heating, Cooling and Air Conditioning Engineers
ANSI American National Standards Institute
AWS Amazon Web Services
CUE Carbon Usage Effectiveness
CEF Carbon Emission Factor
DC Data Center
DCIE Data Center Infrastructure Efficiency
EMP Electromagnetic Pulse
ENIAC Electronic Numerical Integrator and Computer
ICT Information and Communication Technology
IoT Internet of Things
IT Information Technology
kW Kilowatt
kWh Kilowatt hour
LEED Leadership in Energy and Environmental Design
mW Megawatt
OCP Open Compute Project
PUE Power Usage Effectiveness
TIA Telecommunications Industry Association
TCO Total Cost of Ownership
UPS Uninterruptible Power Supply
WHO World Health Organization
WUE Water Usage Effectiveness
ZB Zettabyte

Chapter 7
Feasibility of Green Tourism in Small European Emerging Economies

Aleksandra Bradić-Martinović
https://orcid.org/0000-0002-5930-9278
Institute of Economic Sciences, Serbia

Marija Antonijević
Institute of Economic Sciences, Serbia

Milena Lazić
Institute of Economic Sciences, Serbia

ABSTRACT

Expansion of the tourism sector can lead to environmental deterioration. In response, initiatives for sustainable tourism have emerged, followed by certification schemes to promote sustainable consumption, and align consumer preferences and behavior. However, many destinations struggle to satisfy these standards, particularly in smaller developing countries. This chapter aims to analyze the possibility of certification for a spa destination in Serbia, an emerging economy in South-East Europe, using it as a case study to understand the certification process and draw a conclusion about the capacity of small destinations to meet requirements. The research is focused on green destination standard as the most notable validation of the GSTC criterion in the case of Sokobanja Spa. Although the destination in the case study could not receive certification, the results and examples of successful destinations in the region indicate that certification is achievable with the systematic effort of the destination's management and national-level support, particularly in the infrastructure segment.

DOI: 10.4018/978-1-6684-8140-0.ch007

INTRODUCTION

The expanded development of modern society has influenced the excessive consumption of resources, resulting in high pollution rates in urban areas, the creation of the so-called greenhouse effect, global warming, and climate change that significantly impacts the profile changes of entire areas. In this context, there has been much recent discussion about the "green economy" and the solutions it provides, where "green tourism" and its position in the green economy are of utmost importance, particularly in terms of spreading awareness and "green" solutions.

Sustainable tourism development is not defined as a separate policy but rather as a development idea, a philosophy that penetrates and is applied to all tourism strategies and areas. Therefore, it is not about a particular type of tourism but rather about an ethical commitment to promoting solutions of all forms and types of sustainable tourism. "Green tourism" does not refer to tourist services in a clean, "green" environment. Although "green" is frequently primarily associated with ecological and geographical solutions, it entails care and support systems for enhancing the three pillars of sustainable development. The first is economic, reflected through the multiplier effect in income, new jobs and increasing tourism's direct and indirect revenue in GDP. The second is ecological, which is focused on encouraging the preservation of natural and cultural heritage and represents one of the drivers of the sustainable development concept of the destination. The third is social, which has a very positive impact on balanced local economic growth and the wellbeing of local communities, as well as on increasing the recognizability, reputation and overall image of a tourism destination.

The most prominent and influential worldwide organizations have acknowledged the negative impact of mass tourism on nature and society and have initiated programs to promote green and sustainable tourism and tourist consumption. In the previous period, Organisation for Economic Co-operation and Development (OECD), World Tourism Organization (UNWTO), Global Sustainable Tourism Council (GSTC), European Environment Agency and others provide guidance and indicators for sustainable and green tourism. Other organizations followed the lead and offered various certification schemes for destinations or businesses (e.g., hotels).

Considering that the procedure of acquiring a certificate needs the fulfillment of a number of requirements or criteria, the issue arises as to whether or not it is feasible for destinations in small developing countries to meet them. This chapter aims to empirically explore the potential of destinations in a small European emerging economy to achieve certification based on the case study of Sokobanja Spa in the Republic of Serbia and the Green Destinations Standard as a framework for assessment.

GREEN CONSUMERISM IN TOURISM

Travel and tourism (T&T) is one of the fastest-expanding sectors globally (Moreno-Luna et al., 2021). Considering its global position as the third-largest export sector, after fuels and chemicals (Rasool et al., 2021), it is generally regarded as the engine of socio-economic growth and development (World Tourism Organization [UNWTO], n.d.a). Moreover, T&T goes hand in hand with other economic sectors as an employment and income generator, directly and diffused through the economy (Organization of American States [OAS], n.d.). Its importance has comprehensively been analyzed concerning growth, foreign exchange, sustainability, income, employment, cultural values, infrastructural development, and poverty reduction (Gwenhure & Odhiambo, 2017). However, the sector's correlation to green consumerism, environmental protection, and socio-cultural conservation has recently emerged as a far-reaching topic of interest to policymakers and practitioners (Yfantidou & Matarazzo, 2016).

The current staggering development of global consumption has caused numerous environmental problems. Therefore, it is crucial to manage and control the public's green purchasing intentions and behaviors (Tang et al., 2022). Furthermore, it seems like there has never been a better time to launch a sustainable product, considering the recent change in consumers' preferences toward environmental protection and sustainability (Harward Business Review [HBR], 2019). According to a recent authoritative study (NielsenIQ, 2018), companies with valid sustainability claims perform better across all product categories. Authors Liao et al. (2020) indicated in their research that green customer value has a considerable and beneficial effect on attitudes toward green products. Furthermore, the authors believe green customer value and views about green products positively influence green purchase intention. Likewise, green marketing (i.e., environmental advertising and word-of-mouth) and green psychological advantages (i.e., warm glow, self-expression benefits, and nature experience) influence the relationships between consumer value, green product attitude, and green purchase intention. However, a perplexing contradiction remains at the core of green business: few consumers who express good opinions about eco-friendly products and services buy them. Similarly, as per one recent poll (HBR, 2019), 65 percent of respondents said they desire to buy purpose-driven products that promote sustainability, but roughly 26 percent do so. As can be observed, consumers want to be environmentally conscious, but they expect corporations to lead the way.

According to McKinsey Report (2022), civilization has lately witnessed complex disruptions with disparate origins and long-term consequences. The frequency of crises has notably increased during the last few years, including the COVID-19 pandemic, the energy crisis and the latest Ukrainian conflict. Crises have devastating impacts on people, communities and entire societies. They are predicted to become even more common in the future (International Federation of Red Cross and Red

Crescent Societies [IFRC], n.d.). Above that is an ever-present climate crisis (McKinsey, 2022), whose mitigation urgently calls for the gradual global transition to a low-carbon economy. Considering T&T's contribution to global development, efforts to achieve sustainable development will likely fail if the sector's contribution in this respect and its total alignment with sustainable development policies and procedures are not considered (Yfantidou & Matarazzo, 2016).

Before the COVID-19 pandemic, the T&T sector reached 10.4 percent of the global GDP while employing, on average, one out of four newly generated jobs (World Travel & Tourism Council [WTTC], 2021). However, during the pandemic crisis, the contribution of the T&T sector to global economic growth declined from 4.0 percent in 2019 to 2.0 percent in 2020, with a slight rebound to 2.2 percent in 2021 (UNWTO, 2022a). In addition, the year 2020 has considered "the worst year in the history of tourism" (UNWTO, 2021a). Nevertheless, the projections support the sector's recovery, considering its resilience and propensity to bounce back. WTTC Report (2022) indicates that the sector GDP is expected to grow on average by 5.8 percent annually during 2022-2033, surpassing the overall growth of the global economy, which is predicted at 2.7 percent annually. In the same report, the WTTC data imply that T&T GDP may return to the pre-crisis level by the end of 2023.

Along with the tremendous impact on the T&T sector's economic performance, the COVID-19 pandemic has accelerated the change of the sector's essence. Pre-pandemic, the T&T sector was dominated by a mass, mainly in "sun-and-beach" form (Lazić & Bradić-Martinović, 2022a). Moreover, early T&T literature focused on the economic aspects of tourism and was typically enthusiastic about the impact and overall contribution of the sector to global and local economic development (Giampicoli et al., 2020). Nevertheless, the T&T sector's "mass component" and the extensive usage of natural resources followed by the rapid expansion of both international and domestic travel, the emerging tendency of modern tourists to travel to distant destinations over shorter periods, as well as their preference for using energy-intensive means of transportation led to the sector's non-renewable energy dependency and its contribution to global greenhouse gas emissions of 5 percent (Green Policy Platform, n.d.). T&T sector's CO2 emissions are anticipated to grow 25 percent by 2030 compared to 2016 (The World Counts, n.d.). Accordingly, recent tourism literature indicates the sector's significant adverse environmental consequences, including local natural resource depletion and pollution and waste issues. In that regard, T&T usually utilizes more natural resources than necessary, particularly in already scarce regions. It also significantly impacts how local land is utilized, which might result in soil erosion, increased pollution, the destruction of natural habitats, and increasing pressure on endangered species. These effects may eventually even diminish the environmental resources necessary for tourism (The World Counts, n.d.). Notably, tourist attractions are located in vulnerable landscapes and local communities, where the environmental damage outweighs the economic benefits (Archer et al., 2005).

The origins of sustainable tourism are closely interconnected with the rise of global sustainable development as a broader issue of public concern, first introduced in the World Conservation Strategy in March (1980), and the subsequent establishment of the World Commission on Environment and Development (WCED) (Weeden, 2002). Ecotourism emerged in the 1980s to direct tourism income toward conservation and development (Stronza et al., 2019). A growing body of T&T literature indicates that ecotourism is appealing to a substantial number of tourists (Adlwarth, 2010; Deng et al., 2015), while it has become a trend and a "buzzword" for one of the T&T industry's fastest-expanding divisions (Jaafar & Maideen, 2012; Jamrozy & Lawonk, 2017). Ecotourism is commonly defined as environmentally conscious travel that combines opportunities to learn first-hand about a destination's natural and cultural heritage with the chance to participate in conservation efforts (Crossley & Lee, 1994). Definitions of ecotourism generally highlight the following activities - learning, enjoyment, and adventure in the natural environment (Kim & Park, 2017). Ecotourism differs from purely nature-based tourism in that it is focused on the following three cornerstones: (1) it is nature-based, (2) educational, and (3) sustainably managed (Weaver & Lawton, 2007). While most of the earlier research implies that visitors chose ecotourism for moral reasons, recent data shows that chances to project one's social standing are gaining momentum in decision-making. Likewise, Beall et al. (2021) argue that environmental concerns are not the only reason visitors choose ecotourism alternatives and that ego-enforcing incentives play their roles.

The abovementioned indicates that the relationship between the T&T sector and the environment is direct – tourist infrastructure and facilities directly exploit the environment and natural resources (Marcuta et al., 2021). A typical golf course in a tropical region, for example, consumes the same amount of water as 60,000 rural inhabitants while at the same time employing 1,500kg of chemical fertilizers, insecticides, and herbicides yearly (The World Counts, n.d.). The 21st century has been generally recognized as the century of gradual natural resource contamination (Đukić et al., 2016). In that regard, the COVID-19 pandemic created a chance for the sector to rebuild itself in a more resilient, inclusive, and environmentally sustainable manner (UNWTO, 2021b). "Greening" the tourism sector creates new, green jobs while supporting the local economy and reducing poverty (Green Policy Platform, n.d.). Moreover, there is evidence that T&T entities that successfully qualify for green certification receive various benefits. Schemes, for example, assist companies in becoming more environmentally conscious, protecting vulnerable environmental regions, reducing water consumption, and improving waste management (Honey et al., 2007). Lower energy, water, and waste costs/bills are typical advantages for businesses undertaking environmental improvements (Pizam, 2009; Rivera & deLeon,

2005). However, in some instances, firms enhance their environmental practices to comply with the law (Bhaskaran et al., 2006; Tzschentke et al., 2007).

For the sector to recover its position in the future, the policymakers must look beyond their tendency to adopt strategies solely focused on a return to the pre-COVID-19 turnover and seek how to adapt to the environmental protection process instead (Prideaux et al., 2020). Moreover, significant changes have occurred in the last several decades due to technological advancement, deregulation, and globalization (Lončar et al., 2016). Technological advancements and ICT have altered the nature of risk, forming new ecosystems (Kaličanin & Lazić, 2018). The T&T industry has become more resilient and competitive as a result of increased acceptance and usage of advanced digital solutions (Bradić-Martinović, 2021; Mihailović et al., 2020), which proved to be one of the sector's primary competitive advantages during the COVID-19 pandemic (Opute et al., 2021). Consequently, work towards more sustainable tourism which is resilient to overcome future challenges should be grounded on the following principles (UNWTO, 2021b): (1) diminishing socio-economic effects of the crisis with special care of its influence on vulnerable social categories; (2) boosting the sector's resilience and competitiveness; (3) fostering new ideas and speeding the use of cutting-edge ICT solutions; (4) encouraging sustainability and environmentally friendly growth; and (5) transforming the industry to achieve sustainable development goals (SDGs).

Even though there is no clear answer to the question of how the entire sector may become more sustainable, numerous initiatives, including certification systems, have been established to address the negative effects of tourism. Certification is the process of determining whether a company or product has satisfied a set of voluntary requirements. It was formed by the business sector in reaction to external demand and provided standards and procedures for corporate social responsibility (Dodds & Joppe, 2005). Certification programs can potentially mitigate the negative consequences of tourism by holding industry participants accountable while simultaneously delivering extra advantages to firms that fulfill the recognized criteria. However, each certifying authority has unique characteristics, including differing objectives, criteria, scope, and degree of transparency (Plüss et al., 2012). Although not new, destination certification programs and implementing sustainability standards are rising trends in all regions worldwide. Without a doubt, voluntary guidelines, standards and ecolabels have established baseline norms and indicators that promote socially, culturally, and environmentally sustainable tourism. However, Chan (2021) indicates that despite the positive influence that certificates can have on economic benefits, environment protection, and conservation of cultural property, the advantages of these schemes are still discussed.

Furthermore, research has revealed that the feasibility of sustainability criteria that provide optimal advantages for public and local authorities, policymakers, and tourism enterprises in mature destinations is uncertain (Gkoumas, 2019). Since no universally accepted technique exists, it remains challenging for local destinations to measure tourism-related sustainability and achieve such sustainability standards. Even though certification is acknowledged as an essential tool for mitigating the harmful effects of tourism, the use of destination certification to implement sustainability remains controversial (Font & Harris, 2004).

INDICATORS OF SUSTAINABLE AND GREEN TOURISM

Indicators or parameters that may be measured and monitored to reflect the evolving state of a particular phenomenon are a method for filtering existing data and collecting new data. They indicate the status or the phenomenon, such as tourism or a particular component at a specific time, which is not a definitive but indicative evaluation of the phenomenon's state. In practice, indicators measure information with which decision-makers may reduce the chances of unknowingly making poor decisions. Given the complexity of tourist systems, an endless number of tourism-related indicators are theoretically available, such as policy relevance, the type of approach to sustainability (weak or robust, minimalist or extensive), measurability, financial and other resource limitations, corporate values, level of public support, politics, and other (Butler, 1999). A set of indicators needs to include variables that describe the condition, vitality, and possible impact of the system itself (e.g., number of tourists, annual increase, accommodation capacity, and percentage of the labor force utilized in tourism) as well as variables that determine the effects of the system on the sustainability of other systems (e.g., tourism-related water pollution and greenhouse gas emissions, as well as the amount of domestic and foreign food consumed by the tourism sector). The most important global and European indicators of sustainable tourism are presented, in brief, with the aim of insight into the coverage of the topic by the most important and influential institutions in this field.

UN Sustainable Development Goals and Tourism - Governments' efforts to achieve global development have begun since 2015 by adopting the 2030 Agenda for Sustainable Development and Sustainable Development Goals (SDGs). The United Nations defined seventeen sustainable development goals with belonging targets. Tourism is recognized as essential for achieving these goals directly or indirectly. One of the most harmful factors in the recent period is the COVID-19 emergence, which significantly limited the movement of people and consequently caused a collapse in the T&T sector.

UNWTO Indicators of Sustainable Development for Tourism Destinations - To assess the level of tourism sustainability, it is crucial to use the indicators to measure the improvement in sustainable development. According to the UNWTO, tourism sustainability indicators refer to a group of data that measure the level and state of a tourist destination's sustainability. Indicators play a significant role in determining: 1. achievement of the initial goals, 2. gaps, 3. responsibility for achieved results, and 4. further steps to improve the situation. Indicators provide an opportunity to identify and overcome problems in time by taking appropriate actions. The guidebook UNWTO (2004) presents critical issues related to sustainability and corresponding indicators. The spotlight is on 29 fundamental characteristics significant for most destinations (Dimoska & Petrevska, 2012). These indicators allow for comparisons with other destinations and tracking of the destination's sustainability development over time.

UNWTO Statistical Framework for Measuring the Sustainability of Tourism (SF-MST) - UNWTO, in cooperation with the United Nations Statistics Division (UNSD), initiated the development of the SF-MST. The framework's purpose is to measure tourism's impact on sustainable development regarding three aspects – 1. economic, 2. environmental, and 3. social. The SF-MST has a significant role in providing data adequate for further analysis and comparisons, so relevant bodies can make proper decisions toward reaching SDGs goals. The SF-MST is still developing (UNWTO, 2022b).

The Global Sustainable Tourism Criteria - The Global Sustainable Tourism Criteria are developed by the Global Sustainable Tourism Council (GSTC). Each criterion corresponds to the performance indicators that measure compliance with the criterion, and each criterion relates to at least one Sustainable Development Goal (Global Sustainable Tourism Council [GSTC], n.d.a.).

EarthCheck destination standard - EarthCheck represents the Group that provides certification, training, advisory services, and software solutions for sustainable T&T. It was founded in 1987 to support and help build sustainable destinations. The experts visit the destination to determine its performance against the defined standard, but they also assist in developing authority and policy, benchmarking, and promoting certification levels (EarthCheck, n.d.).

European Tourism Indicators System - The European Commission developed the European Tourism Indicator System (ETIS) in 2013. ETIS aims to estimate a destination's sustainability by using core and optional indicators (27 and 40 indicators, respectively) related to the following aspects: environmental, social, cultural, economic and destination management. Thus, this self-assessment tool helps measure sustainability performance and improvements but does not include certification and minimum required standards (European Commission, 2016).

ETC Framework for Sustainable Tourism Development - In 2021, Green Case Consulting, the Travel Foundation, and Good Place developed a Handbook on sustainable tourism implementation for the European Travel Commission (ETC). The framework is based on 12 sustainability indicators, including environmental, economic, and social dimensions. It consists of four independent modules, and each module includes steps with corresponding activities. The framework helps National Tourism Organization to improve and achieve sustainable tourism development (European Travel Commission, 2021).

Green Destinations Standard - The Green Destinations Standard, recognized by GSTC in 2016, represents the system for measuring and enhancing the destination's sustainability. The first version was introduced in 2016 but was revised and upgraded in 2020 after feedback and readjustment with GSTC Destination Criteria V2. The standard is based on 84 criteria and numerous indicators covering six themes. The certification program is rigorous, considering it includes consultation with stakeholders regarding compliance verification, and everything should be covered by evidence. The certificate is valid for three years (Green Destinations, n.d.). Size and type are two elements that determine the price of the certification. Green Destinations also awards for destinations' efforts to achieve sustainability. The award has a three-year expiration date. There are four award levels 1. Platinum, 2. Gold, 3. Silver, and 4. Bronze.

The destinations go through four stages after enrolling in the program. In the first stage, the Green Destinations secretariat introduces the program and explains how the standards are implemented and how to use the platform for assessment. The second stage involves technical verification and checking the accuracy of the reported compliance. In the third stage, a committee assesses the auditor's findings and gives an award or certification. The final stage includes providing suggestions and recommendations to help the destinations improve their sustainability (Green Destinations, n.d.). A detailed explanation of the Green Destination standard is presented in the Methodology section.

The other indicators schemes that need to be mentioned are TourCert, Green Tourism, Starlight Foundation, QualityCoast (at the global level), and Alpine Pearls, Europarc, Vireo/GSTC (at the European level).

TOWARD GREEN DESTINATION CERTIFICATE: THE CASE OF SOKOBANJA SPA AS A TOURISM DESTINATION—MACRO AND MICRO ENVIRONMENT

Before presenting the case study, it is beneficial to consider the worth and significance of tourism to the entire Republic of Serbia on the macro level and Sokobanja Spa on the micro level. Serbia is a small country in South-East Europe in the Western Balkan region. It covers an area of 88.5 thousand square kilometers with 6.8 million inhabitants (Statistical Office of the Republic of Serbia [SORS], 2022). Due to its abundant natural, cultural, historical resources, and a favorable climate, Serbia has effectively developed its tourism sector since the beginning of the millennium, focusing primarily on mountain, spa, and city tourism products. Numerous factors and initiatives of the state and private sector influenced tourism development, and policymakers identified tourism as one of the priorities with a favorable impact on social and economic growth and development. The effort invested is best viewed through the achieved values of indicators of national tourism development. According to 2019 data (UNWTO, 2022c; World Bank, 2021; WTTC, 2021), the contribution of tourism to the Serbian economy was 0.99 billion USD, and the share of tourism in GDP was 2.36 percent.

Serbian tourism was experiencing unprecedented supply and demand growth in the last fifteen years. The supply structure has been gradually modernized, and accommodation capacities, measured by the number of rooms and beds, grew between 2004 and 2019 at annual rates of 2.2 percent and 2.3 percent, respectively. Tourist demand also recorded significant growth, and the most intensive growth was achieved between 2010 and 2019, with annual increase rates of 7.0 percent and 5.4 percent, respectively. Due to the circumstances caused by the outbreak of the COVID-19 pandemic, Serbia recorded a 38 percent (y/y) decline in the number of overnight travelers in 2020, which is less than the global (-73 percent) and European (-68 percent) averages (Lazić & Antonijević, 2021; Lazić & Bradić-Martinović, 2022b). Also, empirical research conducted by Ivanović and Antonijević (2020) shows that only 1.3 percent of travelers booked travel/accommodation online after the virus appeared in 2020. Demand has gradually recovered during 2022. Unfortunately, despite a quality resource base, tourism development lags significantly behind the leading indicators in resource and market opportunities for its development. One of the reasons is that Serbia's competitive position as a tourism destination mostly depends on the local population's resources and hospitality (Petković et al., 2022). The importance of spa tourism in the tourism sector of the Republic of Serbia is highlighted by the fact that spa tourism accounts for around 30 percent of the country's total tourist traffic. One of the main issues with spa tourism in Serbia is the significant disparity in the supply of accommodation and other resources between spa destinations, which results in two spas, Vrnjačka Banja and Sokobanja, generating over 60 percent of total spa turnover.

The municipality of Sokobanja administratively belongs to the Zaječar district in Timočka Krajina and includes the urban settlement, spa and surrounding villages. The Sokobanja is the only town-type settlement in the municipality and represents the municipality's administrative, economic, tourist, health and cultural-educational center. Sokobanja has the longest tradition of developing spa tourism in Serbia. The first tourist came in 1837, and it has been known as a natural health resort since the Roman time. Sokobanja has the harmony of all the rich factors with which nature has endowed it, which is an essential factor of its competitive position. One of the primary healing resources in Sokobanja is the noble gas radon, which, dispersing in the air, has a beneficial effect on many diseases (bronchial asthma, chronic bronchitis, high blood pressure, diseases of the nervous system and glands with internal secretion) and thermal springs. Favorable ionization, i.e., the presence of negative ions in the air, refreshes and invigorates. Due to air and thermal water, Sokobanja has its market recognition, rich history and a solid resource-attraction basis for taking over one of the leading positions in the active holidays, health and wellness market.

Tourism development of Sokobanja could be presented based on the trend of overnight stays. Figure 1 shows the overnight stay trend in Sokobanja from 2011 to 2022. The general tendency indicates an increasing movement with an annual growth rate of 8.1 percent. The period between 2011 and 2015 is characterized by stagnation and a slight decrease, while from 2016, demand has recovered, and Sokobanja records a very high annual growth rate of 21.6 percent. The most significant observation would be that the COVID-19 crisis did not influence tourism demand in Sokobanja, a remarkably uncommon case and the only such ab example in Serbia. Research shows (Lazić & Bradić-Martinović, 2022b) that this is a consequence of the redirection of domestic guests towards local destinations due to the ban on travel to other countries. Changing the structure of the guests is also extremely important. The share of foreign guests in 2011 was 1 percent, and in 2019 it reached 8 percent. However, this upward trend was interrupted due to the COVID-19 crisis.

METHODOLOGY AND DATA

The case study methodology is used for the research. Although it is crucial to bear in mind that results from a small sample or one example may not entirely generalize to a broader population of tourist destinations in one country, literature offers approaches that would give researchers valuable insight into the problems they were studying. In that regard, the study by Flyvbjerg (2006) indicates that it is appropriate to accept the generalization of conclusions based on case study research. It contains arguments in support of the use of this method. The author points out that drawing general conclusions from a single instance is often possible, considering that the case study is carefully chosen, meaning that the example with the most helpful research qualities should be chosen. Based on facts presented in the previous sub-chapter, the authors conclude that Sokobanja captures one of the top places in Serbian tourism in terms of visits, overnight stays, turnover, employment and other key performance indicators and could be an example of a well-established destination which can compete for the Green Destinations Certificate. In addition,

Table 1. Green destination standards primary and secondary core criteria

Type	#	Criteria title
Theme 1. - Destination Management		
Commitment & Organization		
C15	1.1	Sustainable destination coordinator
Planning & Development		
C15	1.5	Inventory of destination assets
C15	1.7	Destination Management Policy or Strategy
Visitor Management		
C30	1.12	Managing visitor pressure
C30	1.14	Visitor behaviour at sensitive sites
Theme 2: Nature & Scenery		
Nature & Conservation		
C30	2.1	Nature conservation
C15	2.2	Tourism impacts on nature
C15	2.5	Landscape & Scenery
Nature & Animal Experience		
C30	2.8	Captive animal welfare
Theme 3: Environment & Climate		
Land Use & Pollution		
C30	3.1	Noise
C30	3.2	Light pollution
Water Management		
C30	3.7	Wastewater treatment
Waster and Recycle		
C15	3.8	Solid waste reduction
C30	3.9	Waste separation & recycling
Energy, Sustainable Mobility & Climate Change		
C15	3.13	Reducing transport emissions from travel
C15	3.16	Reducing energy consumption
C30	3.17	Renewable Energy
Climate Change Adaptation		
C30	3.19	Responding to climate risks
Theme 4: Culture & Tradition		
Cultural Heritage		
C15	4.1	Tangible cultural heritage
C30	4.2	Managing tourism impacts on culture
People & Tradition		
C15	4.4	Intangible heritage

continued on following page

Table 1. Continued

Type	#	Criteria title
Theme 5: Social Wellbeing		
Human Respect		
C30	5.4	Human rights
Community Participation		
C15	5.7	Community involvement in planning
C30	5.10	Inhabitant satisfaction
Local Economy		
C15	5.12	Supporting local entrepreneurs
C15	5.13	Promoting local products and services
Socio-economic Impact		
C30	5.16	Property exploitation
Health & Safety		
C15	5.17	Health & Safety
Theme 6: Business & Communication		
Business Involvement		
C15	6.1	Promoting sustainability among enterprises
C30	6.2	Sustainability standards

Source: Green Destinations Standard V.2 (2021)

the main slogan of Sokobanja is "*Green Heart of Serbia*", which indirectly implies orientation toward green and sustainable tourism.

The case study is analyzed concerning the Green Destinations Standard V.2 (2021) and its 30 "Core Criteria" used for the yearly Top 100 competition and seen as necessary for achieving fundamental sustainability performance. The Green Destinations Standard recognizes "Primary core criteria" (C15) and "Secondary core criteria" (C30), "Optional criteria" (O) and "Not Applicable" (N/A). For this research, the authors considered Primary and Secondary core criteria, presented in Table 1:

The presented framework is used to analyze sustainable and green tourism within the case study of Sokobanja Spa. The data used in the analysis is drawn from two sources. The first is a list of public policies that can be found on the Sokobanja municipality's official website:

- "Program of Tourism Development of the Municipality of Sokobanja for the period 2023-2027" (shortened "Program of Tourism Development") was created on the initiative and with the support of the Touristic Organization of Sokobanja (TOS), adopted by the Government of the Republic of Serbia in September 2022;

- "Program of Sustainable Development of Winter Tourism in Sokobanja (Serbia) – Varshetz (Bulgaria) for the period 2020-2029" (shortened "Program of Sustainable Development of Winter Tourism"). The document is a delivery of the Interreg - IPA CBC Bulgaria – Serbia project financed by the European Commission;
- "Strategy of Sustainable Development of Sokobanja Municipality for the period 2015-2025" (shortened "Sustainable Development Strategy". The document is a general strategic development plan which provides guidelines and incentives for the future development of the local community and a roadmap for reaching the set goal-vision for both local self-government decision-makers and all public figures and the local community. The strategy is focused on sustainable socio-economic development through the harmonized improvement of the three primary development segments: economy, society and protection and improvement of the environment;
- "Local Plan for Waste Management in Sokobanja Municipality for the period 2022-2032" (shortened "Local Plan") adopted in early 2022. The plan is a comprehensive study of waste management's current and desired state with a detailed financial analysis and action plan; "Environmental Protection Program of the Municipality of Sokobanja for the period 2017-2021" (shortened "Environmental Protection Program");
- "Strategic Guidelines for Land Management as a Contribution Balanced Urban and Rural Development - Municipality of Sokobanja" (shortened "Strategic Guidelines") adopted in 2018;
- "Plan for the Management of Risks from Violation of the Principle of Gender Equality" (shortened "Plan for the Management of Risks") adopted in 2022. The document contains rules and guidelines regarding gender equality in the workplace, raising awareness of proper behavior, gender-sensitive language, etc.;
- "Statute of the Municipality of Sokobanja" (shortened "Statute") adopted in 2019;
- "Program for the use of funds for environmental protection on the territory of the Municipality of Sokobanja" adopted in 2021 and
- "Operational flood defense plan for watercourses II order for the territory of the municipality of Sokobanja for the year 2021".

Another source of qualitative data is transcripts of interviews conducted with a representative of the Tourist Organization of Sokobanja, and two experts engaged in the leading company for the development of public policies in the field of tourism in the Republic of Serbia - Horwath HTL, Belgrade.

FINDINGS

Destination Management

The Assembly is the most important governing and policymaking body in the municipality of Sokobanja. It performs the fundamental tasks of local government mandated by the Constitution, the law, and the municipal Statute (2019). In addition, it is responsible for the planning, coordination, and supervision of tourist development and tourism-related activities, as well as the implementation and adoption of the annual operational plan for the "Sustainable Development Strategy" (2014), while the Department for Economy and Local Economic Development is responsible for monitoring and evaluating the Strategy. The "Program of Tourism Development" (2022), whose implementation starts this year, demands the establishment of the Council for Tourism Sokobanja, which aims to formalize collaboration and communication mechanisms among all stakeholders, especially the corporate sector. Initiatives for sustainable development would be further encouraged through this process. "Program of Tourism Development" (2022) includes a tourism resource-attraction analysis which includes mountains, rivers and lakes, picnic areas, and cultural and historical heritage.

In the last five years, Sokobanja has considerably improved the strategic management of the municipality and the tourism sector. In support of this statement, numerous public policies were adopted and have already been listed above. The most important is the "Program of Tourism Development" (2022) for tourism development. It is a comprehensive document containing part of political, economic, societal and tourism market analysis, detailed guidance for strategic government, but also investment and competitive plans, together with a detailed action plan with activities and an estimated budget. The Strategy is up-to-date, and its implementation started in 2023.

Sokobanja does not have a mechanism to manage visitor pressure. However, this issue is recognized in the "Program of Tourism Development" (2022), as it states that Sokobanja is visited by a substantial number of tourists and visitors during the high season. However, due to a poor management system, there are often too many visitors, which degrades the quality of the traveler's experience. It implies that it is necessary to create a model that will enhance the handling of Sokobanja visitor flow, so two steps should be considered. First step is finding a drop-off and pick-up zone for guest buses within the very center and at numerous significant tourist points, where space will be prepared and permit a brief stay of the bus to accommodate the needs of visitors disembarking and boarding. The second step includes finding a spot for a more extended parking area outside the center, where supervised vehicle parking will be possible, and, with adequate infrastructural support - electric minibuses that would transport tourists to defined tourist spots, possibly enabling the rental of bicycles and electric bicycles. It also includes arranging sanitary facilities, covered areas (protection from rain and sun) and the like. Designing a Park & Ride system for tourists is an additional long-term component that can be achieved in 5-10 years, where the idea is to connect the center of the municipality with parking and other points through an innovative and environmentally sustainable way (bike sharing, e-bus, etc.) of interest to tourists and visitors.

Areas for improvement: establishment of a mechanism to manage visitor pressure and control visitors' behavior at sensitive sites.

Nature and Scenery

In recent years, there has been a significant increase in awareness regarding the protection of nature in Sokobanja, bearing in mind that it is one of the primary tourist resources of this spa, highly correlated with the slogan *"Green Heart of Serbia"*. The main document that concerns this subject is "Environmental Protection Program of the Municipality of Sokobanja for the period 2017-2021 ", but it is now outdated. The main goal for the authors of this policy document was to determine the state of the environment, define the most significant problems, establish goals and develop an action plan to achieve priority goals for five years. As an outcome, the local self-government environmental protection policy was created, which is harmonized with other sectoral policies at the local level, but also with the related policies at the national level. Currently, Sokobanja implements the following local regulations, adopted in 2021:

1) A decision on special compensation for the protection and improvement of the living environment in the territory of the municipality of Sokobanja and
2) A decision on the budget fund for environmental protection of the municipality of Sokobanja which provide a budget for activities related to nature protection.

The "Strategic Guidelines" (2018) also emphasize that municipality should actively participate in the procedures for the protection of natural assets and create mechanisms for the functional implementation of protection measures, including the promotion of the measures to interested parties and the general public, as well as the possibility of further sustainable development following the established protection measures. In addition, the "Program of Tourism Development" (2022) contains guidelines that imply environmental protection and its planned introduction into tourist exploitation. It emphasizes that management needs a system of environmental protection and its planned and controlled introduction into tourist exploitation.

Additionally, the "Strategic Guidelines" (2017) state that Sokobanja has no responsible public policy to control urbanization for landscape preservation. However, there is an awareness of the need to protect the rural area from uncontrolled construction. The goal of the document is to provide balanced development of the urban and rural areas of the municipality of Sokobanja by the specifics of the area and the long-term strategic goals of the destination, with particular reference to the preservation of agricultural land.

Areas for improvement: Sokobanja has to create a system for nature conservation, a mechanism to measure or assess the impact of tourism on nature and a policy for controlling urbanization.

Environment and Climate

The Department of Urban Planning, Local Economic Development and Environmental Protection of Sokobanja Municipality – Decision About Noise Protection Measures includes Acoustic zoning of the spaces of Sokobanja settlement and limiting values of noise indicators in open space by zone. Regarding light pollution, Sokobanja has no measures. However, considering it is a spa destination with a long tradition, there is no source of extended light sources that could harm nature or disrupt guests.

In Sokobanja, 95 percent of households are connected to the sewage network, but wastewater treatment is not carried out in rural areas. Also, technical and sanitary septic tanks are used to collect used water from the area of weekend and village settlements, which represent a risk for pollution of the reservoir and a limiting factor for the development of tourist activities.

Sokobanja also faces issues regarding solid waste collection, disposal, and reduction. The municipality government is aware of this, and as answered in early 2022, the "Local Plan for Waste Management in Sokobanja Municipality for the period 2022-2032" was adopted by the General Assembly. The document points to numerous shortcomings and contains strategic goals, required institutional changes, and financial analysis – costs and sources to improve the situation.

Waste separation and recycling is also a problematic area in Sokobanja. Only PET packaging is sporadically collected separately for recycling, and this issue is also thoroughly addressed by the goals within the "Local Plan for Waste Management".

The municipality also recognizes the significance of reducing transport gas emissions from travel. The main document is the "Air Quality Control Program in the Territory of the Municipality of Sokobanja in 2022", adopted in 2021. On the territory of the municipality of Sokobanja, the program creates a local network of monitoring stations for assessing air pollution levels. It includes the measurement of pollutants in the air and the measurement of allergenic pollen in the air. "Program of Tourism Development" provides measures that will add support to this issue, such as the Development of ecological mobility options (soft mobility for a "car-free" destination).

The municipality started to raise awareness about climate risks. One of the first steps toward responding to this issue is an "Operational Flood Defence Plan for Watercourses II Order for the Territory of the Municipality of Sokobanja for 2021".

Areas for improvement: Sokobanja should create a system for light pollution measurement and reduction if needed; establish an appropriate method for wastewater treatment in rural areas; develop infrastructure for waste collection, disposal, and reduction; promote renewable energy models, recycling and raise awareness about consequences of climate risks, apart from floods.

Culture and Tradition

The "Program for Tourism Development" (2022) finds that Sokobanja has many cultural and historical resources that can be valorized for tourism. However, they are not properly marked and do not provide an appropriate tourist interpretation. It also states the need for urban rehabilitation of the center of Sokobanja and its ambient harmony, which is needed to ensure the long-term overall image of an advanced spa destination whose identity and sophistication are woven into its overall space. Revitalization, restoration and valorization of cultural (material and immaterial), industrial and sacral heritage is a basis for developing the tourist products of cultural tourism. The primary step in the touristic valorization of all localities is their preservation, which safeguards their historical significance and enhances their allure and reputation.

Additionally, it is necessary to categorize the identified localities, identify the cultural and tourist offer and communicate in an organized, standard way. Finally, the valorization of all sites must communicate the core values and appropriate stories associated with the sites to attract visitors' attention. Digital interpretation and visitor participation in the experience consumption at each place constitute the recommended option. As an additional activity/clarification of the previous initiative, the key elements of the concept interpretation of cultural-historical heritage are given separately. It also suggests using Augmented Reality and Virtual Reality technologies, especially in the case of cultural and natural thematic routes (Kovačević et al., 2021).

Sokobanja cherishes its intangible heritage, such as cultural heritage, including local traditions, arts, music, language, and gastronomy, mainly through traditional annual manifestations and events. Also, it is important to mention one of the first initiatives to protect the geographical origin of bee products – Public competition for honey.

Areas for improvement: to start a process of cultural and historical heritage revitalization, restoration and tourism valorization and to introduce a system for impact assessment.

Social Wellbeing

The Municipality of Sokobanja started tackling issues regarding human rights by adopting the "Local action plan for the promotion of gender equality in the municipality of Sokobanja for the period 2021-2024" (2021). Unfortunately, the Republic of Serbia has faced exceptional resistance from many citizens toward LGBT+ and other minorities. In contrast, other topics, such as trafficking, modern slavery and discrimination, are regulated by laws at the national level.

Community involvement in planning is deeply rooted in all decisions regarding Sokobanja. Citizens and stakeholders are involved in all public decisions and are publicly available on the Municipalities web site (https://sokobanja.ls.gov.rs/). The "Program for Tourism Development" (2022) also emphasizes that it is crucial to seek the active participation of the inhabitants of the municipality regarding the development of the tourist offer, especially in making decisions that will significantly affect their quality of life. The process ensures the local community's satisfaction and guides the tourist offer's development, following their expectations to the greatest extent possible.

The promotion of local products in Sokobanja is not systematically organized but done through fairs and events or a sales network based on the private sector's initiative. Unfortunately, there is no systematic effort to support local entrepreneurs, only some initiatives organized by the Touristic Organization of Sokobanja. Also, the destination does not have standards, laws or policies to optimize the socio-economic effects of real estate development and operations, including tourism-related real estate rentals and concessions. Concerning health and safety, Sokobanja has the "Security Council of the Municipality of Sokobanja", formed in April 2021.

Areas for improvement: raising awareness and introducing policies regarding human rights; system for the systematic support of local entrepreneurs and laws or policies to optimize the socio-economic effects of real estate development and operations, including tourism-related real estate rentals and concessions.

Business and Communication

Analysis of the state in this area in Sokobanja shows a lack of systematized promotion of sustainable business among entrepreneurs. Furthermore, Sokobanja does not yet actively push sustainability standards, but there is a principled commitment to this business model.

Table 2. Assessment of green destination criteria fulfillment in the case of Sokobanja Spa

Type	Criteria title	Alignment
Theme 1. - Destination Management		
Commitment & Organisation		
C15	1.1 Sustainable destination coordinator	2
C15	1.5 Inventory of destination assets	1
C15	1.7 Destination Management Policy or Strategy	1
Visitor Management		
C30	1.12 Managing visitor pressure	3+
C30	1.14 Visitor behaviour at sensitive sites	3+
Theme 2: Nature & Scenery		
Nature & Conservation		
C30	2.1 Nature conservation	2
C15	2.2 Tourism impacts on nature	3+
C15	2.5 Landscape & Scenery	2
C30	2.8 Captive animal welfare	3+
Theme 3: Environment & Climate		
Land Use & Pollution		
C30	3.1 Noise	1
C30	3.2 Light pollution	3
Water Management		
C30	3.7 Wastewater treatment	2+
Waster and Recycle		
C15	3.8 Solid waste reduction	2+
C30	3.9 Waste separation & recycling	2+
Energy, Sustainable Mobility & Climate Change		
C15	3.13 Reducing transport emissions from travel	2+
C15	3.16 Reducing energy consumption	3+
C30	3.17 Renewable Energy	3
Climate Change Adaptation		
C30	3.19 Responding to climate risks	3+
Theme 4: Culture & Tradition		
Cultural Heritage		
C15	4.1 Tangible cultural heritage	2+
C30	4.2 Managing tourism impacts on culture	3

continued on following page

Table 2. continued

Type	Criteria title	Alignment
People & Tradition		
C15	4.4 Intangible heritage	2+
Theme 5: Social Wellbeing		
Human Respect		
C30	5.4 Human rights	3+
Community Participation		
C15	5.7 Community involvement in planning	1
C30	5.10 Inhabitant satisfaction	3+
Local Economy		
C15	5.12 Supporting local entrepreneurs	3+
C15	5.13 Promoting local products and services	3+
Socio-economic Impact		
C30	5.16 Property exploitation	3
Health & Safety		
C15	5.17 Health & Safety	2
Theme 6: Business & Communication		
Business Involvement		
C15	6.1 Promoting sustainability among enterprises	3
C30	6.2 Sustainability standards	3

Note: 1 – Fully aligned, 2 – Partly aligned, 3 – Not-aligned and sign + implies the areas where activities are anticipated within the framework of public policies.

Source: Authors

Based on the analysis of public policies and information received from the respondents, an evaluation of the individual criteria of the Green Destinations Standard was performed. The acquired results are presented in Table 2.

DISCUSSION AND CONCLUSION

Encouragement of sustainable business activities is a topic of substantial academic and practical interest. Literature exposes various challenges applicable to sustainable certification programs, with marketing incentives frequently serving as a primary motivation. Factors in operating a sustainable destination include financial savings potential and the role of personal moral duty as a motivation, but also considerable costs, which could be highly challenging for emerging countries. The Sokobanja Spa case study demonstrated the situation quite clearly. Table 1 comprises evaluations of Green Destination Criteria fulfillment. Based on these evaluations, it is possible to conclude that Sokobanja Spa is far from receiving the Green Destination Certificate. The destination has only five areas fully aligned with criteria and eight partly aligned, while most criteria (17) are not aligned, the result can be considered exceedingly undesirable. However, the analysis showed that there is a very high awareness and a clearly directed effort towards reaching the green standard in the medium term, which is indicated by numerous measures and activities foreseen in the local strategic and planning documentation, as well as decisions on the formation of appropriate bodies in charge of certain aspects of sustainable tourism. Despite the optimistic outcomes, it is equally important to consider the phenomena that can impede advancement. The process of Serbia's entrance to the European Union requires the harmonization of laws and regulations. In this context, the national government of Serbia is establishing a new framework that local governments must implement. However, this does not necessarily imply that an implementation control mechanism has been formed for these policies, indicating the possibility that they were adopted simply as a formal response to a national-level request.

The case study of Sokobanja Spa points to the fact that, even for a well-established destination with a rich history, it is extremely difficult to provide all the necessary conditions for certification, even at the basic level. The most sensitive area is an infrastructure for wastewater treatment, waste reduction and energy consumption due to the high costs of construction, modernization, and maintenance. Another challenge is raising the local government's and citizens' understanding of climate hazards, human rights, and sustainable business practices in the private sector. Despite that, the experiences of several regional destinations indicate that this goal is achievable. "Mali Lošinj" in Croatia achieved the "Green Destination Silver Award", while destination "Tivat" in Montenegro achieved the "Green Destination Bronze Award" in 2022. These destinations are on the Adriatic Sea coast and have a high tourism turnover. Also, the destination "Trebinje" in Bosnia and Herzegovina achieved "2022 Top 100 Destinations Sustainability Stories". Unfortunately, small European countries lack certifications besides Slovenia with the national-established Green Destination Award.

Indirectly, the results can reveal the correlation between general social and economic growth and the potential to meet the criteria for sustainable destinations. More developed and wealthier societies have more significant financial resources for developing infrastructure and supporting elements that ensure sustainability and green consumerism. A similar relationship could be found at the level of destinations. Funding for projects focused on sustainable development is easier to acquire in more developed destinations. Therefore, additional case studies across many levels – nations, regions, towns, and resorts – would be a useful comparative tool for gaining a deeper insight into the concept, anatomy, and consequences of constructing and defending green objectives.

ACKNOWLEDGMENT

The research presented in this paper was funded by the Ministry of Science, Technological Development and Innovation of the Republic of Serbia: 451-03-47/2023-01/200005. We also thank the Tourism Organization of Sokobanja and Horwath HTL, Belgrade, for supporting us.

REFERENCES

Adlwarth, W. (2010). Corporate social responsibility–customer expectations and behaviour in the tourism sector. In R. Conrady & M. Buck (Eds.), *Trends and Issues in Global Tourism 2010* (pp. 101–109). Springer. doi:10.1007/978-3-642-10829-7_13

Archer, B., Cooper, C., & Ruhanen, L. (2005). The positive and negative impacts of tourism. In W. F. Theobald (Ed.), *Global tourism* (pp. 79–102). Elsevier. doi:10.1016/B978-0-7506-7789-9.50011-X

Beall, J. M., Boley, B. B., Landon, A. C., & Woosnam, K. M. (2021). What drives ecotourism: Environmental values or symbolic conspicuous consumption? *Journal of Sustainable Tourism*, *29*(8), 1215–1234. doi:10.1080/09669582.2020.1825458

Bhaskaran, S., Polonsky, M., Cary, J., & Fernandez, S. (2006). Environmentally sustainable food production and marketing. *British Food Journal*, *108*(8), 677–690. doi:10.1108/00070700610682355

Bradić-Martinović, A. (2021). Tourism 4.0: Data-Driven Covid-19 Recovery. Innovative Aspects of the Development Service and Tourism. In *Proceedings of IX International scientific-practical conference*. Stavropol State Agrarian University, Faculty of Social and Cultural Service and Tourism.

Butler, R. (1999). Sustainable tourism: A state-of-the-art review. *Tourism Geographies*, *1*(1), 7–25. doi:10.1080/14616689908721291

Chan, T. (2021). *Attitudes and Perception of Destination Certification Towards Sustainable Tourism Development* [Master Thesis, School of Tourism and Maritime Technology of Polytechnic of Leiria]. ProQuest Dissertations and Theses database.

Crossley, J., & Lee, B. (1994). Characteristics of Ecotourists and Mass Tourists. *Visions in Leisure and Business, 13*(2).

Deng, J., & Li, J. (2015). Self-identification of ecotourists. *Journal of Sustainable Tourism, 23*(2), 255–279. doi:10.1080/09669582.2014.934374

Dimoska, T., & Petrevska, B. (2012). Indicators for sustainable tourism development in Macedonia. In *Proceedings of the First International Conference on Business, Economics and Finance "From Liberalization to Globalization: Challenges in the Changing World"*. Faculty of Economics Goce Delcev University.

Dodds, R., & Joppe, M. (2005). *CSR in the tourism industry? The status of and potential for certification, codes of conduct and guidelines*. IFC World Bank.

Đukić, M., Jovanoski, I., Munitlak Ivanović, O., Lazić, M., & Bodroža, D. (2016). Cost-benefit analysis of an infrastructure project and a cost-reflective tariff: A case study for investment in wastewater treatment plant in Serbia. *Renewable & Sustainable Energy Reviews, 59*, 1419–1425. doi:10.1016/j.rser.2016.01.050

EarthCheck. (n.d.). *EarthCheck Sustainable Destinations*. Earthcheck. https://earthcheck.org/what-we-do/certification/sustainable-destinations/

European Commission. (2016). *The European Tourism Indicator System ETIS toolkit for sustainable destination management*. EC. https://ec.europa.eu/docsroom/documents/21749

European Travel Commission. (2021). *Sustainable tourism implementation. A framework and toolkit to support national approaches*. ETC. https://etc-corporate.org/uploads/2021/03/ETC-HANDBOOK-FINAL.pdf

Flyvbjerg, B. (2006). Five Misunderstandings About Case-Study Research. *Qualitative Inquiry, 12*(2), 219–245. doi:10.1177/1077800405284363

Font, X., & Harris, C. (2004). Rethinking standards from green to sustainable. *Annals of Tourism Research, 31*(4), 986–1007. doi:10.1016/j.annals.2004.04.001

Giampiccoli, A., Mtapuri, O., & Dluzewska, A. (2020). Investigating the intersection between sustainable tourism and community-based tourism. *Tourism (Zagreb), 68*(4), 415–433. doi:10.37741/t.68.4.4

Gkoumas, A. (2019). Evaluating a standard for sustainable tourism through the lenses of local industry. *Heliyon, 5*(11), e02707. doi:10.1016/j.heliyon.2019.e02707 PMID:31840122

Global Sustainable Tourism Council. (2019). *GSTC Destination Criteria Version 2.0.* GST Council. https://www.gstcouncil.org/wp-content/uploads/GSTC-Destination-Criteria-v2.0.pdf

Global Sustainable Tourism Council. (n.d.a.). *GSTC Destination Criteria.* GST Council. https://www.gstcouncil.org/gstc-criteria/gstc-destination-criteria/

Global Sustainable Tourism Council. (n.d.b.). *Certified Sustainable Destinations.* GST council. https://www.gstcouncil.org/certified-sustainable-destinations/

Green Destinations. (2021). *Green Destination Standard V2.* Green Destinations. https://tempo.greendestinations.org/wp-content/uploads/2022/11/GD-Standard-V2-2021-GSTC-Recognised.pdf

Green Destinations. (n.d.). *About the Green Destinations Awards & Certification Program.* Green Destinations. https://www.greendestinations.org/awards-certification/

Green Policy Platform. (n.d.). *Tourism.* Green Growth Knowledge. https://www.greengrowthknowledge.org/sectors/tourism

Gwenhure, Y., & Odhiambo, N. M. (2017). Tourism and economic growth: A review of international literature. *Tourism (Zagreb), 65*(1), 33–44.

Harvard Business Review. (2019). The Elusive Green Consumer. *Harvard Business Review.* https://hbr.org/2019/07/the-elusive-green-consumer

Honey, M., Rome, A., Russillo, A., & Bien, A. (2007). *Practical Steps for Marketing Tourism Certification. Handbook 3.* Inter-American Development Bank. https://publications.iadb.org/en/practical-steps-marketing-tourism-certification

International Federation of Red Cross and Red Crescent Societies. (n.d.). *Disasters, climate, and crises.* IFRC. https://www.ifrc.org/our-work/disasters-climate-and-crises

Ivanović, Đ., & Antonijević, M. (2020). The Role of Online Shopping in the Republic of Serbia During Covid-19. *Economic Analysis, 53*(1), 28–41.

Jaafar, M., & Maideen, S. A. (2012). Ecotourism-related products and activities, and the economic sustainability of small and medium island chalets. *Tourism Management, 33*(3), 683–691. doi:10.1016/j.tourman.2011.07.011

Jamrozy, U., & Lawonk, K. (2017). The multiple dimensions of consumption values in ecotourism. *International Journal of Culture, Tourism and Hospitality Research, 11*(1), 18–34. doi:10.1108/IJCTHR-09-2015-0114

Kaličanin, T., & Lazić, M. (2018). Evaluating the Level of Market Concentration in Insurance Sector: the case of Serbia. In Western Balkans Economies in EU Integration: past, present and future. CEMAFI International.

Kim, K. H., & Park, D. B. (2017). Relationships Among Perceived Value, Satisfaction, and Loyalty: Community-Based Ecotourism in Korea. *Journal of Travel & Tourism Marketing, 34*(2), 171–191. doi:10.1080/10548408.2016.1156609

Kovačević, I., Bradić-Martinović, A., & Petković, G. (2021). Covid-19 impact on cultural and natural Pan-European thematic routes. *Ekonomika preduzeća, 69*(5-6), 357-368.

Lazić, M., & Antonijević, M. (2021). The Overview of ECB's and NBS' COVID-19 Containment Measures. In *Macroeconomic stability and improvement of the Western Balkans countries' competitiveness*. Institute of Economic Sciences.

Lazić, M., & Bradić-Martinović, A. (2022a). Analysis of Tourism Demand in Selected WB6 Countries during the COVID-19 Pandemic. In The 6th International Thematic Monograph: Modern Management Tools and Economy of Tourism Sector in Present Era. Association of Economists and Managers of the Balkans - UDEKOM Balkans.

Lazić, M., & Bradić-Martinović, A. (2022b). Analysis of the Impact of the COVID-19 Pandemic on Tourism Demand in the Republic of Serbia – Challenges and Opportunities. In *Proceedings of the National conference with international participation "Challenges and perspective in marketing" - SEMA*. Serbian Marketing Society – SEMA.

Liao, Y.-K., Wu, W.-Y., & Pham, T.-T. (2020). Examining the Moderating Effects of Green Marketing and Green Psychological Benefits on Customers' Green Attitude, Value and Purchase Intention. *Sustainability (Basel), 12*(18), 7461. Advance online publication. doi:10.3390u12187461

Lončar, D., Đorđević, A., Lazić, M., Milošević, S., & Rajić, V. (2016). Interplay Between Market Concentration and Competitive Dynamics in The Banking Sector. *Ekonomika preduzeća, 44*(5/6), 332-346.

Marcuta, L., Popescu, A., Marcuta, A., Tindeche, C., & Smedescu, D. (2021). The impact of the COVID-19 crisis on tourism and its recover possibilities. *Scientific Papers. Series Management, Economic, Engineering in Agriculture and Rural Development, 21*(1), 495–500.

McKinsey. (2022). *Resilience for sustainable, inclusive growth*. https://www.mckinsey.com/capabilities/risk-and-resilience/our-insights/resilience-for-sustainable-inclusive-growth

Mihailović, B., Radić Jean, I., Popović, V., Radosavljević, K., Chroneos Krasavac, B., & Bradić-Martinović, A. (2020). Farm Differentiation Strategies and Sustainable Regional Development. *Sustainability (Basel)*, *12*(17), 1–18. doi:10.3390u12177223

Moreno-Luna, L., Robina-Ramirez, R., Sanchez-Oro Sanchez, M., & Castro-Serrano, J. (2021). Tourism and Sustainability in Times of COVID-19: The Case of Spain. *International Journal of Environmental Research and Public Health*, *18*(4), 1–21. doi:10.3390/ijerph18041859 PMID:33672912

Municipality of Sokobanja. (2015) *Strategy of Sustainable Development of Sokobanja Municipality for the period 2015-202.*. Municipality of Sokobanja.

Municipality of Sokobanja. (2016). *Program of Sustainable Development of Winter Tourism in Sokobanja (Serbia) – Varshetz (Bulgaria) for the period 2020-2029*. Municipality of Sokobanja.

Municipality of Sokobanja. (2016). *Environmental Protection Program of the Municipality of Sokobanja for the period 2017-2021*. Municipality of Sokobanja.

Municipality of Sokobanja. (2018). *Strategic Guidelines for Land Management as a Contribution Balanced Urban and Rural Development - Municipality of Sokobanja*. Municipality of Sokobanja.

Municipality of Sokobanja. (2019). *Statute of the Municipality of Sokobanja*. Municipality of Sokobanja.

Municipality of Sokobanja. (2021). *Operational flood defence plan for watercourses II order for the territory of the municipality of Sokobanja for the year 2021*. Municipality of Sokobanja.

Municipality of Sokobanja. (2021). *Program for the use of funds for environmental protection on the territory of the Municipality of Sokobanja*. Municipality of Sokobanja.

Municipality of Sokobanja. (2021). *Local action plan for the promotion of gender equality in the municipality of Sokobanja for the period 2021-2024*. Municipality of Sokobanja. https://sokobanja.ls.gov.rs/

Municipality of Sokobanja. (2022). *Local Plan for Waste Management in Sokobanja Municipality for the period 2022-2032*. Municipality of Sokobanja.

Municipality of Sokobanja. (2022). *Plan for the Management of Risks from Violation of the Principle of Gender Equality*. Municipality of Sokobanja.

Municipality of Sokobanja and Tourism Organization of Sokobanja. (2022). *Program of Tourism Development of the Municipality of Sokobanja for the period 2023-2027*. Municipality of Sokobanja.

Nielsen IQ. (2018). *Sustainability sells: Linking sustainability claims to sales*. Neilsen IQ. https://nielseniq.com/global/en/insights/report/2018/sustainability-sells-linking-sustainability-claims-to-sales/

Opute, A. P., Irene, B. O., & Iwu, C. G. (2020). Tourism Service and Digital Technologies: A Value Creation Perspective. *African Journal of Hospitality, Tourism and Leisure*, *9*(2), 1–18.

Organization of American States. (n.d.). *Annex 2. Tourism as an economic development tool*. OAS. http://www.oas.org/dsd/publications/unit/oea78e/ch10.htm

Petković, G., Pindžo, R., & Bradić-Martinović, A. (2022). Competitiveness Factors of Serbian Tourism. *Ekonomika preduzeća, 70*(1-2), 113-127.

Pizam, A. (2009). Green hotels: A fad, ploy or fact of life. *International Journal of Hospitality Management*, *28*(1), 1. doi:10.1016/j.ijhm.2008.09.001

Plüss, C., Zotz, A., Monshausen, A., & Kühhas, C. (2012). *Sustainablitiy in Toursm – A Guide Through the Label Jungle*. Naturefriends International.

Prideaux, B., Thompson, M., & Pabel, A. (2020). Lessons from COVID-19 can prepare global tourism for the economic transformation needed to combat climate change. *Tourism Geographies*, *22*(3), 667–678. doi:10.1080/14616688.2020.1762117

Rasool, H., Maqbool, S., & Tarique, M. (2021). The relationship between tourism and economic growth among BRICS countries: A panel cointegration analysis. *Future Business Journal*, *7*(1), 1–11. doi:10.118643093-020-00048-3

Rivera, J., & deLeon, P. (2005). Chief executive officers and voluntary environmental performance: Costa Rica's certification for sustainable tourism. *Policy Sciences*, *38*(2-3), 107–127. doi:10.100711077-005-6590-x

Statistical Office of the Republic of Serbia. (2022). Statistical Yearbook 2022. SORS. https://www.stat.gov.rs/en-us/publikacije/publication/?p=14853

Stronza, A. L., Hunt, C. A., & Fitzgerald, L. A. (2019). *Ecotourism for Conservation?*. *Annual Review of Environment and Resources*. Annual Reviews Inc. https://doi.org/doi:10.1146/annurev-environ-101718-033046

Tang, Ch., Han, Y., & Ng, P. (2022). Green consumption intention and behavior of tourists in urban and rural destinations. *Journal of Environmental Planning and Management*, 1–25. doi:10.1080/09640568.2022.2061927

The World Counts. (n.d.). *Global Challenges*. The World Counts. https://www. theworldcounts.com/challenges/consumption/transport-and-tourism/negative-environmental-impacts-of-tourism

Tourism Organization of Sokobanja. (2019). *Program of Sustainable Development of Winter Tourism in Sokobanja (Serbia) – Varshetz (Bulgaria) for the period 2020-2029*. TOS.

Tzschentke, N., Kirk, D., & Lynch, P. A. (2007). Going green: Decisional factors in small hospitality operations. *International Journal of Hospitality Management*, *27*(1), 126–133. doi:10.1016/j.ijhm.2007.07.010

Weaver, D. B., & Lawton, L. J. (2007). Twenty years on: The state of contemporary ecotourism research. *Tourism Management*, *28*(5), 1168–1179. doi:10.1016/j. tourman.2007.03.004

Weeden, C. (2002). Ethical tourism: An opportunity for competitive advantage? *Journal of Vacation Marketing*, *8*(2), 141–153. doi:10.1177/135676670200800204

World Bank. (2021). *Tcdata360, 2021*. World Bank. https://databank.worldbank. org/home.aspx

World Tourism Organization. (2021a). *2020: Worst year in tourism history with 1 billion fewer international arrivals*. WTO. https://www.unwto.org/news/2020-worst-year-in-tourism-history-with-1-billion-fewer-international-arrivals

World Tourism Organization. (2021b). *Tourism and Covid-19 – Unprecedented Economic Impacts*. WTO. https://www.unwto.org/tourism-and-covid-19-unprecedented-economic-impacts

World Tourism Organization. (2022a). *UNWTO Tourism Education Guidelines*. World Tourism Organization.

World Tourism Organization. (2022b). *Measuring the sustainability of tourism learning from pilots*. WTO. https://webunwto.s3.eu-west-1.amazonaws.com/s3fs-public/2023-01/MST_pilots_learning.pdf

World Tourism Organization. (2022c). *Tourism Statistics Data: Economic Contribution of Tourism and Beyond*. WTO. https://www.unwto.org/statistic-data-economic-contribution-of-tourism-and-beyond

World Tourism Organization. (n.d.a.). *Tourism – an economic and social phenomenon.* WTO. https://www.unwto.org/why-tourism

World Tourism Organization. (n.d.b.). *Tourism in the 2030 agenda.* https://www. unwto.org/tourism-in-2030-agenda

World Tourism Organization. (n.d.c.). *On measuring the sustainability of tourism: MST.* WTO. https://www.unwto.org/tourism-statistics/measuring-sustainability-tourism

World Travel & Tourism Council. (2021). *Travel & Tourism Economic Impact 2021: Global Economic Impacts and Trends 2021.* WTTC. https://wttc.org/Portals/0/ Documents/Reports/2021/Global%20Economic%20Impact%20and%20Trends%20 2021.pdf

World Travel & Tourism Council. (2022). *Travel & Tourism Economic Impact 2022: Global Trends.* WTTC. https://wttc.org/Portals/0/Documents/Reports/2022/ EIR2022-Global%20Trends.pdf

Yfantidou, G., & Matarazzo, M. (2016). The Future of Sustainable Tourism in Developing Countries. *Sustainable Development (Bradford), 25*(6), 459–466. doi:10.1002d.1655

Chapter 8

Unveiling the Impact of Green Marketing Tools on the Consumer Purchasing Behavior of Cosmetic Products:
Evidence From the University of Cape Coast

Dominic Owusu
https://orcid.org/0000-0002-1749-6538
University of Cape Coast, Ghana

Micheal Shant Osei
University of Cape Coast, Ghana

F. O. Boachie-Mensah
University of Cape Coast, Ghana

Alfred Ghartey
University of Cape Coast, Ghana

Rebecca Dei Mensah
University of Cape Coast, Ghana

ABSTRACT

Body and beauty care are considered essential in everyday life of a young adult. This has attracted the attention of the cosmetic industry to respond with products that serve these varying interests. Not only are the youth interested in using cosmetic products, but they also consider the greenness of the cosmetic products. This has

DOI: 10.4018/978-1-6684-8140-0.ch008

forced the corporate world to churn out products that are considered safe for the environment and also engage in practices that are considered green. Drawing on the theory of planned behavior, the chapter assesses how students' exposure to green marketing practices influences their purchase of cosmetic products over time. The chapter uses eco-label, eco-brand, and environmental advertising as predictors of students' purchasing behaviour of cosmetic products. Further, PLS-SEM is used to examine the effect of green marketing tools on students' purchasing decisions. The study's findings suggest that eco-label and environmental advertising influence the purchase of cosmetic products. Implications of the findings are discussed.

1. INTRODUCTION

Body and beauty care are considered key in the everyday life of a young adult. Whereas some want to establish identity and self-esteem, ward off body odor and smell good to be accepted by their peers, others also think about their hair, nails, and the use of cosmetic products to prevent negative attention (Huber et al., 2018). They spend resources searching for various cosmetic products that make them smell good, have nice nails and polished hair, and have good skin. These reasons have attracted several cosmetic companies to provide products that serve these varying interests of the youth. The youth also consider their safety and the environment as paramount in their quest to care for their beauty and body (Pardana et al., 2019). This has exerted considerable pressure on companies within the cosmetic industry to churn out products that are considered safe for the environment (Wear et al., 2018). This is supported by the multiplicity of studies suggesting that consumers prefer eco-friendly products and react positively towards organizations that are perceived to be green (Pardana et al., 2019). However, Govender and Govender (2016) are of the view that the focus of developing countries on green marketing has been on awareness creation and knowledge, trust, and concerns towards environmental degradation rather than on changing the behavior of consumers towards green products.

Ghana's contribution to the growth of the cosmetic industry remains significant. The World Health Organization has projected Ghana as one of the countries to look out for in the cosmetic business. This is partly attributed to the rise in skin-bleaching products largely amongst women in Ghana. The Ghana Health Service in 2005 indicated that nearly 30% and 5% of Ghanaian women and men are engaged in bleaching. It further accentuated that 50 – 60% of Ghanaian adult women are currently involved in bleaching or have engaged in bleaching before (*Ghanaweb*, 2016). This has attracted several local businesses to source for products deemed to be environmentally safe. For example, Forever Clair Beauty Clinic and its product have received considerable attention among customers of cosmetic products (*Taking a Good Look at the Beauty Industry*, 2021)). The company relies on raw materials such as alfalfa powder, barley grass powder, and wheatgrass powder. It uses the environmental benefits of these raw materials to differentiate its cosmetic products from others. In 2013, however, cosmetic companies in Ghana were believed to have contributed to driving customers toward sustainability (Bempong, 2017). Unilever Ghana Limited is engaged in fast-moving consumer goods (FMCG), which are among the companies that have been campaigning for green marketing in Ghana. Unilever products such as Dove, Knorr, and Rexona are examples of sustainable living brands that have contributed significantly to the company's growth (Unilever PLC Annual Report, 2019). The company uses labels of green certification agencies that signify how safe their products are as part of their labeling. Lifebuoy soap, one of the green products of Unilever, has reached over a billion people with its handwashing campaign. They rely on handwashing as the key content of their promotional message to preach environmental sustainability and the need for people to continue to wash their hands. Another example is L'Oreal which includes the label fair trade as part of its labels.

However, as accentuated in the study of Bempong (2017), green marketing focusing on the cosmetic industry remains a grey area that requires more research attention. Similarly, Adinyira and Gligui (2011) indicated that the concept of green marketing is at the development stage, which involves the expansion of literature and theory. Further, the impact of climate change resulting in changing weather patterns has also contributed to the need for firms to engage in green marketing. These changing conditions have implications for the health of consumers. This has contributed to the growing need for consumers to demand products that are considered green. However, businesses need to know the extent of the impact of green marketing on purchasing behavior to position themselves well to take advantage of the growing needs of consumers who prefer green products, hence the need for scientific studies to provide businesses with such answers. This chapter, therefore, assesses how students' exposure to green marketing practices influences their purchase of cosmetic products.

This will therefore help companies who are into green marketing or about to practice green marketing an opportunity to assess its influence on consumer purchasing behavior and determine the opportunities the business can take advantage of.

2. THEORETICAL FRAMEWORK

The Theory of Planned Behavior (TPB) underpins the study. This theory predicts how some factors influence consumer purchase behavior. This theory is further explained subsequently.

2.1 The Theory of Planned Behavior

The TPB is used to explain consumer behavior (Stern, 2000). The theory indicates that people's intention predicts a person's behavior (Ajzen, 2011). As people intend, they begin to gather the information that will enable them to fulfill their intention. They then compare the merits and demerits of several courses of action before selecting the option the consumer believes will help them address their intention (Ajzen, 2011). The theory indicates that for a consumer to make a choice that maximizes his or her benefits, the consumer must have all the needed information. This information is what the consumer uses to assess the cost and advantages of the options available to him or her. Ajzen (2011) posits three determinants explain behavioral intentions: attitude, subjective norm, and perceived behavioral control. The theory further indicates that demographic factors influence behavior through the three determinants of intention. However, it indicates that attitudes, subjective norms and perceived behavioral control are predictors of behavior as they explain behavior intention before behavior occurs.

The motivation for the individual to act in a particular manner is depended on the outcome to be achieved should the person act in that way, behavior exhibited by a person is not only dependent on perceptions that are considered true but also considers the views of others who are close or related and when people act based on the views and perceptions of others, intentions are formed which exhibits the behavior of such persons. The theory, therefore, implies that as people consider protecting the environment important, they are likely to make decisions supporting this intention. This, therefore, explains their behavior.

2.2 Green Marketing

Interest in green marketing continues to attract a lot of attention from companies and society in general. This results from the growing need to ensure our environment is safe. According to Ansar (2013), the key issue distinguishing green marketing from traditional marketing is the issue of environmental safety and the needs of consumers. The focus of marketers involved in green marketing has not only been on how to sell products considered safe but also on how to influence consumers to support and protect the environment. Leonidou et al. (2012) explain green marketing as a means to realize a firm's monetary and strategic goals while reducing the negative impact of a firm's activity on the environment. As such, the focus of firms has been on promoting products that are considered recyclable, ozone-friendly, environmentally friendly, and cruelty-free. However, what is expected in green marketing is the acknowledgment that the marketing efforts should result in acts that save or protect the environment. Kumar and Gangal (2011) sum it up by indicating that regardless of human wants and needs, actions taken to fulfill them should not result in the depletion of natural resources as these resources are limited in supply.

"The obvious assumption of green marketing is that potential consumers will view a product or services" and "greenness" as the reason for making the purchasing behavior (Saini, 2013). This has forced firms to indicate as part of their promotional message that their products are green when that is not the case. Such a practice is referred to as greenwashing. There has been an over-emphasis on promoting products that are considered green. However, issues such as reducing water usage, increasing energy efficiency, and reducing pollution are often ignored as being green. These should also be highlighted as it has been considered part of green marketing.

2.3 Green Marketing Tools

Rahbar et al. (2011) used eco-label, eco-brand, and environmental advertisement as a measure of green marketing. Similarly, Govender and Govender (2016) also identified these same elements as key drivers of perception and determinants of consumer behavior. Consumers are interested in products that are considered green. Such products are considered healthy, natural, of higher quality and help preserve the environment. Researchers suggest that consumers are even willing to pay more as they consider that the benefits of consuming a green product far outweigh the price (Abzari et al., 2013). These tools have weighty prominence in the purchasers' decision regarding products considered to be green.

2.3.1 Eco-Brand

When marketers use the environmental benefit as a basis for identifying and differentiating one's product from that of others, the act can be said to explain eco-brand. According to Rahbar et al. (2011), this will result in a positive reaction from the consumer. An example is the skin gourmet baobab sugar scrub which is considered an eco-brand because it uses materials that are considered natural and organic to distinguish it from other brands. Another example is Burt's Bees which creates cosmetic products that rely primarily on botanical oils, herbs, and beeswax and has a no-waste policy on manufacturing.

2.3.2 Eco-Labels

Eco-label differentiates the products whether these products are environmentally friendly or not. Delafrooz et al. (2014) highlight eco-labels as one of the key elements of green marketing as it contributes to green marketing by providing information and knowledge of the product. Products like L'Oreal, The Body Shop, and Estee

Lauder display fair trade marks on their products. Having the mark of fair trade on their product indicates that these cosmetic products have met the ethical standard of putting people's lives first and engaging in activities that are considered sustainable to the environment. This helps to provide consumers with information about the product's function and value.

2.3.3 Environmental Advertising

There is a growing demand for marketers to consider ways that are deemed to be environmentally friendly in promoting their products. This has resulted in using social media other than traditional means such as newspapers. According to Zinkhan and Carlson (1995), adverts are deemed green when they seek to promote sustainability, have eco-friendly content, and address the desires and wants of green consumers and other stakeholders. The use of fair trade in an advert to signify compliance with ethical systems and improving the lives of the ordinary in emerging economies is an example of an environmental advert.

2.4 Consumer Purchasing Behavior

Purchasing behavior studies have comprehensive coverage in the field of medicine, business, etc., and are mostly linked to human behavior. Kotler and Keller (2016) indicated that when humans decide on what, when, and whom, they are playing the role of the consumer. The authors indicate that purchasing behavior is simply the study of human behavior in the context of a consumer. Han and Kim (2010) also suggest that purchasing behavior studies go beyond just studying human behavior in the consumer context but include issues such as the approaches, intents, and choices made to justify and foretell behavior. Therefore, this suggests that purchasing behavior encompasses all the processes leading to the consumer deciding to buy or not. Marketers need to understand the context in which such decisions are made if they are to influence the process to favor their firms successfully. Studies have suggested that consumers' decision toward green marketing has increased (Han and Kim, 2010). According to Pickett-Baker and Ozaki (2008), the motivation for this surge can be attributed to the consumer's awareness of the need to protect the environment.

Mathur et al. (2007), were of the view that consumers were largely induced by green values and culture. It was further noticed that this is prevalent among Indian youth. This affirms that purchasing behavior is a process and that consumers are likely to be influenced if marketers can build value through green marketing. However, although awareness of green marketing has been low in Ghana, Braimah and Twnenboah-Kodua (2011) indicated that price influenced those who support green products.

2.5 Green Marketing Practices and Their Influence on Consumer Purchasing Behavior

This section focused on trends in research related to green marketing and consumer purchasing behavior. According to Ajzen (2011), the purchasing behavior theory explains an individual's character, depicting the end of a process. Therefore, purchasing a product considered green represents the end of a process. As found in the study of Adinyra and Gligui (2011), consumers' trust in a brand that is regarded as green results in purchasing that product. Lixandru (2017) explained that consumer purchases create an impression about the individual, which defines that individual's character. Daria and Sara (2011) accentuate that consumers are willing to sacrifice more to obtain a product perceived to be green. This supports the earlier assertion that once the consumer anticipates benefiting from patronizing a product, intentions are formed and will therefore be influenced to act in that regard to receive such benefits. Marketers are to reinforce the benefits derived from green products to influence the process leading to a decision. As explained in the study of Delafrooz et al. (2014), the authors asserted that the focus of marketers in recent times is how green marketing practices such as eco-labels, eco-brand, and environmental advertising influence consumers' buying behavior. This, therefore, stresses the need for more research work in the area to explain the extent of influence that green marketing exerts on consumers purchasing behavior.

Rashid (2009) posited that eco-labels positively affect consumers' intent to consider a green product as the labels are to explain how green their products are and are backed by certification. This view is supported by the study of Sung and Woo (2019), which posited that the levels of influence that eco-labels exert on consumers depend on how such a green marketing practice is perceived. The report further suggested that the acceptability of eco-labels is likely to influence consumer purchases. The influence of green products on consumers' purchasing behavior was affirmed in the report of Energy Star score for offices in the United States in 2019, indicating that a green product ranks the highest in influencing customers. A study by Nielsen Holdings (2014) also found that 55 per cent of consumers will offer more to receive services and goods considered harmless for the ecosystem and also observed to be publicly reliable. It further reveals that the acceptability of eco-brands ranks high in countries in Asia-Pacific, Latin America, and the Middle East. Additionally, they found that eco-labels were considered first before eco-brands.

Hilliard et al. (2012) posit that eco-advertising results in affirmative action toward the advertised green product. This presupposes that consumers would favor products that are promoted through green advertising. Similarly, Rahim et al. (2012) also believed that prior knowledge of green living develops a positive attitude toward environmental advertising. Drawing on the TPB, it is anticipated that when marketers use environmental benefits as the basis for differentiating their products, it is likely to raise the consumer's expectations to believe in the product. The belief is based on the expectation that the product if purchased, will benefit the consumer and contribute to protecting the environment. Once this belief is heightened through the use of eco-brand, eco-label, and environmental advertising, it has the potential to reduce the difficulty on the part of the consumer in deciding whether to buy or not. Once the difficulty is reduced, it will likely lead to positive action, resulting in a purchase decision. Hence, it is hypothesized that:

H_1: Green marketing positively influences consumer purchasing behavior.
H_2: Eco-label positively influences consumer purchasing behavior.
H_3: Eco-brand positively influences consumer purchasing behavior.
H_4: Environmental advertising positively influences consumer purchasing behavior.

3. RESEARCH MODEL

Figure 1 illustrates the research model. From the figure, green marketing and its dimensions of eco-label, eco-brand, and environmental advertising lead to a favorable˙ consumer outcome. The model proposes that consumers are likely to behave positively towards firms that are seen as using eco-brand, eco-label, and engaging in environmental advertising.

Figure 1. Research model

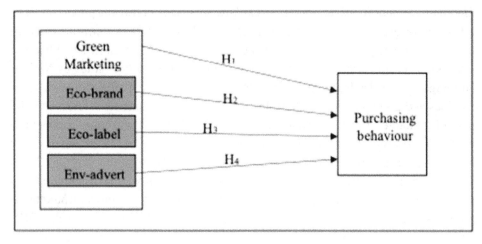

4. METHODOLOGY

4.1 Research Design

The descriptive research design was employed to gather quantitative cross-sectional data. The use of the descriptive design was to provide answers that sought to describe the relationship between the phenomenon being studied (Saunders et al., 2007).

4.2. Participants and Procedures

The focus of the study was to explain whether green marketing influenced the purchasing behavior of students using data from regular students of the University of Cape Coast who are deemed to be youth and understand the concept being investigated. The use of students was premised on the findings in the study of Husain (2018), who established that usage of cosmetic products among students was high. This, therefore, justified why the study focused on tertiary students. However, before undertaking the data collection, a pre-test was carried out at Cape Coast Technical University using fifty students, which assisted in revising the survey instrument in terms of wording and layout. The Student Records and Information Management of the University of Cape Coast, the university's section responsible for managing student records, posited that the total number of regular students at the time of data collection was estimated to be 18,699. This includes students from all four colleges in the university comprising the College of Humanities and Legal Studies, College of Health and Allied Sciences, College of Education Studies and College of Agriculture and Natural Sciences. In all, 377 students were selected using the convenient sampling technique from the four colleges to participate in the study. Data was collected over four weeks. A description of the sample distribution is presented in Table 1.

Table 1. Sample distribution

College	Male	Female	Total	ratio	Sample
College of Agriculture and Natural Sciences	2806	835	3641	0.195	73
College of Education Studies	2985	2196	5181	0.277	105
College of Health and Allied Sciences	1478	1103	2581	0.138	52
College of Humanities and Legal Studies	4199	3097	7296	0.390	147
Total	11468	7231	18699	377	60

4.3 Measures

Three constructs from the study of Magali et al. (2012) and Rahbar and Wahid (2011) formed the basis for using eco-brand, eco-label, and environmental advertising as the measure of green marketing. Five-scale items each were used to assess eco-brand and eco-label, and an eight-scale item was also used to assess environmental advertising. The composite reliability for the constructs was 0.863. Hill et al. (1977) scale on purchasing behavior was used to measure purchasing behavior. The purchasing behavior recorded a Cronbach score of 0.943. A Likert scale was used, ranging from 1-5, indicating strongly disagree to strongly agree.

4.4 Data Analysis

All questionnaires were numbered, allowing easy identification before entering the results in SPSS. Completed questionnaires collected were cross-checked for consistency to allow for the necessary corrections. The data were analyzed using PLS-SEM set to 5000. The validity of the data was checked using the Average Variance Extracted (AVE). Descriptive statistical tools such as frequencies and percentages were used to describe the demographic characteristics of respondents.

4.5 Ethical Consideration

An introductory letter from the Department of Marketing and Supply Chain Management requesting permission to engage students in lecture rooms and other study areas of the university was sought. Participants were also assured of confidentiality, and particulars such as name and address were not included in the instrument for data collection. Students were approached individually, and the purpose of the study was explained to them. Consent was also sought, after which the instrument was given to them to complete. The instrument was carefully framed to avoid ambiguity in the questionnaire.

5. RESULTS

5.1 Socio-Demographic Characteristics of Respondents

Participants' sex, age, and college they belong to, as well as the respondents' level, are discussed in this section of the chapter. Table 2 presents the characteristics of the respondents.

Table 2. Demographic characteristics of the respondents

Variable	Category	Frequency	Percentage
Sex Age College Level	Male	210	60
	Female	140	40
	Total	350	100
	Below 20	41	11.7
	20 – 29 years	298	85.1
	30 – 39 years	11	3.1
	Total	350	100
	Education	97	27.7
	Humanities	137	39.1
	Health and Allied	46	13.1
	Agriculture	70	20
	Total	350	100
	100	125	35.7
	200	85	24.3
	300	40	11.4
	400	100	28.6
	Total	350	100

Table 2 shows that most respondents were males representing 60%, and 40% were females. Most of the respondents (85.1%) were aged between 20 to 29 years, followed by 41 respondents who were below 20 years old, while (11) of the respondents were 30 years and above.

The distribution regarding the college in the university that the students were admitted to is as follows: 137 of the respondents representing 39.1% are from the College of Humanities and Legal Studies, 97 representing 27.7% from the College of Education Studies, and 46 representing 13.1% from the College of Health and Allied Sciences. A more significant number of respondents were in their first year of university education, followed by levels 400, 200, and 300 representing 35.7%, 28.6%, 24.3%, and 11.4%, respectively.

5.2 Effect of Green Marketing on Purchasing Behavior

The main purpose of the study was to determine whether green marketing influenced consumer behavior. First, the study assessed the composite effect of green marketing on consumer behavior. Secondly, the individual effect of green marketing tools on purchasing behavior was also assessed. Details of the outcome of the analysis are shown in the subsequent sections of this paper.

5.2.1 Assessment of Measurement Model

The measurement of the model's outer loadings, composite reliability, Average variance extracted, and discriminant validity was assessed (Hair et al., 2013). Table 3 revealed that all the modified measurement models recorded composite reliability and Average Variance Extracted figures above 0.7 and 0.5, respectively. As recommended by Hair et al. (2013), overall reliability and average variance extracted are acceptable if they are greater than 0.7 and 0.5, respectively.

Figure 2. Model one depicting the composite effect of green marketing on consumer behavior

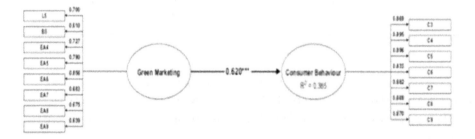

Table 3. Construct reliability

Construct	Dijkstra-Henseler's rho (ρ_A)	Jöreskog's rho (ρ_c)	Cronbach's alpha(α)	Average Variance Extracted (AVE)
Purchasing behavior	0.9163	0.9215	0.8990	0.6303
Green Marketing	0.8803	0.8908	0.8597	0.5077

Table 4. Discriminant Validity: Fornell-Larcker Criterion

Construct	Purchasing behavior	Green Marketing
Purchasing behavior	0.6303	
Green Marketing	0.3849	0.5077

Table 3 shows that the Cronbach's alpha values for all the items exceeded 0.7. It was also found that all the AVE values were within the acceptable threshold of 0.5, confirming convergent validity. Discriminant validity was assessed based on the Fornell-Lacker criterion. The correlations among the constructs were less than the square root of the AVE, indicating discriminant validity.

5.2.2 Structural Model

After the structural model was assessed, there was the need to test the hypothesized relationships proposed in the model. The analysis assessed the relationship between green marketing and consumer purchase behavior

Numbers within the circle shown in Figure 2 indicate how much variance of purchasing behavior is explained by green marketing. The coefficient of determination between green marketing and purchasing behavior compositely showed an R^2 of 0.385, indicating that green marketing explains 38.5% of the variance in consumer behavior. The weight on the path also recorded 0.620, signifying the high predictive value of green marketing on consumer purchasing behavior.

To confirm the significance of the path loading, bootstrapping was run using a two-tailed test with a 5% significance level. The path coefficient was significant as the T-statistics recorded 19.6380 and a significance level of 0.0000, as shown in Table 5. The effect size was also high as it recorded 0.6986, indicating that green marketing highly predicts consumer behavior.

The study assessed the effect of eco-brand, eco-label, and environmental advertising on consumer purchasing behavior. A second model was developed and assessed. The model's AVE and Composite Reliability recorded figures above 0.5. and 0.7, respectively, as presented in Table 6. This was within the threshold suggested by Hair et al. (2013). The Fornell-Lacker criterion also showed that there was an indication of discriminant validity (see Table 7)

The second model recorded an R^2 of 0.410, indicating that the three tools used in measuring green marketing explained 41.0% of the variation in consumer behavior.

Table 5. Direct effects inference

Effect	Original coefficient	Standard bootstrap results						f^2
		Mean value	Standard error	t-value	p-value (2-sided)	p-value (1-sided)		
Green Marketing -> Purchasing behavior	0.6204	0.6241	0.0316	19.6380	0.0000	0.0000	0.6258	

Figure 3. Model depicting the individual effect of the three green marketing tools

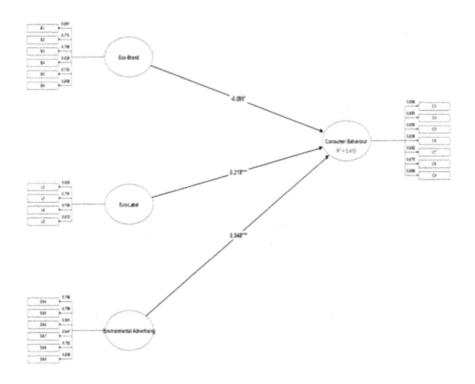

Table 6. Construct reliability

Construct	Dijkstra-Henseler's rho (ρ_A)	Jöreskog's rho (ρ_c)	Cronbach's alpha(α)	Average Variance Extracted (AVE)
Eco-Label	0.7964	0.8388	0.7504	0.5687
Purchasing behavior	0.9155	0.9215	0.8990	0.6302
Eco-Brand	0.8707	0.8901	0.8623	0.5707
Environmental Advertising	0.8611	0.8796	0.8353	0.5517

Table 7. Discriminant validity: Fornell-Larcker criterion

Construct	Eco-Label	Purchasing behavior	Eco-Brand	Environmental Advertising
Eco-Label	0.5687			
Purchasing behavior	0.2226	0.6302		
Eco-Brand	0.2875	0.1061	0.5757	
Environmental Advertising	0.3070	0.3805	0.3063	0.5517

The weights on each path also indicated that of the three tools, environmental advertising recorded the highest path loading of 0.548, eco-label followed with a loading of 0.219. eco-brand recorded a negative path loading of -0.095. To confirm the path loadings, bootstrapping was run. The results indicated that environmental advertising and eco-label recorded T-statistics greater than 1.96, indicating that these two tools were significant with P-values of 0.0002 and 0.0000 for eco-label and environmental advertising, respectively. Eco-brand recorded an insignificant effect with a p-value of 0.0636. Further analysis was done to confirm the predictive effect of the variables using the effect size. Eco-label recorded an effect size of 0.0502, and environmental advertising recorded 0.3060, indicating low and high effect sizes, respectively. The eco-brand also recorded 0.0094, indicating a very low effect size.

6. DISCUSSION

The study posited that when marketers of cosmetic products engage in green marketing, consumers are persuaded to act. The findings of the study supported this assertion that when marketers engage in activities that are perceived to be green, consumers are inclined to act positively towards the product. Hence, the study proposes that greenness exerts considerable influence on consumers' purchase behavior of cosmetics products. This is supported by the study findings, which recorded T-statistics and p-values of 19.6380, and $p<0.05$, respectively. This confirms the findings of Ottoman and Mallen (2014). Therefore, this finding highlights the significance of green marketing tools in consumers' decision-making process of cosmetic products.

The study further sought to find out which specific green marketing tool explains the purchasing behavior of consumers. To this end, eco-label, eco-brand, and environmental advertising, which the study defined as green marketing were examined to determine which accounted for consumers purchasing behavior toward cosmetic products. The findings of the study indicated that eco-brands could not explain the purchasing behavior of consumers as it recorded a T-statistics of 1.8570, with a value greater than 0.05 (p>0.05). Similar findings were established in the study of Braimah (2015), who explained that the Ghanaian consumer does not consider eco-brands when making purchases.

Furthermore, the study posited that eco-label is a key driver when consumers decide to purchase a cosmetic product. This assertion was supported by the study's findings (t=3.5916, p<0.05), indicating consumers consider eco-labels an important tool when purchasing a cosmetic product. This finding supports Delafrooz et al. (2014), who concluded that eco-labels on cosmetics provide consumers with helpful knowledge about the product's green features, which aids consumers in their decision-making process. This implies considerable influence is exerted on the consumer when marketers highlight the merits of having a green product (Peattie, 2001).

The study further assumed environmental advertising plays a key role when consumers make a purchase decision regarding a cosmetic product. The study's findings support this assertion based on the t-statistics and the p-values recorded (t=10.0749, p<0.05) in this study. Similar results were also reported in the study of Ankit and Mayur (2013), who found that environmental advertising significantly influenced consumers' purchasing behavior. This means that by highlighting the greenness of a product as against a product not considered green, consumers tend to favor the green product over the non-green product (Peattie, 2001).

7. CONCLUSION AND IMPLICATIONS

The study concludes that green marketing affects consumers purchasing behavior. However, to determine which green marketing variable is responsible for such influence, the study concludes that eco-label and environmental advertising are the constructs that explain the positive influence of green marketing practices on consumer purchasing decisions. Eco-brand was found not to exert any influence on consumer decision-making. These findings support the TPB's assertions that intentions predict consumers' behaviors. This means that intention predicts behavior, as espoused in the TPB. The findings have implications for businesses that engage in green marketing practices or business that wants to engage in green marketing. This means that when managers only use jargon such as our product is eco-friendly, recyclable, or low energy, it is not enough to exert considerable influence on a consumer to make a purchase. However, when the marketer of cosmetic products focuses on securing certification on the greenness of their product from approved agencies, it is likely to influence a purchase decision. Likewise, using environmentally friendly promotional tools will likely influence a purchase decision. Therefore, the focus should be on these constructs of green marketing emphasizing certification that supports the greenness of their product with labels of the certification agency as part of their labels, using environmentally accepted promotional messages such as "help us fight the impact of cosmetic testing", "stop the abuse", all go a long way in promoting the natural environment. Nonetheless, the findings generally support the proposition that when businesses engage in activities perceived to be green by their customers, it is likely to result in positive consumer feedback.

8. RECOMMENDATIONS FOR STUDIES

Since the study concentrated on only regular students of the University of Cape Coast, future studies can also focus on respondents who are not students and assess how their purchasing behavior may be influenced by firms that practice green marketing. It is also anticipated that the current study would inspire other researchers to examine the influence of situational factors on how they might mediate the relationship between green marketing tools and consumer purchasing behavior.

9. REFERENCES

Abzari, M., Safari Shad, F., Abedi Sharbiyani, A. A., & Parvareshi Morad, A. (2013). Studying the effect of green marketing mix on market share increase. *European Online Journal of Natural and Social Sciences: Proceedings, 2*(3), 641.

Adinyra, N., & Gligui, E. (2011). *Green Marketing Potential as Assessed from Consumers Purchasing Behaviors: The Case of Ghana* [Dissertation, URN]. http://urn.kb.se/resolve?urn=urn:nbn:se:bth-5441

Ajzen, I. (2011). The theory of planned behavior: Reactions and reflections. *Psychology & Health, 26*(9), 1113–1127. doi:10.1080/08870446.2011.613995 PMID:21929476

Ankit, G., & Mayur, R. (2013). Green marketing: Impact of green advertising on consumer purchase intention. *Advances in Management, 6*(9), 14.

Ansar, N. (2013). Impact of green marketing on consumer purchase intention. *Mediterranean Journal of Social Sciences.* Advance online publication. doi:10.5901/mjss.2013.v4n11p650

Bempong, G. B. (2017). *The effect of green branding on consumer purchasing behavior: A study of the Ghanaian cosmetic market* [Unpublished doctoral dissertation, Ashesi University].

Braimah, M. (2015). Green brand awareness and customer purchase intention. *Management Science Letters*, 895–902. doi:10.5267/j.msl.2015.8.007

Braimah, M., & Tweneboah-Koduah, E. Y. (2011). An exploratory study of the impact of green brand awareness on consumer purchase decisions in Ghana. *Journal of Marketing Development and Competitiveness, 5*(7), 11–18.

Daria, B., & Sara, K. S. (2011). *The Influence of Eco-labelled Products on Consumer Buying Behaviour- By focusing on eco-labelled bread.* [Bachelor"s thesis, Mälardalen University College]. http://mdh.diva- portal.org/smash/get/diva2:390922/FULLTEXT01.pdf

Delafrooz, N., Taleghani, M., & Nouri, B. (2014). Effect of green marketing on Consumer Purchase Behavior. *QScience Connect, 2014*(1). doi:10.5339/connect.2014.5

Energy Star score for offices in the United States. (2019). Energy Star. https://www.energystar.gov/sites/default/files/tools/Office_August_2019_508.pdf

Ghanaweb. (2016, May 9). *Skin Bleaching.* Ghanaweb. https://www.ghanaweb.com/GhanaHomePage/entertainment/Skin-bleaching-a-silent-killer-of-the-youth-of-today-441001

Govender, J. P., & Govender, T. L. (2016). The influence of green marketing on consumer purchase behavior. *Environment and Ecology, 7*(2), 77–85. doi:10.21511/ee.07(2).2016.8

Hair, J. F. Jr, Ringle, C. M., & Sarstedt, M. (2013). Partial least squares structural equation modeling: Rigorous applications, better results and higher acceptance. *Long Range Planning, 46*(1–2), 1–12. doi:10.1016/j.lrp.2013.01.001

Han, H., & Kim, Y. (2010). An investigation of green hotel customers' decision formation: Developing an extended model of the theory of planned behavior. *International Journal of Hospitality Management, 29*(4), 659–668. doi:10.1016/j.ijhm.2010.01.001

Hill, R. J., Fishbein, M., & Ajzen, I. (1977). Belief, attitude, intention and behavior: An introduction to theory and research. *Contemporary Sociology, 6*(2), 244. doi:10.2307/2065853

Hilliard, H., Matulich, E., Haytko, D., & Rustogi, H. (2012). An international look at attitude towards advertising, brand considerations, and market expertise: United States, China, and India. *Journal of International Business Research, 11*(1), 29.

Huber, P., Bongartz, A., Cezanne, M. L., & Julius, N. (2018). How far can we predict sensorial feelings by instrumental modeling? *IFSCC Magazine, 1*(21), 13–18.

Husain, K. (2018). A survey on usage of personal care products especially cosmetics among university students in Saudi Arabia. *Journal of Cosmetic Dermatology, 18*(1), 271–277. doi:10.1111/jocd.12773 PMID:30203510

Kotler, P., & Keller, K. L. (2016). Marketing management (15th global ed.). England: Pearson.

Kumar, D. A., & Gangal, P. V. (2011). The impact of 'ambience' and variety on consumer delight: A study on consumer behaviour in Ahmedabad. *Indian Journal of Applied Research, 1*(9), 197–200. doi:10.15373/2249555X/JUN2012/70

Leonidou, C. N., Katsikeas, C. S., & Morgan, N. A. (2012). "greening" The marketing mix: Do firms do it and does it pay off? *Journal of the Academy of Marketing Science, 41*(2), 151–170. doi:10.100711747-012-0317-2

Lixandru, M. G. (2017). Advertising for natural beauty products: The shift in cosmetic industry. *European Scientific Journal, 7881*, 6–13.

Magali, M., Francis, K., & Hulten, P. (2012). *Green marketing: Consumers' attitudes towards eco-friendly products and purchase intention in the fast moving consumer goods sector.* Umea School Of Business Spring Semester.

Mathur, A., Moschis, G. P., & Lee, E. (2007a). A longitudinal study of the effects of life status changes on changes in consumer preferences. *Journal of the Academy of Marketing Science, 36*(2), 234–246. doi:10.100711747-007-0021-9

Nielsen Holdings. (2014). *Global consumers are willing to put their money where their heart is.* Nielsen. http://www.nielsen.com/in/en/press-room/2014/global-consumers-are-willing-to-put-their-money-where-their-heart- is.htm

Ottoman, J., & Mallen, D. (2014), *5 Green marketing strategies to earn consumer trust.* gREENbIZ. https://www.greenbiz.com/blog/2014/01/14/five-strategies-avoid-taint- greenwash-your-business.

Pardana, D., Abdullah, R., Mahmuda, D., Malik, E., Pratiwi, E. T., Dja'wa, A., Abdullah, L. O., Hardin, & Hamid, R. S. (2019). Attitude analysis in the theory of planned behavior: Green marketing against the intention to buy environmentally friendly products. *IOP Conference Series. Earth and Environmental Science, 343*(1), 012128. doi:10.1088/1755-1315/343/1/012128

Peattie, K. (2001). Towards sustainability: The third age of green marketing. *The Marketing Review, 2*(2), 129–146. doi:10.1362/1469347012569869

Pickett-Baker, J., & Ozaki, R. (2008). Pro-environmental products: Marketing influence on consumer purchase decision. *Journal of Consumer Marketing, 25*(5), 281–293. doi:10.1108/07363760810890516

Rahbar, E., Shwu Shyan, T., & Abdul Wahi, N. (2011). Actors influencing the Green Purchase Behavior of Penang Environmental Volunteers. *International Business Management, 5*(1), 38–49. doi:10.3923/ibm.2011.38.49

Rahbar, E., & Wahid, N. A. (2011). Investigation of Green Marketing Tools' effect on consumers' purchase behavior. *Business Strategy Series*, *12*(2), 73–83. doi:10.1108/17515631111114877

Rahim, M. H. A., Zukni, R. Z. A., Ahmad, F., & Lyndon, N. (2012). Green advertising and environmentally responsible consumer behavior: The level of awareness and perception of Malaysian youth. *Asian Social Science*, *8*(5). Advance online publication. doi:10.5539/ass.v8n5p46

Rashid, N. R. (2009). Awareness of eco-label in Malaysia's green marketing initiative. *International Journal of Business and Management*, *4*(8). Advance online publication. doi:10.5539/ijbm.v4n8p132

Saini, B. (2013). Green marketing and its impact on consumer buying behavior. *International Journal of Engineering and Science Invention*, *2*(12), 61–64.

Saunders, M., Lewis, P., & Thornhill, A. (2007). Research methods. Business Students, 6(3), 1-268. Pearson Education Limited, England.

Stern, P. C. (2000). New environmental theories: Toward a coherent theory of environmentally significant behavior. *The Journal of Social Issues*, *56*(3), 407–424. doi:10.1111/0022-4537.00175

Sung, J., & Woo, H. (2019). Investigating male consumers' lifestyle of health and sustainability (LOHAS) and perception toward slow fashion. *Journal of Retailing and Consumer Services*, *49*, 120–128. doi:10.1016/j.jretconser.2019.03.018

Taking a good look at the beauty industry. (2021, July 22). McKinsey & Company. https://www.mckinsey.com/industries/retail/our-insights/taking-a-good-look-at-the-beauty-industry

Unilever PLC Annual Report. (2019, January 31). Unilever PLC. https://www.unilever-ewa.com/files/678bbb68-9105-42cc-ae04-fd0989c22b47/annual-report-and-financial-statements-2019.pdf

Wear, H., Hills, S., Heere, B., & Walker, M. (2018). Communal brand associations as drivers of team identity and consumer behavior. *Journal of Global Sport Management*, *3*(3), 302–320. doi:10.1080/24704067.2018.1432990

Yeng, W. F., & Yazdanifard, R. (2015). Green marketing: A study of consumers buying behavior in relation to green products. *Global Journal of Management and Business Research*.

Zinkhan, G. M., & Carlson, L. (1995). Green advertising and the reluctant consumer. *Journal of Advertising*, *24*(2), 1–6. doi:10.1080/00913367.1995.10673471

APPENDIX

Section A: Background of Respondents

Please tick/indicate where appropriate

1. Sex: a. Male [ ] b. Female [ ]
2. Age: a. below 20 [ ] b. 20-29 [ ] c. 30-39 [ ] d. 40-49 [ ] e. 50-59 [ ] f. 60 and above [ ]
3. College: a. Education[ ] b. Humanities [ ] c. Health and Allied [ ] d. Agriculture[ ]
4. Programme _____
5. Level: a. 100 [ ] b. 200 [ ] c. 300 [ ] d. 400 [ ]

Section B: Green Marketing

6.   Please rank your views using the scale 1-5 by ticking appropriately ($\sqrt{}$)

Scale: *SD= Strongly Disagree D=Disagree U=Undecided A=Agree SA=Strongly Agree*

ECO-LABEL	SD	D	U	A	SA
Eco-labels on cosmetics help with easy identification of its green feature					
I believe that eco-labels are easy to read and understand					
Eco-labels on cosmetics makes them eye catching					
Eco-labels on cosmetics indicates that it is environmental safe					
I have purchased cosmetics based on eco- labels					
ECO-BRAND					
I feel good about buying brands which are less damaging to the environment					
It is important to reuse or recycle the packaging after use					
I acknowledge that the information on packaging is an important criterion					
I think that safe packaging is an important consideration for green customers					
I trust well-known green branded cosmetics in Ghana					
ENVIRONMENTAL ADVERTISING					
Advertising is a reliable source of information about the quality and performance of cosmetics					
I believe environmental advertising is informative					
I depend on getting the truth in most green advertising					
In general, advertising presents a true picture of the product being advertised					
I feel I have been accurately informed after viewing most advertisements on green products					
Most advertising provides consumers with essential information					
green advertising influence people to buy green					
purchased a product because the advertising indicated that it was environmentally safe					

Section C: Consumer Purchase Behavior

7.   Please rank your views using the scale 1-5 by ticking appropriately ($\sqrt{}$)

Scale: *SD= Strongly Disagree D=Disagree U=Undecided A=Agree SA=Strongly Agree*

CONSUMER PURCHASE BEHAVIOR	SD	D	U	A	SA
I purchased green cosmetics because it is needed to save the earth than non-green products					
I make comparisons on cosmetics in deciding on the environmentally friendly one to buy					
I spent much money on green products within the previous month.					
I purchased about three number of green products bought within previous month					
The frequency of buying green products with recyclable or biodegradable packaging increased within the previous month					
I had every opportunity to shopped green products within the previous month					
I feel good about buying brands which are less damaging to the environment					
I feel happy after buying and using green products					

Chapter 9
Towards a Sustainable Transportation System:
Innovative Measures to Alleviate Road Traffic Congestion

Sonia Mrad

iD https://orcid.org/0000-0002-1755-4355
University of Manouba, Tunisia

Rafaa Mraihi
Univesity of Manouba, Tunisia

ABSTRACT

In modern societies, the need for a high degree of mobility in transportation systems is increasingly evident. Consequently, the establishment of a sustainable transport system that aligns with social needs, economic growth, and environmental concerns becomes paramount. This chapter aims to shed light on the role of transport in sustainable development and the challenges associated with achieving sustainable mobility. A thorough analysis of the primary factors contributing to the growing demand for mobility is provided. Additionally, the chapter examines the key decision-makers involved in shaping transportation systems, with a particular focus on the pivotal role of intelligent transportation systems. These systems are considered a vital component in addressing road congestion and enhancing overall traffic performance, such as reducing congestion and noise levels while promoting sustainable mobility.

DOI: 10.4018/978-1-6684-8140-0.ch009

INTRODUCTION

Sustainable transport has long been a complex and sensitive subject involving various stakeholders (Goldman & Gorham, 2006; Litman, 2005; Richardson, 2005; Zhao et al., 2020; Chatziioannou et al., 2020). In modern societies, the need for a high degree of mobility in transportation systems is increasingly evident. For this reason, it is essential to have a sustainable transport system adapted to social needs, economic growth, and environmental concerns (Babaei et al., 2023). However, traffic congestion is a global nagging phenomenon confronting cities, a perpetual problem that challenges the development of sustainable transportation systems (Hussain et al., 2022). From this point of view, the detection of the root cause of congestion (Downs, 2000) as well as its quantification methods are regarded as important for decision-makers, researchers, or transportation experts to implement mitigation policies aimed at improving the overall sustainability of the transportation system, such as efficient traffic management, reducing greenhouse gas emissions, and accurate prediction of congestion (Rao & Rao, 2012; Afrin & Yodo, 2020).

Intelligent transportation systems (ITS) are consistently identified as the panacea to many of the economic, social, and environmental effects associated with private vehicles, including road congestion, urban sprawl, social exclusion, increased costs, emissions, and environmental degradation, due to technological advancements and the availability of big data. (Butler et al., 2020).

It is within this framework that this chapter attempts to introduce the pivotal role of transport in sustainable development as well as the challenge of sustainable mobility. An in-depth analysis of the main factors contributing to the increase in mobility demand and the insufficiency of supply transport is also presented. They provide not only a pedagogical guide but also a scientific reference related to an exhaustive implementation in the field of urban transportation systems and their importance, as well as the phenomenon of congestion as an immediate consequence of the evolution of transport demand. In this chapter also, a review of the main decision-makers is presented, and attention is focused on the key role of intelligent transportation systems as a part of the solution to road congestion.

SUSTAINABLE TRANSPORT

In the last few years, there has been a growing interest in sustainability, sustainable development, sustainable transport, and sustainable mobility. Numerous researchers and state organizations are engaged in efforts to embrace sustainable development in the transport sector. Sustainable development is defined as "development that meets the needs of the present without compromising the ability of future generations to meet their own needs" in the Brundtland Report (Brundtland et al., 1987). Sustainability is commonly acknowledged to have three dimensions: environmental, social, and economic. This definition is one of the reasons why the concept of sustainable transport was born out of sustainable development. Sustainable transportation can be defined in two ways: narrowly and broadly. The former is concerned with environmental issues and resources depletion, whereas the latter is concerned with the aforementioned as well as social and economic well-being (Zhao et al., 2020b). The latter is favoured because it allows individuals to consider all of the effects of the transportation sector (Litman & Burwell, 2006) and motivates them to seek for holistic solutions for sustainable transportation (Zhou, 2012).

According to the 2000 European Conference of Ministers of Transport (ECMT) report on Sustainable transport policy (ECMT 2000), which identifies a set of recommendations, the principal ones are in relation to sustainability (May & Crass, 2007):

- Reducing greenhouse gas emissions
- Improving air quality/reducing noise
- Improving transport safety
- Improving access
- Reducing congestion
- Supporting the economy

Literature review aids to develop a thorough understanding of the subject from multiple angles, such as social, economic, health, urban, technological and so on (Gallo & Marinelli, 2020). The most notable contributions in this field have been made by renowned researchers and scholars. Some key references include the following publications: Gallo and Marinelli (2020), Goldman and Gorham (2006), Holden et al. (2019), Laconte (2012), Litman (2005), López et al. (2019), Pojani and Stead (2015), Raffaud (2003), and Tirachini (2019). These works have greatly influenced the understanding and advancement of the subject matter. In all of the main definitions found in the literature, the following is emphasized for transport sustainable policy:

- On the one hand, its impacts on sustainable development are associated with social or economic benefits, but on the other hand, it involves the need to minimize the adverse effects of the developments (Cheba & Saniuk, 2016).
- It is indispensable for the economy and its expansion. It should also be affordable for each generation. It is also a powerful means of ensuring the harmonious economic development of a nation and of integrating it to play its role in the world's economic structure.

Figure 1. Sustainable transport goals
(*Kimura et al., 2017*)

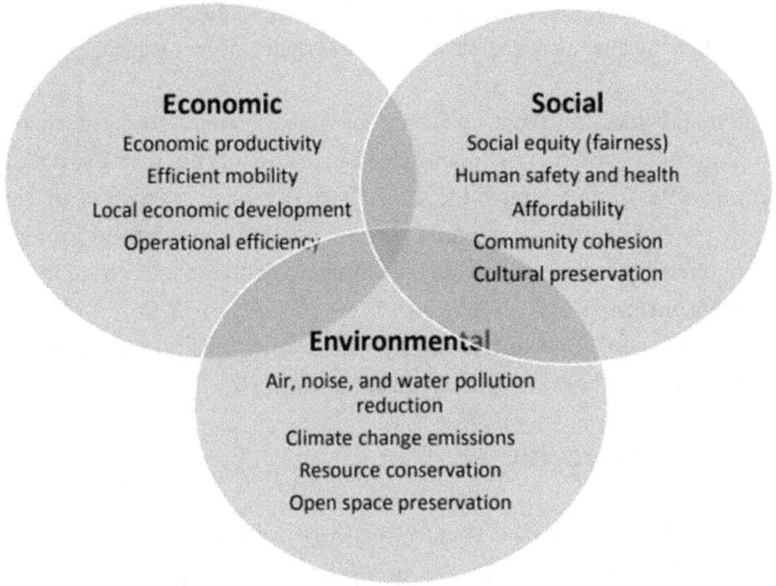

- Must avoid the common transportation policy trap of ignoring the larger systems in which transport activities are located (Goldman & Gorham, 2006).
- A sustainable transport system is mainly oriented towards three elements that need to be implemented: planning, policies, and used technologies (Banister, 2008).
- The goal of sustainable transportation may be better served by a number of organic innovations in transportation practice, such as New Mobility, City Logistics, Intelligent System Management, and Livability (Badassa et al., 2020).

All these objectives can be illustrated in Figure 1.

URBAN DEMAND TRANSPORTATION: EVOLUTION, IMPORTANCE AND CHALLENGES

In rapid urban development, motorization goes hand in hand with the growth in economic growth and travel passenger demand. This is due in part to rising incomes making the diffusion of personal mobility more accessible but also to inadequate provision of public transport to meet rising travel demand (Litman, 2006; Portugal-Pereira et al., 2013). Jones (2014) argued that this increasing mobility can be seen as the outcome of a complex and changing set of interactions. According to these authors, this growing mobility can be seen as the result of a complex and changing set of interactions.

On the demand side, contributing factors include varying demographic patterns linked to economic growth and societal changes resulting in new patterns of consumption, while on the supply side, there have been major changes in transport infrastructure provision, often associated with advances in technology (Jones, 2014). In fact, urban mobility can be classified into three categories: collective, individual, and freight transportation.

Several factors contribute to the steady increase in transport demand and can generate congestion in the long or short term, such as:

Socio-Economic Growth

The main focus of economic and social growth is in large urban areas, where the majority of activities, income, and capital are based and can interconnect. These circumstances have an impact on transport needs, resulting in increased transport demand and the possibility of congestion on urban transport networks (Organisation for Economic Co-operation and Development et al., 2007). When it came to highlighting the role of transport in economic growth, a number of researchers showed that transportation infrastructure development impacts economic growth through increased labour and capital productivity, cost savings, industrial agglomeration, and changing aggregate market demand. Understanding these factors is crucial for successful infrastructure development (Zhang & Cheng, 2023).

Rapid Population Growth and Car Ownership

Over the 20th century, the world's urban population grew from 751 million in 1950 to 4.2 billion in 2018[1]. By 2050, it is forecast that there will be 6.9 billion people living in urban areas, comprising 70% of the global population (May & Marsden, 2010). The impacts of population growth on travel and the daily use of cars are highlighted by the increase in car ownership (Dargay, 2002). In fact, in his research study, Dargay (2002) anticipated the evolution of the numbers of cars per capita and the volume of traffic per capita in the different regions of the world. The data was based on recently observed growth rates, estimated shifts in GDP, and population growth. The author assumes that vehicle use remains constant over time and that traffic increase in proportion to the number of vehicles.

Rapid Urbanization

Transport not only favours economic development but also has an impact on spatial organization. Throughout history, transport networks have structured space at different scales (Rodrigue, 2016). The recent explosion in the rate of urbanization has been largely based on the extension of urban networks and the going trend of motorization; this spatial dilatation has given rise to a new form of urbanity called the urban sprawl, dependent on the automobile. The abundant provision of building land or new, cheap housing, assistance for home ownership, and the creation of business parks and centres in the outer suburbs are leading to a massive use of private cars.

The Increase in the Standard of Living

The increase in the standard of living has multiplied the opportunities for shopping, leisure, personal affairs to be dealt with, social relations, etc., and therefore for travel. On the other hand, at the company level, the evolution of activities towards tertiaryization has led to an increase in the exchange of information and business travel. Finally, the reduction in working hours and the general increase in purchasing power in developed and developing countries have had a significant impact on urban travel for reasons other than home to work: shopping, leisure, personal affairs, etc.

Car Ownership and Dependency

Since automobile use is linked to a numerous benefits, such as accessibility, demand mobility, comfort, speed and convenience (Rodrigue, 2016). Generally, urban form plays a crucial role in creating and preserving the necessity to use the private car.

These advantages jointly illustrate why automobile ownership continues to expand globally, especially in urban areas. When given a choice and the opportunity, most individuals will prefer using an automobile. Accordingly to Newman and Kenworthy (1999), urban form and the availability of alternative transport modes are important in determining the degree of car dependency. If more than 75% of trips are made by the car, this dependence is regarded as high.

CONGESTION: THE MAIN TRANSPORTATION PROBLEM AND ITS IMPACTS ON SUSTAINBILITY

Researchers have defined congestion from different points of view in order to state an adequate measure of the level of congestion. Nevertheless, there is no universally accepted definition of traffic congestion since it is extremely variable in time and space (Downs, 2005).

The most common definition of the state of traffic flow is stated by Aftabuzzaman (2007) as when travel demand exceeds road capacity. Ye (2012) defined congestion as the unbalanced transportation of supply and demand almost every weekday morning and evening during rush hours. Congestion is classified as one of the most serious problems of modern life, generating undesirable effects at all levels: social, economic, political, and environmental.

Furthermore, this issue is particularly severe on road networks. Congestion is a fact that every traveler must face at least once in their lives. It impacts thousands of people worldwide and has numerous implications (Kerner, 1999). Congestion, in general, causes a significant slowdown of vehicles, particularly in long traffic jams, and causes delays. Individual users and businesses are both affected by these delays. Users who are subjected to regular traffic congestion have stress and anxiety issues, as well as increased chance of accidents. Furthermore, congestion has a direct impact on the rise in energy use. Congestion, for society, degrades the quality of the environment by causing overconsumption of non-renewable energy. According to the scientific literature, the authors Aftabuzzaman (2007) and Nguyen-Phuoc et al. (2020) have presented a review in the classification of the definition of traffic congestion based on three main groups in terms of causes and effects: From a demand perspective (Rosenbloom, 1978; Rothenberg, 1985; Vaziri, 2002; Lesteven, 2012), when demand exceeds capacity, it can be considered the cause of congestion.

From a delay-related perspective (Meyer, 1997; Downs, 2005; Falcocchio & Levinson, 2015; Systematics, 2005), when the normal flow of traffic is interrupted by a high density of vehicles, resulting in excess travel time, and from a cost-related perspective (Kockelman & Kalmanje, 2005; Naude & Tsolakis, 2005), when there is a disruption in the flow of traffic, an increase in cost is attributed to the road user. On the other hand, congestion can be specified as a range of indirect impacts, including quality of life, security, and impacts on road space for non-vehicular users, such as users of sidewalks. The different definitions are presented in Table 1.

A variety of reasons are responsible for creating congestion in most urban areas. Depending on these different reasons, congestion can be clustered into recurring and non-recurring categories (Downs, 2000b). Recurrent congestion occurs regularly on a daily, weekly, or annual cycle. On the other hand, non-recurrent congestion occurs, especially with unpredictable events such as traffic accidents, stop-and-go, work zones, weather conditions, etc. (Falcocchio & Levinson, 2015; Afrin & Yodo, 2020).

Table 1. Alternate definitions of congestion

	Authors	Definition
Demand-capacity related	(Rosenbloom, 1978)	Traffic congestion occurs when travel demand exceeds the existing road system's capacity
	(Rothenberg, 1985)	Congestion denotes any condition in which demand for a facility exceeds flow capacity at maximum design speed.
	(Vaziri, 2002)	The definition and quantification of congestion have been related to its causes and effects. Congestion occurs when traffic demand approaches and exceeds highway capacity. The definition and quantification of congestion have been related to its causes and effects. Congestion occurs when traffic demand approaches and exceeds highway capacity. Inadequacies of roadway systems and traffic management are the main causes of recurring congestion.
Delay-travel time related	(Meyer, 1997)	Congestion means there are more people trying to use a given transportation facility during a specific period of time than the facility can handle with what are considered acceptable levels of delays or inconvenience.
	(Downs, 2005)	Traffic congestion occurs when traffic is moving at speeds below the designed capacity of a roadway.
	(Falcocchio & Levinson, 2015b)	Congestion in transportation occurs when the occupancy of spaces (roadways, sidewalks, transit lines and terminals) by vehicles or people reaches unacceptable levels of discomfort and delay.
Cost- related	(Kockelman & Kalmanje, 2005)	Congestion can be viewed as the result from underpricing of the road network and marginal cost pricing can be used internalize the congestion externality.
	(Naude & Tsolakis, 2005)	Congestion may be regarded as the point at which an additional road user joins the traffic flow and affects marginal cost in such a way that marginal social cost of road use exceeds the marginal private cost of road

CURRENT APPROACHES OF CONGESTION MEASURES

Several approaches have been developed to measure the level of traffic congestion on roadways in urban areas. As pointed out in Lomax et al. (1997) and Aftabuzzaman (2007), there is a debate about what is the most appropriate measure of traffic congestion. A selection of performance criteria has been suggested to measure congestion. Based on these criteria, the congestion measures can be classified into five broad categories: (i) speed, (ii) travel time, (iii) delay, (iv) level of service (LoS), (v) congestion indices, and (vi) Annual average daily traffic (AADT), as shown in Figure 2. It should be noted that the measures presented in this section are not exhaustive.

Figure 2. Congestion measures in different categories

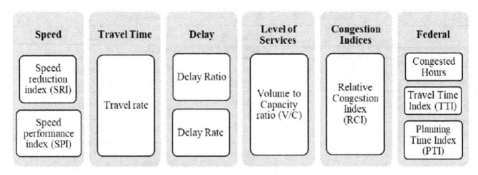

Speed	Travel Time	Delay	Level of Services	Congestion Indices	Federal
Speed reduction index (SRI)		Delay Ratio			Congested Hours
	Travel rate		Volume to Capacity ratio (V/C)	Relative Congestion Index (RCI)	Travel Time Index (TTI)
Speed performance index (SPI)		Delay Rate			Planning Time Index (PTI)

Speed Performance Index (SPI)

In order to evaluate the traffic conditions on urban roads, the SPI was developed (He et al., 2016). The value of the SPI (ranging from 0 to 100) can be defined by the ratio of the vehicle speed to the maximum speed allowed. The SPI is represented by the following equation:

$$SPI = \left(\frac{v_{avg}}{v_{max}} \right) *100$$

Where SPI denotes the performance speed index, v_avg denotes the average travel speed, and v_max indicates the maximum speed allowed on the road. To measure the traffic condition on the road with this index, the traffic condition level can be classified with three threshold values (20, 50, and 75). The classification criterion of the urban road state is shown in Table 2 (He et al., 2016; Afrin & Yodo, 2020).

Table 2. The evaluation criterion of the speed performance index

Speed Performance Index	Traffic State Level	Description of Traffic State
(0,20)	Heavy congestion	Low average speed, poor road traffic state
(25,50)	Medium congestion	Lower average speed, road traffic state bit weak
(50,75)	Smooth	Higher the average speed, road traffic state better
(75,100)	Very smooth	High average speed, road traffic state good

Travel Rate (TR in Minutes Per Mile)

The TR is an indicator of travel time, which makes it relevant to travellers. The inverse of speed can also be used to calculate the travel rate.

$$TR\left(\min/\ mile\right) = \frac{travel\ time\left(\min\right)}{segment\ length\left(mile\right)}$$

Delay Rate

The delay rate is the time loss for vehicles operating during congestion conditions for a specific roadway segment or trip (Aftabuzzaman, 2007; Afrin & Yodo, 2020). This indicator can estimate the difference between system performance and expectations for those system elements, which can be used to rank alternative improvements (Lomax et al., 1997). The DR is:

$$DR = TR_{ac} - TR_{ap}$$

With
TR_{ac}: actual travel rate (minute per mile)
TR_{ap}: accesptable travel time (minute per mile)

Level of Service

In 1985, Highway Capacity Manual (Roess et al, 1985) (Manual, 1985), the first that has adopted the use of level of service (LOS) as an indicator of road performance. It has considered the most popular measures of traffic congestion. The LOS of a facility is determined by traffic flow characteristics such as vehicle density, volume - to - capacity ratio, average speed and intersection delay. The scale of LOS measure has six discrete classes ranging from A to F (He et al., 2016; Afrin & Yodo, 2020).

$$\frac{V}{C} = \frac{N_v}{N_{max}}$$

Where, N_v is the spatial mean volume, and N_{max} denotes the maximum number of vehicles that a segment is able to contain as the capacity.

Road Congestion Index (RCI)

The RCI, developed by Schrank et al. (1993), is an indicator that measure the length of the peak period based on the ratio of total traffic flow per day to the road network supply. It is considered as the only that measures the overall performance of the system and provides comparisons between the metropolitan areas (freeways or arterial roadway), as shown below,

$$RCI = \frac{\left[Freeway_{VMT\left(\ln/mile\right)} * Freeway_{VMT}\right] + \left[PAS_{VMT\left(\ln/mile\right)} + PAS_{VMT}\right]}{\left[a * Freeway_{VMT}\right] + \left[b * PAS_{VMT}\right]}$$

Where, PAS VMT is the Principal Arterial Street Vehicle Mile Traveled, a and b two parameters varying depending on the type of line. Freeway VMT: Freeway Daily Vehicle Miles Traveled.

An RCI value of 1.0 or greater indicates an undesirable congestion level. However, it is difficult for travellers to relate this index to their experience, nor is it easy to predict future conditions. From this measure, it is not possible to deduce what traffic improvement schemas to mitigate congestion (Hamad & Kikuchi, 2002).

Throughout the course of research into the measures of traffic congestion, certain authors pointed out the appropriate indicators that take into account all the aspects that characterize congestion (Aftabuzzaman, 2007). Consequently, several measures have been developed. Earlier studies tend to use travel time measurement and delay as the most popular indices for defining congestion. In other line of view, some author used alternative measure (surrogate measure), which indirectly define congestion, when resources are not available to conduct specific congestion studies, or when the prediction of future congestion trends (Lomax et al., 1997; Lomax, 1997) and Report 398. The most commonly reported surrogate measure was traffic volume typically the AADT or their derivatives (Veh/km). The AADT is the annual average daily traffic is an important indicator for the level of demand on each section of the road network.

Accessibility is perceived as another important piece of information. The concept of accessibility refers to the time it takes to complete travel objectives at a certain geographical location. Travel objectives are defined as trips to work, shopping, home, or other destinations of interest. This measure is the sum of the objective opportunities where the travel time is less than or equal to the acceptable travel time. This measure can be used with any mode of transport, but it is most often used to assess the quality of public transport services.

REVIEW ON THE IMPACTS OF TRAFFIC CONGESTION

The effects of traffic congestion can be classified into four mains categories of environmental, economic, health and social (Mahmud et al., 2012; Kiunsi, 2013; Agyapong & Ojo, 2018). The nature, scale and gravity of impact varies from one city to another, depending on, for example, the size of the city, the capacity and road layout, spatial distribution of land uses, transit and private modes and travel behavior (Kiunsi, 2013). Figure 3 presents an overview of the principal effects of traffic congestion.

Figure 3. The principal effects of traffic congestion

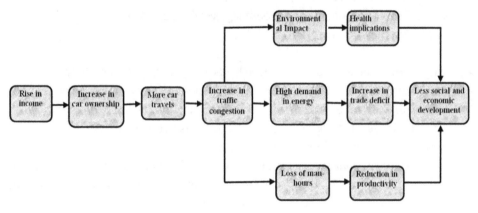

Environmental Effects

According to World Health Organization[2], urban traffic causes 4.2 million deaths each years (2016), due to exposure to ambient (outdoor) air pollution. The same organization classifies the fuel combustion from motor vehicles (e.g. cars and heavy-duty vehicles) as one of the main sources of the environmental noise, especially of particulate matter (PM) and nitrogen dioxide (NO2).

The issue of traffic congestion is still relevant from a literary perspective, and research on its effects on the environment is continually expanding. Kiunsi, (2013) showed that the general environmental impacts due to traffic congestion include air and noise pollution and visual intrusion. Air pollution leads to increase of Greenhouse Gases (GHG) in the atmosphere thus contributing to climate change. Accordingly to Bharadwaj et al. (2017), the traffic congestion on city roads not only increases the fuel consumption but consequently leads to increase in carbon dioxide emissions, outdoor air pollution as well as increase in the exposure time of the passengers.

In an analysis of the top hundred largest US urban centers, Chang et al. (2017) found that road congestion generates 19.524 billion kilograms of CO2 emissions in 2011, up from 3.94 billion kilograms in 1982. In another investigation, Shi et al. (2018) applied the detrended cross-correlation analysis to examine the relationships between NO2 pollution and traffic congestion. Lu et al. (2021) conclude that the extent of the influence of traffic congestion and public transport on atmospheric pollution is unknown.

Economic Effects

Road congestion has even a high cost and an externality in terms of economic efficiency. It generates economic impacts that leads to higher transportation costs, loss of working time, delay in the delivery service and difficult accessibility to economic activities (Kiunsi, 2013).

- Higher travel costs: road congestion leads to longer travel times, higher vehicle operating costs for drivers and an associated increase in energy consumption. The value of time, travel time reliability factors, vehicle operating costs and the costs of congestion related accidents are the key measures of the efficiency of the travel system. In a study conducted in 2011, Schrank et al., (2012) showed that congestion in the United States caused about 5.5. billion hours of delay and 2.9 billion gallons of additional fuel consumption at a total cost of a \$121 billion (Schrank et al., 2012).
- Waste of productivity: given the critical importance of productivity on the Gross Domestic Product (GDP) growth, it is economically worthwhile, and of policy importance to recognize the negative effect of traffic congestion on productivity (Harriet et al., 2013). Road congestion can have negative impacts on a firm's productivity (Abdo, 2011). This is due not only to delay in getting people to their workplaces, but also to additional costs associated with late deliveries of services. Indeed, delays in the delivery of goods are time-sensitive and can in some result in additional inventory costs, logistics costs and reliability costs. This has a direct impact on productivity and socio-economic development.
- Reduce of income growth: Jin and Rafferty (2017) show that traffic congestion negatively affects income growth and employment growth. In the same vein, Hymel (2009) proved also that the high levels of congestion dampen employment growth.

Social Effects

In addition to the environmental and economic consequences, congestion has a negative effect on society. From a social point of view, the costs of congestion are the costs to society as a whole of resources that are attributable to traffic congestion and could have been used for more valuable socio-economic activities. Road users depreciate the time lost to congestion: additional travel time that should have been spent for more productive and useful social activities, such as work and family.

The users of transport networks pay the costs of vehicle use, air pollution, congestion related accident costs and additional greenhouse gas emissions (Harriet et al., 2013). Road congestion has direct consequences on the increase of energy consumption. It leads to a decrease in the purchasing power of consumers, a decrease in social relations between people and a deterioration in the quality of life.

Health Effects

Drivers who are subject to frequent jams, exposure to polluted air and unnecessarily long periods spent on roads, are mental stress, anxiety, tiredness, and headache (Kiunsi, 2013; Agyapong & Ojo, 2018).

CURRENT POLICY INSTRUMENTS

Effective congestion management requires both a comprehensive and integrated strategy that goes beyond the visible impact of congestion to the management of the urban region as a whole. There are many possible measures that can be deployed to alleviate congestion, such as pricing, access management, modification or construction of new infrastructure, improvement of public transport, parking management, incentives for walking and cycling, and intelligent transportation systems. In this section, a review of the main decision-making processes and policies that can be applied to enhance sustainable mobility is presented.

Pricing Mechanisms

Congestion charging is seen as a strategic means of influencing travel demand and allowing more efficient use of road infrastructure capacity. For example, variable charges for road use based on driver location, route length, time of day, and vehicle type could influence the mode of travel, the time, and the length of trip chosen. Congestion charging is based on the use of financial instruments in the interest of alleviating road congestion and predicting the appropriate user price for one or all lanes of the road. Indeed, it can take many forms depending on the roads to which it is applied, its technical implementation, and the method of charging (de Palma & Lindsey, 2011). It can apply to all roads in a region, to cities, or be limited to motorways. Generally, the motivations for road pricing can be divided between traffic regulation and investment financing. In recent years, interest in the concept of road pricing has grown. Its implementation has been widely applied in some cities, such as Singapore, London, Stockholm, and Milan, and shows promising results. For example, a reduction of 18%, 18%, 18%, and 14.2% in traffic entering the congestion zone during the charging hours, respectively, was estimated (Viauroux, 2011; Li & Hensher, 2012; Shatanawi et al., 2020; Selmoune et al., 2020). Pricing has been confirmed as an effective way to reduce congestion in major urban areas (Selmoune et al., 2020).

Fuel Taxation

Taxation policies for fuels or private cars (Santos, 2017; Steinsland et al., 2018), which vary according to their impact on environmental and greenhouse gas emissions (Sterner, 2007). Fuel taxation is the highest direct costs incurred by motorists to internalize the externalities of transport (Newbery, 2001; Small, 2010). This type of tax is widely introduced in Europe. The objective is to encourage people to adopt more responsible behaviour in their choice of vehicle, tending to penalize those who buy vehicles with a greater environmental impact. In certain cases, such as electric cars, the registration tax is eliminated or considerably reduced to encourage their purchase (Lah, 2019).

Access Management

This instrument aims to restrict vehicle access to certain areas (e.g., historical centres) or road links. The overall objective here is to reduce road congestion. Access management involves a number of important policies and measures, such as:

- Alternating traffic is a restriction strategy for car users and large vehicles, such as trucks. For example, alternating traffic on trucks is a ban on traffic in a given direction for a limited period of time (from a few minutes to several hours). Traffic restriction zones should be coupled with a range of complementary measures, such as the provision of quality public transport, parking control, and pricing, to ensure the reduction of traffic.
- Road signs allow for efficient road operation. It automatically indicates, based on traffic density, which lanes to use and in which direction (Organisation for Economic Co-operation and Development, 2007).

- The speed limitation can be applied on freeways as well as urban roads. Traffic disturbances are detected by sensors, and then speed reductions will be displayed to drivers on variable message signs.

Investing in Public Transport

A reliable and affordable public transport system is a key element of sustainable urban transport. While providing a similar level of mobility, public transport only requires a fraction of the energy and space compared to a private car (Lah, 2019). The development of public transport can be an adequate solution to the problem of road congestion, as it offers drivers an alternative mode of transport. It is about twice as expensive as private car transport.

As illustrated in the book Leblanc (2010), public transport has allowed Montreal households to earn $800 million in relation to their personal expenses. This permanent public service leads to a decrease in car use in the city. It has the potential to carry more passengers using much less road space than is required to move the same number of passengers by private car. Public transport uses about six times less road space than private transport (Reymond, 2005).

To ensure an attractive public transport provision, it needs to offer a quality of service that is close to that provided by a private car. Passengers must feel that the range and quality of services provided to them are sufficient to avoid using the car, especially at peak times, and thus to complete their journey with private transport.

The several measures to improve the attractiveness and performance of public transport systems will need to address, according to Reymond (2005), the costs perceived by users, ease and comfort of travel, accessibility, reliability, safety and security, speed, and the creation of parking on the periphery of cities. Investment in public transport is an effective strategy for reducing road congestion and increasing the fluidity of road traffic. It reduces travel times for the population (Organisation for Economic Co-operation and Development, 2007). Public transport facilitates the movement of users to work, school, or shopping areas (Litman, 2006). At the same time, it is an important factor in employment.

In reviewing the principles and issues for public transportation investment, Litman (2006) demonstrated that, based on 2003 data, the overall cost of congestion in the Montreal metropolitan area is estimated to be $1.4 billion per year, equivalent to 1% of Montreal's GDP, and that increasing the modal share of public transportation by 3% represents 43.2 million fewer annual car trips. This would reduce annual congestion costs by $63.8 million and contribute to $75.7 million in transportation savings for households. Although investment in transit transport may lead to short-term reductions in congestion due to "the substitution effect", in the long term it may be less effective due to the "induced demand effect" (Beaudoin et al., 2015). From a literary point of view, previous empirical studies have examined the relationship between transit supply and traffic congestion. We can conclude that the findings differ. For example, Beaudoin & Lawell, (2017) developed a theory model to evaluate whether public transit investment has a role in reducing congestion in a second-best setting. Stopher (2004), and Rubin and Mansour (2013) are wary of the potential of public transport to reduce congestion and consider that public investment is an ineffective tool, whereas Litman (2014) supports investment in public transport.

Litman (2014) in his research study, critiques the demonstration of Rubin and Mansour (2013) that found a positive correlation between public transit supply and traffic congestion level. The author argues that Rubin and Mansour (2013) have underestimated the congestion reductions provided by high-quality transit because they have used only congestion intensity indicators rather than congestion costs indicators and so ignored some indicators such as city size, density, and employment rates (Litman, 2014). The author concludes that high-quality public transit can help reduce congestion.

Parking Management and Regulation

Although efficient, parking management and regulatory strategies are rarely used. Despite being readily available to authorities, parking management and control are crucial because they have the power to change demand on a regional level. However, they frequently seem underutilized to address congestion.[3] (Organisation for Economic Co-operation and Development, 2007). Similar to road charging and other demand-oriented approaches, parking management, and regulation can contribute to the reduction of congestion by diminishing the demand of traffic in the concerned areas. By lowering the demand for travel in the affected areas, parking management and regulation, like road charging and other demand-oriented strategies, can help to lessen congestion.

Given the great political and operational flexibility available, parking regulation can also be quite specifically targeted in that it can be applied on the basis of location and time. Furthermore, parking regulations have relatively low implementation costs, are better accepted by the public than road pricing, and can be controlled directly by local authorities (Button, 2006; Litman, 2016; Gallo & Marinelli, 2020).

Increase the Amount of Infrastructure

Since the 1960s and 1970s, a common approach to solving congestion and other urban transport problems was to increase the overall length and number of routes (which included tunnels) (Pojani & Stead, 2018). In recent years, it has become clear that increased capacity can lead to increased demand due to generated travel (also called "latent demand" or induced demand) (Pojani & Stead, 2015). The theory of induced demand can be explained by analogy to the simple economic principle of supply and demand. When any good, say demand, is reduced in cost, the quantity demanded of that good increases. A change in a transport condition, such as a capacity increase, can reduce the generalized costs of travel. Consequently, there is a growing demand for travel. The optimum point may have been reached in some places, and in other places, the optimum was probably reached a long time ago (Goodwin, 1996; Noland, 2001).

In response, three types of divergence occur on the improved road (freeway or urban road): (1) many drivers who previously used alternative routes during peak hours move to the improved road; (2) many drivers who previously travelled just before or after peak hours begin to travel during these divergence hours; and (3) some commuters who used public transport during peak hours no longer travel by car (Downs, 2000b).

The result is that congestion levels quickly return to previous levels during the expansion, and little time savings are realized. Road investments also have long-term negative effects on traffic congestion. They generate new displacement due to land (urban sprawl) that improves access by car. In addition, road construction is inherently disruptive for densely built-up urban areas (Downs, 2000b; Pojani & Stead, 2015).

Indeed, this strategy may initially facilitate travel, but, over time, the more fluid traffic encourages other people to use their private cars. Thus, we return to the starting point, or even to a worse situation. Since then, this approach has suffered from declining interest due to its induced traffic but also due to its high costs in terms of money and space.

Technological Solutions

In addition to investments in transport infrastructure, policymakers have started to exploit Information and Communication Technologies (ICTs), such as data processing and data-driven decision-making (Bull, 2015), for the management of transport networks and to deal with the major interrelated transportation problems, especially congestion and pollution.

The role of technology is important as it impacts the efficiency of transport directly by ensuring that the best available technology is being used in terms of design, alternative fuels, the use of renewable energy sources, and the development of new patterns of travel (Goldman & Gorham, 2006; Banister, 2008; May, 2013). Due to the advances in ICTs, data-driven decision-making models have significantly developed in recent years (Oladimeji et al., 2023). In addition, measuring and analyzing tools have significantly increased, thereby providing immediate and reliable information about traffic flow conditions, resulting in the emergence of the concept of "Intelligent Transport systems," or ITS (Chen & Miles, 2004).

Such intelligent devices are capable of providing decision-makers with real-time measurements of the traffic at a given point of the road network. ITS can be applied to all modes of transport and takes into account all elements of the transport system, that is, the infrastructure, the mobile, and the driver, which interact together in a dynamic way. As a consequence, the operation of the whole transport system is expected to improve, leading to better use of resources and a more rational coordination of physical flows (Mangiaracina et al., 2017).

The interaction and integration of ITS are described in Figure 4. ITS makes use of vehicle-to-vehicle (V2V) and vehicle-to-Infrastructure (V2I) applications. ITS can help manage and operate the transport system and ensure the smooth flow of passengers and freight. According to Lemoine (2011), the basic principle of these intelligent transport systems is to "adapt traffic rules to traffic conditions in real time". This requires, on the one hand, accurate information about the situation on

Figure 4. Intelligent Transportation Systems
(Yilmaz et al., 2016)

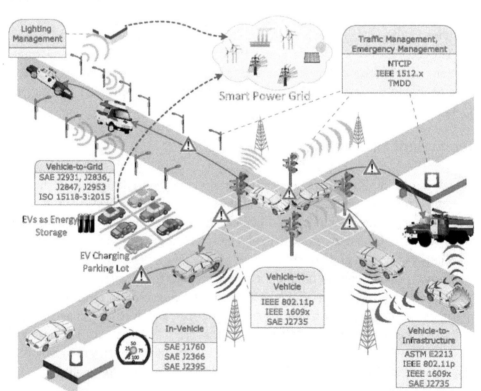

the network and, on the other hand, the means to react quickly and influence driver behaviour". Governments around the world, including those in Europe, the United States, Japan, and Canada, are investing in ITS solutions to solve transport problems. In line with this vision, it is crucial to have a complete and clear overview of ITS competencies, both for passengers and goods.

From a literary perspective, there are several contributions, each focusing on a specific topic. As Khisty & Sriraj (2002) state "ITSs are composed of many aspects geared towards the task of improving network efficiency and sustainability". These aspects include smart mobility, smart parking management, Advanced Traffic Management Systems (ATMS), Advanced traveller Information Systems (ATIS), intelligent traffic signal control systems, motorway management systems, transit management systems, incident management systems, electronic toll collection systems, emergency response systems, travel information systems, route guidance systems, etc (Chen & Miles, 2004; Sussman, 2005). On top of them, all these elements are the pillars of Smart Cities (Albino et al., 2015).

Smart city (Xiong et al., 2012; Benevolo et al., 2016; Bamwesigye & Hlavackova, 2019) refers to using various information technologies or innovative concepts to open up and integrate urban systems and services, improve the efficiency of resource utilization, optimize urban management and services, and improve the quality of life of citizens. Traffic construction is the first step in urban construction, transportation is the artery of urban economic development, and an intelligent transportation system is an important part of smart city construction (Liu, 2020).

The following are some of these components of the ITS (Cheng et al., 2020; Zhang et al., 2011).

- Influencing Driver Behavior: the distribution of various information for motorists before they start their journey can be very useful. This real-time information provided by ITS, such as information on traffic flow conditions, road maintenance work, the reservation of a vacant parking space, journey times, diversion routes in the event of a temporary closure of a road section, helps users to avoid congestion and to make decisions on their chosen mode of transport (Reymond, 2005). Some regulatory measures can also be used by governments to change driver behavior, such as partial or total bans on car use, and spatial organization through the provision of routes indicated by directional signs.
- Environmental Protection: the application of Intelligent Transport Systems contributes to the reduction of CO2 emissions (Ifsttar, 2014). The reduction of road congestion problems contributes to reducing pollution and greenhouse gas emissions. Several reports have assessed the potential of these technologies

and suggest that they could contribute to about half of the required reduction in CO2 emissions by 2050.

- Incident Management: According to CEMT/ITF (2007) (Organisation for Economic Co-operation and Development, 2007), incident management is "a process of planning and coordinating that detects, responds to and removes the impediments caused by traffic incidents and re-establishes road capacity as quickly as safe and feasible" (Organisation for Economic Co-operation and Development et al., 2007). Intelligent transport systems aim to facilitate the process of detecting incident information (vehicle breakdown, works, accident, traffic jam, unexpected weather conditions, etc.) quickly and efficiently. Response organizations are guided precisely to the location of the event thanks to the precise location of the incident site, established by means of on-board satellite navigation systems such as GPS.

- Improving Road Safety: safety is at the center of many applications of intelligent transport systems (Jacob & Abdulhai, 2006), the main aim of which is to reduce the risk of accidents (collision warning, brake assistance). The use of the Internet and the installation of terminals on the infrastructure make it possible to exchange messages between vehicles, thus helping drivers to avoid an accident or to minimise its consequences. In addition to passenger safety, the protection of personnel working on the road could also be improved by the local dissemination of information on the presence of maintenance teams at the roadside (Ifsttar, 2014).

- Parking Management: as an integral part of the transport planning process, parking management is not new, it has been discussed and promoted for a long time, by Johnson in 1997 (Johnson, 1997). In recent years, advancement of technology, the use of parking management is associated with the development of intelligent transportation system. In order to propose a smart parking guidance that supports drivers to find the most appropriate parking considering real time status, walking distance from parking facility to destination, expected parking cost, and traffic congestion due to parking guidance (Shin & Jun, 2014). In the same line, Vianna et al. (2004) propose a methodological procedure that underpins the feasibility of implementing an integrated parking system based on telematics resources. The authors develop a procedure that include a logic architecture for processing and transferring data and information to being transmitted to the users through variable message signs (VMS) (Jacob & Abdulhai, 2006).

- Dynamic traffic management uses technologies for real-time traffic monitoring, network-wide traffic management of traffic flow, and traffic adaptive control to respond to changing traffic conditions. For example, at a traffic control station, ITS assists operators in choosing the traffic management strategies they will apply (Ifsttar, 2014). When traffic increases on motorways and/or urban expressways, managers must take certain measures to avoid congestion. They introduce a set of precautions that offer an effective alternative for reducing congestion and that aim to balance supply (infrastructure capacity) with demand, either by varying the allocation of lanes for road traffic on a temporary basis or by alternating the use of lanes depending on the time of day. Another alternative is the opening of car-sharing lanes, dynamic speed limits to better distribute traffic, the temporary use of hard shoulder lanes, dynamic lane management, and strategic traffic diversion. According to Jacob and Abdulhai (2006), smart mobility solutions combined with demand management can help to reduce congestion.

- Traffic Management Systems (TMS): can help reducing these negative effects by managing the road network, allocating resources, deploying strategies and notifying the users accordingly. Traffic forecasting is a fundamental area of TMS has been widely researched in the last decades.

Over the last years, significant progress has been made in the new technologies used to install the intelligent transport system. These technologies are used in the design, construction, management and operation of transport systems. Some examples of ITS technologies (Jacob & Abdulhai, 2006): closed circuit television (CCTV) camera; variable message signs (VMS) (Organisation for Economic Co-operation and Development, 2007) that provide passengers with up-to-data information on traffic conditions; in-pavement sensors and wireless communication systems that transit traffic data and other information to the various actors in the transport system; radio technologies that inform users of delays and alternatives routes, automatic speed cameras, video surveillance (CEMT/ITF, 2007). From a general point of view, the representative information flow of ITS is as follows: Data collection, communication, processing and, services.

However, like with every scientific study, there are certain limitations. For example, the report summarizes only current road traffic congestion measures and provides constructive insight into the construction of a sustainable and robust traffic management system. Therefore, given its importance, future research directions would include:

Take into consideration the problem of climate change and its environmental impacts on transportation sustainability and inclusive growth.

Include social sustainability in transportation systems, which refers to social equity, safety, social protection, social value, and social inclusion.

CONCLUSION

The transportation sector is vital to human society, but it also contributes significantly to congestion, global GHG emissions and petroleum consumption. Sustainable transport has piqued the interest of academics, industry practitioners, and governments as a means for the transportation sector to embrace the concept of sustainable development. Since the year 2000, there have been numerous studies conducted in the field of sustainable transportation. It is vital to consult with relevant stakeholders or to involve stakeholders in the policymaking process. Today, with the aid of technological advancements and the availability of big data, intelligent transportation systems (ITS), essentially traffic demand management, have emerged to provide solutions to congestion problems and support all the objectives for sustainable mobility. Traffic forecasting is a data-driven decision-making model that forecasts future traffic demand based on history and real-time data. A high level of accuracy in traffic prediction can generate precise travel information for urban citizens and help in the implementation of ITS applications.

REFERENCES

Afrin, T., & Yodo, N. (2020). A survey of road traffic congestion measures towards a sustainable and resilient transportation system. *Sustainability (Basel)*, *12*(11), 4660. doi:10.3390u12114660

Aftabuzzaman, M. (2007). Measuring traffic congestion-a critical review. *30th Australasian Transport Research Forum*, (pp. 1-16).

Agyapong, F., & Ojo, T. K. (2018). Managing traffic congestion in the Accra central market, Ghana. *Journal of Urban Management*, *7*(2), 85–96. doi:10.1016/j.jum.2018.04.002

Albino, V., Berardi, U., & Dangelico, R. M. (2015). Smart cities : Definitions, dimensions, performance, and initiatives. *Journal of Urban Technology*, *22*(1), 3–21. doi:10.1080/10630732.2014.942092

Babaei, A., Khedmati, M., Jokar, M. R. A., & Tirkolaee, E. B. (2023). An integrated decision support system to achieve sustainable development in transportation routes with traffic flow. *Environmental Science and Pollution Research International*, *30*(21), 1–16. doi:10.100711356-023-26644-8 PMID:37022553

Badassa, B. B., Sun, B., & Qiao, L. (2020). Sustainable Transport Infrastructure and Economic Returns : A Bibliometric and Visualization Analysis. *Sustainability (Basel), 12*(5), 2033. doi:10.3390u12052033

Bamwesigye, D., & Hlavackova, P. (2019). Analysis of sustainable transport for smart cities. *Sustainability (Basel), 11*(7), 2140. doi:10.3390u11072140

Banister, D. (2008). The sustainable mobility paradigm. *Transport Policy, 15*(2), 73–80. doi:10.1016/j.tranpol.2007.10.005

Beaudoin, J., Farzin, Y. H., & Lawell, C.-Y. C. L. (2015). Public transit investment and sustainable transportation : A review of studies of transit's impact on traffic congestion and air quality. *Research in Transportation Economics, 52*, 15–22. doi:10.1016/j.retrec.2015.10.004

Beaudoin, J., & Lawell, C.-Y. L. (2017). The effects of urban public transit investment on traffic congestion and air quality. *Urban Transport Systems, 111*.

Benevolo, C., Dameri, R. P., & D'auria, B. (2016). Smart mobility in smart city. In *Empowering Organizations* (pp. 13–28). Springer. doi:10.1007/978-3-319-23784-8_2

Bharadwaj, S., Ballare, S., Rohit, & Chandel, M. K. (2017). Impact of congestion on greenhouse gas emissions for road transport in Mumbai metropolitan region. *Transportation Research Procedia, 25*, 3538–3551. doi:10.1016/j.trpro.2017.05.282

Brundtland, G. H., Khalid, M., Agnelli, S., Al-Athel, S. A., Chidzero, B., Fadika, L. M., Hauff, V., Lang, I., Ma, S., & Botero, M. M. de. (1987). *Our common future; by world commission on environment and development.* UN.

Bull, R. (2015). ICT as an enabler for sustainable development : Reflections on opportunities and barriers. *Journal of Information, Communication and Ethics in Society*.

Butler, L., Yigitcanlar, T., & Paz, A. (2020). Smart urban mobility innovations : A comprehensive review and evaluation. *IEEE Access : Practical Innovations, Open Solutions, 8*, 196034–196049. doi:10.1109/ACCESS.2020.3034596

Button, K. (2006). The political economy of parking charges in "first" and "second-best" worlds. *Transport Policy, 13*(6), 470–478. doi:10.1016/j.tranpol.2006.05.004

Chang, Y. S., Lee, Y. J., & Choi, S. S. B. (2017). Is there more traffic congestion in larger cities?-Scaling analysis of the 101 largest US urban centers. *Transport Policy, 59*, 54–63. doi:10.1016/j.tranpol.2017.07.002

Chatziioannou, I., Alvarez-Icaza, L., Bakogiannis, E., Kyriakidis, C., & Chias-Becerril, L. (2020). A Structural Analysis for the Categorization of the Negative Externalities of Transport and the Hierarchical Organization of Sustainable Mobility's Strategies. *Sustainability (Basel)*, *12*(15), 6011. doi:10.3390u12156011

Cheba, K., & Saniuk, S. (2016). Sustainable urban transport–the concept of measurement in the field of city logistics. *Transportation Research Procedia*, *16*, 35–45. doi:10.1016/j.trpro.2016.11.005

Chen, K., & Miles, J. C. (2004). *ITS handbook 2004 : Recommendations from the world road association*. PIARC.

Cheng, Z., Pang, M.-S., & Pavlou, P. A. (2020). Mitigating traffic congestion : The role of intelligent transportation systems. *Information Systems Research*, *31*(3), 653–674. doi:10.1287/isre.2019.0894

Dargay, J. (2002). Road vehicles : Future growth in developed and developing countries. *Proceedings of the Institution of Civil Engineers. Municipal Engineer*, *151*(1), 3–11. doi:10.1680/muen.2002.151.1.3

de Palma, A., & Lindsey, R. (2011). Traffic congestion pricing methodologies and technologies. *Transportation Research Part C, Emerging Technologies*, *19*(6), 1377–1399. doi:10.1016/j.trc.2011.02.010

Downs, A. (2000). *Stuck in traffic : Coping with peak-hour traffic congestion*. Brookings Institution Press.

Falcocchio, J. C., & Levinson, H. S. (2015). *Road traffic congestion : A concise guide* (Vol. 7). Springer. doi:10.1007/978-3-319-15165-6

Gallo, M., & Marinelli, M. (2020). Sustainable mobility : A review of possible actions and policies. *Sustainability (Basel)*, *12*(18), 7499. doi:10.3390u12187499

Goldman, T., & Gorham, R. (2006). Sustainable urban transport : Four innovative directions. *Technology in Society*, *28*(1-2), 261–273. doi:10.1016/j.techsoc.2005.10.007

Goodwin, P. B. (1996). Empirical evidence on induced traffic. *Transportation*, *23*(1), 35–54. doi:10.1007/BF00166218

Hamad, K., & Kikuchi, S. (2002). Developing a measure of traffic congestion : Fuzzy inference approach. *Transportation Research Record: Journal of the Transportation Research Board*, *1802*(1), 77–85. doi:10.3141/1802-10

Harriet, T., Poku, K., & Emmanuel, A. K. (2013). An assessment of traffic congestion and its effect on productivity in urban Ghana. *International Journal of Business and Social Science*, *4*(3).

He, F., Yan, X., Liu, Y., & Ma, L. (2016). A traffic congestion assessment method for urban road networks based on speed performance index. *Procedia Engineering*, *137*, 425–433. doi:10.1016/j.proeng.2016.01.277

Holden, E., Gilpin, G., & Banister, D. (2019). Sustainable mobility at thirty. *Sustainability (Basel)*, *11*(7), 1965. doi:10.3390u11071965

Hussain, Z., Xia, Z., & Li, Y. (2022). Estimating sustainable transport efficiency and socioeconomic factors : Application of non-parametric approach. *Transportation Letters*, 1–13. doi:10.1080/19427867.2022.2082004

Hymel, K. (2009). Does traffic congestion reduce employment growth? *Journal of Urban Economics*, *65*(2), 127–135. doi:10.1016/j.jue.2008.11.002

Jacob, C., & Abdulhai, B. (2006). Automated adaptive traffic corridor control using reinforcement learning : Approach and case studies. *Transportation Research Record: Journal of the Transportation Research Board*, *1959*(1), 1–8. doi:10.1177/0361198106195900101

Jin, J., & Rafferty, P. (2017). Does congestion negatively affect income growth and employment growth? Empirical evidence from US metropolitan regions. *Transport Policy*, *55*, 1–8. doi:10.1016/j.tranpol.2016.12.003

Johnson, C. M. (1997). The national ITS program : Where we've been and where we're going. *Public Roads, 61*(2).

Jones, P. (2014). The evolution of urban mobility : The interplay of academic and policy perspectives. *IATSS Research*, *38*(1), 7–13. doi:10.1016/j.iatssr.2014.06.001

Kerner, B. S. (1999). Congested Traffic Flow : Observations and Theory. *Transportation Research Record: Journal of the Transportation Research Board*, *1678*(1), 160–167. doi:10.3141/1678-20

Khisty, C. J., & Sriraj, P. S. (2002). Taming the problems of hypermobility through synergy. In *Synergy Matters* (pp. 271–276). Springer. doi:10.1007/0-306-47467-0_46

Kimura, S., Pacudan, R., & Phoumin, H. (2017). *Development of the eco town model in the ASEAN region through adoption of energy-efficient building technologies, sustainable transport, and smart grids*. Economic Research Institute.

Kiunsi, R. B. (2013). A review of traffic congestion in Dar es Salaam city from the physical planning perspective. *Journal of Sustainable Development*, *6*(2), 94. doi:10.5539/jsd.v6n2p94

Kockelman, K. M., & Kalmanje, S. (2005). Credit-based congestion pricing : A policy proposal and the public's response. *Transportation Research Part A, Policy and Practice*, *39*(7-9), 671–690. doi:10.1016/j.tra.2005.02.014

Laconte, P. (2012). Towards sustainability in European cities contrasts between the overall effects of European Union policies and achievements at the level of individual cities. *ISOCARP Review*, *8*, 2–17.

Lah, O. (2019). Sustainable urban mobility in action. In *Sustainable Urban Mobility Pathways* (pp. 133–282). Elsevier. doi:10.1016/B978-0-12-814897-6.00007-7

Lesteven, G. (2012). Les stratégies d'adaptation à la congestion automobile dans les grandes métropoles: Analyse à partir des cas de Paris, São Paulo et Mumbai. *Confins. Revue franco-brésilienne de géographie/Revista franco-brasilera de geografia, 15*.

Li, Z., & Hensher, D. A. (2012). Congestion charging and car use : A review of stated preference and opinion studies and market monitoring evidence. *Transport Policy*, *20*, 47–61. doi:10.1016/j.tranpol.2011.12.004

Litman, T. (2005). *Well measured : Developing indicators for comprehensive and sustainable transportation planning*. Victoria Transportation Policy Institute.

Litman, T. (2006). Changing travel demand : Implications for transport planning. *Institute of Transportation Engineers. ITE Journal*, *76*(9), 27.

Litman, T. (2014). *Critique of" Transit Utilization and Traffic Congestion : Is There a Connection?* Reason Foundation.

Litman, T. (2016). *Parking management : Strategies, evaluation and planning*. Victoria Transport Policy Institute Victoria.

Litman, T., & Burwell, D. (2006). Issues in sustainable transportation. *International Journal of Global Environmental Issues*, *6*(4), 331–347. doi:10.1504/IJGENVI.2006.010889

Liu, H. (2020). *Smart Cities : Big Data Prediction Methods and Applications*. Springer. doi:10.1007/978-981-15-2837-8

Lomax, T., Turner, S., Shunk, G., Levinson, H. S., Pratt, R. H., Bay, P. N., & Douglas, G. B. (1997). *Quantifying Congestion* (Vol. 2). User's Guide.

Lomax, T. J. (1997). *Quantifying congestion* (Vol. 398). Transportation Research Board.

López, C., Ruíz-Benítez, R., & Vargas-Machuca, C. (2019). On the environmental and social sustainability of technological innovations in urban bus transport : The EU case. *Sustainability (Basel)*, *11*(5), 1413. doi:10.3390u11051413

Lu, J., Li, B., Li, H., & Al-Barakani, A. (2021). Expansion of city scale, traffic modes, traffic congestion, and air pollution. *Cities (London, England)*, *108*, 102974. doi:10.1016/j.cities.2020.102974

Mahmud, K., Gope, K., & Chowdhury, S. M. R. (2012). Possible causes & solutions of traffic jam and their impact on the economy of Dhaka City. *Journal of Management and Sustainability*, *2*(2), 112. doi:10.5539/jms.v2n2p112

Mangiaracina, R., Perego, A., Salvadori, G., & Tumino, A. (2017). A comprehensive view of intelligent transport systems for urban smart mobility. *International Journal of Logistics*, *20*(1), 39–52. doi:10.1080/13675567.2016.1241220

Manual, H. C. (1985). *Special report 209*. Transportation Research Board, Washington, DC.

May, A., & Marsden, G. (2010). *Urban transport and mobility*. Semantic Scholar.

May, A. D. (2013). Urban transport and sustainability: The key challenges. *International Journal of Sustainable Transportation*, *7*(3), 170–185. doi:10.1080/15568318.2013.710136

May, T., & Crass, M. (2007). Sustainability in transport: Implications for policy makers. *Transportation Research Record: Journal of the Transportation Research Board*, *2017*(1), 1–9. doi:10.3141/2017-01

Meyer, M. D. (1997). *A toolbox for alleviating traffic congestion and enhancing mobility*. Federal Highway Administration.

Naude, C., & Tsolakis, D. (2005). *Defining transport congestion*. TRB. https://trid.trb.org/view/1156189

Newbery, D. M. (2001). Harmonizing energy Taxes in the EU. conference Tax Policy in the European Union, Ministry of Finance. The Hague, 17-19.

Newman, P., & Kenworthy, J. (1999). *Sustainability and cities : Overcoming automobile dependence*. Island press.

Nguyen-Phuoc, D. Q., Young, W., Currie, G., & De Gruyter, C. (2020). Traffic congestion relief associated with public transport : State-of-the-art. *Public Transport (Berlin)*, *12*(2), 455–481. doi:10.100712469-020-00231-3

Noland, R. B. (2001). Relationships between highway capacity and induced vehicle travel. *Transportation Research Part A, Policy and Practice*, *35*(1), 47–72. doi:10.1016/S0965-8564(99)00047-6

Oladimeji, D., Gupta, K., Kose, N. A., Gundogan, K., Ge, L., & Liang, F. (2023). Smart transportation : An overview of technologies and applications. *Sensors (Basel)*, *23*(8), 3880. doi:10.339023083880 PMID:37112221

Organisation for Economic Co-operation and Development. European Conference of Ministers of Transport, & Transport Research Centre (Éds.). (2007). *Managing urban traffic congestion*. OECD: ECMT.

Pojani, D., & Stead, D. (2015). Sustainable urban transport in the developing world: Beyond megacities. *Sustainability (Basel)*, *7*(6), 7784–7805. doi:10.3390u7067784

Pojani, D., & Stead, D. (2018). Policy design for sustainable urban transport in the global south. *Policy Design and Practice*, *1*(2), 90–102. doi:10.1080/25741292.2 018.1454291

Portugal-Pereira, J. O., Doll, C. N. H., Suwa, A., & Puppim de Oliveira, J. A. (2013). The sustainable mobility-congestion nexus : A co-benefits approach to finding win-win solutions. *Transport and Communications Bulletin for Asia and the Pacific*, *82*, 19–31.

Raffaud, F. (2003). *L'URBAIN, L'ENVIRONNEMENT ET LE DEVELOPPEMENT DURABLE EN FRANCE Essai d'analyse–Revue Urbanisme-1964-2000*. Université de Pau et des Pays de l'Adour.

Rao, A. M., & Rao, K. R. (2012). Measuring urban traffic congestion-a review. *IJTTE. International Journal for Traffic and Transport Engineering*, *2*(4).

Reymond. M. (2005). *La tarification de la congestion automobile: Acceptabilité sociale et redistribution des recettes du péage*. [Thèse de doctorat en sciences économiques, Montpellier, université Montpellier 1].

Richardson, B. C. (2005). Sustainable transport: Analysis frameworks. *Journal of Transport Geography*, *13*(1), 29–39. doi:10.1016/j.jtrangeo.2004.11.005

Rodrigue, J.-P. (2016). *The geography of transport systems*. Taylor & Francis. doi:10.4324/9781315618159

Rosenbloom, S. (1978). Peak-period traffic congestion: A state-of-the-art analysis and evaluation of effective solutions. *Transportation, 7*(2), 167–191. doi:10.1007/BF00184638

Rothenberg, M. J. (1985). *Urban traffic congestion: what does the future hold? Urban congestion in the united states: what does the future hold?* TRB. https://trid.trb.org/view/274659

Rubin, T. A., & Mansour, F. (2013). *Transit Utilization and Traffic Congestion: Is There a Connection?* Santos, G. (2017). Road fuel taxes in Europe: Do they internalize road transport externalities? *Transport Policy, 53*, 120–134.

Schrank, D., Lomax, T., & Eisele, B. (2012). *2012 urban mobility report.* Texas Transportation Institute. http://mobility. tamu. edu/ums/report

Schrank, D. L., Turner, S. M., & Lomax, T. J. (1993). *Estimates of urban roadway congestion, 1990.*

Selmoune, A., Cheng, Q., Wang, L., & Liu, Z. (2020). Influencing factors in congestion pricing acceptability: A literature review. *Journal of Advanced Transportation, 2020*, 2020. doi:10.1155/2020/4242964

Shatanawi, M., Abdelkhalek, F., & Mészáros, F. (2020). Urban Congestion Charging Acceptability: An International Comparative Study. *Sustainability (Basel), 12*(12), 5044. doi:10.3390u12125044

Shi, K., Di, B., Zhang, K., Feng, C., & Svirchev, L. (2018). Detrended cross-correlation analysis of urban traffic congestion and NO 2 concentrations in Chengdu. *Transportation Research Part D, Transport and Environment, 61*, 165–173. doi:10.1016/j.trd.2016.12.012

Shin, J.-H., & Jun, H.-B. (2014). A study on smart parking guidance algorithm. *Transportation Research Part C, Emerging Technologies, 44*, 299–317. doi:10.1016/j.trc.2014.04.010

Small, K. A. (2010). *Energy Policies for Automobile Transportation.* Resources for the Future.

Steinsland, C., Fridstrøm, L., Madslien, A., & Minken, H. (2018). The climate, economic and equity effects of fuel tax, road toll and commuter tax credit. *Transport Policy, 72*, 225–241. doi:10.1016/j.tranpol.2018.04.019

Sterner, T. (2007). Fuel taxes: An important instrument for climate policy. *Energy Policy, 35*(6), 3194–3202. doi:10.1016/j.enpol.2006.10.025

Stopher, P. R. (2004). Reducing road congestion: A reality check. *Transport Policy*, *11*(2), 117–131. doi:10.1016/j.tranpol.2003.09.002

Sussman, J. M. (2005). Intelligent Transportation Systems at the Turning Point: Preparing for Integrated, Regional, and Market-Driven Deployment. *Perspectives on Intelligent Transportation Systems (ITS)*, 173-187.

Systematics, C. (2005). *Traffic congestion and reliability: Trends and advanced strategies for congestion mitigation.* Federal Highway Administration.

Tirachini, A. (2019). Ride-hailing, travel behaviour and sustainable mobility : An international review. *Transportation*, 1–37.

Vaziri, M. (2002). Development of highway congestion index with fuzzy set models. *Transportation Research Record: Journal of the Transportation Research Board*, *1802*(1), 16–22. doi:10.3141/1802-03

Vianna, M. M. B., da Silva Portugal, L., & Balassiano, R. (2004). Intelligent transportation systems and parking management: Implementation potential in a Brazilian city. *Cities (London, England)*, *21*(2), 137–148. doi:10.1016/j.cities.2004.01.001

Viauroux, C. (2011). Pricing urban congestion: A structural random utility model with traffic anticipation. *European Economic Review*, *55*(7), 877–902. doi:10.1016/j.euroecorev.2011.04.001

Yılmaz, Y., Uludağ, S., Dilek, E., & Ayizen, Y. E. (2016). A preliminary work on predicting travel times and optimal routes using Istanbul's real traffic data. 9th transist transport congress and exhibition.

Xiong, Z., Sheng, H., Rong, W., & Cooper, D. E. (2012). Intelligent transportation systems for smart cities: A progress review. *Science China. Information Sciences*, *55*(12), 2908–2914. doi:10.100711432-012-4725-1

Ye, S. (2012). Research on Urban Road Traffic Congestion Charging Based on Sustainable Development. *Physics Procedia*, *24*, 1567–1572. doi:10.1016/j.phpro.2012.02.231

Zhang, J., Wang, F.-Y., Wang, K., Lin, W.-H., Xu, X., & Chen, C. (2011). Data-driven intelligent transportation systems: A survey. *IEEE Transactions on Intelligent Transportation Systems*, *12*(4), 1624–1639. doi:10.1109/TITS.2011.2158001

Zhang, Y., & Cheng, L. (2023). The role of transport infrastructure in economic growth : Empirical evidence in the UK. *Transport Policy*, *133*, 223–233. doi:10.1016/j.tranpol.2023.01.017

Zhao, X., Ke, Y., Zuo, J., Xiong, W., & Wu, P. (2020a). Evaluation of sustainable transport research in 2000–2019. *Journal of Cleaner Production, 256*, 120404. doi:10.1016/j.jclepro.2020.120404

Zhao, X., Ke, Y., Zuo, J., Xiong, W., & Wu, P. (2020b). Evaluation of sustainable transport research in 2000–2019. *Journal of Cleaner Production, 256*, 120404. doi:10.1016/j.jclepro.2020.120404

Zhou, J. (2012). Sustainable transportation in the US: A review of proposals, policies, and programs since 2000. *Frontiers of Architectural Research, 1*(2), 150–165. doi:10.1016/j.foar.2012.02.012

ENDNOTES

[1]   https://www.un.org/development/desa/en/news/population/2018-revision-of-world-urbanization-prospects.html

[2]   https://www.who.int/news-room/fact-sheets/detail/ambient-(outdoor)-air-quality-and-health

[3]   The European Conference of Ministers of Transport (ECMT) 2007

[4]   https://www.un.org/development/desa/en/news/population/2018-revision-of-world-urbanization-prospects.html

[5]   https://www.who.int/news-room/fact-sheets/detail/ambient-(outdoor)-air-quality-and-health

[6]   The European Conference of Ministers of Transport (ECMT) 2007

Chapter 10

Petri Nets–Based Optimization of Multi-Level Marketing Schemes for the Green Economy

Girish Rao Salanke
R.V. College of Engineering, India

Girish Rao Salanke
R.V. College of Engineering, India

Ashok Kumar A. R.
R.V. College of Engineering, India

ShivaKumar Dalali
PES University, India

ABSTRACT

Green economy and its relevant concepts have gained popularity during the last decade to promote and support equitable and sustainable development. Developing countries have deliberately undertaken initiatives that float responsible development, valuing the magnanimity and foresight of these principles despite their barriers to the progress of a developing nation. The repeating idea of placing a tax on the production, use, and emission of carbon by industry has been recognized and implemented by governments worldwide. The principle addressed in this chapter advocates for the implementation of carbon tax measures in a selective and authoritative manner, which historically led to non-conformity, restlessness, and inefficiency. The objective of this article is to utilize Petri Nets to legalize the behavior of a multi-level marketing system to assure an effective carbon tax hierarchy to promote a green economy, to optimize it, and to model it.

DOI: 10.4018/978-1-6684-8140-0.ch010

INTRODUCTION

Sustainable Development and a Green Economy

A model of sustainable development is a paradigm that has been encouraged, incentivized and sometimes, even imposed on developing and developed nations, to direct growth that promoted minimized impact on the environment. As a result, sustainable development can be explained in various forms. In simplest terms, as quoted from the Brundtland Report, "Sustainable development is development that meets the needs of the present without compromising the ability of future generations to meet their own needs" (United Nations, 1987, p. 37).

A green economy is seen as the most tangible, realistic and goal-oriented approach to embrace sustainable development and revolutionizing the environmental sector. There is a greater demand and public awareness for sustainable goods and services, engendered by government policy, incentives and regulatory environments. Henceforth, companies worldwide have begun using the 'greenness' of their initiatives as a unique selling point of their goods and services (Nathalie, 2022).

In retrospect, the green economy encompasses all aspects that relate to the production of green products and services including the inputs, outputs, processes and outcomes. It also serves to aggregate all the activities operating with the primary intention of minimizing all forms of environmental impact by reducing conventional levels of resource consumption and harmful emissions. It aims to undertake proactive efforts to repair and rethink future efforts to address and implement the reduction of negative production, distribution and consumption patterns in the economy. ECO Canada (2010) defines a green organization as an organization that produces and designs goods and services to minimize environmental impact, and a green job as one that requires a skill set pertaining to the above.

Governments worldwide have tried incessantly to inculcate the values of sustainability in the society and entrench principles of green economy amongst industries. Global warming and the greenhouse effect tarnished the environment beyond repair, and countries made frantic attempts to control the damage by taxing carbon consumption. Carbon dioxide is one of the most detrimental greenhouse gases that arises from coal and carbon. Carbon fuels industries, homes and a country's development. However, its ill-effects have forced even governments of developing nations to place development on a backseat, and rethink futuristic strategies that have lesser negative production and leave a smaller carbon footprint.

Carbon Tax

A carbon tax may be a unique charge or a number of excise duty levies on the extraction, production and consumption of and by-products of carbon. The process assures the greater cost to pump carbon dioxide into the atmosphere so that the globe utilizes cleaner and greener solutions (Letzter, 2016).

At the annual American Geophysical Union (AGU), billionaire entrepreneur and reputed renewable energy enthusiast - Elon Musk advocated for instituting a carbon tax to migrate to cleaner forms of renewable energy and mitigate the climate change (Wall, 2015).

The following Table 1 has been constructed to consolidate the current operation and implementation of carbon taxes around the world and invoke a comparative study of the emission trading schemes in various countries today (Carbon Tax Centre, n.d.; SBS News, 2016).

Analyzing the aforementioned statistics reveals that around 80% of the nations have imposed a national carbon price. It is very commendable that many of these countries are developing nations. In applying a nationwide tax, advanced nations looked more cautious and carbon prices are exclusive to select states or provinces. South Africa is apparently unique for setting a higher tax time limit, whereas Australia appears after two years of operation to have withdrawn the carbon tax. Figure 1, provides a comprehensive representational map of carbon tax schemes around the world.

Multi-Level Marketing

"Marketing at multilevel or "network" is a business strategy aimed at raising money through a recruitment scheme including the recruitment of new members suggested by existing scheme members. It employs these independent representatives to offer items or services to others through the company's favourable word of mouth, which allows for free exposure and marketing. The representative receives commissions or discounts from his or her retail sales, as well as from other persons he or she employs for retail sales. Amway and Mary Kay Cosmetics are examples of renowned multi-level marketing firms (Michigan Department of Attorney General, n.d.).

Multi-level marketing schemes do not collect an entry fee for an individual to join the network, and is a lawful and legitimate business method. They are frequently mistaken with pyramid schemes that also entail recruiting and a heavy charge. Pyramid schemes violate the law and are called unlawful as the structure of a pyramid system assures rapid market saturation, making people immensely affluent at the highest levels in the pyramid, while close to 90% of the other members are misplaced.

Table 1. A Summary of carbon tax schemes around the world

Sl no.	Country	Year of Implementation	Jurisdiction	Status	Tax Amount in USD per tonne of Carbon
1	China	2017	State-based	To be implemented	-NA-
2	USA	2009	State-based	In practice in some states	-NA-
3	Canada	2006	State-based	In practice in some states	-NA-
4	India	2010	Nation-wide	In practice	1-8
5	Ireland	2010	Nation-wide	In practice	43
6	Chile	2014	Nation-wide	In practice	5
7	Zimbabwe	-NA-	Nation-wide	In practice	0.03 or 3% of fuel cost
8	New Zealand	2008	Nation-wide	In practice	-NA-
9	South Korea	2015	Nation-wide	In practice	-NA-
10	Japan	2012	Nation-wide	In practice	4
11	Europe	2025	State-based	To be implemented	5-32
12	Finland	1990	Nation-wide	In practice	21
13	Netherlands	1990	Nation-wide	In practice	-NA-
14	Sweden	1991	Nation-wide	In practice	150
15	Norway	1991	Nation-wide	In practice	-NA-
16	Denmark	2002	Nation-wide	In practice	18
17	Switzerland	2008	Nation-wide	In practice	36
18	Costa Rica	1997	Nation-wide	In practice	3.5% of market value of fossil fuel
19	South Africa	2017-2020	Nation-wide	In practice	15
20	Australia	2012-2014	Nation-wide	Repealed	20

Pyramid scheme promoters promise recruits of making large sums of money if they join the scheme by paying a nominal entry fee and convince 6 more members to do so. Typical marketing strategies would involve lines such as "Pay 1000$, get 36000$ in return!". Having originated from a source involving one individual who would not have paid anything to join the scheme, he recruits 6 members who pay 1000$ each, who in turn recruit 6 members each. At this stage, the person at the top of the pyramid leaves the scheme, collecting the newly earned 36000$, while the pyramid is now split into 6 pyramids each having one person at the top, waiting

Figure 1. A representation of existing, emerging and potential regional, national and sub-national carbon pricing initiatives (ETS and tax)
Courtesy - World Bank ("State and Trends of Carbon Pricing, 2016"). Note, ETS refers to emissions trading schemes (i.e., cap-and-trade).
Source: Carbon Tax Centre (n.d.)

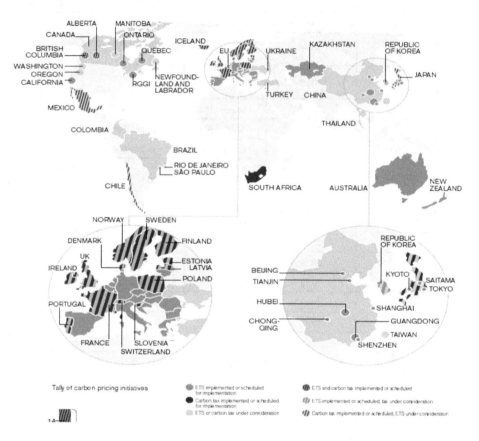

to fill the next 216 recruits, as shown in Figure 2. The detrimental problem with this scheme is its exponential structure which ensures that the number of recruits at the 13th level would have to exceed the population of the world. Due to the sheer impossibility and absence of subsequent levels, the people at the 12th and 13th level will make no money. In other words, around 90% of the members will be duped.

Multi-level marketing schemes do not place rigid requirements on the number of people to recruit as shown in Figure 3 and Figure 4, nor does it collect an entry fee to be recruited. Money paid as a part of the scheme acts as a complete or partial compensation for goods or services.

Figure 2. Market saturation in pyramid schemes
Courtesy - Security and Exchange commission, U.S. Federal Govt.

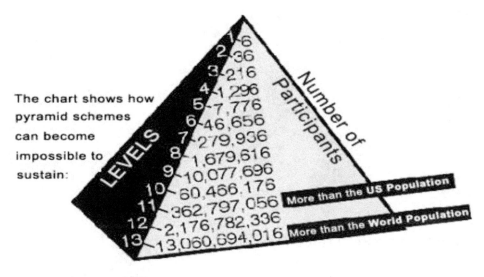

The methodology proposed in this paper involves using a multi-level marketing scheme with a restriction on the number of recruits, to build a carbon tax hierarchy that is modeled using Petri Nets.

Figure 3. Multi-level marketing
Courtesy – One Happy Hubbard

Figure 4. The spatial structure of a multi-level marketing scheme

Programming Petri Nets

A Petri Net in the broadest sense, is a mechanism that is used to model the behavior of real-world systems that operate in a concurrent environment with limited resources. Ever since their inception by Carl Adam Petri in 1962, Petri Nets and their concepts have been used to model, develop, optimize and extend applications in a variety of areas such as work-flows, automation, telecommunications, manufacturing, networks and real-time systems (Petri Nets, n.d.).

A Petri Net is a bipartite graph G: (V, E), where V is the set of vertices and E is the set of edges. It is to be noted that the set of vertices consists of places P and transitions T, such that $V = P \cup T$ and $P \cap T \neq \emptyset$. Edges E consists of a collection of directed arcs connecting transitions and places. Places hold tokens, which represent the number of resources present. A marked Petri Net consists of tokens assigned to places, as shown in Figure 5 (Dennis, 2011; Folz-Weinstein et al., 2023; Petri Nets, n.d.).

Places indicate states, transitions indicate processes and tokens denote resources in a real time concurrent environment. A place having a directed arc from itself to a transition serves as an input place, else it is termed as an output place. A transition is said to be enabled if all of its input places contain at least one token, as shown in Figure 6(a). An enabled transition can fire, denoting the execution of a particular transition or process. This results in a Petri Net as shown in Figure 6(b), with one token deducted from each input place, and one token added to each of the output places. It must be noted that multiple transitions can fired simultaneously provided they are all enabled. This idea helps to implement Petri Nets for concurrent environments like the proposed carbon tax model.

Figure 5. A marked Petri Net

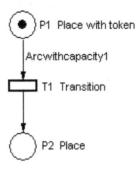

Figure 6. (a) Marked Petri Net with enabled input places (b) firing Complete

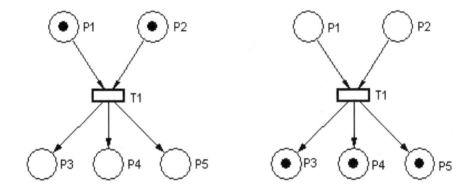

METHODOLOGY

The arbitrary and unidirectional nature of the tax regime was highlighted by an analysis of carbon tax regimes throughout the world. Corporate actors and industries have frequently been noted to be hesitant participants of the carbon tax system, which explains why industrialized nations have no federal carbon tax schemes. In emerging countries, it seems to be unjust to place limitations on the board of growth because these countries are moving quickly in order to achieve equal status with industrialized ones. On the other side, governments are responsible for supporting sustainability and for promoting green projects. This requires a profit-making carbon tax mechanism which proves profitable for both industry and governments and the environment by extension. Retrospectively, carbon tax defaults are numerous, and a carbon price promotes and implements little to the final aim of true sustainable development and an efficient green economic with minimal environmental effect.

The proposed model is often called as 8-ball model in a multi-level marketing scheme. The aim is to construct multi-level marketing scheme to build a carbon tax hierarchy, modeled using Petri Nets. The 8-ball model consists of the first player, denoted in blue in Figure 7, who is required to recruit two members into the scheme. Abiding by the rules of network marketing, there is no entry fee involved to enter the scheme. The number of recruits per member is restricted to two, to prevent collapse and congestion in early stages. Each member is required to satisfy a set of basic conditions to enter the scheme, and then required to recruit two members, to reap benefits from the scheme.

Figure 7. The proposed structure

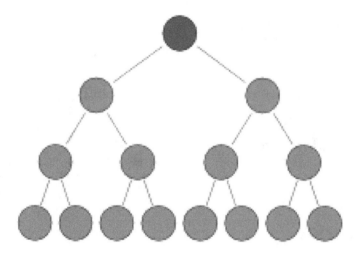

The proposed model is now represented using Petri Nets to gain better clarity, as shown in Figure 6. First of all, a carbon tax recruiting plan was announced by the government. The initiatives' policies can be described succinctly as follows.

i.   By enrolling with a Government site, industry, corporations and organizations can register without entrance fees into the plan.
ii.   In order to qualify and continue forward, companies must then apply green ways to minimize carbon footprint and emissions by means of innovation, research and growth, and production, consumption, distribution, packaging and disposal.

iii.   The scheme must be adopted on the first completed and first serving basis as a 'Certified Green Organization' by organizations that fulfil all the Government's certificates and emission controls and environmental metrics. Each 'Certified Green Organization' is then required to recruit and encourage two more organizations to join the scheme.

iv.   The former receives a Carbon Tax Exemption when recruiting the full certification and turning it into "Certified Green Organizations."

v.   The maintenance of green practices should be reviewed automatically by all organizations which have entered the system after two years of accession. Once the certification has been renewed, they are reassembled in the network and have two members recruit for carbon tax exemption.

The above policy has been represented and modeled in the Figure 8(a), using Petri Nets. These programmed Petri Nets will operate on the backend of the government portal to ensure the smooth functioning of the scheme. Each place P1, P2, P3, P4, P5, P6 and P7 denote the organizations that have registered in the scheme. P1 starts the network. Upon receiving certification as a 'Certified Green Organization', it can execute transitions t1 and t2, firing both of them.

P1 consists of only two tokens, to allow it to recruit only two members. After firing is complete, P1 gets an exemption on carbon tax, as shown in figure 8(b). P2 and P3 will now have to get certified to enable their transitions, and then fire them by recruiting two members each, thereby obtaining an exemption.

Figure 8a. Detailed METHODOLOGY

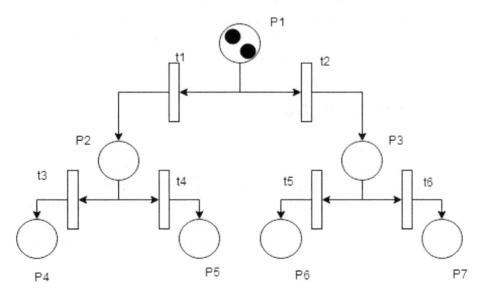

Figure 8b. Firing complete

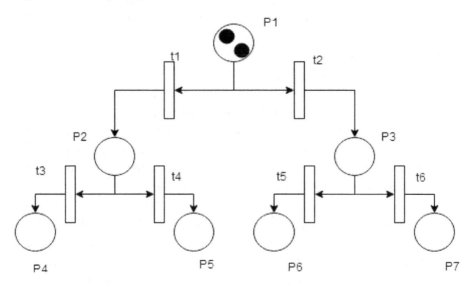

The advantage of using multi-level marketing increases two-fold when multiple organizations wish to start the scheme, instead of a single source. The nature of multi-level marketing guarantees a spatial web, and the functionality of Petri Nets validates concurrency. Besides, the idea of employing a spatial recruitment scheme to develop a carbon tax hierarchy is more beneficial and enforceable, as opposed to an arbitrary taxation scheme using similar policies as above. A recruitment scheme establishes an ideology of recommendation, where the recommender is readily endorsing the initiative, thereby promoting better enthusiasm amongst organizations to join. The prototype of recruitment encourages participation amongst industries. In arbitrary taxation, corporations are seen to wait until key contemporaries make a move, before they decide to accept a proposal.

EXPERIMENTAL ANALYSIS

An analysis of the enforcement of carbon tax and emission trading schemes around the world has been illustrated below. Figure 9 is a time graph that elaborates on the year of enforcement of carbon taxes in various countries. While Scandinavian nations have been at the forefront of introducing carbon taxes, a lot of the other countries have enforced carbon legislation over the last decade. As a consequence, while countries noted a decrease in their carbon emissions, some of them reported increased emissions, due to defaulters.

Figure 9. Year of implementation of Carbon Tax Scheme

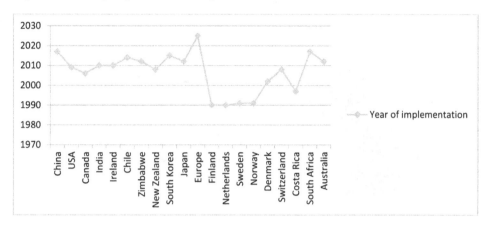

An observable trend is that 80% of the nations that have implemented carbon legislation have enforced federal laws, with most of them being developing nations, as shown in Figure 10. The developed nations follow state-based restrictions, with some provinces levying a tax, while others do not. This anomalous behavior has foiled reasonable efforts to minimize environmental impact.

Figure 11 elucidates on the fact that only three quarters of the nations that have placed carbon taxation on the agenda, have enforced it in practice. The remaining countries are yet to implement them, or have revoked them, owing to pressurized opposition and poor implementation.

The analysis enlightens the reason for the underlying lackluster performance of carbon taxes worldwide, which is poor enforcement and tax model. The model

Figure 10. Carbon tax policy in nations

Figure 11. Status of implementation of carbon tax

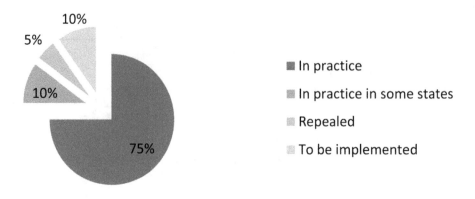

- In practice
- In practice in some states
- Repealed
- To be implemented

proposed in this paper offers an efficient alternative, and the illustration below explains its benefits.

Table 2. Illustration of financial implication of proposed model

Sl. no	Metric	Value
1	Total number of companies	80
2	Number of companies willing to pay Carbon tax under present scheme	8 (10%)
3	Investment on capital per company	Rs. 100000
4	Carbon Tax paid per company	Rs. 20000
5	Revenue received by the government	Rs. 160000
6	Number of companies willing to go green, thereby will get recruited in the current scheme	64 (80%)
7	Reduced Tax offered by government for companies that recruit two new members	5%
8	Model of new scheme	
9	Carbon Tax paid per company under proposed scheme	Rs. 5000
10	Number of companies benefited by special tax	32
11	Number of companies in lowermost level of the scheme	32
12	Carbon Tax paid per company until it recruits more members under proposed scheme	Rs. 10000 (10%)
13	Revenue received by the government	Rs. 480000
14	Number of years after which companies undergo review	2 years

This instance has been considered in the situation of India, a developing country. India collects a carbon tax of Rs. 400. (~$6). That is over 20% of the carbon cost per tonne, and a tax of 20% on the capital spent. In India, most firms are said to pay 0 percent of tax, as they are all paid on profits. But the carbon tax is an issue, because it is paid by 20% on capital. To illustrate this, it was imagined that India had a total of 80 firms. A report found that just 10% of Indian firms earned profits and hence paid carbon taxes. However, 80 percent of firms indicated their wish to become green since their reputation would grow on the market. Table 2 shows the financial potential of the model suggested. Every firm was projected to invest Rs. 100,000 on capital.

Henceforth, the efficiency of the scheme has been illustrated to understand the win-win model for the industries that pay lesser tax with better satisfaction, the government that could make more revenue, and the environment, which is conserved better.

CONCLUSION

i.   A detailed study of sustainable development was carried out to understand the effects and enforcement of a green economy that is tangible, realistic and futuristic.

ii. A comprehensive, comparative analysis of carbon taxes and legislation was performed to correlate the implementation of Carbon taxes for a greener economy.

iii. Experimental analysis on the carbon legislation in countries around the world revealed that it is poorly enforced with little impact on environmental conservation. While only three quarters of the countries have an enforced law, 80% of the countries had a federal law in place.

iv. A model was proposed to construct a carbon tax hierarchy, that uses multi-level marketing schemes to recruit organizations to go green, thereby gaining carbon tax exemption.

v.   Petri Nets were programmed to model and illustrate the behavior of the scheme, which serves as a win-win situation for industries, governments and the environment, thereby putting forth an efficient, enforceable, sustainable, innovative and financially stable carbon tax model.

REFERENCES

ECO Canada. (2010). *Defining the green economy*. Eco Canada. https://eco.ca/new-reports/defining-the-green-economy

Carbon Tax Centre. (n.d.). *Where carbon is taxed*. Carbon Tax. https://www.carbontax.org/where-carbon-is-taxed-overview/

Dennis, J. B. (2011). Petri Nets. In D. Padua (Ed.), *Encyclopedia of Parallel Computing*. Springer.

Folz-Weinstein, S., Bergenthum, R., Desel, J., & Kovář, J. (2023, May). ILP2 Miner–Process Discovery for Partially Ordered Event Logs Using Integer Linear Programming. In *International Conference on Applications and Theory of Petri Nets and Concurrency* (pp. 59-76). Cham: Springer Nature Switzerland. 10.1007/978-3-031-33620-1_4

Letzter, R. (2016, November 2). One of the most influential economists in the world explains why a carbon tax is a good idea. *Insider*. https://www.businessinsider.com/gregory-mankiw-harvard-professor-carbon-tax-2016-11

Michigan Department of Attorney General. (n.d.). *Multi-level marketing or illegal pyramid scheme*. MI Department of Attorney General. https://www.michigan.gov/ag/consumer-protection/Consumer-Alerts/consumer-alerts/invest/mlm-illegal-pyramid-scheme

Nathalie, B. O. (2022). Sustainable development. *International Institute for Sustainable Development*. https://www.iisd.org/mission-and-goals/sustainable-development

News, S. B. S. (2016, December 8). *Factbox: Carbon taxes and emission trading schemes around the world*. SBS. https://www.sbs.com.au/news/article/2016/12/08/factbox-carbon-taxes-and-emission-trading-schemes-around-world

Petri Nets. (n.d.). *Intro*. Bielefeld University. https://www.techfak.uni-bielefeld.de/~mchen/BioPNML/Intro/pnfaq.html

United Nations. (1987). *Our common future*. UN. https://www.are.admin.ch/are/en/home/media/publications/sustainable-development/brundtland-report.html

Wall, M. (2015, December 17). The world needs a carbon tax, Elon Musk says. *Live Science*. https://www.livescience.com/53113-elon-musk-carbon-tax.html

Compilation of References

Abd Hamid, M., & Mohd Isa, S. (2020). Exploring the sustainable tourism practices among tour operators in Malaysia. *Journal of Sustainability Science and Management*, *15*, 68–80.

Abdel Wahed Ahmed, M. M., & Abd El Monem, N. (2020). Sustainable and green transportation for better quality of life case study greater Cairo–Egypt. *HBRC Journal*, *16*(1), 17–37. doi:10.1 080/16874048.2020.1719340

Abduljabbar, R., Dia, H., Liyanage, S., & Bagloee, S. A. (2019). Applications of artificial intelligence in transport: An overview. *Sustainability (Basel)*, *11*(1), 189. doi:10.3390u11010189

AbdullahiS. I. (2018). Nigerian economy: Business, governance and investment in period of crisis. *Social Science Research Network*. https://ssrn.com/abstract=3310120

Abdullahi, S. I., & Shuaibu, M. (2022). Can Stock Market Capitalization and Financial Development Predict Household Consumption in Nigeria? *CBN Bullion*, *46*(2), 39–48.

Abebe, R., Adamic, L., & Kleinberg, J. (2018). Mitigating Overexposure in Viral Marketing. *Proceedings of the AAAI Conference on Artificial Intelligence*, *32*(1). doi:10.1609/aaai.v32i1.11282

Abur, C. C., Angahar, J. S., & Terande, T. J. (2022). Electricity Generation and Economic Growth in Nigeria: Is There Any Link? *Asian Journal of Current Research*, *7*(1), 1–7. doi:10.56557/ajocr/2022/v7i17560

Abzari, M., Safari Shad, F., Abedi Sharbiyani, A. A., & Parvareshi Morad, A. (2013). Studying the effect of green marketing mix on market share increase. *European Online Journal of Natural and Social Sciences: Proceedings, 2*(3), 641.

Adedokun, A. (2015). Can Electricity Consumption be Useful in Predicting Nigerian Economic Growth? Evidence From Error Correction Model. *OPEC Energy Review*, *39*(2), 125–140. doi:10.1111/opec.12042

Adinyra, N., & Gligui, E. (2011). *Green Marketing Potential as Assessed from Consumers Purchasing Behaviors: The Case of Ghana* [Dissertation, URN]. http://urn.kb.se/resolve?urn=urn:nbn:se:bth-5441

Adlwarth, W. (2010). Corporate social responsibility–customer expectations and behaviour in the tourism sector. In R. Conrady & M. Buck (Eds.), *Trends and Issues in Global Tourism 2010* (pp. 101–109). Springer. doi:10.1007/978-3-642-10829-7_13

Afrin, T., & Yodo, N. (2020). A survey of road traffic congestion measures towards a sustainable and resilient transportation system. *Sustainability (Basel)*, *12*(11), 4660. doi:10.3390u12114660

Aftabuzzaman, M. (2007). Measuring traffic congestion-a critical review. *30th Australasian Transport Research Forum*, (pp. 1-16).

Agrawal, R., & Gupta, S. (2018). Consuming Responsibly: Exploring Environmentally Responsible Consumption Behaviors. *Journal of Global Marketing*, *31*(4), 231–245. doi:10.1080/0891176 2.2017.1415402

Agyapong, F., & Ojo, T. K. (2018). Managing traffic congestion in the Accra central market, Ghana. *Journal of Urban Management*, *7*(2), 85–96. doi:10.1016/j.jum.2018.04.002

Ajzen, I. (1991). The theory of planned behavior. *Organizational Behavior and Human Decision Processes*, *50*(2), 179–211. doi:10.1016/0749-5978(91)90020-T

Ajzen, I. (2011). The theory of planned behavior: Reactions and reflections. *Psychology & Health*, *26*(9), 1113–1127. doi:10.1080/08870446.2011.613995 PMID:21929476

AKCP. (2022, February). *The Amount of Datacenter Energy Use.* AKCP Monitoring. https://www.akcp.com/blog/the-real-amount-of-energy-a-data-center-use/

Akehurst, G., Afonso, C., & Martins Gonçalves, H. (2012). Re-examining green purchase behaviour and the green consumer profile: New evidences. *Management Decision*, *50*(5), 972–988. doi:10.1108/00251741211227726

Akhtar, R., Sultana, S., Masud, M. M., Jafrin, N., & Al-Mamun, A. (2021). Consumers' environmental ethics, willingness, and green consumerism between lower and higher income groups. *Resources, Conservation and Recycling*, *168*, 105274. doi:10.1016/j.resconrec.2020.105274

Akilli Hayat 2030 Blog. (2022, March 25). *Yeşil mutabakat nedir?* Zorlu. https://www.zorlu.com.tr/akillihayat2030/yazilar/yesil-mutabakat-nedir

Akomolafe, K. J., & Danladi, J. D. (2014). Electricity Consumption and Economic Growth in Nigeria: A Multivariate Investigation. *International Journal of Economics Financial Management*, *3*(1), 143–159.

Albino, V., Berardi, U., & Dangelico, R. M. (2015). Smart cities : Definitions, dimensions, performance, and initiatives. *Journal of Urban Technology*, *22*(1), 3–21. doi:10.1080/1063073 2.2014.942092

Ali, H. S., Nathaniel, S. P., Uzuner, G., Bekun, F. V., & Sarkodie, S. A. (2020). Trivariate modelling of the nexus between electricity consumption, urbanization and economic growth in Nigeria: Fresh insights from Maki Cointegration and causality tests. *Heliyon*, *6*(2), e03400. doi:10.1016/j.heliyon.2020.e03400 PMID:32123762

Alizadeh, T. (2015). A policy analysis of digital strategies: Brisbane vs. Vancouver. *International Journal of Knowledge-Based Development*, 6(2), 85–103. doi:10.1504/IJKBD.2015.071469

Amazon. (2020, June 17). Four trends driving global utility digitization. *Amazon AWS Blog*. Amazon. https://aws.amazon.com/tr/blogs/industries/four-trends-driving-global-utility-digitization/

Andersen, B., & Skrede, J. (2017). Planning for a sustainable Oslo: The challenge of turning urban theory into practice. *Local Environment*, 22(5), 581–594. doi:10.1080/13549839.2016.1236783

Andrews, C. J., & Friis, R. H. (n.d.). Green Living: Reducing the Individual's Carbon Footprint. In. (Eds.), The Praeger Handbook of Environmental Health (pp. 455-475).

Ankit, G., & Mayur, R. (2013). Green marketing: Impact of green advertising on consumer purchase intention. *Advances in Management*, 6(9), 14.

Ansar, N. (2013). Impact of green marketing on consumer purchase intention. *Mediterranean Journal of Social Sciences*. Advance online publication. doi:10.5901/mjss.2013.v4n11p650

ANSI. (2022). *ANSI/TIA-942 Standard*. TIA Online. https://tiaonline.org/products-and-services/tia942certification/ansi-tia-942-standard/

Apinran, M. O., Usman, N., Akadiri, S. S., & Onuzo, C. T. (2022). The Role of Electricity Consumption, Capital, Labor Force, Carbon Emissions on Economic Growth: Implication for Environmental Sustainability Targets in Nigeria. *Environmental Science and Pollution Research International*, 29(11), 15955–15965. doi:10.100711356-021-16584-6 PMID:34636018

Archer, B., Cooper, C., & Ruhanen, L. (2005). The positive and negative impacts of tourism. In W. F. Theobald (Ed.), *Global tourism* (pp. 79–102). Elsevier. doi:10.1016/B978-0-7506-7789-9.50011-X

Aschemann-Witzel, J., & Zielke, S. (2017). Can't Buy Me Green? A Review of Consumer Perceptions of and Behavior Toward the Price of Organic Food. *The Journal of Consumer Affairs*, 51(1), 211–251. doi:10.1111/joca.12092

ASHRAE. (2021). *2021 Thermal Guidelines for Air Cooling*. Kasım. https://www.ashrae.org/file%20library/technical%20resources/bookstore/supplemental%20files/referencecard_2021thermalguidelines.pdf

Avelar, V., Azevedo, D., & French, A. (2012, October 02). *White Paper #49 - PUE: A Comprehensive Examination of the Metric*. The Green Grid. https://www.thegreengrid.org/en/resources/library-and-tools/237-PUE%3A-A-Comprehensive-Examination-of-the-Metric

Awad, T. (2011). Environmental segmentation alternatives: Buyers' profiles and implications. *Journal of Islamic Marketing*, 2(1), 55–73. doi:10.1108/17590831111115240

Azam, A., Rafiq, M., Shafique, M., Ateeq, M., & Yuan, J. (2020). Causality Relationship Between Electricity Supply and Economic Growth: Evidence From Pakistan. *Energies, 13*, 837. doi: 13040837. doi:10.3390/en

Babaei, A., Khedmati, M., Jokar, M. R. A., & Tirkolaee, E. B. (2023). An integrated decision support system to achieve sustainable development in transportation routes with traffic flow. *Environmental Science and Pollution Research International*, *30*(21), 1–16. doi:10.100711356-023-26644-8 PMID:37022553

Badassa, B. B., Sun, B., & Qiao, L. (2020). Sustainable Transport Infrastructure and Economic Returns : A Bibliometric and Visualization Analysis. *Sustainability (Basel)*, *12*(5), 2033. doi:10.3390u12052033

Bakıcı, T., Almirall, E., & Wareham, J. (2013). A smart city initiative: The case of Barcelona. *Journal of the Knowledge Economy*, *4*(2), 135–148. doi:10.100713132-012-0084-9

Bakker, S., Major, M., Mejia, A., & Banomyong, R. (2017). ASEAN cooperation on sustainable transport: Progress and options. *Transport and Communications Bulletin for Asia and the Pacific*, *87*, 1–16.

Balderjahn, I. (1988). Personality variables and environmental attitudes as predictors of ecologically responsible consumption patterns. *Journal of Business Research*, *17*(1), 51–56. doi:10.1016/0148-2963(88)90022-7

Ballantine, P. W., & Creery, S. (2010). The consumption and disposition behaviour of voluntary simplifiers. *Journal of Consumer Behaviour*, *9*(1), 45–56. doi:10.1002/cb.302

Bamwesigye, D., & Hlavackova, P. (2019). Analysis of sustainable transport for smart cities. *Sustainability (Basel)*, *11*(7), 2140. doi:10.3390u11072140

Banister, D. (2008). The sustainable mobility paradigm. *Transport Policy*, *15*(2), 73–80. doi:10.1016/j.tranpol.2007.10.005

Barbosa, G. S., Drach, P. R., & Corbella, O. D. (2014). A conceptual review of the terms sustainable development and sustainability. *Journal of Social Sciences*, *3*(2), 1.

Barr, S. (2007). Factors influencing environmental attitudes and behaviors: A U.K. case study of household waste management. In Environment and Behavior, 39(4). doi:10.1177/0013916505283421

Barro, R. J. (1996). *Determinants of economic growth: A cross-country empirical study*. National Bureau of Economic Research.

Bartels, A. (2011, August 31). *[INFOGRAPHIC] Data Center Evolution: 1960 to 2000*. Rackspace Blog. https://web.archive.org/web/20181024232055/https://blog.rackspace.com/datacenter-evolution-1960-to-2000

Baumeister, R. F., & Leary, M. R. (1997). Writing Narrative Literature Reviews. *Review of General Psychology*, *1*(3), 311–320. doi:10.1037/1089-2680.1.3.311

Beall, J. M., Boley, B. B., Landon, A. C., & Woosnam, K. M. (2021). What drives ecotourism: Environmental values or symbolic conspicuous consumption? *Journal of Sustainable Tourism*, *29*(8), 1215–1234. doi:10.1080/09669582.2020.1825458

Beaudoin, J., & Lawell, C.-Y. L. (2017). The effects of urban public transit investment on traffic congestion and air quality. *Urban Transport Systems, 111.*

Beaudoin, J., Farzin, Y. H., & Lawell, C.-Y. C. L. (2015). Public transit investment and sustainable transportation : A review of studies of transit's impact on traffic congestion and air quality. *Research in Transportation Economics, 52,* 15–22. doi:10.1016/j.retrec.2015.10.004

Belady, C. (2010, December 02). *Carbon Usage Effectiveness (CUE): A Green Grid Data Center Sustainability Metric.* [White paper 32]. The Green Grid. https://www.thegreengrid.org/en/resources/library-and-tools/241-Carbon-Usage-Effectiveness-%28CUE%29%3A-A-Green-Grid-Data-Center-Sustainability-Metric

Bempong, G. B. (2017). *The effect of green branding on consumer purchasing behavior: A study of the Ghanaian cosmetic market* [Unpublished doctoral dissertation, Ashesi University].

Benevolo, C., Dameri, R. P., & D'auria, B. (2016). Smart mobility in smart city. In *Empowering Organizations* (pp. 13–28). Springer. doi:10.1007/978-3-319-23784-8_2

Bharadwaj, S., Ballare, S., Rohit, & Chandel, M. K. (2017). Impact of congestion on greenhouse gas emissions for road transport in Mumbai metropolitan region. *Transportation Research Procedia, 25,* 3538–3551. doi:10.1016/j.trpro.2017.05.282

Bhaskaran, S., Polonsky, M., Cary, J., & Fernandez, S. (2006). Environmentally sustainable food production and marketing. *British Food Journal, 108*(8), 677–690. doi:10.1108/00070700610682355

Bhutto, M. Y., Zeng, F., Soomro, Y. A., & Khan, M. A. (2019). Young chinese consumer decision making in buying green products: An application of theory of planned behavior with gender and price transparency. *Pakistan Journal of Commerce and Social Science, 13*(3), 599–619.

Biswas, A., & Roy, M. (2015). Green products: An exploratory study on the consumer behaviour in emerging economies of the East. *Journal of Cleaner Production, 87*(1), 463–468. doi:10.1016/j.jclepro.2014.09.075

Boenig-Liptsin, M. (2017). AI and robotics for the city: Imagining and transforming social infrastructure in San Francisco, Yokohama, and Lviv. *Field Actions Science Reports. The journal of field actions,* (17), 16-21.

Bradić-Martinović, A. (2021). Tourism 4.0: Data-Driven Covid-19 Recovery. Innovative Aspects of the Development Service and Tourism. In *Proceedings of IX International scientific-practical conference.* Stavropol State Agrarian University, Faculty of Social and Cultural Service and Tourism.

Braimah, M. (2015). Green brand awareness and customer purchase intention. *Management Science Letters,* 895–902. doi:10.5267/j.msl.2015.8.007

Braimah, M., & Tweneboah-Koduah, E. Y. (2011). An exploratory study of the impact of green brand awareness on consumer purchase decisions in Ghana. *Journal of Marketing Development and Competitiveness, 5*(7), 11–18.

Brundtland, G. H., Khalid, M., Agnelli, S., Al-Athel, S. A., Chidzero, B., Fadika, L. M., Hauff, V., Lang, I., Ma, S., & Botero, M. M. de. (1987). *Our common future; by world commission on environment and development.* UN.

Buerke, A., Straatmann, T., Lin-Hi, N., & Müller, K. (2017). Consumer awareness and sustainability-focused value orientation as motivating factors of responsible consumer behavior. *Review of Managerial Science, 11*(4), 959–991. doi:10.100711846-016-0211-2

Bull, R. (2015). ICT as an enabler for sustainable development : Reflections on opportunities and barriers. *Journal of Information, Communication and Ethics in Society.*

Burrington, I. (2015, December 16). *The Enviromental Impact of Data-Center Industry.* The Atlantic. https://www.theatlantic.com/technology/archive/2015/12/there-are-no-clean-clouds/420744/

Butler, L., Yigitcanlar, T., & Paz, A. (2020). Smart urban mobility innovations : A comprehensive review and evaluation. *IEEE Access : Practical Innovations, Open Solutions, 8,* 196034–196049. doi:10.1109/ACCESS.2020.3034596

Butler, R. (1999). Sustainable tourism: A state-of-the-art review. *Tourism Geographies, 1*(1), 7–25. doi:10.1080/14616689908721291

Button, K. (2006). The political economy of parking charges in "first" and "second-best" worlds. *Transport Policy, 13*(6), 470–478. doi:10.1016/j.tranpol.2006.05.004

Bwalya, K. J. (2019). The smart city of Johannesburg, South Africa. In *Smart city emergence* (pp. 407–419). Elsevier. doi:10.1016/B978-0-12-816169-2.00020-1

California Goverment. (2022). *What Is E-Waste?* CalRecycle. https://calrecycle.ca.gov/electronics/whatisewaste/

Carbon Tax Centre. (n.d.). *Where carbon is taxed.* Carbon Tax. https://www.carbontax.org/where-carbon-is-taxed-overview/

Carfora, V., Cavallo, C., Caso, D., Del Giudice, T., De Devitiis, B., Viscecchia, R., Nardone, G., & Cicia, G. (2019). Explaining consumer purchase behavior for organic milk: Including trust and green self-identity within the theory of planned behavior. *Food Quality and Preference, 76*(March), 1–9. doi:10.1016/j.foodqual.2019.03.006

Centobelli, P., Cerchione, R., Esposito, E., & Shashi. (2020). Evaluating environmental sustainability strategies in freight transport and logistics industry. *Business Strategy and the Environment, 29*(3), 1563–1574. doi:10.1002/bse.2453

Cervero, R., & Sullivan, C. (2011). Green TODs: Marrying transit-oriented development and green urbanism. *International Journal of Sustainable Development and World Ecology, 18*(3), 210–218. doi:10.1080/13504509.2011.570801

Chan, T. (2021). *Attitudes and Perception of Destination Certification Towards Sustainable Tourism Development* [Master Thesis, School of Tourism and Maritime Technology of Polytechnic of Leiria]. ProQuest Dissertations and Theses database.

Chang, C. (2011). Feeling ambivalent about going green: Implications for green advertising processing. *Journal of Advertising*, *40*(4), 19–31. doi:10.2753/JOA0091-3367400402

Chang, Y. S., Lee, Y. J., & Choi, S. S. B. (2017). Is there more traffic congestion in larger cities?-Scaling analysis of the 101 largest US urban centers. *Transport Policy*, *59*, 54–63. doi:10.1016/j.tranpol.2017.07.002

Chanpaneri, A., & Jog, D. (2020). The role of consumer typology on the consumers' green involvement and its effect on green purchase behaviour. *4th International Marketing Conference Marketing Technology and Society*. Indian Institute of Management Kozhikode.

Chatziioannou, I., Alvarez-Icaza, L., Bakogiannis, E., Kyriakidis, C., & Chias-Becerril, L. (2020). A Structural Analysis for the Categorization of the Negative Externalities of Transport and the Hierarchical Organization of Sustainable Mobility's Strategies. *Sustainability (Basel)*, *12*(15), 6011. doi:10.3390u12156011

Cheba, K., & Saniuk, S. (2016). Sustainable urban transport–the concept of measurement in the field of city logistics. *Transportation Research Procedia*, *16*, 35–45. doi:10.1016/j.trpro.2016.11.005

Chen, C. (2001). Design for the Environment: A Quality-Based Model for Green Product Development. *Management Science*, *47*(2), 250–263. doi:10.1287/mnsc.47.2.250.9841

Cheng, Z., Pang, M.-S., & Pavlou, P. A. (2020). Mitigating traffic congestion : The role of intelligent transportation systems. *Information Systems Research*, *31*(3), 653–674. doi:10.1287/isre.2019.0894

Chen, K., & Miles, J. C. (2004). *ITS handbook 2004 : Recommendations from the world road association*. PIARC.

Chitedze, I., Nwedeh, C. C., Adeola, A., & Abonyi, D. C. (2021). An econometric analysis of electricity consumption and real sector performance in Nigeria. *International Journal of Energy Sector Management*, *15*(4), 855–873. doi:10.1108/IJESM-04-2020-0003

Chiu, Y. T. H., Lee, W.-I., & Chen, T.-H. (2014). Environmentally responsible behavior in ecotourism: Antecedents and implications. *Tourism Management*, *40*, 321–329. doi:10.1016/j.tourman.2013.06.013

Climate Neutral Data Center Pact. (2022). *Self-Regulatory Initative*. Aralık. https://www.climateneutraldatacentre.net/wp-content/uploads/2022/07/20220725__Self-Regulatory-Initiative.pdf

CNBCTV18. (2021). Explained: Why inflation rates are increasing across the globe. *CNBCTV18*. https://www.cnbctv18.com/economy/explained-why-inflation-rates-are-increasing-across-the-globe-11565352.htm

Corraliza, J. A., & Berenguer, J. (2000). Environmental values, beliefs, and actions: A situational approach. *Environment and Behavior, 32*(6), 832–848. doi:10.1177/00139160021972829

Crossley, J., & Lee, B. (1994). Characteristics of Ecotourists and Mass Tourists. *Visions in Leisure and Business, 13*(2).

Cruz, C. O., & Sarmento, J. M. (2020). "Mobility as a service" platforms: A critical path towards increasing the sustainability of transportation systems. *Sustainability (Basel), 12*(16), 6368. doi:10.3390u12166368

D'Souza, C., Taghian, M., Lamb, P., & Peretiatkos, R. (2006). Green products and corporate strategy: An empirical investigation. *Society and Business Review, 1*(2), 144–157. doi:10.1108/17465680610669825

Dangelico, R. M., & Vocalelli, D. (2017). "Green Marketing": An analysis of definitions, strategy steps, and tools through a systematic review of the literature. *Journal of Cleaner Production, 165*, 1263–1279. doi:10.1016/j.jclepro.2017.07.184

Danilina, N., & Slepnev, M. (2018, June). Managing smart-city transportation planning of "Park-and-ride" system: Case of Moscow metropolitan. *IOP Conference Series. Materials Science and Engineering, 365*(2), 022002. doi:10.1088/1757-899X/365/2/022002

Dargay, J. (2002). Road vehicles : Future growth in developed and developing countries. *Proceedings of the Institution of Civil Engineers. Municipal Engineer, 151*(1), 3–11. doi:10.1680/muen.2002.151.1.3

Daria, B., & Sara, K. S. (2011). *The Influence of Eco-labelled Products on Consumer Buying Behaviour- By focusing on eco-labelled bread.* [Bachelor"s thesis, Mälardalen University College]. http://mdh.diva- portal.org/smash/get/diva2:390922/FULLTEXT01.pdf

Dasgupta, P., & Maler, K. (1991). *The environment and emerging development issues.* The World Bank.

Davey, L. (2022). *15 Green marketing examples to inspire you in 2022.* GIVZ. https://www.givz.com/blog/green-marketing-examples

Davis, J., Bizo, D., Lawrence, A., Rogers, O., & Smolaks, M. (2022). *Global Data Center Survey 2022.* Uptime Institute.

de Bakker, F. G. A. (2009). Book Review: Jennifer Howard-Grenville. Corporate culture and environmental practice: Making change at a high-technology manufacturer. Cheltenham, UK: Edward Elgar, 2007. *Organization & Environment, 22*(2), 257–260. doi:10.1177/1086026609338170

de Brito, M. P., Carbone, V., & Blanquart, C. M. (2008). Towards a sustainable fashion retail supply chain in Europe: Organisation and performance. *International Journal of Production Economics, 114*(2), 534–553. doi:10.1016/j.ijpe.2007.06.012

de Palma, A., & Lindsey, R. (2011). Traffic congestion pricing methodologies and technologies. *Transportation Research Part C, Emerging Technologies, 19*(6), 1377–1399. doi:10.1016/j.trc.2011.02.010

De Young, R. (1985). *Encouraging environmentally appropriate behavior: The role of intrinsic motivation.*

Delafrooz, N., Taleghani, M., & Nouri, B. (2014). Effect of green marketing on Consumer Purchase Behavior. *QScience Connect, 2014*(1). doi:10.5339/connect.2014.5

Delgado-Ballester, E., & Munuera-Alemán, J. L. (2005). Does brand trust matter to brand equity? *Journal of Product and Brand Management, 14*(3), 187–196. doi:10.1108/10610420510601058

Delmas, M. A., & Burbano, V. C. (2011). The drivers of greenwashing. *California Management Review, 54*(1), 64–87. doi:10.1525/cmr.2011.54.1.64

Deloitte. (2023). *How consumers are embracing sustainability.* Deloitte. https://www2.deloitte.com/uk/en/pages/consumer-business/articles/sustainable-consumer.html

Deng, J., & Li, J. (2015). Self-identification of ecotourists. *Journal of Sustainable Tourism, 23*(2), 255–279. doi:10.1080/09669582.2014.934374

Dennis, J. B. (2011). Petri Nets. In D. Padua (Ed.), *Encyclopedia of Parallel Computing.* Springer.

DigitalRealty. (2023). *Driving Efficiency in Design and Performance through Sustainability.* Digital Realty - Green Datacenters. https://www.digitalrealty.com/data-center-solutions/green-data-centers

Dillon, V. (2021). Ben and Jerry: Founders striving towards sustainability. *The Momentum.* https://www.themomentum.com/articles/ben-and-jerry-founders-striving-towards-sustainability

Dilotsotlhe, N. (2021). Factors influencing the green purchase behaviour of millennials: An emerging country perspective. *Cogent Business and Management, 8*(1), 1908745. doi:10.1080/23311975.2021.1908745

Dimoska, T., & Petrevska, B. (2012). Indicators for sustainable tourism development in Macedonia. In *Proceedings of the First International Conference on Business, Economics and Finance "From Liberalization to Globalization: Challenges in the Changing World".* Faculty of Economics Goce Delcev University.

Dodds, R., & Joppe, M. (2005). *CSR in the tourism industry? The status of and potential for certification, codes of conduct and guidelines.* IFC World Bank.

Doğuş Marketing. (2022). *PUE Değeri Nedir, Ne İşe Yarar?* Doğuş Marketing. https://dogus.com.tr/pue-degeri-nedir-nasil-dusurulur/

Donthu, N., Kumar, S., Mukherjee, D., Pandey, N., & Lim, W. M. (2021). How to conduct a bibliometric analysis: An overview and guidelines. *Journal of Business Research, 133*, 285–296. doi:10.1016/j.jbusres.2021.04.070

Dorce, L. C., da Silva, M. C., Mauad, J. R. C., de Faria Domingues, C. H., & Borges, J. A. R. (2021). Extending the theory of planned behavior to understand consumer purchase behavior for organic vegetables in Brazil: The role of perceived health benefits, perceived sustainability benefits and perceived price. *Food Quality and Preference, 91*. doi:10.1016/j.foodqual.2021.104191

Downs, A. (2000). *Stuck in traffic : Coping with peak-hour traffic congestion.* Brookings Institution Press.

Dubey, R., & Gunasekaran, A. (2015). The role of truck driver on sustainable transportation and logistics. *Industrial and Commercial Training, 47*(3), 127–134. doi:10.1108/ICT-08-2014-0053

Đukić, M., Jovanoski, I., Munitlak Ivanović, O., Lazić, M., & Bodroža, D. (2016). Cost-benefit analysis of an infrastructure project and a cost-reflective tariff: A case study for investment in wastewater treatment plant in Serbia. *Renewable & Sustainable Energy Reviews, 59*, 1419–1425. doi:10.1016/j.rser.2016.01.050

Duong, C. D., Doan, X. H., Vu, D. M., Ha, N. T., & Van Dam, K. (2022). The Role of Perceived Environmental Responsibility and Environmental Concern on Shaping Green Purchase Intention. *Vision (Basel)*, 1–15. doi:10.1177/09722629221092117

Durieux, V., & Gevenois, P. A. (2010). Bibliometric indicators: Quality measurements of scientific publication. *Radiology, 255*(2), 342–351. doi:10.1148/radiol.09090626 PMID:20413749

Durmaz, Y., & Akdoğan, L. (2023). The effect of environmental responsibility on green the effect of environmental responsibility on green consumption intention: The moderator role of price sensitivity and the mediator role of environmental concern. A case study in Turkey. *Environment, Development and Sustainability, 0123456789*. Advance online publication. doi:10.100710668-023-03083-6

EarthCheck. (n.d.). *EarthCheck Sustainable Destinations.* Earthcheck. https://earthcheck.org/what-we-do/certification/sustainable-destinations/

Echegaray, F., & Hansstein, F. V. (2017). Assessing the intention-behavior gap in electronic waste recycling: The case of Brazil. *Journal of Cleaner Production, 142*, 180–190. doi:10.1016/j.jclepro.2016.05.064

ECO Canada. (2010). *Defining the green economy.* Eco Canada. https://eco.ca/new-reports/defining-the-green-economy

Eisenman, A. (2012). *Sustainable streets and highways: an analysis of green roads rating systems.* Bureau of Transportation Statistics.

Ekeocha, P. C., Penzin, D. J., & Ogbuabor, J. E. (2020). Energy Consumption and Economic Growth in Nigeria: A Test of Alternative Specifications. *International Journal of Energy Economics and Policy, 10*(3), 369–379. doi:10.32479/ijeep.8902

Emeritus. (2022). *What is the Importance of Marketing for Businesses? Discover the Undiscovered.* Emeritus. https://emeritus.org/blog/what-is-the-importance-of-marketing-for-business/

Energy Star score for offices in the United States . (2019). Energy Star. https://www.energystar.gov/sites/default/files/tools/Office_August_2019_508.pdf

Equinix. (2021). *2021 Sustainability Report*. Kapost. https://cloud.kapostcontent.net/pub/fae282ef-8d29-4266-96cd-b1bc91164299/sustainability-report-fy2021?kui=nKl648GVlEjEXFAjNIzzuw

Esposito, G., Clement, J., Mora, L., & Crutzen, N. (2021). One size does not fit all: Framing smart city policy narratives within regional socio-economic contexts in Brussels and Wallonia. *Cities (London, England), 118*, 103329. doi:10.1016/j.cities.2021.103329

Eurobarometer. (2008). *Attitudes of Europeans towards the Environment*. European Union. https://europa.eu/eurobarometer/surveys/detail/673

European Commission. (2016). *The European Tourism Indicator System ETIS toolkit for sustainable destination management*. EC. https://ec.europa.eu/docsroom/documents/21749

European Commission. (2021, July 14). *A European Green Deal*. European Commission. https://commission.europa.eu/strategy-and-policy/priorities-2019-2024/european-green-deal_en

European Travel Commission. (2021). *Sustainable tourism implementation. A framework and toolkit to support national approaches*. ETC. https://etc-corporate.org/uploads/2021/03/ETC-HANDBOOK-FINAL.pdf

Falcocchio, J. C., & Levinson, H. S. (2015). *Road traffic congestion : A concise guide* (Vol. 7). Springer. doi:10.1007/978-3-319-15165-6

Fazal, S., Gillani, S., Amjad, M., & Haider, Z. (2020). Impact of the Renewable-Energy Consumption on Thailand's Economic Development: Evidence from Cointegration Test. *Pakistan Journal of Humanities and Social Sciences*, 857-67. https://doi.org/. doi:1052131/pjhss.2020.0802.0103

Feng, L., Liu, F., & Shi, Y. (2018, May). City brain, a new architecture of smart city based on the Internet brain. In *2018 IEEE 22nd International Conference on Computer Supported Cooperative Work in Design ((CSCWD))* (pp. 624-629). IEEE. 10.1109/CSCWD.2018.8465164

Feucht, Y., & Zander, K. (2017). Consumers' attitudes on carbon footprint labelling: Results of the SUSDIET project. *Thünen Working Paper, No. 78, Johann Heinrich von Thünen-Institut, Braunschweig*. DNB. doi:10.3220/WP1507534833000

Finisterra do Paço, A. M., Barata Raposo, M. L., & Filho, W. L. (2009). Identifying the green consumer: A segmentation study. *Journal of Targeting. Measurement and Analysis for Marketing, 17*(1), 17–25. doi:10.1057/jt.2008.28

Finisterra do Paço, A. M., & Raposo, M. L. B. (2008). Determining the characteristics to profile the "green" consumer: An exploratory approach. *International Review on Public and Nonprofit Marketing, 5*(2), 129–140. doi:10.100712208-008-0010-9

Fishbein, M., Ajzen, I., & Belief, A. (1975). *Intention and Behavior: An introduction to theory and research*. Addison-Wesley.

Fisk, G. (1973). Criteria for a Theory of Responsible Consumption. *Journal of Marketing*, *37*(2), 24–31. doi:10.1177/002224297303700206

Flyvbjerg, B. (2006). Five Misunderstandings About Case-Study Research. *Qualitative Inquiry*, *12*(2), 219–245. doi:10.1177/1077800405284363

Follows, S. B., & Jobber, D. (2000). Environmentally responsible purchase behaviour: A test of a consumer model. *European Journal of Marketing*, *34*(5/6), 723–746. doi:10.1108/03090560010322009

Folz-Weinstein, S., Bergenthum, R., Desel, J., & Kovář, J. (2023, May). ILP2 Miner–Process Discovery for Partially Ordered Event Logs Using Integer Linear Programming. In *International Conference on Applications and Theory of Petri Nets and Concurrency* (pp. 59-76). Cham: Springer Nature Switzerland. 10.1007/978-3-031-33620-1_4

Font, X., & Harris, C. (2004). Rethinking standards from green to sustainable. *Annals of Tourism Research*, *31*(4), 986–1007. doi:10.1016/j.annals.2004.04.001

Francois-Lecompte, A., & Roberts, J. A. (2006). Developing a measure of socially responsible consumption in France. *Marketing Management Journal, 16*(2).

Furlow, N. E. (2010). Greenwashing in the new millennium. *The Journal of Applied Business and Economics*, *10*(6), 22–25.

Gaffney, C., & Robertson, C. (2018). Smarter than smart: Rio de Janeiro's flawed emergence as a smart city. *Journal of Urban Technology*, *25*(3), 47–64. doi:10.1080/10630732.2015.1102423

Gallo, M., & Marinelli, M. (2020). Sustainable mobility : A review of possible actions and policies. *Sustainability (Basel)*, *12*(18), 7499. doi:10.3390u12187499

GeSI. (2008, June). *Smart 2020: Enabling the low carbon economy in the information age.* GeSI. https://gesi.org/research/smart-2020-enabling-the-low-carbon-economy-in-the-information-age

Ghanaweb. (2016, May 9). *Skin Bleaching.* Ghanaweb. https://www.ghanaweb.com/GhanaHomePage/entertainment/Skin-bleaching-a-silent-killer-of-the-youth-of-today-441001

Ghvanidze, S., Velikova, N., Dodd, T. H., & Oldewage-Theron, W. (2016). Consumers' environmental and ethical consciousness and the use of the related food products information: The role of perceived consumer effectiveness. *Appetite*, *107*, 311–322. doi:10.1016/j.appet.2016.08.097 PMID:27554182

Giampiccoli, A., Mtapuri, O., & Dluzewska, A. (2020). Investigating the intersection between sustainable tourism and community-based tourism. *Tourism (Zagreb)*, *68*(4), 415–433. doi:10.37741/t.68.4.4

Ginsberg, J. M., & Bloom, P. N. (2004). Choosing the right green marketing strategy. *MIT Sloan Management Review*, *46*(1), 79–84.

Girardi, P., & Temporelli, A. (2017). Smartainability: A methodology for assessing the sustainability of the smart city. *Energy Procedia*, *111*, 810–816. doi:10.1016/j.egypro.2017.03.243

Gkoumas, A. (2019). Evaluating a standard for sustainable tourism through the lenses of local industry. *Heliyon*, *5*(11), e02707. doi:10.1016/j.heliyon.2019.e02707 PMID:31840122

Gleim, M. R., Smith, J. S., Andrews, D., & Cronin, J. J. Jr. (2013). Against the Green: A Multi-method Examination of the Barriers to Green Consumption. *Journal of Retailing*, *89*(1), 44–61. doi:10.1016/j.jretai.2012.10.001

Global Sustainable Tourism Council. (2019). *GSTC Destination Criteria Version 2.0*. GST Council. https://www.gstcouncil.org/wp-content/uploads/GSTC-Destination-Criteria-v2.0.pdf

Global Sustainable Tourism Council. (n.d.a.). *GSTC Destination Criteria*. GST Council. https://www.gstcouncil.org/gstc-criteria/gstc-destination-criteria/

Global Sustainable Tourism Council. (n.d.b.). *Certified Sustainable Destinations*. GST council. https://www.gstcouncil.org/certified-sustainable-destinations/

Goldman, T., & Gorham, R. (2006). Sustainable urban transport : Four innovative directions. *Technology in Society*, *28*(1-2), 261–273. doi:10.1016/j.techsoc.2005.10.007

Golubchikov, O., & Thornbush, M. (2020). Artificial intelligence and robotics in smart city strategies and planned smart development. *Smart Cities, 3*(4).

Goodwin, P. B. (1996). Empirical evidence on induced traffic. *Transportation*, *23*(1), 35–54. doi:10.1007/BF00166218

Google. (2023). *Google*. Efficiency Datacenters. https://www.google.com/about/datacenters/efficiency/

Govender, J. P., & Govender, T. L. (2016). The influence of green marketing on consumer purchase behavior. *Environment and Ecology*, *7*(2), 77–85. doi:10.21511/ee.07(2).2016.8

Granger, C. W. J. (1969). Investigating causal relations by econometric models and cross-spectral methods. *Econometrica*, *37*(3), 424–438. doi:10.2307/1912791

Green Destinations. (2021). *Green Destination Standard V2*. Green Destinations. https://tempo.greendestinations.org/wp-content/uploads/2022/11/GD-Standard-V2-2021-GSTC-Recognised.pdf

Green Destinations. (n.d.). *About the Green Destinations Awards & Certification Program*. Green Destinations. https://www.greendestinations.org/awards-certification/

Green Policy Platform. (n.d.). *Tourism*. Green Growth Knowledge. https://www.greengrowthknowledge.org/sectors/tourism

Groening, C., Sarkis, J., & Zhu, Q. (2018). Green marketing consumer-level theory review: A compendium of applied theories and further research directions. *Journal of Cleaner Production*, *172*, 1848–1866. doi:10.1016/j.jclepro.2017.12.002

Gudmundsson, H., & Regmi, M. B. (2017). Developing the sustainable urban transport index. *Transport and sustainable development goals*, 35.

Gupta, S., & Agrawal, R. (2018). Environmentally responsible consumption: Construct definition, scale development, and validation. *Corporate Social Responsibility and Environmental Management, 25*(4), 523–536. doi:10.1002/csr.1476

Gurkaynak, G., Yilmaz, I., & Haksever, G. (2016). Stifling artificial intelligence: Human perils. *Computer Law & Security Report, 32*(5), 749–758. doi:10.1016/j.clsr.2016.05.003

Gwenhure, Y., & Odhiambo, N. M. (2017). Tourism and economic growth: A review of international literature. *Tourism (Zagreb), 65*(1), 33–44.

Hair, J. F. Jr, Ringle, C. M., & Sarstedt, M. (2013). Partial least squares structural equation modeling: Rigorous applications, better results and higher acceptance. *Long Range Planning, 46*(1–2), 1–12. doi:10.1016/j.lrp.2013.01.001

Håkansson, H., & Waluszewski, A. (2005). Developing a new understanding of markets: Reinterpreting the 4Ps. *Journal of Business and Industrial Marketing, 20*(3), 110–117. doi:10.1108/08858620510592722

Hamad, K., & Kikuchi, S. (2002). Developing a measure of traffic congestion : Fuzzy inference approach. *Transportation Research Record: Journal of the Transportation Research Board, 1802*(1), 77–85. doi:10.3141/1802-10

Hämäläinen, M. (2020). A framework for a smart city design: Digital transformation in the Helsinki smart city. *Entrepreneurship and the community: a multidisciplinary perspective on creativity, social challenges, and business*, 63-86.

Han, H., & Kim, Y. (2010). An investigation of green hotel customers' decision formation: Developing an extended model of the theory of planned behavior. *International Journal of Hospitality Management, 29*(4), 659–668. doi:10.1016/j.ijhm.2010.01.001

Harriet, T., Poku, K., & Emmanuel, A. K. (2013). An assessment of traffic congestion and its effect on productivity in urban Ghana. *International Journal of Business and Social Science, 4*(3).

Harvard Business Review. (2019). The Elusive Green Consumer. *Harvard Business Review*. https://hbr.org/2019/07/the-elusive-green-consumer

He, F., Yan, X., Liu, Y., & Ma, L. (2016). A traffic congestion assessment method for urban road networks based on speed performance index. *Procedia Engineering, 137*, 425–433. doi:10.1016/j.proeng.2016.01.277

Henion, K. E., & Kinnear, T. C. (1976). *A guide to ecological marketing. Ecological Marketing*. American Marketing Association.

Hepkul, A., & Polatoğlu, V. (2013). Türkiye'de Kurumsal Sosyal Sorumluluk Olarak E-Atıkların Bertarafı. *Social Business@Anadolu*, 169-170.

Hernández-Zelaya, S. L., Reyes-Reina, F., & Rodríguez Benito, M. E. (2021). Evolution and Future of the Marketing and Sustainability Linkage: Towards a Civil Marketing Approach. In Financial Management and Risk Analysis Strategies for Business Sustainability (pp. 105-123). IGI Global.

Herremans, I. M., & Reid, R. E. (2002). Developing awareness of the sustainability concept. *The Journal of Environmental Education, 34*(1), 16–20. doi:10.1080/00958960209603477

Hilliard, H., Matulich, E., Haytko, D., & Rustogi, H. (2012). An international look at attitude towards advertising, brand considerations, and market expertise: United States, China, and India. *Journal of International Business Research, 11*(1), 29.

Hill, R. J., Fishbein, M., & Ajzen, I. (1977). Belief, attitude, intention and behavior: An introduction to theory and research. *Contemporary Sociology, 6*(2), 244. doi:10.2307/2065853

Hofmeister-Toth, G., Kasza-Kelemen, K., & Piskti, M. (2011). The shades of green living in Hungary. *International Journal of Management Cases, 13*(2), 5–14. doi:10.5848/APBJ.2011.00027

Ho, L. T., & Goethals, P. L. (2019). Opportunities and challenges for the sustainability of lakes and reservoirs in relation to the Sustainable Development Goals (SDGs). *Water (Basel), 11*(07), 1462. doi:10.3390/w11071462

Holden, E., Gilpin, G., & Banister, D. (2019). Sustainable mobility at thirty. *Sustainability (Basel), 11*(7), 1965. doi:10.3390u11071965

Holdgate, M. W. (1987). Our Common Future: The Report of the World Commission on Environment and Development. Oxford University Press, Oxford & New York: xv+ 347+ 35 pp., 20.25× 13.25× 1.75 cm, Oxford Paperback,£ 5.95 net in UK, 1987. *Environmental Conservation, 14*(3), 282–282. doi:10.1017/S0376892900016702

Honey, M., Rome, A., Russillo, A., & Bien, A. (2007). *Practical Steps for Marketing Tourism Certification. Handbook 3.* Inter-American Development Bank. https://publications.iadb.org/en/practical-steps-marketing-tourism-certification

Hosta, M., & Zabkar, V. (2021a). Antecedents of Environmentally and Socially Responsible Sustainable Consumer Behavior. *Journal of Business Ethics, 171*(2), 273–293. doi:10.100710551-019-04416-0

Hsu, C. L., Chang, C. Y., & Yansritakul, C. (2017). Exploring purchase intention of green skincare products using the theory of planned behavior: Testing the moderating effects of country of origin and price sensitivity. *Journal of Retailing and Consumer Services, 34*, 145–152. doi:10.1016/j.jretconser.2016.10.006

Huber, P., Bongartz, A., Cezanne, M. L., & Julius, N. (2018). How far can we predict sensorial feelings by instrumental modeling? *IFSCC Magazine, 1*(21), 13–18.

Husain, K. (2018). A survey on usage of personal care products especially cosmetics among university students in Saudi Arabia. *Journal of Cosmetic Dermatology, 18*(1), 271–277. doi:10.1111/jocd.12773 PMID:30203510

Hussain, Z., Xia, Z., & Li, Y. (2022). Estimating sustainable transport efficiency and socioeconomic factors : Application of non-parametric approach. *Transportation Letters*, 1–13. doi:10.1080/1 9427867.2022.2082004

Hymel, K. (2009). Does traffic congestion reduce employment growth? *Journal of Urban Economics*, *65*(2), 127–135. doi:10.1016/j.jue.2008.11.002

International Energy Agency. (2016, November). *Energy, Climate Change and Environment 2016 Insights*. International Energy Agency. https://www.iea.org/reports/energy-climate-change-and-environment-2016-insights

International Energy Agency. (2022, September). *Data Centres and Data Transmission Networks*. International Energy Agency. https://www.iea.org/reports/data-centres-and-data-transmission-networks

International Federation of Red Cross and Red Crescent Societies. (n.d.). *Disasters, climate, and crises*. IFRC. https://www.ifrc.org/our-work/disasters-climate-and-crises

IPCC. (2021). *Climate Change 2021 The Physical Science Basis*. IPCC. https://report.ipcc.ch/ar6/wg1/IPCC_AR6_WGI_FullReport.pdf

IPCC. (2022). *Climate Change 2022: Mitigation of Climate Change (The Working Group III Report)*. IPCC. https://www.ipcc.ch/report/ar6/wg3/downloads/report/IPCC_AR6_WGIII_FullReport.pdf

Ivanova, O., Flores-Zamora, J., Khelladi, I., & Ivanaj, S. (2019). The generational cohort effect in the context of responsible consumption. *Management Decision*, *57*(5), 1162–1183. doi:10.1108/MD-12-2016-0915

Ivanović, Đ., & Antonijević, M. (2020). The Role of Online Shopping in the Republic of Serbia During Covid-19. *Economic Analysis*, *53*(1), 28–41.

Iyke, B. N. (2014). *Electricity consumption and economic growth in Nigeria: A revisit of the energy-growth debate*. MPRA Paper No. 70001. https://mpra.ub.unimuenchen.de/70001/

Jaafar, M., & Maideen, S. A. (2012). Ecotourism-related products and activities, and the economic sustainability of small and medium island chalets. *Tourism Management*, *33*(3), 683–691. doi:10.1016/j.tourman.2011.07.011

Jacob, C., & Abdulhai, B. (2006). Automated adaptive traffic corridor control using reinforcement learning : Approach and case studies. *Transportation Research Record: Journal of the Transportation Research Board*, *1959*(1), 1–8. doi:10.1177/0361198106195900101

Jamrozy, U., & Lawonk, K. (2017). The multiple dimensions of consumption values in ecotourism. *International Journal of Culture, Tourism and Hospitality Research*, *11*(1), 18–34. doi:10.1108/IJCTHR-09-2015-0114

Jin, J., & Rafferty, P. (2017). Does congestion negatively affect income growth and employment growth? Empirical evidence from US metropolitan regions. *Transport Policy*, *55*, 1–8. doi:10.1016/j.tranpol.2016.12.003

Johnson, C. M. (1997). The national ITS program : Where we've been and where we're going. *Public Roads, 61*(2).

Jones, P. (2014). The evolution of urban mobility : The interplay of academic and policy perspectives. *IATSS Research, 38*(1), 7–13. doi:10.1016/j.iatssr.2014.06.001

Joseph, S. I. T., Velliangiri, S., & Chandra, C. S. (2020). Investigation of deep learning methodologies in intelligent green transportation system. *Journal of Green Engineering, 10*, 931–950.

Jouma, C., & Kadry, S. (2012). Green IT: Case Studies. *2012 International Conference on Future Energy, Environment and Materials, (vol.* 16, pp. 1052-1058). Energy Procedia.

Kachaner, N., Nielsen, J., Portafaix, A., & Rodzko, F. (2020). *The Pandemic Is Heightening Environmental Awareness.* Boston Consulting Group.

Kaiser, F. G., & Wilson, M. (2004). Goal-directed conservation behavior: The specific composition of a general performance. *Personality and Individual Differences, 36*(7), 1531–1544. doi:10.1016/j.paid.2003.06.003

Kalama, E. (2007). *Green marketing practices by Kenya petroleum refineries: A study of the perception of the management of oil marketing companies in Kenya* [Doctoral dissertation, University of NAIROBI].

Kaličanin, T., & Lazić, M. (2018). Evaluating the Level of Market Concentration in Insurance Sector: the case of Serbia. In Western Balkans Economies in EU Integration: past, present and future. CEMAFI International.

Kantawateera, K., Naipinit, A., Sakolnakorn, T. P. N., & Kroeksakul, P. (2015). Tourist transportation problems and guidelines for developing the tourism industry in Khon Kaen, Thailand. *Asian Social Science, 11*(2), 89.

Karuppannan, S., & Sivam, A. (2009). *Sustainable development and housing affordability, institute of sustainable systems and technologies.* University of South Australia. https://tasa.org.au/wp-content/uploads/2008/12/Sivam-Alpana_-Karuppannan-Sadasivam.pdf

Kautish, P., & Sharma, R. (2019). Value orientation, green attitude and green behavioral intentions: An empirical investigation among young consumers. *Young Consumers, 20*(4), 338–358. doi:10.1108/YC-11-2018-0881

Keegan, W. J., & Green, M. S. (2000). *Global marketing* (2nd ed.). Prentice-Hall.

Kenji. (2020). "Don't Buy This Jacket" — Patagonia's Daring Campaign. *Medium.* https://bettermarketing.pub/dont-buy-this-jacket-patagonia-s-daring-campaign-2b37e145046b

Kerner, B. S. (1999). Congested Traffic Flow : Observations and Theory. *Transportation Research Record: Journal of the Transportation Research Board, 1678*(1), 160–167. doi:10.3141/1678-20

Keynes, J. M. (1936). *The General Theory of Employment, Interest and Money.* Macmillan.

Khare, A. (2014). Consumers' susceptibility to interpersonal influence as a determining factor of ecologically conscious behaviour. *Marketing Intelligence & Planning, 32*(1), 2–20. doi:10.1108/MIP-04-2013-0062

Khare, A. (2015). Antecedents to green buying behaviour: A study on consumers in an emerging economy. *Marketing Intelligence & Planning, 33*(3), 309–329. doi:10.1108/MIP-05-2014-0083

Khare, A., & Pandey, S. (2017). Role of green self-identity and peer influence in fostering trust towards organic food retailers. *International Journal of Retail & Distribution Management, 45*(9), 969–990. doi:10.1108/IJRDM-07-2016-0109

Khisty, C. J., & Sriraj, P. S. (2002). Taming the problems of hypermobility through synergy. In *Synergy Matters* (pp. 271–276). Springer. doi:10.1007/0-306-47467-0_46

Khobai, H. (2018). *The Causal Linkages Between Renewable Electricity Generation and Economic Growth in South Africa*. MPRA Paper No. 86485, UTC.

Kilbourne, W. E., & Beckmann, S. C. (1998). Review and critical assessment of research on marketing and the environment. *Journal of Marketing Management, 14*(6), 513–532. doi:10.1362/026725798784867716

Kim, K. H., & Park, D. B. (2017). Relationships Among Perceived Value, Satisfaction, and Loyalty: Community-Based Ecotourism in Korea. *Journal of Travel & Tourism Marketing, 34*(2), 171–191. doi:10.1080/10548408.2016.1156609

Kimura, S., Pacudan, R., & Phoumin, H. (2017). *Development of the eco town model in the ASEAN region through adoption of energy-efficient building technologies, sustainable transport, and smart grids*. Economic Research Institute.

Kiunsi, R. B. (2013). A review of traffic congestion in Dar es Salaam city from the physical planning perspective. *Journal of Sustainable Development, 6*(2), 94. doi:10.5539/jsd.v6n2p94

Kluckhohn, F. R., & Strodtbeck, F. L. (1961). *Variations in value orientations*. Grand Valley State University.

Kockelman, K. M., & Kalmanje, S. (2005). Credit-based congestion pricing : A policy proposal and the public's response. *Transportation Research Part A, Policy and Practice, 39*(7-9), 671–690. doi:10.1016/j.tra.2005.02.014

Kotchen, M. J., & Reiling, S. D. (2000). Environmental attitudes, motivations, and contingent valuation of nonuse values: A case study involving endangered species. *Ecological Economics, 32*(1), 93–107. doi:10.1016/S0921-8009(99)00069-5

Kotler, P., & Armstrong, G. (2023). Principles of Marketing. Pearson College Div.

Kotler, P., & Keller, K. L. (2016). Marketing management (15th global ed.). England: Pearson.

Kotler, P., Burton, S., Brown, L., & Armstrong, G. (2015). *Marketing*. Pearson Higher Education AU.

Kovačević, I., Bradić-Martinović, A., & Petković, G. (2021). Covid-19 impact on cultural and natural Pan-European thematic routes. *Ekonomika preduzeća, 69*(5-6), 357-368.

Kumar, A., Prakash, G., & Kumar, G. (2021). Does environmentally responsible purchase intention matter for consumers? A predictive sustainable model developed through an empirical study. *Journal of Retailing and Consumer Services, 58*, 102270. doi:10.1016/j.jretconser.2020.102270

Kumar, D. A., & Gangal, P. V. (2011). The impact of 'ambience' and variety on consumer delight: A study on consumer behaviour in Ahmedabad. *Indian Journal of Applied Research, 1*(9), 197–200. doi:10.15373/2249555X/JUN2012/70

Kumar, P., & Ghodeswar, B. (2015). Factors affecting consumers' green product purchase decisions. *Marketing Intelligence & Planning, 33*(3), 330–347. doi:10.1108/MIP-03-2014-0068

Laconte, P. (2012). Towards sustainability in European cities contrasts between the overall effects of European Union policies and achievements at the level of individual cities. *ISOCARP Review, 8*, 2–17.

Lah, O. (2019). Sustainable urban mobility in action. In *Sustainable Urban Mobility Pathways* (pp. 133–282). Elsevier. doi:10.1016/B978-0-12-814897-6.00007-7

Landman, A. (2010, May 3). *BP's "Beyond Petroleum" Campaign Losing its Sheen*. Prwatch.

Larina, I. V., Larin, A. N., Kiriliuk, O., & Ingaldi, M. (2021). Green logistics-modern transportation process technology. *Production Engineering Archives, 27*(3), 184–190. doi:10.30657/pea.2021.27.24

Law, A., DeLacy, T., & McGrath, G. M. (2017). A green economy indicator framework for tourism destinations. *Journal of Sustainable Tourism, 25*(10), 1434–1455. doi:10.1080/09669582.2017.1284857

Lazić, M., & Bradić-Martinović, A. (2022a). Analysis of Tourism Demand in Selected WB6 Countries during the COVID-19 Pandemic. In The 6th International Thematic Monograph: Modern Management Tools and Economy of Tourism Sector in Present Era. Association of Economists and Managers of the Balkans - UDEKOM Balkans.

Lazić, M., & Bradić-Martinović, A. (2022b). Analysis of the Impact of the COVID-19 Pandemic on Tourism Demand in the Republic of Serbia – Challenges and Opportunities. In *Proceedings of the National conference with international participation "Challenges and perspective in marketing" - SEMA*. Serbian Marketing Society – SEMA.

Lazić, M., & Antonijević, M. (2021). The Overview of ECB's and NBS' COVID-19 Containment Measures. In *Macroeconomic stability and improvement of the Western Balkans countries' competitiveness*. Institute of Economic Sciences.

Lee, J., & Cho, M. (2020). The Effects of Consumers' Media Exposure, Attention, and Credibility on Pro-environmental Behaviors. *Journal of Promotion Management, 26*(3), 434–455. doi:10.1080/10496491.2019.1699629

Lefdal Mine Datacenter. (2022, December 1). *Cooling*. Lefdal Mine Datacenter. https://www. lefdalmine.com/facility-2/cooling/

Leonidou, C. N., Katsikeas, C. S., & Morgan, N. A. (2012). "greening" The marketing mix: Do firms do it and does it pay off? *Journal of the Academy of Marketing Science, 41*(2), 151–170. doi:10.100711747-012-0317-2

Lesteven, G. (2012). Les stratégies d'adaptation à la congestion automobile dans les grandes métropoles: Analyse à partir des cas de Paris, São Paulo et Mumbai. *Confins. Revue franco-brésilienne de géographie/Revista franco-brasilera de geografia, 15.*

Letzter, R. (2016, November 2). One of the most influential economists in the world explains why a carbon tax is a good idea. *Insider.* https://www.businessinsider.com/gregory-mankiw-harvard-professor-carbon-tax-2016-11

Liao, Y.-K., Wu, W.-Y., & Pham, T.-T. (2020). Examining the Moderating Effects of Green Marketing and Green Psychological Benefits on Customers' Green Attitude, Value and Purchase Intention. *Sustainability (Basel), 12*(18), 7461. Advance online publication. doi:10.3390u12187461

Li, H. R. (2016). Study on green transportation system of international metropolises. *Procedia Engineering, 137,* 762–771. doi:10.1016/j.proeng.2016.01.314

Li, H., & Cai, W. (2009). Green marketing and sustainable development of garment industry-A game between cost and profit. *International Journal of Biometrics, 3,* 81.

Lim, H. S. M., & Taeihagh, A. (2018). Autonomous vehicles for smart and sustainable cities: An in-depth exploration of privacy and cybersecurity implications. *Energies, 11*(5), 1062. doi:10.3390/en11051062

Lin, L. P. (2018). How would the contextual features of a destination function together with individual factors to enhance tourists' intention toward ST in Taiwan? *Journal of Sustainable Tourism, 26*(9), 1625–1646. doi:10.1080/09669582.2018.1491586

Lin, P. H., & Chen, W. H. (2022). Factors That Influence Consumers' Sustainable Apparel Purchase Intention: The Moderating Effect of Generational Cohorts. *Sustainability (Basel), 14*(14), 8950. doi:10.3390u14148950

Litman, T. (2014). *Critique of" Transit Utilization and Traffic Congestion : Is There a Connection?* Reason Foundation.

Litman, T. (2005). *Well measured : Developing indicators for comprehensive and sustainable transportation planning.* Victoria Transportation Policy Institute.

Litman, T. (2006). Changing travel demand : Implications for transport planning. *Institute of Transportation Engineers. ITE Journal, 76*(9), 27.

Litman, T. (2016). *Parking management : Strategies, evaluation and planning.* Victoria Transport Policy Institute Victoria.

Litman, T., & Burwell, D. (2006). Issues in sustainable transportation. *International Journal of Global Environmental Issues*, *6*(4), 331–347. doi:10.1504/IJGENVI.2006.010889

Liu, H. (2020). *Smart Cities : Big Data Prediction Methods and Applications.* Springer. doi:10.1007/978-981-15-2837-8

Lixandru, M. G. (2017). Advertising for natural beauty products: The shift in cosmetic industry. *European Scientific Journal*, *7881*, 6–13.

Li, Z., & Hensher, D. A. (2012). Congestion charging and car use : A review of stated preference and opinion studies and market monitoring evidence. *Transport Policy*, *20*, 47–61. doi:10.1016/j.tranpol.2011.12.004

Lomax, T. J. (1997). *Quantifying congestion* (Vol. 398). Transportation Research Board.

Lomax, T., Turner, S., Shunk, G., Levinson, H. S., Pratt, R. H., Bay, P. N., & Douglas, G. B. (1997). *Quantifying Congestion* (Vol. 2). User's Guide.

Lončar, D., Đorđević, A., Lazić, M., Milošević, S., & Rajić, V. (2016). Interplay Between Market Concentration and Competitive Dynamics in The Banking Sector. *Ekonomika preduzeća, 44*(5/6), 332-346.

López, C., Ruíz-Benítez, R., & Vargas-Machuca, C. (2019). On the environmental and social sustainability of technological innovations in urban bus transport : The EU case. *Sustainability (Basel)*, *11*(5), 1413. doi:10.3390u11051413

Lu, J., Li, B., Li, H., & Al-Barakani, A. (2021). Expansion of city scale, traffic modes, traffic congestion, and air pollution. *Cities (London, England)*, *108*, 102974. doi:10.1016/j.cities.2020.102974

Lumley, S., & Armstrong, P. (2004). Some of the nineteenth century origins of the sustainability concept. *Environment, Development and Sustainability*, *6*(3), 367–378. doi:10.1023/B:ENVI.0000029901.02470.a7

Lumsdon, L. (2000). Transport and tourism: Cycle tourism–a model for sustainable development? *Journal of Sustainable Tourism*, *8*(5), 361–377. doi:10.1080/09669580008667373

Mabugu, M., & Inglesi-Lotz, R. (2022). *Energy Sources. Part B, Economics, Planning, and Policy*, 1–18.

Macrorie, R., Marvin, S., & While, A. (2021). Robotics and automation in the city: A research agenda. *Urban Geography*, *42*(2), 197–217. doi:10.1080/02723638.2019.1698868

Magali, M., Francis, K., & Hulten, P. (2012). *Green marketing: Consumers' attitudes towards eco-friendly products and purchase intention in the fast moving consumer goods sector.* Umea School Of Business Spring Semester.

Mahmoud, T. O. (2018). Impact of green marketing mix on purchase intention. *International Journal of Advanced and Applied Sciences*, *5*(2), 127–135. doi:10.21833/ijaas.2018.02.020

Mahmud, K., Gope, K., & Chowdhury, S. M. R. (2012). Possible causes & solutions of traffic jam and their impact on the economy of Dhaka City. *Journal of Management and Sustainability*, 2(2), 112. doi:10.5539/jms.v2n2p112

Mainieri, T., Barnett, E. G., Valdero, T. R., Unipan, J. B., & Oskamp, S. (1997). Green Buying: The Influence of Environmental Concern on Consumer Behavior. *The Journal of Social Psychology*, 137(2), 189–204. doi:10.1080/00224549709595430

Malone, C., & Belady, C. L. (2006). *Metrics to Characterize Data Center & IT Equipment Energy Use.* Digital Power Forum, Richardson, TX.

Mangiaracina, R., Perego, A., Salvadori, G., & Tumino, A. (2017). A comprehensive view of intelligent transport systems for urban smart mobility. *International Journal of Logistics*, 20(1), 39–52. doi:10.1080/13675567.2016.1241220

Manual, H. C. (1985). *Special report 209.* Transportation Research Board, Washington, DC.

Ma, R., & Lam, P. T. (2019). Investigating the barriers faced by stakeholders in open data development: A study on Hong Kong as a "smart city". *Cities (London, England)*, 92, 36–46. doi:10.1016/j.cities.2019.03.009

Marcuta, L., Popescu, A., Marcuta, A., Tindeche, C., & Smedescu, D. (2021). The impact of the COVID-19 crisis on tourism and its recover possibilities. *Scientific Papers. Series Management, Economic, Engineering in Agriculture and Rural Development*, 21(1), 495–500.

Marinchak, C. M., Forrest, E., & Hoanca, B. (2018). Artificial intelligence: Redefining marketing management and the customer experience. [IJEEI]. *International Journal of E-Entrepreneurship and Innovation*, 8(2), 14–24. doi:10.4018/IJEEI.2018070102

Mathur, A., Moschis, G. P., & Lee, E. (2007a). A longitudinal study of the effects of life status changes on changes in consumer preferences. *Journal of the Academy of Marketing Science*, 36(2), 234–246. doi:10.100711747-007-0021-9

May, A., & Marsden, G. (2010). *Urban transport and mobility.* Semantic Scholar.

May, A. D. (2013). Urban transport and sustainability: The key challenges. *International Journal of Sustainable Transportation*, 7(3), 170–185. doi:10.1080/15568318.2013.710136

Mayer, R. N. (1976). The socially conscious consumer—Another look at the data. *The Journal of Consumer Research*, 3(2), 113–115. doi:10.1086/208659

May, T., & Crass, M. (2007). Sustainability in transport: Implications for policy makers. *Transportation Research Record: Journal of the Transportation Research Board*, 2017(1), 1–9. doi:10.3141/2017-01

McCarthy, J. (2007). From here to human-level AI. *Artificial Intelligence*, 171(18), 1174–1182. doi:10.1016/j.artint.2007.10.009

McKinsey. (2022). *Resilience for sustainable, inclusive growth.* https://www.mckinsey.com/capabilities/risk-and-resilience/our-insights/resilience-for-sustainable-inclusive-growth

Meyer, M. D. (1997). *A toolbox for alleviating traffic congestion and enhancing mobility.* Federal Highway Administration.

Michigan Department of Attorney General. (n.d.). *Multi-level marketing or illegal pyramid scheme.* MI Department of Attorney General. https://www.michigan.gov/ag/consumer-protection/Consumer-Alerts/consumer-alerts/invest/mlm-illegal-pyramid-scheme

Microsoft. (2022, December 14). *Project Natick Phase 2.* Project Natick Research. https://natick.research.microsoft.com/

Mihailović, B., Radić Jean, I., Popović, V., Radosavljević, K., Chroneos Krasavac, B., & Bradić-Martinović, A. (2020). Farm Differentiation Strategies and Sustainable Regional Development. *Sustainability (Basel), 12*(17), 1–18. doi:10.3390u12177223

Mishra, P., & Sharma, P. (2010). Green marketing in India: Emerging opportunities and challenges. *Journal of Engineering. Science and Management Education, 3,* 9–14.

Mohammed, F., Idries, A., Mohamed, N., Al-Jaroodi, J., & Jawhar, I. (2014, March). Opportunities and challenges of using UAVs for dubai smart city. In *2014 6th international conference on new technologies, mobility and security (NTMS)* (pp. 1-4). IEEE. 10.1109/NTMS.2014.6814041

Mora, L., & Bolici, R. (2015). How to become a smart city: Learning from Amsterdam. Bisello A., Vettorato D., Stephens R., Elisei P.(eds) Smart and sustainable planning for cities and regions. Edinburgh University.

Moreno-Luna, L., Robina-Ramirez, R., Sanchez-Oro Sanchez, M., & Castro-Serrano, J. (2021). Tourism and Sustainability in Times of COVID-19: The Case of Spain. *International Journal of Environmental Research and Public Health, 18*(4), 1–21. doi:10.3390/ijerph18041859 PMID:33672912

Muench, S. T., Anderson, J. L., & Söderlund, M. (2010). Greenroads: A sustainability performance metric for roadways. *Journal of Green Building, 5*(2), 114–128. doi:10.3992/jgb.5.2.114

Mukhtar, S., Abdullahi, S. I., & Murtala, I. (2020). Do Energy Consumption, Interest Rate and Import affect Household Consumption in Nigeria: What did the Empirical Evidence says? *Lapai Journal of Economics, 4*(2), 98–106.

Municipality of Sokobanja and Tourism Organization of Sokobanja. (2022). *Program of Tourism Development of the Municipality of Sokobanja for the period 2023-2027.* Municipality of Sokobanja.

Municipality of Sokobanja. (2015) *Strategy of Sustainable Development of Sokobanja Municipality for the period 2015-202..* Municipality of Sokobanja.

Municipality of Sokobanja. (2016). *Environmental Protection Program of the Municipality of Sokobanja for the period 2017-2021.* Municipality of Sokobanja.

Municipality of Sokobanja. (2016). *Program of Sustainable Development of Winter Tourism in Sokobanja (Serbia) – Varshetz (Bulgaria) for the period 2020-2029.* Municipality of Sokobanja.

Municipality of Sokobanja. (2018). *Strategic Guidelines for Land Management as a Contribution Balanced Urban and Rural Development - Municipality of Sokobanja.* Municipality of Sokobanja.

Municipality of Sokobanja. (2019). *Statute of the Municipality of Sokobanja.* Municipality of Sokobanja.

Municipality of Sokobanja. (2021). *Local action plan for the promotion of gender equality in the municipality of Sokobanja for the period 2021-2024.* Municipality of Sokobanja. https://sokobanja.ls.gov.rs/

Municipality of Sokobanja. (2021). *Operational flood defence plan for watercourses II order for the territory of the municipality of Sokobanja for the year 2021.* Municipality of Sokobanja.

Municipality of Sokobanja. (2021). *Program for the use of funds for environmental protection on the territory of the Municipality of Sokobanja.* Municipality of Sokobanja.

Municipality of Sokobanja. (2022). *Local Plan for Waste Management in Sokobanja Municipality for the period 2022-2032.* Municipality of Sokobanja.

Municipality of Sokobanja. (2022). *Plan for the Management of Risks from Violation of the Principle of Gender Equality.* Municipality of Sokobanja.

Nathalie, B. O. (2022). Sustainable development. *International Institute for Sustainable Development.* https://www.iisd.org/mission-and-goals/sustainable-development

Nathaniel, S. P., & Bekun, F. V. (2020). *Electricity consumption, urbanization and economic growth in Nigeria: New insights from combined cointegration amidst structural breaks.* AGDI Working Paper, No. WP/20/013, African Governance and Development Institute (AGDI), Yaoundé.

Naude, C., & Tsolakis, D. (2005). *Defining transport congestion.* TRB. https://trid.trb.org/view/1156189

Neves, J., & Oliveira, T. (2021). Understanding energy-efficient heating appliance behavior change: The moderating impact of the green self-identity. *Energy, 225,* 120169. doi:10.1016/j.energy.2021.120169

Newbery, D. M. (2001). Harmonizing energy Taxes in the EU. conference Tax Policy in the European Union, Ministry of Finance. The Hague, 17-19.

Newman, P., & Kenworthy, J. (1999). *Sustainability and cities : Overcoming automobile dependence.* Island press.

News, S. B. S. (2016, December 8). *Factbox: Carbon taxes and emission trading schemes around the world.* SBS. https://www.sbs.com.au/news/article/2016/12/08/factbox-carbon-taxes-and-emission-trading-schemes-around-world

Ng, M. K., Koksal, C., Wong, C., & Tang, Y. (2022). Smart and sustainable development from a Spatial planning perspective: The case of Shenzhen and Greater Manchester. *Sustainability (Basel), 14*(6), 3509. doi:10.3390u14063509

Nguyen, N. H., & Nguyen, D. N. (2018). Impacts of green marketing on the green brand image and equity in banking sector. *WSEAS Transactions on Business and Economics, 15*, 452–460.

Nguyen-Phuoc, D. Q., Young, W., Currie, G., & De Gruyter, C. (2020). Traffic congestion relief associated with public transport : State-of-the-art. *Public Transport (Berlin), 12*(2), 455–481. doi:10.100712469-020-00231-3

Nielsen Holdings. (2014). *Global consumers are willing to put their money where their heart is.* Nielsen. http://www.nielsen.com/in/en/press-room/2014/global- consumers-are-willing-to-put-their-money-where-their-heart- is.htm

Nielsen IQ. (2018). *Sustainability sells: Linking sustainability claims to sales.* Neilsen IQ. https://nielseniq.com/global/en/insights/report/2018/sustainability-sells-linking-sustainability-claims-to-sales/

Niinimäki, K. (2010). Eco-clothing, consumer identity and ideology. *Sustainable Development (Bradford), 18*(3), 150–162. doi:10.1002d.455

Nikitas, A., Michalakopoulou, K., Njoya, E. T., & Karampatzakis, D. (2020). Artificial intelligence, transport and the smart city: Definitions and dimensions of a new mobility era. *Sustainability (Basel), 12*(7), 2789. doi:10.3390u12072789

NJMEP. (2016). *How Green Manufacturing & Sustainability Reduces Costs & Improves Efficiencies.* NJMEP. https://www.njmep.org/blog/how-green-manufacturing-sustainability-reduces-costs-improves-efficiencies/

Nnaji, Chukwu, & Moses. (2013). Electricity Supply, Fossil fuel Consumption, Co2 Emissions and Economic Growth: Implications and Policy Options for Sustainable Development in Nigeria. *International Journal of Energy Economics and Policy, 3*(3), 262–271.

Noh, S. M., Kang, H. S., & Jang, S. Y. (2020). The Effects of Smart Tolling for the Improvement of Traffic Flow on the Seoul Tollgate with ARENA. *Journal of Advanced Simulation in Science and Engineering, 7*(2), 279–290. doi:10.15748/jasse.7.279

Noland, R. B. (2001). Relationships between highway capacity and induced vehicle travel. *Transportation Research Part A, Policy and Practice, 35*(1), 47–72. doi:10.1016/S0965-8564(99)00047-6

NREL. (2023). *National Renewable Energy Laboratory.* High-Performance Computing Data Center. https://www.nrel.gov/computational-science/hpc-data-center.html

Nundy, S., Ghosh, A., Mesloub, A., Albaqawy, G. A., & Alnaim, M. M. (2021). Impact of COVID-19 pandemic on socio-economic, energy-environment and transport sector globally and sustainable development goal (SDG). *Journal of Cleaner Production, 312*, 127705. doi:10.1016/j.jclepro.2021.127705 PMID:36471816

Ogbonna, O. S., Idenyi, O. S., & Nick, A. (2016). Power Generation Capacity and Economic Growth in Nigeria: A Causality Approach. *European Journal of Business and Management*, *8*(32), 74–90.

Ogundipe, A. A., Akinyemi, O., & Ogundipe, O. M. (2016). Electricity Consumption and Economic Development in Nigeria. *International Journal of Energy Economics and Policy*, *6*(1), 134–143.

Okoye, L. U., Omankhanlen, A. E., Okoh, J. I., Adeleye, N. B., Ezeji, F. N., Ezu, G. K., & Ehikioya, B. I. (2021). Analyzing the Energy Consumption and Economic Growth Nexus in Nigeria. *International Journal of Energy Economics and Policy*, *11*(1), 378–387. doi:10.32479/ijeep.10768

Oladimeji, D., Gupta, K., Kose, N. A., Gundogan, K., Ge, L., & Liang, F. (2023). Smart transportation : An overview of technologies and applications. *Sensors (Basel)*, *23*(8), 3880. doi:10.339023083880 PMID:37112221

Oliveira, C., & Sousa, B. (2019). Green consumer behavior and its implications on brand marketing strategy. In V. Naidoo & R. Verma (Eds.), *Green marketing as a positive driver toward business sustainability* (pp. 69–95). IGI Global. doi:10.4018/978-1-5225-9558-8.ch004

Omar, N., Osman, L., Alam, S. S., & Othman, A. (2015). Ecological conscious behaviour in Malaysia: The case of environmental friendly products. *Malaysian Journal of Consumer and Family Economics*, *18*, 17–34.

Onakoya, A. B., Onakoya, A. O., Salami, O. A., & Odedairo, B. O. (2013). Energy consumption and Nigerian economic growth: An empirical analysis. *European Scientific Journal*, *9*(4), 25–40.

Onayemi, S. O., Olomola, P. A., Alege, P. O., & Onayemi, O. O. (2020). Foreign Direct Investment, Electricity Power Supply and Economic Growth in Nigeria. *International Journal of Energy Economics and Policy*, *10*(5), 243–247. doi:10.32479/ijeep.7774

OpenCompute. (2023). *Sustainability*. Open Compute Project. https://www.opencompute.org/projects/sustainability

Opute, A. P., Irene, B. O., & Iwu, C. G. (2020). Tourism Service and Digital Technologies: A Value Creation Perspective. *African Journal of Hospitality, Tourism and Leisure*, *9*(2), 1–18.

Organisation for Economic Co-operation and Development. European Conference of Ministers of Transport, & Transport Research Centre (Éds.). (2007). *Managing urban traffic congestion*. OECD: ECMT.

Organization of American States. (n.d.). *Annex 2. Tourism as an economic development tool*. OAS. http://www.oas.org/dsd/publications/unit/oea78e/ch10.htm

Osareh, F. (1996). Bibliometrics, citation analysis and co-citation analysis: A review of literature I. *Libri*, *46*(3), 149–158. doi:10.1515/libr.1996.46.3.149

Ottman, J., & Eisen, M. (2010). *Green Marketing Myopia and the SunChips Snacklash*. Green Marketing. http://www.greenmarketing.com/site/green-marketing-myopia-and-the-sunchips-snacklash/

Ottman, J. (1998). *Green Marketing: Opportunity for Innovation* (2nd ed.). NTC/Contemporary Publishing Company.

Ottman, J. A., Stafford, E. R., & Hartman, C. L. (2006). Avoiding Green Marketing Myopia: Ways to Improve Consumer Appeal for Environmentally Preferable Products. *Environment*, *48*(5), 22–36. doi:10.3200/ENVT.48.5.22-36

Ottoman, J., & Mallen, D. (2014), *5 Green marketing strategies to earn consumer trust*. gREENbIZ. https://www.greenbiz.com/blog/2014/01/14/five-strategies-avoid-taint- greenwash-your-business.

Oyaromade, R., Mathew, A., & Abalaba, B. P. (2014). Energy Consumption and Economic Growth in Nigeria: A Causality Analysis. *International Journal of Sustainable Energy and Environmental Research*, *3*(1), 53–61.

Özdemir, V., & Hekim, N. (2018). Birth of industry 5.0: Making sense of big data with artificial intelligence, "the internet of things" and next-generation technology policy. *OMICS: A Journal of Integrative Biology*, *22*(1), 65–76. doi:10.1089/omi.2017.0194 PMID:29293405

Ozturk, I. (2010). Literature survey on energy–growth nexus. *Energy Policy*, *38*(1), 340–349. doi:10.1016/j.enpol.2009.09.024

Paço, A. (2009). Adam werbach, strategy for sustainability. A business manifesto. *International Review on Public and Nonprofit Marketing*, *6*(2), 187–188. doi:10.100712208-009-0039-4

Pal, K. (2018, May 3). *How Green Computing Can Improve Energy Efficiency in IT*. Technopedia. https://www.techopedia.com/how-green-computing-can-improve-energy-efficiency-in-it/2/32212

Pande, K (2017). Mainstreaming sdgs in national policies: the case of transport sector in nepal. *Transport and Sustainable Development Goals*, *16*.

Pardana, D., Abdullah, R., Mahmuda, D., Malik, E., Pratiwi, E. T., Dja'wa, A., Abdullah, L. O., Hardin, & Hamid, R. S. (2019). Attitude analysis in the theory of planned behavior: Green marketing against the intention to buy environmentally friendly products. *IOP Conference Series. Earth and Environmental Science*, *343*(1), 012128. doi:10.1088/1755-1315/343/1/012128

Pearce, D. W., & Warford, J. J. (1993). *World without end: Economics, environment and sustainable development – A summary*. World Bank.

Peattie, K. (1995). *Environmental Marketing Management*. Pitman.

Peattie, K. (2001). Towards sustainability: The third age of green marketing. *The Marketing Review*, *2*(2), 129–146. doi:10.1362/1469347012569869

Peattie, K., & Charter, M. (2002). Green marketing. In M. Baker (Ed.), *The marketing book* (5th ed.). Routledge.

Pekerti, A. A., & Arli, D. (2017). Do Cultural and Generational Cohorts Matter to Ideologies and Consumer Ethics? A Comparative Study of Australians, Indonesians, and Indonesian Migrants in Australia. *Journal of Business Ethics, 143*(2), 387–404. doi:10.100710551-015-2777-z

Petković, G., Pindžo, R., & Bradić-Martinović, A. (2022). Competitiveness Factors of Serbian Tourism. *Ekonomika preduzeća, 70*(1-2), 113-127.

Petri Nets. (n.d.). *Intro.* Bielefeld University. https://www.techfak.uni-bielefeld.de/~mchen/BioPNML/Intro/pnfaq.html

Pfeffer, K. P., Zuidgeest, M. Z., van Maarseveen Maarseveen, M., & Brussel, M. B. (2019). Access or Accessibility? A Critique of the Urban Transport SDG Indicator.

Pickett-Baker, J., & Ozaki, R. (2008). Pro-environmental products: Marketing influence on consumer purchase decision. *Journal of Consumer Marketing, 25*(5), 281–293. doi:10.1108/07363760810890516

Piercy, N. F. (1998). Marketing implementation: The implications of marketing paradigm weakness for the strategy execution process. *Journal of the Academy of Marketing Science, 26*(3), 222–236. doi:10.1177/0092070398263004

Pindyck, R. S., & Rubinfeld, D. L. (1998). *Econometric models and economic forecasts.* McGraw.

Pizam, A. (2009). Green hotels: A fad, ploy or fact of life. *International Journal of Hospitality Management, 28*(1), 1. doi:10.1016/j.ijhm.2008.09.001

Plüss, C., Zotz, A., Monshausen, A., & Kühhas, C. (2012). *Sustainablitiy in Toursm – A Guide Through the Label Jungle.* Naturefriends International.

Pojani, D., & Stead, D. (2015). Sustainable urban transport in the developing world: Beyond megacities. *Sustainability (Basel), 7*(6), 7784–7805. doi:10.3390u7067784

Pojani, D., & Stead, D. (2018). Policy design for sustainable urban transport in the global south. *Policy Design and Practice, 1*(2), 90–102. doi:10.1080/25741292.2018.1454291

Polonsky, M. J. (1994). An introduction to green marketing. *Electronic Green Journal, 1*(2). Advance online publication. doi:10.5070/G31210177

Porter, M. E. (1998). *The competitive advantage: Creating and sustaining superior performance.* Free Press. doi:10.1007/978-1-349-14865-3

Portugal-Pereira, J. O., Doll, C. N. H., Suwa, A., & Puppim de Oliveira, J. A. (2013). The sustainable mobility-congestion nexus : A co-benefits approach to finding win-win solutions. *Transport and Communications Bulletin for Asia and the Pacific, 82*, 19–31.

Prasad, D., Alizadeh, T., & Dowling, R. (2021). Multiscalar smart city governance in India. *Geoforum, 121*, 173–180. doi:10.1016/j.geoforum.2021.03.001

Prideaux, B., Thompson, M., & Pabel, A. (2020). Lessons from COVID-19 can prepare global tourism for the economic transformation needed to combat climate change. *Tourism Geographies*, *22*(3), 667–678. doi:10.1080/14616688.2020.1762117

Purvis, B., Mao, Y., & Robinson, D. (2019). Three pillars of sustainability: In search of conceptual origins. *Sustainability Science*, *14*(3), 681–695. doi:10.100711625-018-0627-5

Raffaud, F. (2003). *L'URBAIN, L'ENVIRONNEMENT ET LE DEVELOPPEMENT DURABLE EN FRANCE Essai d'analyse–Revue Urbanisme-1964-2000*. Université de Pau et des Pays de l'Adour.

Rahbar, E., Shwu Shyan, T., & Abdul Wahi, N. (2011). Actors influencing the Green Purchase Behavior of Penang Environmental Volunteers. *International Business Management*, *5*(1), 38–49. doi:10.3923/ibm.2011.38.49

Rahbar, E., & Wahid, N. A. (2011). Investigation of Green Marketing Tools' effect on consumers' purchase behavior. *Business Strategy Series*, *12*(2), 73–83. doi:10.1108/17515631111114877

Rahim, M. H. A., Zukni, R. Z. A., Ahmad, F., & Lyndon, N. (2012). Green advertising and environmentally responsible consumer behavior: The level of awareness and perception of Malaysian youth. *Asian Social Science*, *8*(5). Advance online publication. doi:10.5539/ass.v8n5p46

Ramadoss, T. S., Alam, H., & Seeram, R. (2018). Artificial intelligence and Internet of Things enabled circular economy. *The International Journal of Engineering and Science*, *7*(9), 55–63.

Ramírez-Moreno, M. A., Keshtkar, S., Padilla-Reyes, D. A., Ramos-López, E., García-Martínez, M., Hernández-Luna, M. C., Mogro, A. E., Mahlknecht, J., Huertas, J. I., Peimbert-García, R. E., Ramírez-Mendoza, R. A., Mangini, A. M., Roccotelli, M., Pérez-Henríquez, B. L., Mukhopadhyay, S. C., & Lozoya-Santos, J. D. J. (2021). Sensors for sustainable smart cities: A review. *Applied Sciences (Basel, Switzerland)*, *11*(17), 8198. doi:10.3390/app11178198

Rao, A. M., & Rao, K. R. (2012). Measuring urban traffic congestion-a review. *IJTTE. International Journal for Traffic and Transport Engineering*, *2*(4).

Rashid, N. R. (2009). Awareness of eco-label in Malaysia's green marketing initiative. *International Journal of Business and Management*, *4*(8). Advance online publication. doi:10.5539/ijbm.v4n8p132

Rasool, H., Maqbool, S., & Tarique, M. (2021). The relationship between tourism and economic growth among BRICS countries: A panel cointegration analysis. *Future Business Journal*, *7*(1), 1–11. doi:10.118643093-020-00048-3

Rehena, Z., & Janssen, M. (2019). The smart city of Pune. In *Smart City Emergence* (pp. 261–282). Elsevier. doi:10.1016/B978-0-12-816169-2.00012-2

Rex, E., & Baumann, H. (2007). Beyond ecolabels: What green marketing can learn from conventional marketing. *Journal of Cleaner Production*, *15*(6), 567–576. doi:10.1016/j.jclepro.2006.05.013

Reymond. M. (2005). *La tarification de la congestion automobile: Acceptabilité sociale et redistribution des recettes du péage.* [Thèse de doctorat en sciences économiques, Montpellier, université Montpellier 1].

Richardson, B. C. (2005). Sustainable transport: Analysis frameworks. *Journal of Transport Geography*, *13*(1), 29–39. doi:10.1016/j.jtrangeo.2004.11.005

Rivera, J., & deLeon, P. (2005). Chief executive officers and voluntary environmental performance: Costa Rica's certification for sustainable tourism. *Policy Sciences*, *38*(2-3), 107–127. doi:10.100711077-005-6590-x

Robert, J., Kubler, S., Kolbe, N., Cerioni, A., Gastaud, E., & Främling, K. (2017). Open IoT ecosystem for enhanced interoperability in smart cities—Example of Métropole De Lyon. *Sensors (Basel)*, *17*(12), 2849. doi:10.339017122849 PMID:29292719

Roberts, J. A. (1995). Profiling Levels of Socially Responsible Consumer Behavior: A Cluster Analytic Approach and Its Implications for Marketing. *Journal of Marketing Theory and Practice*, *3*(4), 97–117. doi:10.1080/10696679.1995.11501709

Roberts, J. A., & Bacon, D. R. (1997). Exploring the Subtle Relationships between Environmental Concern and Ecologically Conscious Consumer Behavior. *Journal of Business Research*, *40*(1), 79–89. doi:10.1016/S0148-2963(96)00280-9

Rock Content. (2021, August 21). *What is green marketing? 5 examples to inspire your business.* Rock Content. https://rockcontent.com/blog/green-marketing-examples/

Rodrigue, J.-P. (2016). *The geography of transport systems.* Taylor & Francis. doi:10.4324/9781315618159

Romer, P. M. (1982). The Origins of endogenous growth. *The Journal of Economic Perspectives*, *8*(1), 3–22. doi:10.1257/jep.8.1.3

Romer, P. M. (1986). Increasing returns and long run growth. *Journal of Political Economy*, *94*(5), 1002–1038. doi:10.1086/261420

Roome, N. (1992). Developing environmental management strategies. *Business Strategy and the Environment*, *1*(1), 11–24. doi:10.1002/bse.3280010104

Rosenbloom, S. (1978). Peak-period traffic congestion: A state-of-the-art analysis and evaluation of effective solutions. *Transportation*, *7*(2), 167–191. doi:10.1007/BF00184638

Rothenberg, M. J. (1985). *Urban traffic congestion: what does the future hold? Urban congestion in the united states: what does the future hold?* TRB. https://trid.trb.org/view/274659

Rubin, T. A., & Mansour, F. (2013). *Transit Utilization and Traffic Congestion: Is There a Connection?* Santos, G. (2017). Road fuel taxes in Europe: Do they internalize road transport externalities? *Transport Policy*, *53*, 120–134.

Saad, L. (2007, March 26). *Environmental concern holds firm during past year.* Gallup News Service. https://news.gallup.com/poll/26971/environmental-concern-holds-firm-during-past-year.aspx

Saini, B. (2013). Green marketing and its impact on consumer buying behavior. *International Journal of Engineering and Science Invention, 2*(12), 61–64.

Sajid, K. S., Hussain, S., Hussain, R. I., & Mustafa, B. (2022). The Effect of Fear of COVID-19 on Green Purchase Behavior in Pakistan: A Multi-Group Analysis Between Infected and Non-infected. *Frontiers in Psychology, 13*, 826870. doi:10.3389/fpsyg.2022.826870 PMID:35422735

Salomonson, N., & Fellesson, M. (2014). Tricks and tactics used against troublesome travelers—Frontline staff's experiences from Swedish buses and trains. *Research in Transportation Business & Management, 10*, 53–59. doi:10.1016/j.rtbm.2014.04.002

Samarasinghe, R. (2012). A green segmentation: Identifying the green consumer demographic profiles in Sri Lanka. *Int. J. Mark. Technol., 2*(4), 318–331.

Saunders, M., Lewis, P., & Thornhill, A. (2007). Research methods. Business Students, 6(3), 1-268. Pearson Education Limited, England.

Schrank, D. L., Turner, S. M., & Lomax, T. J. (1993). *Estimates of urban roadway congestion, 1990.*

Schrank, D., Lomax, T., & Eisele, B. (2012). *2012 urban mobility report.* Texas Transportation Institute. http://mobility. tamu. edu/ums/report

Schwartz, S. H. (1977). In L. Berkowitz (Ed.), *Normative Influences on Altruism,* pp. 221–279. Academic Press.

Sechrist, S. (2022, May 18). *Understanding the Differences Between 5 Common Types of Data Centers.* Datacenter Frontier. https://www.datacenterfrontier.com/voices-of-the-industry/article/11427373/understanding-the-differences-between-5-common-types-of-data-centers

Selmoune, A., Cheng, Q., Wang, L., & Liu, Z. (2020). Influencing factors in congestion pricing acceptability: A literature review. *Journal of Advanced Transportation, 2020*, 2020. doi:10.1155/2020/4242964

Seroka-Stolka, O. (2016). Green initiatives in environmental management of logistics companies. *Transportation Research Procedia, 16*, 483–489. doi:10.1016/j.trpro.2016.11.045

Seyhan, F., & Özzeybek Taş, M. (2021). Sağlık turizmi konusunda yapılan çalışmaların "R tabanlı" bibliyometrix analizi. *Social Sciences Studies Journal, 7*(81), 1569–1586. doi:10.26449ssj.3117

Sharma, N. K., & Sharma, B. (2014). Ethical marketing as a tool for developing customer relations: An empirical analysis. *International Journal on Customer Relations, 2*(2), 26.

Sharma, R., & Jha, M. (2017). Values influencing sustainable consumption behaviour: Exploring the contextual relationship. *Journal of Business Research, 76*, 77–88. . doi:10.1016/j.jbusres.2017.03.010

Shatanawi, M., Abdelkhalek, F., & Mészáros, F. (2020). Urban Congestion Charging Acceptability: An International Comparative Study. *Sustainability (Basel)*, *12*(12), 5044. doi:10.3390u12125044

Sheoran, M., & Kumar, D. (2022). Conceptualisation of sustainable consumer behaviour: Converging the theory of planned behaviour and consumption cycle. *Qualitative Research in Organizations and Management*, *17*(1), 103–135. doi:10.1108/QROM-05-2020-1940

Shi, K., Di, B., Zhang, K., Feng, C., & Svirchev, L. (2018). Detrended cross-correlation analysis of urban traffic congestion and NO 2 concentrations in Chengdu. *Transportation Research Part D, Transport and Environment*, *61*, 165–173. doi:10.1016/j.trd.2016.12.012

Shinde, S., Nalawade, S., & Nalawade, A. (2013). Ekim). Green Computing: Go Green and Save Energy. *International Journal of Advanced Research in Computer Science and Software Engineering*, *3*(7), 1033–1037.

Shin, J.-H., & Jun, H.-B. (2014). A study on smart parking guidance algorithm. *Transportation Research Part C, Emerging Technologies*, *44*, 299–317. doi:10.1016/j.trc.2014.04.010

Shiva, V. (1992). Recovering the real meaning of sustainability. D. Cooper and J. Palmer (eds.), The environment question: Ethics and global issues. Taylor and Francis.

Shuaibu, M., Yusufu, M., Abdullahi, S. I., Shehu, K. K., & Adamu, M. B. (2021). What explains economic growth in Nigeria in the last three decades?—A dynamic modelling approach. *East African Scholars Multidiscip Bull*, *4*, 75–84.

Sinnappan, P., & Rasdi, R. M. (2013). Corporate social responsibility: Adoption of green marketing by hotel industry. *Asian Social Science*, *9*(17), 79. doi:10.5539/ass.v9n17p79

Small, K. A. (2010). *Energy Policies for Automobile Transportation*. Resources for the Future.

Solow, R. M. (1956). A Contribution to the Theory of Economic Growth. *The Quarterly Journal of Economics*, *70*(1), 65–94. doi:10.2307/1884513

Somoye, O. A., Ozdeser, H., & Seraj, M. (2022). The Impact of Renewable Energy Consumption on Economic Growth in Nigeria: Fresh Evidence from a Non-linear ARDL Approach. *Environmental Science and Pollution Research International*, *29*(41), 62611–62625. doi:10.100711356-022-20110-7 PMID:35404038

Soomro, R. B., Mirani, I. A., Sajid Ali, M., & Marvi, S. (2020). Exploring the green purchasing behavior of young generation in Pakistan: Opportunities for green entrepreneurship. *Asia Pacific Journal of Innovation and Entrepreneurship*, *14*(3), 289–302. doi:10.1108/APJIE-12-2019-0093

SRG. (2021, September 13). *Hyperscale Data Center Count Grows to 659 – ByteDance Joins the Leading Group*. Synergy Research Group. https://www.srgresearch.com/articles/hyperscale-data-center-count-grows-to-659-bytedance-joins-the-leading-group

Staff, W. B. E. (2022, October 25). Green marketing. *Website Builder Expert*. https://www.websitebuilderexpert.com/grow-online/green-marketing-examples/

Stall-Meadows, C., & Davey, A. (2013). Green marketing of apparel: Consumers' price sensitivity to environmental marketing claims. *Journal of Global Fashion Marketing*, *4*(1), 33–43. doi:10 .1080/20932685.2012.753293

Statistical Office of the Republic of Serbia. (2022). Statistical Yearbook 2022. SORS. https:// www.stat.gov.rs/en-us/publikacije/publication/?p=14853

Steinsland, C., Fridstrøm, L., Madslien, A., & Minken, H. (2018). The climate, economic and equity effects of fuel tax, road toll and commuter tax credit. *Transport Policy*, *72*, 225–241. doi:10.1016/j.tranpol.2018.04.019

Stern, D. I. (2004). Factors affecting linkage Between energy and growth. Encyclopedia of Energy, 2.

Stern, D. (2000). A multivariate cointegration analysis of the role of energy in the US economy. *Energy Economics*, *22*(2), 267–283. doi:10.1016/S0140-9883(99)00028-6

Stern, D. I. (1993). Energy and economic growth in the USA: A multivariate approach. *Energy Economics*, *15*(2), 137–150. doi:10.1016/0140-9883(93)90033-N

Stern, D. I. (1997). Limits to substitution and irreversibility in production and consumption: A neoclassical interpretation of ecological economics. *Ecological Economics*, *21*(3), 197–215. doi:10.1016/S0921-8009(96)00103-6

Sterner, T. (2007). Fuel taxes: An important instrument for climate policy. *Energy Policy*, *35*(6), 3194–3202. doi:10.1016/j.enpol.2006.10.025

Stern, P. C. (2000). New environmental theories: Toward a coherent theory of environmentally significant behavior. *The Journal of Social Issues*, *56*(3), 407–424. doi:10.1111/0022-4537.00175

Stopher, P. R. (2004). Reducing road congestion: A reality check. *Transport Policy*, *11*(2), 117–131. doi:10.1016/j.tranpol.2003.09.002

Stronza, A. L., Hunt, C. A., & Fitzgerald, L. A. (2019). *Ecotourism for Conservation?*. *Annual Review of Environment and Resources*. Annual Reviews Inc. https://doi.org/ doi:10.1146/annurev-environ-101718-033046

Stungwa, S., Hlongwane, N. W., & Daw, O. D. (2022). Consumption and Supply of Electricity on Economic Growth in South Africa: An Econometric Approach. *International Journal of Energy Economics and Policy*, *12*(1), 266–274. doi:10.32479/ijeep.12542

Sudbury-Riley, L., & Kohlbacher, F. (2016). Ethically minded consumer behavior: Scale review, development, and validation. *Journal of Business Research*, *69*(8), 2697–2710. doi:10.1016/j. jbusres.2015.11.005

Sung, J., & Woo, H. (2019). Investigating male consumers' lifestyle of health and sustainability (LOHAS) and perception toward slow fashion. *Journal of Retailing and Consumer Services*, *49*, 120–128. doi:10.1016/j.jretconser.2019.03.018

Sussman, J. M. (2005). Intelligent Transportation Systems at the Turning Point: Preparing for Integrated, Regional, and Market-Driven Deployment. *Perspectives on Intelligent Transportation Systems (ITS)*, 173-187.

Swarbrooke, J. (1999). *Sustainable tourism management*. Cabi. doi:10.1079/9780851993140.0000

Systematics, C. (2005). *Traffic congestion and reliability: Trends and advanced strategies for congestion mitigation*. Federal Highway Administration.

Szabo, S., & Webster, J. (2020). Perceived greenwashing: The effects of green marketing on environmental and product perceptions. *Journal of Business Ethics*, *171*(4), 719–739. doi:10.100710551-020-04461-0

Taking a good look at the beauty industry. (2021, July 22). McKinsey & Company. https://www.mckinsey.com/industries/retail/our-insights/taking-a-good-look-at-the-beauty-industry

Tandon, A., Dhir, A., Kaur, P., Kushwah, S., & Salo, J. (2020). Why do people buy organic food? The moderating role of environmental concerns and trust. *Journal of Retailing and Consumer Services, 57*, 102247. doi:10.1016/j.jretconser.2020.102247

Tang, Ch., Han, Y., & Ng, P. (2022). Green consumption intention and behavior of tourists in urban and rural destinations. *Journal of Environmental Planning and Management*, 1–25. doi:10.1080/09640568.2022.2061927

Tanwari, A. (2020). A study on assessing the relationship between green marketing and brand loyalty in manufacturing sector of Greece: A moderating role of green supply chain practices. *Journal of Business Management and Accounting*, *4*(1), 44–55.

Taş, M. A., & Akcan, S. (2022). *Investigation of green criteria with clustering analysis in green supplier selection* (pp. 207–228). IGI Global. doi:10.4018/978-1-7998-8900-7.ch012

Taufique, K. M. R., & Islam, S. (2020). Green marketing in emerging Asia: Antecedents of green consumer behavior among younger millennials. *Journal of Asia Business Studies*, *15*(4), 541–558. doi:10.1108/JABS-03-2020-0094

The World Counts. (n.d.). *Global Challenges*. The World Counts. https://www.theworldcounts.com/challenges/consumption/transport-and-tourism/negative-environmental-impacts-of-tourism

Tinne, W. S. (2013). Green Washing: An Alarming Issue. *ASA University Review*, *7*(1), 81–88.

Tirachini, A. (2019). Ride-hailing, travel behaviour and sustainable mobility : An international review. *Transportation*, 1–37.

Tiwari, S., Tripathi, D. M., Srivastava, U., & Yadav, P. K. (2011). Green marketing-emerging dimensions. *Journal of Business Excellence*, *2*(1), 18–23.

Tobin, J., & Golub, S. S. (1998). *Money credit and capital*. McGraw-Hill international.

Todaro, M. P., & Smith, S. C. (2003). *Economic development*. Pearson Education.

Tourism Organization of Sokobanja. (2019). *Program of Sustainable Development of Winter Tourism in Sokobanja (Serbia) – Varshetz (Bulgaria) for the period 2020-2029.* TOS.

Trandafilovic, I., Conic, V., & Blagojevic, A. (2017). Impact of demographic factors on environmentally conscious purchase behavior. *Ekonomika Poljoprivrede, 64*(4), 1365–1377. doi:10.5937/ekoPolj1704365T

Tussyadiah, I. (2020). A review of research into automation in tourism: Launching the Annals of Tourism Research Curated Collection on Artificial Intelligence and Robotics in Tourism. *Annals of Tourism Research, 81,* 102883. doi:10.1016/j.annals.2020.102883

Twin, A. (2022). *Competitive Advantage Definition with Types and Examples.* Investopedia. https://www.investopedia.com/terms/c/competitive_advantage.asp

Tzschentke, N., Kirk, D., & Lynch, P. A. (2007). Going green: Decisional factors in small hospitality operations. *International Journal of Hospitality Management, 27*(1), 126–133. doi:10.1016/j.ijhm.2007.07.010

U.S. Green Building Council. (2022). *U.S. Green Building Council.* LEED Project Profiles. https://www.usgbc.org/projects/?Country=%5B%22Turkey%22%5D

Ugbaka, M. A., Awujola, A., & Isa, G. H. (2019). Electricity Supply and Economic Growth in Nigeria: A Bound Testing and Co-integration Approach. *Lapai Journal Economics; 3*(2).

Umeji, G., Agu, A. O., Eleanya, E. E., Chinedum, E. M., Nwabugwu, O. O., & Obumnene, M. T. (2023). Renewable Energy Consumption and Economic Growth in Nigeria. *African Journal of Social Science and Humanities Research., 6*(1), 34–48. doi:10.52589/AJSSHR-BNHM472F

Unilever PLC Annual Report. (2019, January 31). Unilever PLC. https://www.unilever-ewa.com/files/678bbb68-9105-42cc-ae04-fd0989c22b47/annual-report-and-financial-statements-2019.pdf

United Nations. (1987). *Our common future.* UN. https://www.are.admin.ch/are/en/home/media/publications/sustainable-development/brundtland-report.html

Uptime Entitüsü. (2022). *Uptime Institute Issued Awards.* Uptime Institute. https://uptimeinstitute.com/uptime-institute-awards/achievements

Vaibhav, R., Bhalerao, V., & Deshmukh, A. (2015). Green marketing: Greening the 4 Ps of marketing. *International Journal of Knowledge and Research in Management and E-Commerce, 5,* 5–8.

Vaziri, M. (2002). Development of highway congestion index with fuzzy set models. *Transportation Research Record: Journal of the Transportation Research Board, 1802*(1), 16–22. doi:10.3141/1802-03

Vianna, M. M. B., da Silva Portugal, L., & Balassiano, R. (2004). Intelligent transportation systems and parking management: Implementation potential in a Brazilian city. *Cities (London, England), 21*(2), 137–148. doi:10.1016/j.cities.2004.01.001

Viauroux, C. (2011). Pricing urban congestion: A structural random utility model with traffic anticipation. *European Economic Review*, *55*(7), 877–902. doi:10.1016/j.euroecorev.2011.04.001

Vilkaite-Vaitone, N., & Skackauskiene, I. (2019). Green marketing orientation: Evolution, conceptualization and potential benefits. *Open Economics*, *2*(1), 53–62. doi:10.1515/openec-2019-0006

Vogt, M., & Weber, C. (2019). Current challenges to the concept of sustainability. *Global Sustainability*, *2*, e4. doi:10.1017us.2019.1

Vu, D. M., Ha, N. T., Ngo, T. V. N., Pham, H. T., & Duong, C. D. (2021). Environmental corporate social responsibility initiatives and green purchase intention: An application of the extended theory of planned behavior. *Social Responsibility Journal*. doi:10.1108/SRJ-06-2021-0220

Wall, M. (2015, December 17). The world needs a carbon tax, Elon Musk says. *Live Science*. https://www.livescience.com/53113-elon-musk-carbon-tax.html

Walsh, N. (2022, 4 22). *How Microsoft measures datacenter water and energy use to improve Azure Cloud sustainability*. Microsoft Azure. https://azure.microsoft.com/en-us/blog/how-microsoft-measures-datacenter-water-and-energy-use-to-improve-azure-cloud-sustainability/

Watkins, E. (2013, July). What is WUE (water usage effectiveness)? . *TechTarget*. https://www.techtarget.com/searchdatacenter/definition/WUE-water-usage-effectiveness

Wear, H., Hills, S., Heere, B., & Walker, M. (2018). Communal brand associations as drivers of team identity and consumer behavior. *Journal of Global Sport Management*, *3*(3), 302–320. doi:10.1080/24704067.2018.1432990

Weaver, D. B., & Lawton, L. J. (2007). Twenty years on: The state of contemporary ecotourism research. *Tourism Management*, *28*(5), 1168–1179. doi:10.1016/j.tourman.2007.03.004

Webster, F. E. Jr. (1975). Determining the Characteristics of the Socially Conscious Consumer. *The Journal of Consumer Research*, *2*(3), 188. doi:10.1086/208631

Weeden, C. (2002). Ethical tourism: An opportunity for competitive advantage? *Journal of Vacation Marketing*, *8*(2), 141–153. doi:10.1177/135676670200800204

Weisman, J. (2023, January 12). 9 green marketing examples to inspire you. *Content Writers*. https://contentwriters.com/blog/brands-doing-green-marketing-right/

Wikipedia. (2022). *Green Computing*. Retrieved December 2022, from Wikipedia: https://en.wikipedia.org/wiki/Green_computing

Wiseman, Y. (2017). Remote parking for autonomous vehicles. *International Journal of Hybrid Information Technology*, *10*(1), 313–324. doi:10.14257/ijhit.2017.10.1.27

Wiseman, Y. (2022). Autonomous vehicles. In *Research Anthology on Cross-Disciplinary Designs and Applications of Automation* (pp. 878–889). IGI Global. doi:10.4018/978-1-6684-3694-3.ch043

World Bank. (2021). *Tcdata360, 2021*. World Bank. https://databank.worldbank.org/home.aspx

World Commission on Environment and Development. (1987). *Our common future*. Oxford University Press.

World Energy Council. (2019). *WEC Trilemma: Country Profile*. World Energy Council.

World Health Organization. (2021, June 15). *Soaring e-waste affects the health of millions of children, WHO warns*. World Health Organization. https://www.who.int/news/item/15-06-2021-soaring-e-waste-affects-the-health-of-millions-of-children-who-warns

World Tourism Organization. (2021a). *2020: Worst year in tourism history with 1 billion fewer international arrivals*. WTO. https://www.unwto.org/news/2020-worst-year-in-tourism-history-with-1-billion-fewer-international-arrivals

World Tourism Organization. (2021b). *Tourism and Covid-19 – Unprecedented Economic Impacts*. WTO. https://www.unwto.org/tourism-and-covid-19-unprecedented-economic-impacts

World Tourism Organization. (2022a). *UNWTO Tourism Education Guidelines*. World Tourism Organization.

World Tourism Organization. (2022b). *Measuring the sustainability of tourism learning from pilots*. WTO. https://webunwto.s3.eu-west-1.amazonaws.com/s3fs-public/2023-01/MST_pilots_learning.pdf

World Tourism Organization. (2022c). *Tourism Statistics Data: Economic Contribution of Tourism and Beyond*. WTO. https://www.unwto.org/statistic-data-economic-contribution-of-tourism-and-beyond

World Tourism Organization. (n.d.a.). *Tourism – an economic and social phenomenon*. WTO. https://www.unwto.org/why-tourism

World Tourism Organization. (n.d.b.). *Tourism in the 2030 agenda*. https://www.unwto.org/tourism-in-2030-agenda

World Tourism Organization. (n.d.c.). *On measuring the sustainability of tourism: MST*. WTO. https://www.unwto.org/tourism-statistics/measuring-sustainability-tourism

World Travel & Tourism Council. (2021). *Travel & Tourism Economic Impact 2021: Global Economic Impacts and Trends 2021*. WTTC. https://wttc.org/Portals/0/Documents/Reports/2021/Global%20Economic%20Impact%20and%20Trends%202021.pdf

World Travel & Tourism Council. (2022). *Travel & Tourism Economic Impact 2022: Global Trends*. WTTC. https://wttc.org/Portals/0/Documents/Reports/2022/EIR2022-Global%20Trends.pdf

Wu, W. N. (2020). Features of smart city services in the local government context: a case study of San Francisco 311 system. In *HCI in Business, Government and Organizations: 7th International Conference, HCIBGO 2020*, *22*, (pp. 216–227). ACM.

Xiong, Z., Sheng, H., Rong, W., & Cooper, D. E. (2012). Intelligent transportation systems for smart cities: A progress review. *Science China. Information Sciences*, *55*(12), 2908–2914. doi:10.100711432-012-4725-1

Yadav, R., & Pathak, G. S. (2017). Determinants of Consumers' Green Purchase Behavior in a Developing Nation: Applying and Extending the Theory of Planned Behavior. *Ecological Economics*, *134*, 114–122. doi:10.1016/j.ecolecon.2016.12.019

Yakubu, Y., Manu, S. B., & Bala, U. (2015). Electricity Supply and Manufacturing Output in Nigeria: Autoregressive Distributed Lag (ARDL) Bound Testing Approach. *Journal of Economics and Sustainable Development*, *6*(17).

Yang, X., & Zhang, L. (2021). Understanding residents' green purchasing behavior from a perspective of the ecological personality traits: The moderating role of gender. *The Social Science Journal*, *00*(00), 1–18. doi:10.1080/03623319.2020.1850121

Yeng, W. F., & Yazdanifard, R. (2015). Green marketing: A study of consumers buying behavior in relation to green products. *Global Journal of Management and Business Research*.

Ye, S. (2012). Research on Urban Road Traffic Congestion Charging Based on Sustainable Development. *Physics Procedia*, *24*, 1567–1572. doi:10.1016/j.phpro.2012.02.231

Yfantidou, G., & Matarazzo, M. (2016). The Future of Sustainable Tourism in Developing Countries. *Sustainable Development (Bradford)*, *25*(6), 459–466. doi:10.1002d.1655

Yigitcanlar, T., & Cugurullo, F. (2020). The sustainability of artificial intelligence: An urbanistic viewpoint from the lens of smart and sustainable cities. *Sustainability (Basel)*, *12*(20), 8548. doi:10.3390u12208548

Yigitcanlar, T., Desouza, K. C., Butler, L., & Roozkhosh, F. (2020). Contributions and risks of artificial intelligence (AI) in building smarter cities: Insights from a systematic review of the literature. *Energies*, *13*(6), 1473. doi:10.3390/en13061473

Yigitcanlar, T., Kankanamge, N., & Vella, K. (2021). How are smart city concepts and technologies perceived and utilized? A systematic geo-Twitter analysis of smart cities in Australia. *Journal of Urban Technology*, *28*(1-2), 135–154. doi:10.1080/10630732.2020.1753483

Yılmaz, G., Damar, M., & Doğan, O. (2016, October). *Yeşil Bilişim: Bir Kamu Kurumu Örneği ve Politika Önerileri*. 673-686. Ege Akademik Bakış.

Yılmaz, Y., Uludağ, S., Dilek, E., & Ayizen, Y. E. (2016). A preliminary work on predicting travel times and optimal routes using Istanbul's real traffic data. 9th transist transport congress and exhibition.

YouMatter. (2020). *What Is A Carbon Footprint? A Carbon Footprint Definition*. Retrieved Aralık 2022, from YouMatter. https://youmatter.world/en/definition/definitions-carbon-footprint/

Yürük-Kayapınar, P., Kayapınar, Ö., & Ergan, S. (2019). Tüketicilerin yeşil ürün satın alma davranışlarının kuşaklar bakımından incelenmesi. *OPUS Uluslararası Toplum Araştırmaları Dergisi, 11*(18), 2055–2070. doi:10.26466/opus.565155

Yusof, N. A., Abidin, N. Z., Zailani, S. H. M., Govindan, K., & Iranmanesh, M. (2016). Linking the environmental practice of construction firms and the environmental behaviour of practitioners in construction projects. *Journal of Cleaner Production, 121*, 64–71. doi:10.1016/j. jclepro.2016.01.090

Yüzgeç, U., & Günel, A. (2015). Üniversitelere Yönelik Bir Veri Merkezinin Enerji Planlaması. *Bilecik Şeyh Edebali Üniversitesi Fen Bilimleri Dergisi, 2*(2), 18–19.

Zhang, J., Wang, F.-Y., Wang, K., Lin, W.-H., Xu, X., & Chen, C. (2011). Data-driven intelligent transportation systems: A survey. *IEEE Transactions on Intelligent Transportation Systems, 12*(4), 1624–1639. doi:10.1109/TITS.2011.2158001

Zhang, Y., & Cheng, L. (2023). The role of transport infrastructure in economic growth : Empirical evidence in the UK. *Transport Policy, 133*, 223–233. doi:10.1016/j.tranpol.2023.01.017

Zhao, X., Ke, Y., Zuo, J., Xiong, W., & Wu, P. (2020a). Evaluation of sustainable transport research in 2000–2019. *Journal of Cleaner Production, 256*, 120404. doi:10.1016/j.jclepro.2020.120404

Zhen, J. S. S., & Mansori, S. (2012). Young female motivations for purchase of organic food in Malaysia. *International Journal of Contemporary Business Studies, 3*(5), 61–72.

Zhou, J. (2012). Sustainable transportation in the US: A review of proposals, policies, and programs since 2000. *Frontiers of Architectural Research, 1*(2), 150–165. doi:10.1016/j.foar.2012.02.012

Zinkhan, G. M., & Carlson, L. (1995). Green advertising and the reluctant consumer. *Journal of Advertising, 24*(2), 1–6. doi:10.1080/00913367.1995.10673471

Zupic, I., & Čater, T. (2015). Bibliometric methods in management and organization. *Organizational Research Methods, 18*(3), 429–472. doi:10.1177/1094428114562629

About the Contributors

Punitha Sinnappan holds a Ph.D. degree in Tourism, which she obtained from University Putra Malaysia in 2017. Prior to that, she pursued a Master's degree in Business Administration (Marketing) from the same university, completing it in 2011. She kick-started her academic journey by attaining a Bachelor's degree in Business Administration (Marketing) from University Tenaga Nasional in 2008. Currently, Punitha serves as an academician at the Sunway University in Malaysia. In addition to her teaching responsibilities, she has also been entrusted with a leadership role as the Program Leader at her current institution. Her expertise and research interests span across various fields, including marketing, consumer behavior, tourism, hospitality, and sustainability. With her multifaceted background, she actively contributes to the academic community, imparting knowledge, conducting research, and advancing the understanding of these disciplines. Her passion for the environment and her deep concern for nature drive her to actively seek out community projects aimed at preserving and protecting the environment. She is very much interested in initiatives that promote sustainability and contribute to the well-being of the environment.

***

Ashok Kumar A. R. obtained his Ph.D. from IIT Guwahati. Presently he is working as an Associate Professor in the Department of Computer Science and Engineering of RVCE. His research interest includes - Distributed Computing, Data Center Networks, and Software Defined Networks.

Shafiu Ibrahim Abdullahi is an academic researcher with specialization in Consumption, Development economics, Islamic economics and finance, International finance, Monetary economics, Marketing & Advertising, Econometrics applications, Field surveys, Mathematical modelling, Statistics. He has peer reviewed for journals/books published by IGI, Wiley and Emerald. His academic works have been published by SCOPUS Indexed journals. He has published two books on Islamic finance and Nigerian economy. He has over 17 years work experience in academic, banking and media.

Mohammed Bashir Adamu was born in Gombi LGA on 3 10 1984; had Bsc Economic ADSU MUBI 2012, Msc Economic Mautech Yola 2018. He has published in local and international journals. He is currently studying for his PhD in Economics.

Marija Antonijević is a Research Assistant at the Institute of Economic Sciences in Belgrade, Serbia. She is a PhD candidate at the Faculty of Economics, University of Belgrade. Her research interests include Banking, FDI, and ICT skills. Marija has published numerous scientific papers in mentioned research areas. One of the most relevant projects she participated in was HORIZON 2020 - Strength2Food: Strengthening European Food Chain Sustainability by Quality and Procurement Policy.

F. O. Boachie-Mensah is an Associate Professor of Marketing and Entrepreneurship in the School of Business, College of Humanities and Legal Studies, University of Cape Coast. He is currently on a post-retirement contract at the same university. He loves to teach and supervise students writing their thesis/dissertation in marketing. He has a number of publications in marketing and entrepreneurship and has also written a number of books in these two fields.

Aleksandra Bradić-Martinović, PhD is a Senior Research Associate at the Institute of Economic Sciences, Belgrade. Her scientific interests are Tourism Management, Digital Economy, and Innovations with a focus on Digital Skills. Aleksandra is also a data analyst in the Horwath HTL (Belgrade Office), the world's largest and most experienced hospitality consulting multinational company. She is also a national key expert in the field of scientific data management in the social sciences. Aleksandra published numerous papers and was a part of projects funded by European Union, as a coordinator for Serbia or team member. Aleksandra Bradić-Martinović, PhD is a Senior Research Associate at the Institute of Economic Sciences, Belgrade. Her scientific interests are Tourism Management, Digital Economy, and Innovations with a focus on Digital Skills. Aleksandra is also a data analyst in the Horwath HTL (Belgrade Office), the world's largest and most experienced hospitality consulting multinational company. She is also a national key expert in the field of scientific data management in the social sciences. Aleksandra published numerous papers and was a part of projects funded by European Union, as a coordinator for Serbia or team member. Aleksandra Bradić-Martinović, PhD is a Senior Research Associate at the Institute of Economic Sciences, Belgrade. Her scientific interests are Tourism Management, Digital Economy, and Innovations with a focus on Digital Skills. Aleksandra is also a data analyst in the Horwath HTL (Belgrade Office), the world's largest and most experienced hospitality consulting multinational company. She is also a national key expert in the field of scientific data management in the social sciences. Aleksandra published numerous papers and was a part of projects funded by European Union, as a coordinator for Serbia or team member. Aleksandra Bradić-Martinović, PhD is a Senior Research Associate at the Institute of Economic Sciences, Belgrade. Her scientific interests are Tourism Management, Digital Economy, and Innovations with a focus on Digital Skills. Aleksandra is also a data analyst in the Horwath HTL (Belgrade Office), the world's largest and most experienced hospitality consulting multinational company. She is also a national key expert in the field of scientific data management in the social sciences. Aleksandra published numerous papers and was a part of projects funded by European Union, as a coordinator for Serbia or team member.

Preethi D., currently is pursuing higher education in Christ (Deemed to be University). Preethi has a strong desire to discover the answers to the questions about the surrounding world. This has sparked a strong interest in research. Preethi believes there is always room for improvement and opportunity in research, and is eager to be part of it.

Shiva Kumar Dalali is an Associate Professor, Dept. of CSE, PESU, Bangalore.

Alfred Ghartey is the Senior Assistant Registrar/Executive Secretary, Pro Vice-Chancellor's Office, University of Cape Coast. He is a member of the Chartered Institute of Administrators and Management Consultants – Ghana and a member of the Ghana Association of University Administrators. He holds a master of degree in marketing from the University of Cape Coast. He has a number of publications in Marketing. His research interest is in marketing in higher education, student support services in higher education, publishing and sustainable marketing.

Başak GÖK (Ph.D) holds undergraduate and graduate degrees in physics education from Gazi University. Her interest in multidisciplinary research led him to management information systems. She holds a second master's and doctorate degrees in management information systems. Her research interests include new technologies, management information systems, data mining, data analysis, performance evaluation, distance education, service quality, productivity analysis, scale development and structural equation modeling. She has been working as a lecturer at Gazi University since 2009. She worked as a post-doctoral visiting researcher at Texas Tech University in the USA for 6 months. She served as a visiting lecturer at Ankara Hacı Bayram Veli University, Faculty of Economics and Administrative Sciences, Department of Management Information Systems. She still continues to work as a lecturer in Management Information Systems at Gazi University, Faculty of Applied Sciences.

Hadi Gökçen graduated from the Industrial Engineering Department at Gazi University In 1987. In the years of 1989 and 1994, he received the M.S and Ph.D degrees in Industrial Engineering from Gazi University. Dr. Gökçen received the title of Associate Professor from manufacturing and services systems in 1998 and title of Professor in 2004. His research interests include Optimization Theory and Methods, Multiobjective Optimization, Linear Programming, Integer and Mix Integer Programming, Production Planning and Control, Decision Support Systems, Supply Chain and Logistics Management.

Sandhya H. is pursuing PhD in Tourism Management from Christ University Bangalore. She successfully completed her Mphil and Masters in Tourism Administration (MTA) from Christ University Bangalore by securing the first rank. She has industry experience of one year having worked with one of the leading multinational tour operations companies, Kuoni SOTC, Bangalore and teaching experience of over 6 years having associated with some of the prestigious academic institutions and colleges in Kerala. She has worked as Research Associate of the Major Research Project on the lines of Destination Management Organisations. She is a very passionate and keen researcher and her research interests include Destination Management, Destination Branding and Smart Tourism. She is currently working as Academic Auditor and Deputy Academic Coordinator at Kairos Institute, Cochin, Kerala.

Anisa Jan, PhD, is an Associate Professor in the Department of Management Studies, Islamic university of science and technology Awantipora, India. Dr. Anisa jan has more than 15 years of experience in academia. Focus of her research are areas of service marketing, social media marketing, green marketing, consumer experience and branding. Her publications have appeared in reputed international journals, including the International Journal of Business and Management, International Journal of Trend in Scientific Research and Development, International journal of Research and Analytical Reviews, International Journal of Advance and Innovation Research, among others.

Sejana Jose V. is pursuing PhD in Tourism Management from Christ University, Bangalore. She has successfully completed her Mphil and Masters in Tourism Administration from Christ University, Bangalore. She is currently working as Lecturer at Mount Carmel College, Bangalore. She has one year of industry experience working in a tour operation company and teaching experience for four years. Her research interest includes Green Transportation, Sustainable Tourism, Organizational behaviour, and Tourism Logistics.

Ahmet Bilgehan Kandemir is has graduated degree from Gazi University in master of managment information systems education in 2023. His research interests include new technologies, management information systems, cloud computing, data centers, it infrastructure, system managment, virtualization. He has been experienced system administrator with a demonstrated history of working in the internet industry. He skilled in linux system administration, network administration, network security, database administration, remote managment, object storage technologies and private clouds. He still working Senior System Administrator at Nokta.

Milena Lazić, PhD is a Research Associate at the Institute of Economic Sciences, Belgrade. Her scientific interest includes Macroeconomics, National Competitiveness and Branding, Digital Economy and ICT in Tourism, and Marketing Management. She has published numerous papers related to previous topics. She is a member of the Serbian Marketing Association SeMA, the Society of Economists of Belgrade and the Scientific Society of Economists of Serbia.

Rebecca Dei Mensah is an associate professor in Human Resource Management, School of Business, University of Cape Coast. She holds a Ph.D. in Business Administration. She teaches on a range of undergraduate and postgraduate courses at the University of Cape Coast. Rebecca is an Associate Member of the Chartered Institute of Personnel and Development (CIPD) and a Full Member of the Chartered Institute of Human Resource Management, (CIHRM) Ghana.

Sonia Mrad obtained her Ph.D. from the High School of Business (University of Manouba). He currently works as an associate professor in the Department of Economics. His research focuses on issues related to transport and urban mobility, such as road traffic forecasting, congestion, and energy consumption. In this context, we use data-driven methods such as wavelets, neural networks and other forecasting techniques. His research interest includes Sustainable Transportation, Smart mobility, and Intelligent Transportation Systems.

Husayn Mahmud Muhammad is a lecturer with Federal College of Education Yola. He has many years of teaching experience. He has published in local and international journals. He was Head of Department of Economics FCE Yola. He has an M.Sc. from UK.

Burcu Ören Özer is a lecturer in Trakya University Technology Transfer Research and Implementation Center.

Micheal Shant Osei is currently the territorial office manager for Christ Apostolic Church International, Western C, Tarkwa. Micheal Shant completed both his masters and undergraduate program from the university of cape coast. He holds a masters degree in master of commerce, marketing and a bachelor of management studies degree respectively. He also has a professional qualifcation in Accounting from the chaterred institute of Accountants, Ghana.

Dominic Owusu is currently a Senior Lecturer in the Department of Marketing and Supply Chain Management, School of Business, University of Cape Coast. Dominic Owusu holds a PhD in Hospitality Management, a Master of Commerce Degree in Marketing and a Bachelor's degree in Management Studies from the university of Cape Coast, Ghana. His research and teaching interest span across various fields including Marketing, hospitality management, entrepreneurship, project management, supply chain management and law.

Rafaa Mraihi is a Full professor at the High School of Business (University of Manouba). He works on issues related to transport and urban mobility, such as forecasting road traffic, its energy consumption, and its emissions of atmospheric pollutants. In this context, we use image processing methods, wavelets, neural networks, and other forecasting techniques. We are also working on the performance of public transport operators in response to public regulations. In this case, we use the methods of microeconometrics applied to panel data (parametric and nonparametric methods).

Nandana Ranjith is a dedicated student researcher passionate about exploring innovative ideas and making meaningful contributions to this field. Currently pursuing a master's degree in commerce at Christ (Deemed to be University) Bangalore. Ranjith's research interests lie in the realm of sustainable marketing and its impact on consumer behaviour.

Mehvish Riyaz, MBA, is a full-time Research Scholar, pursuing her PhD from the Department of Management Studies, Islamic university of science and technology Awantipora, India . Her research interest spans green marketing, socially responsible marketing and consumer behavior.

Krishna Prasath Shanmugam is working as an assistant professor who teaches Marketing, Branding and Technology in the Department of Commerce. He has a teaching experience of more than eight years and industrial experience of 3 years. He was associated with All India Radio as a radio jockey for almost 8 years. He writes cases articles, poems and copyrights his innovative pedagogies. He is a certified digital marketer recognised by Government of India and is associated with projects partnered with the State Governments of Karnataka and Kerala. He is also a mentor and consultant with a couple of start-ups based in Southern India.

Kamal Kabiru Shehu is Muslim by religion and Hausa by tribe, from Kano State, Nigeria. Shehu was born on the 13th of January 1984 and attended Tarauni Special Primary School from 1989 to 1995, and Government Secondary School Tarauni from 1995 to 2001; College of Arts, Science and Remedial Studies Kano for IJMB programme from 2002 to 2004; Bayero University Kano for B.A (Ed) Economics from 2006 to 2009; SRM University Chennai India, for M.Sc Econometrics, from 2013 to 2015. Shehu is presently a lecturer in the Department of Economics and Development Studies at Federal University of Kashere, Gombe State, Nigeria.

Bindi Varghese is a Doctorate in Commerce, specializing in Tourism. As an academician and tourism professional, she has over 18 years of Academic and one year of Industrial experience. Currently, she is affiliated with Christ University, as an Associate Professor and is the Research Coordinator at School of Business Studies and Social Sciences. She has served many educational institutions in South India and has served as a national and international expert, for a decade among the educational institutions of India. Currently, she is actively associated with Indian Tourism Congress (ITC) and Kerala Development Society (KDS), New Delhi. The active researches undertaken include Impact Assessment Studies, Medical Tourism, Destination Management Organization and Ecological Studies. Dr. Bindi completed a major research project on the title "Strategic Intervention of Destination Management Organizations to Enhance Competitiveness of Tourism Destinations– A Model for Karnataka" funded by Christ University. Along with her academic expertise, she is also an Section editor for 'ATNA- Journal of Tourism Studies', published by Christ University, Bengaluru. She has authored one book; on Medical Tourism in India: by an international publisher in Germany, and has also contributed chapters to edited books and has published several articles in areas of Destination Management, Governance, Medical Tourism, E-Tourism etc. To her credit, she has edited a book on "Evolving Paradigms in Tourism and Hospitality in Developing Countries: A Case Study of India". The book is published by CRC Press, Taylor and Francis group - international publisher in US and released in 2018.

Index

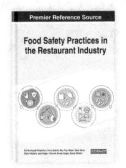

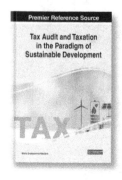

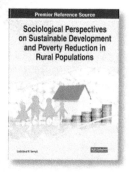

CPSIA information can be obtained
at www.ICGtesting.com
Printed in the USA
LVHW061820190723
752810LV00005B/207